CONTENTS

TABLES

ELECTIONS AND POLITICAL DEVELOPMENT

The South Asian Experience

Elections and Political Development

The South Asian Experience

by Norman D. Palmer

DUKE UNIVERSITY PRESS
DURHAM, NORTH CAROLINA

Published in the United States of America by
Duke University Press,
6697 College Station, Durham, North Carolina 27708

LCC card number 75-4032
ISBN 0-8223-0341-8

Printed in Great Britain

PREFACE

Elections seem to be a subject of particular and peculiar fascination for modern students of political science. The electoral process, and the role of elections in the political system, have been the focus of extensive research, from many points of view, employing different methodological techniques and theoretical approaches. This research has, however, been carried on mainly by Western scholars, living in Western democratic polities, and has centered on the Western democratic experience. More recently, considerable attention has been given to the role and functions of elections in non-democratic political systems and in the few countries of the non-Western world where democratic institutions and practices have continued to survive in actuality as well as in theory.

Along with an expansion of the scope of electoral inquiry has gone a real revolution in the methods of electoral research. A tremendous amount of aggregate data on elections in various political systems has been accumulated, and intensive micro studies, using such techniques as detailed and systematic interviewing and other forms of survey research, have added further valuable material to the store of existing knowledge. Through the use of computers and quantitative techniques of analysis this formidable stockpile of information can be processed and winnowed, thus supplementing and enriching historical, descriptive, and other kinds of more conventional studies. The fruits are available in innumerable voting behavior studies in many political systems, and in a few significant cross-national studies which have used electoral data for comparative political analysis.

It may seem hard to imagine that any significant aspects of the much-discussed subject of elections has remained underdeveloped. This may be true in the Western democratic world, but it is certainly not the case in non-Western systems, of whatever type. Much more extensive and sophisticated research, for example, is needed on the role of elections in the political evolution of the new states of the Third World, with particular reference to the real place and functions of elections in the evolving political systems of these new states, and to the contribution of elections to political development – or to political decay.

The point should never be forgotten that studies of voting behavior in Western countries and studies of political development by Western scholars may have limited value and validity with reference to Asian needs and experience. Such important political phenomena as elections and political development may have quite a different meaning and significance and may function quite differently in different political and cultural milieus. Certainly strange things happen to Western ideas and institutions – and to Westerners – when they are transplanted in the Asian environment.

Quite insufficient attention has been given to the subject of elections and political development. At a time when the study of political development is in a stage of re-assessment and revision, when many Western and non-Western students of the subject are questioning the value of some of the previous approaches and interpretations and are seeking new approaches that are at once more relevant, more useful, and more sophisticated from both a theoretical and practical point of view, it would seem appropriate to give more attention to the central role of an essentially Western import, with some indigenous roots and many indigenous applications, in the developmental process. In short, the study of elections should be an integral part of the study of political development, and the developmental approach to elections, especially in the so-called developing countries, should be emphasized much more than it has been to date. The study of both elections and political development will be enriched and broadened by comparative analysis and cross-fertilization. Cross-national and cross-cultural studies can give added dimensions to this kind of research.

The purpose of this study is to examine the electoral experience of the countries of South Asia, from a comparative and developmental point of view. This will involve a consideration of the different roles and functions of elections in various South Asian states – in an area where electoral experience has varied greatly – and the contributions of elections to the political development, or political decay, of the countries of South Asia. It will also involve a study of the South Asian experience within the broader framework of comparative analysis, drawing upon the information and insights that are available from the experience of other political systems and from the works of various students of elections and political development, not focused on South Asia. In particular, an effort will be made to apply methods and approaches that have proved to be useful in the study of other political systems to the South Asian polities, and also to draw upon the increasingly extensive studies and data, much of it unknown outside of South Asia and much still unpublished, which have been produced by students of South Asian affairs, indigenous and foreign. South Asia offers a particularly extensive and particularly fascinating laboratory for research on such themes as elections and political development.

I have been interested in the comparative study of elections and political development, as well as of South Asian politics, for many years. The extensive literature that has accumulated in these fields of inquiry has been an invaluable source of information and ideas. In the area of political development I have drawn heavily on the writings of specialists in many countries. Among the election studies that I have found most useful, in addition to the classic contributions of such older scholars as Duverger, Tingsten, and V. O. Key, Jr., are the empirically-based volumes which have been produced by the remarkable group of 'psephologists' at Columbia University (Lazarsfeld, Berelson, *et al.*) and the University of Michigan (Campbell, Miller, Stokes, and others associated with the Survey Research Center) and at Nuffield College, Oxford University (especially David E. Butler, whose writings on British elections and on the political process in Britain have been a source of inspiration to me, and who generously shared some of his thoughts on electoral analysis with me), and various European experts on empirical research and electoral studies, especially Stein Rokkan. I have also made a special effort to study the electoral experience in developing countries outside of South Asia, and the literature on elections and political development with reference to these countries.

In South Asia I have been studying elections and political development for a quarter of a century. I was in India immediately after the first general elections in 1951–2, before, during, and after the second, third, and fourth general elections in 1957, 1962, and 1967, and the State Assembly elections of 1972. I also visited Pakistan shortly before the only nationwide general elections in 1970, as well as on several other occasions. I was in Ceylon* just after the general elections of 1952, and again in 1972, and in Bangladesh in 1972 (in addition to previous visits to East Pakistan). I have interviewed the Chief Election Commissioners in India, Pakistan, and Ceylon, and the acting Election Commissioner in Bangladesh, and I have spent considerable time in the office of the Election Commission in New Delhi. I have also interviewed election officials at State, district, and local levels, as well as large numbers of Members of Parliament, Members of State Legislative Assemblies, party leaders, and candidates in various parts of India, and to a lesser extent in other South Asian states. Observing election campaigns and voting at first hand in many parts of India has been an invaluable experience, which has made me more aware of the human aspects of the electoral story and has given me a profound respect for the Indian voter, whatever his limitations or level of political development.

* Since all of Ceylon's nationwide general elections were held before the name of the country was changed to Sri Lanka in 1972, the country is referred to as Ceylon in this study.

My greatest debt is owed to the many students of politics in India – scholars at universities and research centers, journalists, and some practicing politicians and officials with scholarly interests – who have long been engaged in studying elections within the context of their continuing work on Indian politics, and who have been making increasingly valuable and insightful studies in the areas of my special interests. I believe that I have followed these studies as closely as any other non-Indian student of Indian politics. I have been given access to a great deal of unpublished material which I have found invaluable for this particular study. I welcome this opportunity to pay tribute to the Indian scholars who are working in this field, many of whom are my long-time personal friends. Most of them must remain anonymous, but I must express my personal appreciation to some. These include the remarkable group of younger social scientists at the Centre for the Study of Developing Societies in Delhi, who, under the direction of Dr. Rajni Kothari, have made the Centre an oasis of political research in India. My particular thanks are due to the following scholars at the Centre: Rajni Kothari, Gopal Krishna, Bashiruddin Ahmed, Ramashray Roy, D. L. Sheth, and Ashish Nandi. I have benefited greatly from my discussions with them, from their insightful writings, and from the masses of data that they have accumulated. I am also grateful to scholars at universities where special work on elections and development has been carried on, notably at the University of Rajasthan, the University of Poona, Gujarat University, the University of Bombay, and the University of Trivandrum. My special thanks go to Dr. S. P. Verma, Dr. Iqbal Narain, and their associates at the University of Rajasthan; Dr. V. M. Sirsikar of the University of Poona; Dr. D. N. Pathak, Dr. K. D. Desai, and Mr. Pravin L. Sheth of Gujarat University; Dr. Aloo Dastur of Bombay University; and Dr. Sukumaran Nair and Dr. Ramakrishnan Nair of the University of Trivandrum. I have benefited greatly from my contacts and friendship with Dr. A. H. Somjee, formerly at Baroda University (now at Simon Fraser University), and Mrs. Somjee, and especially from their thorough and long-term research on political and socio-economic aspects of development in Anand in the Kaira District of Gujarat, which I have had the opportunity to examine and observe at first hand. Dr. Yogesh Atal and Dr. Narayan Rao of the Indian Council of Social Science Research, and Dr. Imtiaz Ahmed of the Jawaharlal Nehru University in New Delhi were kind enough to let me examine unpublished materials. My debt to Dr. Atal's ground-breaking study of elections and political development in three communities in a district in Uttar Pradesh is obvious in the following pages.

For information on elections in Pakistan I have drawn extensively on the writings of various Pakistani and foreign scholars, including Keith Callard and Khalid Bin Sayeed, and on my discussions with these two scholars and with many others in the universities of Pakistan. My first work on elections in Ceylon was done in 1952–3, when I benefited greatly from talks with Sir Ivor Jennings, then Vice-Chancellor of the University of Ceylon, and Dr. I. D. S. Weerawardene, one of the pioneers in election studies in Ceylon. Since then I have been following political developments in Ceylon as closely as possible. During my last visit, in 1972, I was given many insights into the political process by political leaders and scholars, including Dr. Colvin de Silva, Minister of Constitutional Affairs, Dr. N. M. Perera, Minister of Finance, Dr. Peter Kueneman, Minister of Housing, Mr. J. R. Jayawardene, Leader of the Opposition in the Ceylonese House of Representatives, and Dr. S. U. Kodikara, formerly President of the University of Ceylon at Peradiniya. For some special insights and information on the politics of Ceylon I am grateful to Dr. Urmila Phadnis of the School of International Studies of the Jawaharlal Nehru University, one of the leading Indian authorities on Ceylon.

In East Pakistan and Bangladesh I am especially indebted to several scholars at Dacca and Chittagong Universities and the Academy of Rural Development at Comilla, and especially to Dr. G. W. Choudhury and Dr. M. Rashiduzzaman, who were long associated with Dacca University. For information on Nepal I have relied primarily on the writings of Dr. Leo E. Rose, perhaps the leading American authority on the politics of Nepal, and of those who have been associated with him in Nepal studies, especially Dr. Margaret Fisher, Dr. Bhuwan Lal Joshi, and Dr. B. M. Regmi. I am also particularly indebted to Dr. Malla and other scholars at the Tribhuvan University in Kathmandu, to Dr. Rishikesh Shah, a well-known political leader as well as scholar, to Dr. Jagadish Sharma, and to Dr. Pashupati Shamsher, formerly Director of the Institute of Economic Development in Kathmandu.

Much of my library research was carried out at the libraries of the University of Pennsylvania and of the Indian Council of World Affairs and the School of International Studies of the Jawaharlal Nehru University in New Delhi. I am indebted to the librarians and other staff members of these fine libraries, and also of the India Office Library and the libraries of the University of London and the Institute of Commonwealth Studies in London, the Jawaharlal Nehru Library and the Documentation Centre of the Indian Council of Social Science Research in New Delhi, and of many other libraries in the United States and the countries of South Asia where I spent all-too-brief periods of research in connection with this study.

In many respects the most important resources of all for me were the hundreds of people, from top officials to ordinary citizens, in all parts of South Asia whom I have met over the years, and the opportunity which I have had to roam the highways and byways of

South Asia and especially to observe the actual process of campaigning and voting in different States in different parts of India. A combination of extensive field work and extensive library research is absolutely essential for a study of this kind, even though it is difficult, time-consuming, and often exhausting, and even though it is often impossible to reconcile what one reads in the printed pages in a library environment with what one sees with one's own eyes in various parts of the vast subcontinent. Nowhere is the gulf between theory and practice more apparent than in South Asia, and nowhere is the search for truth – or Truth, to borrow Gandhi's capitalized spelling – more compelling and more elusive. I hope that I have been able to convey some of the human dimensions of the story, and to provide some useful insights into the actual working of the electoral and developmental process in South Asia, without losing sight of the broader comparative and theoretical aspects of the subject.

The final revision of my manuscript was done during a month in the incomparable surroundings of the Rockefeller Foundation's Study and Conference Center at the Villa Serbelloni, Bellagio (Como), Italy. For this I am greatly indebted to the Rockefeller Foundation. The beauty of the physical setting, the magnificence of the facilities, the opportunity for uninterrupted work free from the usual responsibilities and distractions, the good companionship with scholars in various disciplines from several countries, and the hospitality of the Director and his wife, Dr. and Mrs. William C. Olson, combine to make a residence at the Villa Serbelloni a memorable, and indeed an unforgettable, experience.

My research in the preparation of this volume was made possible by sabbatical leaves from the University of Pennsylvania and by a number of grants, most recently from the American Institute of Indian Studies, for field work in India, and the American Council of Learned Societies, for work in other countries of South Asia and in the United States and England.

My wife, Evelyn, has been with me during all of my longer sojourns in South Asia, has helped in various ways in the collection of information and in the preparation of this volume, and has borne with me with a patience and endurance which only the long-suffering wives of academic scholars bent on writing still another book can fully appreciate.

NORMAN D. PALMER

Leopard Lake
Berwyn, Pa., U.S.A.
15 August 1974

1

ELECTIONS AND THE POLITICAL SYSTEM

Elections are particularly conspicuous and revealing aspects of most contemporary political systems. They highlight and dramatize a political system, bringing its nature into sharp relief, and providing insights into other aspects of the system and the basic nature and actual functioning of the system as a whole. During an election, so to speak, a political system is on display, even though the features that are most obviously on display may be only a small part of the iceberg that lies beneath.

Elections are complex events involving individual and collective decisions which directly affect, and are affected by, the total political and social process. They open up channels between the polity and the society, between the elites and the masses, between the individual and his government. They are major agencies of political socialization and political participation.

The Study of Elections

The study of elections provides an opportunity to study a political system in action, using various techniques and methods from survey research and participant observation studies to the analysis of aggregate data. Elections may be studied from the point of view of both macro- and micro-political analysis, and of the linkages between these two forms of analysis. Such studies can include a variety of methodological and theoretical approaches, using historical, psychological, sociological, political, statistical, and other methodologies, and both normative and empirical theory. They may range from individual and localized case studies to the use of aggregate data, comparative studies, and trend analysis to throw light on broad ecological and systemic factors and patterns.

To use the jargon of contemporary political science, elections have generally been conceived as a dependent variable – as the end-product of a political process, shaped by the nature and operations of the larger political system, and especially by the party system – or, less frequently, as an intervening variable, linking the citizen and the polity, the parties and the government, but seldom as an independent variable which has a profound effect on parties, the government, the political system, and the general nature and spirit of political life. Yet in fact elections may be usefully studied from all three approaches – as dependent, as intervening, and as independent variables in a political system. This point is suggestively advanced by James N. Rosenau, in his fascinating book-length essay on *The Dramas of Politics*: 'An election . . . might be viewed as an independent variable in a model explaining the strength of political parties, as an intervening variable in a hypothesis anticipating the nature of public policies and as a dependent variable in a proposition predicting the consequences of political campaigns. In a feedback model, moreover, the same attribute, attitude, or behavior might be conceived to operate simultaneously as all three types of variables.'[1]

Like Rosenau, we can find drama in the study of elections, even when we are concerned with aggregate data and methodological research. Elections are truly exciting phenomena, which political science research should document and highlight – perhaps even dramatize – rather than deaden and obscure.

Elections, broadly considered, are complicated political processes which must be analyzed within the context of the total political and social system. 'An election itself,' wrote V. O. Key, Jr., 'is a formal act of collective decision that occurs in a stream of connected antecedent and subsequent behavior;'[2] and, as David E. Butler and Anthony King observed of the British general election of 1964, it is 'not a single event but a concatenation of thousands of events, some of great significance, some more trivial.'[3]

Robert Lane has developed a useful 'Paradigm for the Study of Electoral Behavior,' which calls attention to the broader dimensions of the electoral process and to a variety of types, attributes, and factors which may be considered as either dependent or independent variables. The types of political behavior listed under 'Responses' represent, 'collectively and individually, the dependent variables.' The 'psychological attributes of the individual' listed under 'Organism' and 'the social or environmental factors' listed under 'Stimuli' represent the independent variables.[4]

Conventionally, in voting behavior and other types of electoral studies, elections have been analyzed on the basis of the factors influencing, and the motivations of, the individual voter, the electorate as a collectivity, the representatives chosen through the electoral process, the process itself, the kind of government that is produced and the nature and degree of its actual responsibility to the electorate, and the role of elections in the functioning and development of the political system. The latter aspect has, at least until recently, been the most

Table 1.i

PARADIGM FOR THE STUDY OF ELECTORAL BEHAVIOR

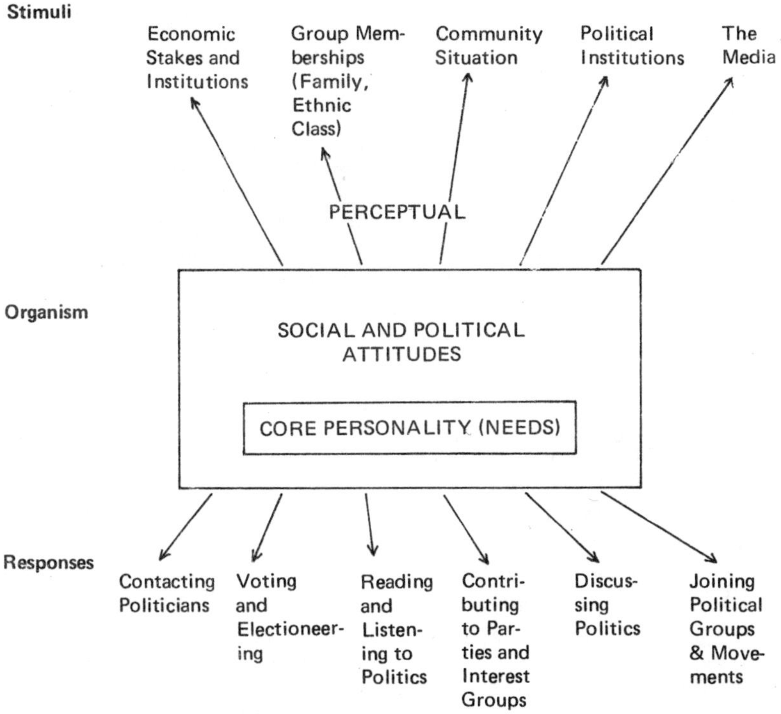

Source: Robert E. Lane, *Political Life: Why People Get Involved in Politics* (Glencoe, Ill.: The Free Press, 1959), p. 6.

neglected phase of electoral analysis. As Richard Rose and Harve Mossawir pointed out in 1967, 'The study of voting and elections is now one of the major growth areas within the field of political science. . . . Limited consideration, however, is given to the relevance of voting and elections for the political system as a whole.'[5]

The relative neglect of the study of elections, within the framework of comparative and systemic analysis, is easily understandable. Until recently most electoral studies were confined to individual elections in a single country, and often had limited comparative value and replicability. Nationwide studies of elections, using modern techniques of research, were undertaken in the United States only in the 1940s and became significant, from a cumulative and comparative point of view, only after a number of these studies had been made.[6] In England such studies date from the end of World War II, as illustrated by the famous Nuffield studies of every British election since the 'turning-point election' of 1945, and by the contributions to election analysis of some of the scholars who have been associated with these studies.[7] In Norway, Sweden, France, and a few other European countries similar studies, using sophisticated methods and techniques, have been available since the early post-war years.[8] In most other parts of the world electoral studies of comparable scope and rigor are almost lacking, although in recent years scholars in many countries have been making significant contributions to the study of voting experience and behavior. In India, for example, with a few exceptions, systematic electoral studies of high quality were initiated only at the time of the fourth general elections in 1967;[9] and even today, in a country that rightly boasts of staging 'the world's largest democratic elections,' electoral studies of high quality are still rare, even though Indian political scientists are probably giving more attention, at least in group research projects, to the study of elections than to any other aspect of political research.

In 1958 one of the ablest British students of 'psephology,'[10] Professor W. J. M. Mackenzie, wrote: 'The question of elections is at the centre of politics everywhere.'[11] It would be more accurate to revise this statement to assert that the question of elections is of central concern to almost all democratic states, and is given considerable attention even in more controlled sytems; but it seems clear that elections have some kind of a place in almost all contemporary political systems, and that indeed they provide an excellent focal point for the study of virtually all types of systems.

Voting and the Electoral Process

Voting is the most common, the most conspicuous, and the most frequently studied act of political participation, but as many students of elections have emphasized, it may not be a very meaningful act of participation at all.[12] It may be hardly more than a rather meaningless ritual, a symbolic gesture, performed for reasons of social conformity or because of social pressures, rather than a conscious, informed, and studied exercise of political choice. Moreover, it is particularly 'difficult to study and assess, for since the advent of the secret ballot – a fundamental feature of free elections – it has become impossible to observe in its final stages, assuming that the conventional safeguards of secrecy are preserved.' In one sense, therefore, as Stein Rokkan has pointed out, 'the vote is no longer a *responsible* act; the citizen could no longer be taken to account for what he had done, neither by his superiors nor by his peers.' The reason for this, as Rokkan noted, is clear. 'The vote is a datum of human behavior but it is an *anonymous* datum.'[13]

While the anonymous and secret nature of the act of voting makes it difficult to study the way in which individual voters exercise their right of franchise, it does not minimize the importance of this act, nor does it prevent ready access to voting results. How an individual actually votes may not be known, but how the voters collectively have voted becomes well known, for aggregate data on voting results, on a polling booth by polling booth or constituency by constituency basis as well as on the basis of overall national returns, are readily available in most political systems. More significantly, voting is only the final stage the dramatic climax – of the electoral process, and the electoral process, which is a complicated and multi-stage process in any political system where elections are held, is the central mechanism of the even broader and more complex electoral system.

This brings up the problem of what Maurice Duverger, in a famous article written a generation ago, called 'the influence of the electoral system on political life.' Influence is one of the most difficult concepts in political science to define, and especially to operationalize. Duverger does not even attempt to do this, but he does insist in general terms on the importance of the electoral system:

> It is obvious that the electoral system must influence political life. The radical changes brought about in the structure of various States by the adoption of universal suffrage or the machinery of arranged elections, for instance, sufficiently indicate the importance of this factor. It is, however, extremely difficult to analyze that influence scientifically. The factors conditioning the political life of a country are very closely interrelated, so that any study of the effects of one of those factors considered in isolation is necessarily artificial. All such a study can do is to define tendencies, likely to be influenced by the operation of the other factors.[14]

Since a premise of this study – which seems to be supported by a substantial body of evidence and experience – is that elections are significant and meaningful, and therefore influential, aspects of the political systems of the South Asian countries – particularly of India and Ceylon* throughout their existence as independent states, and of Pakistan and Bangladesh today – the concept of influence must be borne constantly in mind. The empirical evidence that has been presented seems to confirm one's overall impression that in at least some of the South Asian countries elections have been influential and have contributed significantly to political development. In some countries, in some periods, however, they have been either non-existent or quite peripheral to the political system, and when they have been introduced they have had destabilizing effects, contributing, at least in the short run, to political decay rather than to political

* See footnote on page vii, above.

development. Even in these cases, the long-run effects of elections may be more constructive. However destabilizing their immediate consequences, they may in the longer perspective be as necessary for the transition from unstable political structures of an essentially non-participatory and authoritarian type to more stable systems which are more deeply rooted in the political and social milieu and which are more genuinely participatory and more enduring.

Ubiquity of Elections

Of the ubiquity of elections in contemporary political systems there can be no question. 'Elections are among the most ubiquitous of contemporary political institutions, and voting is the single act of political participation undertaken by a majority of adults in a majority of the nations today.'[15] In most of the democratic states of the West, in the few non-Western democracies, and in some non-democratic polities, elections have become a normal feature of the political system, even though their role and place in the system, and their actual significance, may vary greatly. Between 1954 and 1958 sixty-eight countries held elections.

In 1970–1 national elections were held in twenty-three countries, and local elections in many more. In five of these countries – Austria, Ceylon, Chile, Great Britain, and Mexico – the elections led to important changes in government, and in Pakistan the first nationwide elections on the basis of universal suffrage precipitated the developments leading to civil war and the break-up of the nation. Obviously not all of these elections were competitive elections. In Albania the list of candidates for the People's Assembly received 100 per cent of the votes, and in elections of the Supreme Soviet in the Soviet Union there was only one candidate for each seat.

Although in Asia competitive national elections were alien to the political culture and experience, they have been tried in most Asian countries and have apparently become an accepted political institution in at least five or six of these countries. As John Badgley has pointed out, 'within this century nineteen of the twenty-one Asian states have experienced one or more competitive elections for legislative or lower levels of political office. Considering the alien nature of the electoral process, this represents rapid cultural penetration. One is hard put to locate any other Western institution that has enjoyed, or suffered, depending on one's values, such widespread experimentation, if not acceptance.'[16] Up to 1972 Ceylon, India, Japan, Laos, the Philippines, and South Korea had held five or more nation-wide general elections on the basis of universal suffrage; Burma, Cambodia, Malaysia, and Thailand had held four; Singapore had held three; Indonesia and South

Vietnam two; and Afghanistan, Nepal, and Pakistan, one each. The Communist states of Asia – North Korea, North Vietnam, Mongolia, and the People's Republic of China – have never held competitive nationwide elections, nor has the Republic of China on Taiwan.[17] A study of the electoral experience of all of the Asian countries, and of each of the national and perhaps also some of the local elections, would be a fascinating exercise that would undoubtedly provide many insights into the nature and working of the political systems of the Asian states.

Role of Elections in Different Political Systems

Elections obviously have different meanings and play different roles in different political systems. In some they are central, in others peripheral; in some they have definitely stabilizing effects, in others definitely destabilizing; in some they seem clearly to contribute to political development, in others to political decay. They may be used as thinly veiled disguises for various forms of authoritarian rule, as institutionalized procedures for system maintenance in established democratic societies, or as instruments for the increasing democratization of political systems. They may be considered variously as devices for legitimacy, identification, integration, communication, participation, socialization, and mobilization, as well as for political choice and political control. Because elections serve many purposes and because they cannot be understood except in a systematic context, they should be analyzed not only with relation to the general theory and the general knowledge that have accumulated as a result of extensive voting behavior and other electoral studies in many political systems, but also with relation both to political systems generally and to the distinctive characteristics, traditions, experience, values, and goals of individual systems.

The case for considering elections within the framework of political systems is therefore a compelling one. It has in fact been more or less taken for granted for some time by students of 'psephology.' It was stated forcefully some years ago in what is still probably the most influential and best known study of voting behavior: '. . . the voting behavior of a mass electorate can be seen within the context of a larger political system. The electoral process is a means of decision that lies within a broader political order, and in research on voting it is valuable to have explicitly in view the wider political system in which the electoral process is found.'[18] Since *The American Voter* was published, the role of elections in the political system has been given increasing attention, as a part of the developing study of political systems, but it is still a relatively underdeveloped aspect of 'one of the major growth areas within the field of political science.'[19]

Elections and Political Development

Even more neglected is the place of elections in the process of political development. It is surprising how little attention is given to this subject in the burgeoning literature on political development. Yet the relevance of elections to political development seems quite obvious. Although the concept has been defined, and operationalized, in many ways, almost any definition or effort at concept clarification suggests that political development refers to the increasing capacity of a political system to meet the increasing demands being made upon it. The members of the Comparative Politics Committee of the Social Science Research Council in the United States, who have made the most extensive coordinated study of political development, leading to a library of excellent works and to many significant intellectual by-products, have 'suggested that it may be useful to conceptualize the processes of political development as involving essentially six crises that may be met in different sequences but all of which must be successfully dealt with for a society to become a modern nation-state.'[20] These are the crises of identity, legitimacy, penetration, participation, integration, and distribution. Elections provide a central mechanism for dealing with all of these 'crises of development.' Moreover, the place of elections in a political system may be quite thoroughly analyzed in terms of their contribution to this kind of crisis resolution.

In analyzing 'those characteristics of political development which seem to be most widely held and most fundamental in the general thinking about problems of development,' the members of the Comparative Politics Committee noted three 'broadly shared' characteristics: (1) problems of equality, which 'are generally related to the *political culture* and sentiments about legitimacy and commitment to the system;' (2) problems of the capacity of a political system, which 'are generally related to the performance of the *authoritative* structures of government;' and (3) problems of differentiation and specialization, which 'touch mainly on the performance of the *non-authoritative* structures and the general political process in the society at large.' 'This suggests that in the last analysis the problems of political development revolve around the relationships between the political culture, the authoritative structures, and the general political process.'[21]

Here, too, elections would seem to be obviously related to political development. They have to be considered in the context of 'the *political culture* and sentiments about legitimacy and commitment to the system;' they have a direct and often decisive bearing on the capacity of a political system and on 'the performance of the *authoritative* structures of government' in many political systems; and they have a central role in 'the *non-authoritative* structures and the general political process.'

Elections introduce the important element of accountability into a political system, and provide a means by which such accountability is achieved in greater or lesser degree. Accountability also seems to be related to political development. As John Badgley has reasoned: 'A civil polity is one in which the public interest is served by men accountable to their community. . . . Enlarging the scope of the civil polity in order to include multiple local communities and still retain the sense of political obligation and accountability is the process by which political development, in fact, occurs.'[22]

A 'Responsible Electorate'?

One of the perennial dilemmas of the democratic process is that so much depends on the quality and extent of the participation of the citizens of a state, as individuals and as a collectivity. There is ample and even alarming evidence that even in the most advanced democracies both the quality and the extent of citizen participation are shockingly inadequate and limited. How can a genuine democracy be based on a generally uninformed, selfishly-motivated and highly non-participant electorate? Can collective wisdom emerge out of individual ignorance, selfishness, and apathy? Or are these obvious characteristics of so many voters, even in democratic systems, overbalanced by other characteristics of the voters and the political system which make it possible for the citizens to exercise a genuine and meaningful degree of political choice and political control, and for the system itself to remain genuinely democratic and sufficiently effective as an instrument of governance?

These questions are, of course, as old as democracy itself, however considered. They were posed by the Greek political thinkers, as they have been by almost every student of political systems. The doubts to which they give rise have persisted, even though the experience of modern democracies during the past two centuries and less has tended to indicate that the democratic way is a viable and flexible one, and can function under many different forms of political institutions and under seemingly adverse conditions and circumstances.

This perennial dilemma has been posed anew – and for the first time on a world-wide scale – by the emergence of many new nations, especially in Asia and Africa, in the postwar era. No new nation is ever 'ready' for democracy – or perhaps for any other system of government that is not based on traditional and usually authoritarian practices. Many of the new nations originally accepted various forms of the democratic system; but within a few years the 'erosion of democracy' set in in most of these new states, and today there are few which can properly be described as democratic. Few, for example, can meet the test of genuinely free, fair, direct elections on the basis of universal suffrage. The tradition, political culture, and social institutions of the new states, the circumstances of their emergence into independent nationhood, their political experience since the attainment of independence, the overall political and social environment, and the pressures and challenges from outside their borders in a generally unfavorable international environment have been heavy obstacles to overcome in evolving any kind of adequate and enduring political system. They have been particularly formidable obstacles in the democratic path, even when the political leaders genuinely desire to follow this path.

Within this more general framework, the concept of what V. O. Key, Jr. has called 'the responsible electorate' takes on a special meaning and relevance. Even in the political system which Professor Key studied most intensively – the American system – there is extensive evidence of 'irresponsibility' of the electorate. But Professor Key nevertheless concluded that in spite of all the evidence to the contrary the American electorate was on the whole a responsible one. 'Voters,' he testified almost as an article of faith, 'are not fools. To be sure many individual voters act in odd ways indeed; yet in the large the electorate behaves about as rationally and responsibly as we should expect, given the clarity of the alternatives presented to it and the character of the information available to it.' He insisted that the American voter is not 'strait-jacketed by social determinants or moved by subconscious urges triggered by devilishly skillful propagandists.' On the contrary, he was convinced that the electorate is 'moved by concern about central and relevant questions of public policy, of government performance, and of executive personality.'[23]

This is a remarkably and uncharacteristically optimistic conclusion, even with regard to an old and well-developed democratic system, in 'the first new nation.' It would be challenged by many students of American politics, and is seemingly controverted by much empirical evidence, although the broad conclusion, less optimistically expressed, would seem to be justified. To what extent can it be said that in the newer democratic nations – those which have emerged in the post-war years and which have clung to the institutions of democracy – the electorate has proved to be truly responsible? More specifically, with particular reference to this study, to what extent is the electorate in the South Asian countries – all of which claim to be democracies, although in some instances the claim is a dubious one – a responsible one? Much of the detailed evidence in the following chapters will suggest a negative answer, but the more general evidence, and the broader findings, will suggest that in India and Ceylon, to some extent in Pakistan and Bangladesh, and to a more limited extent in Nepal, the electorate, however illiterate, tradition-bound, inexperienced, and politically apathetic, have oftentimes shown a surprising degree of political awareness, astuteness, and responsibility, and that this tendency seems to be increasing. One leading student of Indian politics has even advanced conclusions regarding the Indian electorate which are strikingly similar to those suggested by Professor Key regarding the American voters. This is a theme which will recur in the following pages, and which is of central importance in this study.

The findings of micro-analysis – in India even more than in America – seem to suggest a much more pessimistic picture than do those of macro-analysis. How can this seeming paradox be resolved? It is, perhaps, a paradox of democracy itself. In any event, the study of elections may provide some clues to the resolution – or at least the explanation – of the seeming paradox. Possibly, as a prominent Indian politician and socialist theoretician who was all too familiar with the mercurial and undependable behavior of the Indian voters once observed: 'Elections are the alchemy of politics – they turn base metals into gold.'[24]

Elections and National Consensus

The larger possible significance of elections in the context of political development should not be overlooked. It has been well stated by one of the senior members of the Centre for the Study of Developing Societies in New Delhi, which has been carrying on some of the most extensive and most sophisticated electoral research that has been undertaken in India: 'In a democratic political system the periodic elections provide opportunities for the expression of the electorate's judgment on the performance of the government. But more than that they become instrumental in developing new political alignments, generating new political attitudes and over a period reorganizing the political society. The politically creative role of elections has been far less understood than it ought to have been, even by profound students of the Indian political process.'[25]

Whereas, as Seymour Martin Lipset has noted, students of elections have tended to concentrate more on cleavages than on consensus, voting may nevertheless be conceived as 'the key mechanism of consensus in democratic society.' 'The study of the integrative aspects of electoral behavior . . . fills important lacunae in our understanding of democracy as a system.'[26] In many developing countries, especially those in Asia, consensus has been a fundamental value in the social system.

'In all such countries where elections are held,' as Richard Harris has astutely observed, 'the strongest electoral impulse is a desire to identify a nationalist consensus. A consensus, after all, is the oldest political assumption of tribal man. . . . It is worth noting that even in those states where monarchical absolutism or military dictatorship have [*sic*] not been replaced even by a rudimentary democracy their rulers are anxious to pay their respects to the creed.'[27] Elections, which may be considered as a link between the society and the polity, between traditional social systems and evolving political structures, may be a vehicle for the employment of the traditionally sanctified device of consensus as a means of achieving national integration in societies where no amount of emphasis on consensus can conceal the deep-seated cleavages, some of ancient origin and frightening persistence, others resulting from the strains of modernization and the crises of development.

The emphasis on consensus is only one of the aspects of the political culture or social traditions of Asian countries which give elections – a Westernized institution grafted onto Asian political and social systems – distinctive features in the Asian context, even though they seem to have universally recognizable characteristics and to function, at least to some extent, in culture-free ways.

Stabilizing and De-Stabilizing Effects of Elections: The South Asian Experience

The stabilizing effects of free competitive elections are apparent in many kinds of political systems. Without them the legitimacy of the government and the people's identification with, and support of, the political system are almost always in question. In countries where elections are taken for granted because they are routinized institutions of the political system, their stabilizing effects may also be taken for granted and receive little notice; but in countries where the political system is still in an early stage of development the stabilizing effects may be more evident and more widely appreciated.

Yet elections may have destabilizing as well as stabilizing effects. This seems to be particularly true in so-called developing countries, where the 'primordial' loyalties are usually stronger than the more 'modern' processes, where the infra-structure of an electoral system is usually flimsy and inadequate, and where elections often serve more as ritualistic or legitimizing devices than as instruments of genuine popular participation and control.

As Samuel Huntington has observed, 'In many, if not most, modernizing countries elections serve only to enhance the power of disruptive and often reactionary social forces and to tear down the structure of public authority.'[28] This may indeed be the effect, although Huntington's statement seems to be exaggerated and internally inconsistent. Elections in 'modernizing countries' have seldom served 'only to enhance the power of disruptive and often reactionary social forces,' except on a short-run basis. These forces have either had to make significant adjustments and concessions to political realities, including the demands for greater popular participation and the requirements of nation-building in the modern world, or they have attempted to turn the clock back, sometimes successfully in the short run, by authoritarian measures, with free elections as one of the first casualties, or they have become less disruptive and have led the way to progressive modernization, or they have been pushed aside by new elites and more progressive forces. If 'the structure of public authority' is controlled by 'reactionary social forces,' its tearing down may be a necessary preliminary step in the path of political development and modernization; if the new structure is to serve the needs of a new democratic order, elections may provide the means for giving it legitimacy and identifying new social forces with, and for involving them in, the political system, and thus for diverting them from disruptive to constructive efforts at nation-building and political development.

In South Asia elections have had both stabilizing and destabilizing effects. Indeed, the electoral experience in South Asia offers many fascinating case studies of the role of elections in political development or political decay. One such case study is provided by the differing effects of free elections in India, Pakistan, and Ceylon in 1970–2.[29]

Focus on Free, Direct, General Elections

In considering the electoral experience in the countries of South Asia, in relation to political development and the political system, we shall be concerned mainly with nationwide general elections to the lower house of the national Parliament, and to a lesser extent, in India and Pakistan, to the State or provincial Legislative Assemblies as well. Many other kinds of elections have been held in the South Asian countries, especially in India, Pakistan, and Ceylon, at local, state (or provincial), and national levels; but while these have been important features of the political experience of these countries, and have doubtless had significant cumulative effects, it seems safe to act on the proposition that the nationwide general elections have been the climatic events in the total electoral process and that they have had the greatest impact on the nature of the political system and on political development. Such elections have activated the South Asian political systems at all levels, and may be analyzed from both micro and macro points of view. In this study we have benefited greatly from micro-studies of various kinds of elections at various levels of the political system and at various times; but we are primarily concerned with systemic analysis, using a developmental approach.

Happily for the researcher, all of the nationwide general elections in South Asian countries since their independence – six in Ceylon, five in India (plus a mid-term election in five States in 1969 and Assembly elections in all but three of the States in 1972), and one each in Nepal, Pakistan, and Bangladesh – have been free, competitive elections on the basis of universal adult suffrage, employing the secret ballot on a one-man-one-vote basis and the simple plurality form of the 'first-past-the-post' system. There have been some minor modifications of this system, such as the special provisions in India for adequate representation of the underprivileged 'untouchables' (the Scheduled Castes) and tribals (the Scheduled Tribes), but not extending to the granting of separate electorates, which had been conceded, on a limited scale, in the years prior to independence. There have also been indirect and limited elections that have purported to be nationwide in character and representing the 'popular will', notably the so-called national elections in Pakistan under the system of Basic Democracies, with the 'Basic Democrats' – the elected members of the basic units of the BD structure, numbering at first 80,000 and then 120,000 – functioning as an electoral college for the choice of members of the provincial Assemblies in the two 'wings' of Pakistan, East and West, and the President of the country. Another example is the Panchayat Democracy system in Nepal, instituted by King Mahendra, not long after he had dismissed the government which had come into power as a result of Nepal's only nationwide general elections, in 1959. In India elections for President, Vice-President, members of the Rajya Sabha, the upper house of the national Parliament, and Legislative Councils, or Vidhan Parishads, the upper houses of the legislatures in some of the States, are held be very complicated procedures of indirect elections, in accordance with the system of proportional representation by means of the single transferable vote.

Ceylon has held direct, competitive, elections on the basis of universal suffrage ever since 1931, and India since 1951–2, and the only truly nationwide general elections in Nepal and Pakistan were held on the same basis, and all of them, procedurally speaking, were conducted with remarkable success. This in itself is an extraordinary political fact, given the alien nature of such elections in the political cultures and experience of the South Asian countries, the high degree of illiteracy, the strong hold of 'primordial' loyalties and forces, the ties of kinship, caste, religion, language, and the generally authoritarian and restrictive social patterns and culture. Many doubts were expressed when such elections were first decided upon, and some have been voiced subsequently; but on the whole this kind of election for the highest officials of the South Asian states was accepted, although by no means routinized, in Pakistan both before and after the long period of military rule, and experimented with and accepted in the new nation of Bangladesh, and accepted, and then abandoned, in Nepal.

In considering elections in South Asia it does not seem to be necessary to attempt to analyze them on the basis of standard types of electoral systems, direct and indirect, including variations of the 'first-past-the-post' system and of proportional representation – and various systems of indirect elections – although, as has been noted, such forms and systems are employed at various levels in the South Asian countries and their relative merit and applicability to South Asian conditions and needs are vigorously discussed, and debated.[30] It is perhaps fortunate for the student of elections in South Asia that the major nationwide elections have all been conducted on the basis of essentially the same system of direct and universal franchise. There are, however, enough differences in the operation and the consequences of this system in the national elections in the various countries of South Asia, and enough experience with other electoral systems at different levels in different countries, to make South Asia a happy hunting ground for the psephologist, whether he is interested primarily in the classic form of electoral systems or in psychological, sociological, ecological, or methodological aspects of the electoral process.

Classifications of Elections

One approach to types of elections that may be useful in the South Asian context, as it has been in studying electoral systems, as well as specific elections, in Western democracies, is the theory or concept of 'critical elections.' This concept is not a new one. It was used, for example, by André Siegfried more than sixty years ago to analyse the effects of 'crisis elections' on voter turnout in France during the period 1876–1906.[31] It was given widespread attention after the publication of V. O. Key's seminal article, 'A Theory of Critical Elections,' in 1955.[32]

A 'critical election,' according to Professor Key, is one 'in which the depth and intensity of electoral involvement are high, in which more or less profound readjustments occur in the relation of power within the community, and in which new and durable electoral groupings are formed.' He mentioned the American presidential elections of 1896 and 1928 as examples of 'crisis elections.'[33] The same concept has been applied to British elections. Professor Richard Rose has argued that 'since 1885 only three elections, those of 1886, 1906, and 1945 may be associated directly with major governmental adaptation.'[34] David E. Butler and Anthony King agree that the elections of 1906 and 1945 were 'turning point' elections, and they suggest that the elections of 1964 might also be included in this category. They also call attention to the usefulness of studying certain 'inconclusive elections' as well, such as those of 1923 and 1950 in Britain.[35]

Another useful classification is suggested by Angus Campbell and associates in *Elections and the Political Order*, published in 1966. They refer to 'maintaining', 'deviating', and 'realigning' elections in the United States, and they classify the Presidential elections of 1948 and 1960 as 'maintaining' elections, those of 1952 and 1956 as 'deviating' elections, and those of 1896 and 1928 as 'realigning' elections (note that these are the same as Professor Key's cited examples of 'critical elections' in the United States).[36]

Examples of each of these classifications could be found in the South Asian experience. Perhaps the clearest example of a 'critical' or 'realigning' election, resulting from fundamental social changes and leading to a major realignment in the electorate, was the general election in Ceylon in 1956. This produced a change of government and of party – the first example in the electoral history of South Asia where one party was succeeded by another through the electoral process (the only other examples are provided by Ceylon, in the general elections of 1960, 1965, and 1970) – and demonstrated that more nationalistic and nativistic groups were becoming important political forces. The fourth general elections in India in 1967, which seemed to mark the end of the one-party dominant system and which ushered in a period of political instability and coalition politics, seemed at the time to be a 'critical' election; but in retrospect, in view of the restoration of Congress dominance, in a new form, four years later, the 1967 election may perhaps be more accurately described as a 'deviating' election. The fifth general elections in 1971 may turn out to have been more truly a 'critical' election, for it came at a critical period in India's post-independence experience and turned an unstable and uncertain political situation into one of considerable strength and stability. In these elections Mrs. Gandhi by-passed or downgraded many of the traditional support groups and party bosses and appealed more directly, and with great success, to new groups and forces, while she was winning back the allegiance to the Congress of some groups which had been turning away from the Congress in previous years. The election of March 1960, in Ceylon was clearly an inconclusive election, and the second and third general elections in India, held in 1957 and 1962, and the election in Ceylon in June 1960 – the second general election in that year – may be described as 'maintaining' elections. The 1971 elections in India might also be characterized as a 'restoring' election.

Elections and Political Parties

The relationship between elections and political parties is a close one in almost every type of political system. During elections parties are most prominently on display, or, to put it in another way, on trial. As David Butler has observed, 'an election provides an unrivalled opportunity to examine the organization, the personnel, and the policies of the parties.'[37] Parties are the main agencies for organizing and for providing political direction to the electorate, and for political choice. As Maurice Duverger pointed out a generation ago, 'The electoral system affects the political life of a country mainly through the parties.'[38] Elections, in turn, are mechanisms which parties use to maintain their support bases and to establish links between the society, mainly non-political, and the political system, in which parties function and of which they are a part.

Thus the relations between electoral and party systems are mutually interacting. For example, a simple majority single-ballot system is generally interpreted as likely to lead in time to a two-party system, whereas a system of proportional representation is likely to lead to a multiple party system. There are many illustrations of these tendencies. Anglo-Saxon countries, where the simple-majority single-ballot system has long been in vogue, have generally had a two-party system, with long periods of gestation in the early years of the development of the party system and with occasional aberrations, as in the case of Britain for two decades or so in the twentieth century, before the Labor Party clearly replaced the Liberal Party as the only party other than the Conservatives that really mattered. Most of the democratic states of Western Europe have systems of proportional representation, and most have multiple party systems. However, it is not difficult to find exceptions to these generalizations. India, for instance, has the simple majority single-ballot system for its major state and national elections, but it does not have, and does not seem likely to have in the foreseeable future, a two party system. PR is not always associated with a multiple party system, nor does it always lead to this kind of party system. A more accurate analysis is suggested by Maurice Duverger: 'Generally speaking, PR keeps more or less unchanged the party situation in being at the time of its introduction. It never has the disruptive effect that some attribute to it.'[39]

Elections and the Social System

It is also essential to consider the relation of the electoral system not only to the party system but also to other key aspects and mechanisms of the political system, such as interest groups and other associational activities, the governmental apparatus at various levels, embracing the bureaucracy as well as the political representatives and leaders, and perhaps also the military and the 'military-industrial establishment.' But even this is not really enough. In addition to the need for studying elections and voting behavior within the context of the political system.

one must not overlook the historical, social, psychological, and ecological setting which bears directly on the electoral process. Elections and voting are not only among the most political of political acts, they are also conditioned by deep-seated historical and societal factors. Hence it is essential to give due consideration to the non-political aspects of the electoral process.

Viewed from another perspective, elections may sometimes be conceived not as 'among the most political of political acts,' or as the major form of political participation, but conversely as hardly as a political act at all. This approach would be a particularly challenging, and perhaps a particularly relevant and revealing one within the South Asian context. As one of the most perceptive students of Indian politics has observed, 'it may well be that by and large the voting act is devoid of political content.... Indeed, the decision to vote for one candidate rather than another may be governed entirely by nonpolitical considerations and the voter may often be unaware of the political choice he makes through the act of voting.' Oftentimes, 'the voting act is not in any significant manner related either to the pursuit of interests.'[40] This is a challenging and unconventional approach, which could find much basis for support in the South Asian environment.

The need for studying elections within the context of historical developments and trends has long been recognized, and is, in fact, an important aspect of earlier studies of elections and voting behavior. Some empirical studies also, such as the Nuffield studies of British elections since 1945, have been able to utilize statistical, survey research, and other sophisticated techniques of electoral analysis without neglecting the historical setting. In their study of the British elections of 1964, for example, David Butler and Anthony King included this significant statement: 'A chronicle of British history between 1959 and 1964 which confined itself to the world of politics would not only fail to take account of the divisive factors that influence men's votes. It would also neglect the profound sea-change in articulate opinion which occurred during these years. The mood of buoyant self-satisfaction which had characterized Britain during the fifties suddenly, it seemed, gave way to a mood of self-doubt and angry introspection.'[41] This change in mood obviously had a profound effect on the British political system, and accounted in large part for the rather surprising results of the general elections of 1964, which brought the Labor Party into power for the first time in thirteen years. Similar analyses of fundamental changes in the fortunes of nations and the mood of their peoples would be essential for an understanding of the results of 'critical' elections in other countries, such as the 1932 elections in the United States, which brought in Franklin D. Roosevelt, the Democratic Party, and the 'New Deal,' the 1958 elections in

France, which gave a resounding mandate to General de Gaulle, and the 1971 elections in India, which gave Mrs. Gandhi the mandate she was seeking.

The importance of considering the electoral process within the societal as well as the political framework, and the role of elections as providing a crucial link between the society and the polity, have already been pointed out. This calls attention to the relationship between the political and the social system, a subject that is much discussed by sociologists and increasingly by political scientists, but which is still relatively underdeveloped.[42] Its relevance to electoral analysis is obvious, even if it is not well spelled out. It is illustrated by one of the most generally discussed of electoral propositions, namely that 'social characteristics determine political preference.'[43]

'In truth,' concluded Professor V. O. Key, Jr., one of the leading students of parties and elections in Western political systems, 'a considerable proportion of the study of electoral behavior bears only a tenuous relation to politics.'[44] This conclusion would seem to be even more applicable to non-Western systems, where the boundaries and distinctions between political and non-political seem to be unclear; but perhaps a sounder conclusion, which electoral studies in Western political systems have already confirmed and which similar studies in non-Western political systems have reinforced, would be that all kinds of social institutions and practices have political consequences and that many of the seemingly non-political aspects of the larger social system have far more than 'a tenuous relation to politics.'

The ecological approach to the study of elections must never be ignored. Elections must be considered not only within the context of the political system, but also within the context of the larger social system, of which the political system is a part. This is particularly true in Asian countries, where elections – like all Western imports – function in both recognizable and unrecognizable ways, especially as viewed from the perspective and experience of Western students of Asian politics and society.[45]

2

ELECTIONS AND THE POLITICAL SYSTEM: INDIA

India's extensive experience with democratic elections, as D. L. Sheth has asserted, 'cannot be ignored while formulating any perspective of the Indian political system.'[1] Unlike the situation in many – perhaps most – of the new states of the so-called developing world, elections in India have been central, and not peripheral, to the system. They have been truly meaningful, and not mainly ritualistic, acts. They have undoubtedly been shaped and conditioned by the nature of the political and social system, and by general environmental factors; but they have also served as links between the polity and the society, between the 'traditional' and the more 'modern' aspects of Indian life and behavior, between the individual citizen and the government, and they have had a considerable effect on the political behavior of the Indian people, on the nature of the emerging mass politics, and indeed upon the nature and evolution of the entire political system. In other words, they may be variously considered as dependent, intervening, and independent variables.

Much more attention has been given to elections as dependent variables in the Indian political system, but their important functions as intervening and independent variables should not be overlooked. This shift in balance or approach is particularly important to note in analyzing the place of elections in the Indian political system, and the contributions of elections to Indian political development. Imtiaz Ahmed has referred to 'the immense transformational impact of our electoral system.'[2] Other careful students have referred to elections in India as 'creative processes' and as 'integrative processes.'[3]

Elections in India: A Developmental Approach

Since the Indian electoral experience has been so vast, and since so many case studies and other micro-studies of particular elections in particular constituencies or districts or States have been made, it seems particularly important to bear in mind the larger aspects and significance of the electoral process in India. This perspective can be best achieved by stressing systemic and developmental analysis. Fortunately many of the Indian and foreign scholars who have done the most detailed work on Indian elections over a considerable period of time have called attention to the macro-political significance of these elections as revealed in their specialized studies and in their efforts to relate these studies to the larger dimensions of the Indian political system. It is perhaps not surprising that elections have been analysed on a more comprehensive and widespread scale than almost any other aspects of Indian politics. This may be explained not only by the availability of aggregate data and the opportunity to do systematic survey research, interviewing, and other kinds of micro-studies, but also by the obvious centrality and significance of elections in the Indian political system.

In a detailed 'ecological electoral investigation' a British and an Indian scholar made these observations concerning the broader significance of India's election story:

> Elections in India provide the occasion for the widest degree of popular participation; they constitute the most important single arena for genuine competition between political groups; they are the principal agency through which recruitment to a significant part of the political elite is affected; and the skills and resources which they especially call forth figure prominently in political life in general. . . . elections in India can now be seen not merely as useful indicators but actually as the events through which the party system and hence, in a measure, the political system achieve their evolution.[4]

As V. M. Sirsikar has stated, elections have become 'a part and parcel of the Indian political life. Elections are now taken for granted.'[5] This is an extraordinary and noteworthy political fact. It is particularly surprising in view of the limited electoral experience in India prior to the first general elections in 1951–2, the relatively short time that has elapsed since the first general elections, and, above all, the difficulties in grafting a system of universal adult franchise onto a new polity in an ancient, heterogeneous, basically traditional, and in many respects highly undemocratic social system. In no other developing country, however, do elections seem to be so central, so meaningful, and so firmly entrenched in the evolving political system.

As in every other country where elections are an integral part of the political system, the electoral process in India has many distinctive features, and is carried on within a distinctive social and political environment. In form it seems generally familiar to any student of psephology, but in operation it can be understood only within its natural habitat. India rightly boasts of having successfully held 'the world's largest democratic elections', including five nationwide general elections and one 'de-linked' State Assembly election in all but three of the Indian States. This experience provides a fascinating case study of the most impressive effort to graft the institutions of modern democracy onto the politics of a mass society. It is particularly impressive because of its dimensions, the relative inexperience of the people with elections, the illiteracy of the great majority of the voters, the generally non-democratic nature of the social system, and other formidable social, physical, and psychological handicaps.

Elections in India, whether for local, State, or national office, are massive spectacles, or '*tamashas*'. They serve important social and entertainment functions, and they also mobilize millions of people into the political process. They are in some ways the most exciting and universal national acts in which the masses engage. They bring politics within the sphere of the citizen, and the citizen into the political arena, if only in a mildly participatory way. National elections are the apex of the election pyramid in a country which has experienced perhaps too frequent elections at various levels. They serve educative functions for the voters and integrative functions for the system. Periodically they throw the spotlight on parties and candidates and political leaders. Miraculously, they are, as Morris-Jones has observed, 'one of the things Indians . . . do well.'[6]

These somewhat euphoric comments on the Indian electoral experience and on the place and significance of elections in India seem to be justified by actual experience, and not simply by the interpretations of those who have benefited by the electoral process or by those scholars whose election studies have tended to support the claims of the political élite. They should, however, be taken with all kinds of qualifications and reservations. The study of elections would seem to be a useful approach to the study of the Indian political system and of India's political development, but it is only one approach, and not necessarily the most useful or revealing.[7]

As long as the Indian political system survives in its present form, elections will continue to be among its essential characteristics. If they cease to be central to the system, then the system itself will be threatened, and probably will not long endure. If for other reasons the system is altered fundamentally, elections will then have a different role and significance, if they are preserved at all in a meaningful way. The system itself is being subjected to many stresses and strains, from within and from without, and various alternative systems or alternative futures for India are possible.

In spite of many pressures and difficulties, the Indian political system is functioning impressively and seems to be developing stronger roots. Within this system the electoral process seems to have functioned with increasing effectiveness and acceptance, and the Indian voter seems to be developing a surprising degree of maturity and sophistication. Or, to put it more accurately, India seems to be developing a 'responsible electorate,' in V. O. Key, Jr.'s words,[8] if not a really mature and sophisticated one.

A study of elections soon leads the analyst to the much-discussed questions of the relations between the polity and the society in India today, the various levels and the different idioms of Indian politics, and the roles and relationships of 'tradition' and 'modernity.' According to conventional interpretations, the Indian polity is more 'modern' than the society. If the polity is considered in terms of vertical organization, presumably it becomes more 'modern' the higher one goes in the political hierarchy; hence politics at the State and regional levels is more 'modern' than at district and local levels, and less 'modern' than at the national level. Presumably, also, it is more 'modern' in urban than in rural areas. Again, however, many exceptions can be found to these observations, although they seem to be generally valid. So too with the 'idioms' of Indian political life. What W. H. Morris-Jones has called the 'traditional,' and to some extent the 'saintly,' idioms are found more commonly at local levels and in rural areas, while the 'modern' idiom prevails at the national level, with the state, and increasingly the district, level standing at the meeting-place of the three idioms, and of the 'traditional' and 'modern' sectors of Indian politics.[9]

Elections are generally thought of as integral features of most modern political systems, and they are usually linked with political parties and other non-ascriptive organizations and processes. In India they are both 'modern' and 'modernizing' agencies, but they also serve as links between 'modern' and 'traditional' sectors of Indian life, and they are profoundly influenced by, as well as exert a profound influence upon, the nature of the Indian political culture. That culture cannot accurately be described as either 'traditional' or 'modern', and the term 'transitional' is too vague to have much utility. It is, as V. M. Sirsikar has described it, a 'mixed political culture.' 'It would be necessary,' wrote Sirsikar in one of the first case studies of an Indian election using the panel interview approach, 'to understand the act of voting in India as operating in a mixed political culture of a traditional society, experiencing modernising influence of the western impact'[10] – and also, he might have added, experiencing countervailing influences of the more 'traditional' sectors of Indian society.

The electoral process is indeed a pervasive one. It extends to the highest levels of political life, and often is the process through which the character of the political leadership and institutions is determined; but it also permeates the social order, at almost every level, and at least to some extent involves people who are generally outside of the reach of politics in political life at basic levels. Hence elections have proved to be powerful instruments of mass education and of political socialization. The Indian experience has proved that they can function in essentially 'traditional' social systems, with an overwhelmingly illiterate population, and still serve the modern political goals of integration, nation-building, and development. In the process the social order becomes more closely identified with the political system, and the political system develops a broader social base.

Many Indian and foreign political scientists, using both anthropological studies and their own detailed research findings for purposes of political analysis, have demonstrated that the Indian political culture is, as Sirsikar described it, a 'mixed' one, in which the elements of 'tradition' and 'modernity' are not sharply differentiated and are in fact quite mixed, in varying degrees, throughout the polity.[11] On the whole, one might say that elections are essentially 'modern' political institutions, and have had a 'modernizing' impact on Indian political behavior; but it would be almost equally true to add that far from contributing to the increasing 'modernization' of Indian politics on a steadily accelerating scale, elections show some signs of becoming more 'traditionalized' in the Indian setting.

This trend has been confirmed in many detailed studies. It is particularly manifest in the changing character of Indian political leadership. On the whole, this leadership is changing significantly, with a declining role and influence of the westernized, educated, urbanized, high-caste, 'modern' élite that spearheaded the Indian independence movement and that provided most of the top leadership to India in the first two decades of its independence, and an increasing role and influence of a middle-caste, less educated, less westernized, more rural, and locally-based élite. Elections have been a major agency for the recruitment and emergence of this new élite. Thus they have served as a vehicle for bringing a more traditional elite into a more central role in the political system, increasingly at all levels.

The phenomenon of the 'modern' institution of competitive, democratic elections having a 'traditionalizing' and 'ruralizing' effect after the first years of independence has been noted in many developing countries. Samuel P. Huntington is one of the many students of political development to call attention to this important trend:

> The extension of the suffrage to the rural masses in a society which otherwise remains highly traditional strengthens and legitimizes the authority of the traditional élite. . . . Electoral competition in postcolonial countries thus seems to direct the attention of political leaders from the urban to the rural voters, to make political appeals and governmental policies less modern and more traditional, to replace highly educated cosmopolitan political leaders with less

educated local and provincial leaders, and to enhance the power of local and provincial government at the expense of the national government.[12]

This general trend has been in evidence in Indian politics for some years, with many countervailing trends. (As Huntington pointed out, 'the assimilation of the rural masses into politics occurs, if at all, in a disjointed and halting manner.')[15]

> Electoral competition in India tended to hasten the replacement of the nationalist, cosmopolitan, Western-educated leaders by more provincial, less well-educated, local-oriented leaders. In the 1962 elections 'virtually everywhere there was a concern by the voter for electing local men who could mediate between the voter and the complex and often slow moving governmental machinery, rather than state-wide or national public figures who could speak on issues of public policy.'[14]

Analyses of the changing membership in State legislative assemblies and in the Lok Sabha (the lower house of the Indian Parliament) have revealed the kind of trends that Huntington and Weiner have described. A recent doctoral dissertation at the Punjab University in Chandigarh on political development in Himachal Pradesh contained this confirmation: 'The introduction of the mass francise has forced the (Congress) party to shift attention from a few urban centres of Himachal Pradesh to the smaller towns and larger villages with the result that middle class agriculturalists have begun to displace, though slowly, the older dominance of the educated upper caste, and the party is becoming more rural in orientation as well as composition.'[15] This study added an important qualification to this overall interpretation of the trend toward the 'traditionalizing' or 'ruralizing' of politics. To be sure, 'the new élites are congressmen who have succeeded in the competitive politics of the Pradesh and also represent largely the more traditional forces in the society. Yet they are not necessarily traditional themselves. Having been brought into touch with the older type of leadership, they have been forced to view the problems in a broader context and in terms of modernized leadership. They are, then, a blend of the modern and traditional, and as such, are perhaps more sensitive to the demands of their supporters.'[16]

The electoral process therefore has brought masses of people into closer contact with the political system, and in turn has brought the political parties into closer contact with the masses. The politics of a mass society, to use Kornhauser's term, inevitably rests on an essentially traditional base; but it also functions through 'modern' agencies, such as political parties, and serves 'modern' political goals.

Elections, as Surindar Suri has pointed out, may be conceived of 'as a process of creative interaction between the political parties and the body of citizens.'[17] This role of parties, and of elections, in the context of the 'polity and society' and the 'tradition and modernity' syndromes has been emphasized by Gopal Krishna in his perceptive essay on 'One Party Dominance – Development and Trends:'

> The introduction of universal adult franchise for the elections to the State and Central legislatures brought the political parties into an intimate and direct relationship with Indian society, whose principal features are the relatively low level of social integration and essentially agglomerative character. . . . A new dimension thus came to be added to the activities of the political parties making them mediating agencies between the largely traditional and politically diffuse electorate and the modern state system. . . . The interpenetration of politics and the social order compelled the parties to come to terms with, and in the process help to moderate and modify, the traditional group orientation in Indian public life. Even when the struggle for power and influence appeared to encourage them to make use of group sentiment, thus increasing and solidifying the already powerful parochial tendencies, the parties in effect contributed to the making of the national community by drawing many non-modern groups into the modern sector of political activity.[18]

Elections and Political Parties

Thus the role of parties, and the interactions of parties and elections, are central to any study of elections. As Duverger has observed, 'the electoral system affects the political life of a country mainly through the parties;'[19] and in most countries, including all democratic countries, parties are deeply involved in the electoral process, and in fact depend upon it to promote their goals and objectives. It is of course theoretically conceivable that elections can be held without parties, and that parties can function without elections. It is also true that in some countries parties are mere political facades, and elections largely ritualistic acts. But no modern democratic country has been able to function without both elections and parties, as meaningful institutions in the political system. India confirms rather than denies or qualifies the validity of this proposition, even though both parties and elections are frequently criticized in a land where a strong tradition of 'consensus' prevails and where there is some continuing sentiment in favor of a system of 'partyless democracy' within a framework of 'democratic decentralization.'[20]

In India, as in other democratic polities, political parties must seek support from the people through periodic elections, and their influence and effectiveness are determined in large part by the verdict of the polls. Elections thus are an index of the relative political standing of various parties, and they both reflect and shape the trend of events and forces in the underlying social and political order. Among other things, they throw a great deal of light on the nature of the party system, and of the changes that are taking place in that system.

Fortunately it is not necessary to go into the details of the Indian party system, but a few broad aspects and trends, which are directly related to elections, should be noted. India obviously does not have a well organized party system, but it does have a very active one, in spite of certain currents of opinion, reflecting either more traditional or more authoritarian views, which are opposed to parties, in theory or in practice. The prevailing model or thesis that has gained currency is that of one-party dominance, or the one-dominant party model. This is a useful characterization, in that it calls attention to the obvious fact that in India one party – the Indian National Congress, the party of Gandhi and Nehru, the spearhead of the independence movement (the relative roles of 'movement' and 'party' have always been rather unclear in the case of the Congress), and the party that has been continuously in power at the center and that has usually been in power in most of the States since independence – is truly dominant. This also serves as a reminder that India is neither a one-party nor a two-party system, or in fact a multi-party system, although many parties exist within the framework of one-party dominance. (The existence of many parties is possible in a one-dominant party system as well as in a truly multiparty system.)

Maurice Duverger has called attention to the 'tendency of the simple majority vote with one ballot to lead to a two-party system.'[21] This tendency, as he notes, is particularly obvious in Anglo-Saxon countries, and it also may be observed in other political systems which have this type of direct elections on the basis of universal franchise. India has clearly been an exception to this trend. Its electoral system is based on 'the simple majority vote with one ballot,' but in the course of nearly a quarter of a century since it first instituted the system on a universal scale it has neither developed a two-party system nor shown strong tendencies in that direction. Instead it has experienced a system of one party dominance, with some ups and downs, with many parties functioning rather ineffectively and with varying fortunes within the framework of the prevailing Congress system, or lack of system.

Many observers have predicted that a polarization of forces will lead to the emergence of a two-party system in India; but thus far this has not occurred, nor has it even come close to occurring. A premise of those who foresaw the emergence of a two-party system was that the 'right wing' of the Congress would break away and form a conservative party in coalition with right-wing opposition parties, and that the 'left wing' inside the Congress would become the nucleus of a leftist party, including the non-Communist socialists in opposition parties and perhaps even some Communists. In 1969 the Congress Party did split, but this led, after a few years of political instability and uncertainty, to the re-emergence of the one-dominant-party system in a somewhat different form, and to the weakening of almost all the opposition parties to the right and to the left, with the possible exception of the two Communist parties but definitely including the other and more conservative wing of the Congress Party.

Opposition parties have proliferated in India, although they have had little success in national politics and in only a few of the Indian States. In the first general elections, in 1951–2, there were no fewer than fourteen recognized 'national' parties, fifty-nine 'state' parties, and several other recognized 'parties,' most of which were hardly parties at all, in any precise sense.[22] After the first general elections the Election Commission decided to recognize as 'national' parties only those parties that received at least three per cent of the vote on a nationwide basis in the previous elections. This decision reduced the number of recognized national parties to four in 1957, but the number rose to six in 1962 and to eight in 1967 and 1971. In the fifth general elections, in 1971, some twenty recognized parties returned one or more members to the Lok Sabha, but only seven of these returned ten or more members, and only one of these seven, the Congress Party, won more than twenty-five seats. The Congress alone won 350 seats, thus giving it a two-thirds majority in the entire House.

Election data help to reveal the varying fortunes of political parties at national, state, and local (including constituency) levels, and also general trends in the political system. The results of the parliamentary elections clearly reveal certain major trends, including the dominance of the Congress Party, which has never gained less than a majority of seats in any general election (usually, in fact, it obtained nearly two-thirds of the total number of seats), the sharp decline in its representation in the Lok Sabha as a result of the fourth general elections in 1967 (when it still won more than half of the total number of seats), the strength of the 'new' Congress led by Mrs. Gandhi, as shown by the results of fifth general elections in 1971 (reconfirmed by the outcome of the State assembly elections in 1972), the declining fortunes of most opposition parties, the marked discrepancy between percentages of votes cast and of seats won (the Congress Party, for example, has never won a majority of the popular votes), and the generally unbalanced nature of the party system. Similar trends can be seen in most States, although in some the opposition to the Congress has been stronger and in a few non-Congress governments have been formed from time to time, and in most constituencies, although at the constituency level there are many examples of pockets of non-Congress opposition.

Because of its dominant position data regarding the electoral fortunes of the Congress party are particularly significant. These reaffirm the thesis of one-party dominance, subject to some fluctuations, and also throw light on underlying political trends. As Douglas Madsen has observed, 'variations in the political environment to which all parties must react are conveniently indexed by the electoral successes and failures of Congress, both within the electorate as a whole and within its various components.'[23]

But even on the national political level election data would have to be analyzed very carefully and in great detail in order to test the validity of conventional interpretations and the findings suggested by the general results of various elections; and, as has often been pointed out in election studies in other countries, electoral data are rather crude and unsatisfactory sources of information on the real trends in a political system, and often lead to oversimplified and even misleading conclusions. This is certainly true with regard to electoral analysis in India based on aggregate electoral data.

Even the familiar thesis of one-party dominance, which seems to be conclusively confirmed by aggregate electoral data, is subject to all kinds of reservations and qualifications. It has often concealed important trends and nuances in the Indian political system. It does not indicate the nature of the opposition, or of the process of opposition, in India, which has often been carried on as much within the Congress Party, always a heterogeneous organization of an umbrella type, as outside, and in which opposition parties, and interest groups, have at times played a much more effective role than their numbers and apparent strength would suggest.[24] Above all, it gives little insight into the nature of politics in India, especially below the national level, where much of the politics of the country is carried on. Election data, however, especially when tested and supplemented by survey research and interviewing and other standard methods of voting behavior and public opinion studies, can be helpful in analyzing detailed developments and underlying trends at local and constituency levels.

Aggregate election data obviously should be used cautiously, and should be supplemented by other sources of information. Such data, for example, would not reveal the reasons for the severe Congress reverses in the fourth general elections in 1967, although they would help to document and highlight these reverses. They would not in themselves show how and why the Congress Party, which seemed to be slipping badly by 1967, disappeared from the political scene in 1969, in the form in which it had previously existed, and how and why one of the splinter groups that emerged, the 'new Congress' led by Mrs. Indira

Gandhi, won out against the other wing of the Congress and in 1971 became even stronger than the undivided Congress had been in its heyday. The election results would, however, document the success of the new Congress, and could also be used to show how the one-party-dominant system, which seemed to be challenged in years 1967–71, re-emerged in a vigorous form in and after 1971; but they would not reveal the limitations of this overall interpretation, or the reasons for the general trends. Nor would they show the changes that were taking place in the Indian political and social system, which largely determined the election results.

Great changes occurred in the parties during the course of India's electoral history. After independence the Congress changed from a national movement to a political party, in spite of Gandhi's famous advice that it become a purely social welfare organization. After the death of Sardar Patel in 1951 it was clearly dominated by one man, Jawaharlal Nehru, until his death in 1964, or at least until shortly before his death; it seemed to experience increasing difficulties, due in part to internal divisions and rivalries, from 1964 to 1971, and these difficulties were reflected in such major developments as the reverses in the fourth general elections, which brought non-Congress governments, political instability, serious breakdowns of law and order, periods of President's Rule in several States, and the split in the Congress Party in 1969. This split left the victorious faction led by Mrs. Gandhi in a minority position in the Lok Sabha and in several States and seemed to presage the end of Congress dominance in the wake of the demise of the Congress in its undivided form. The new Congress of Mrs. Gandhi, however, with an overwhelming mandate in the national elections of 1971 and the State elections of 1972, has emerged in a dominant role, but it is not the same Congress as existed in pre-independence and post-independence days, up to 1969. Nor are any of the other so-called national parties. Indeed, 'an interesting feature of the Indian political party system is that none of the recognized all-India parties posed for elections in 1971, was what it was during the first general elections, two decades ago. Every one has changed its shape. . . . In fact, each of them has been split.'[25]

Electoral statistics, especially when used in conjunction with the kind of socio-economic and demographic data that can be obtained from census reports and more specialized studies, can throw considerable light on the support bases of the various political parties. Using such data, several Indian and foreign scholars have been able to provide empirical confirmation of some generally accepted assumptions and to suggest the need to re-examine others. Quite obviously, 'the Congress party has a relatively more heterogeneous and differentiated social, economic and demographic support base, compared to all other parties.'[26] Its support has come from nearly all regions and nearly all social and occupational groups, with less overall support from the young, the highly educated, the urban voters, the upper castes, and the higher income groups than from other sectors of the society. By 1967 it seemed to be losing its hold on young voters and on certain minority groups, such as the Muslims and the Sikhs, but the results of the 1971 elections showed that the traditional support bases among minorities had been recaptured, and that young voters, for the first time in several years, were rallying behind the youthful and vigorous image of Mrs. Gandhi. All other parties have a much less diversified and heterogeneous support base. The Communists draw their main support from certain regions, notably West Bengal, Andhra Pradesh, and Kerala, and from certain groups, such as new and young voters, lower castes, the industrial and agricultural working class, middle class professionals, and white collar workers; the Socialists from 'young voters between 26 and 35 years of age, the illiterates, the landless labourers and the cultivators with small land holdings, the low caste groups, the Harijans and the tribals, and the very low income groups;' the Jana Sangh from upper caste, highly educated, urban, professional, middle and upper income groups, and from white collar workers and middle and large landowners; the Swatantra from landowners and landless laborers, upper and lower castes, and illiterates and less educated people; the regional parties from particular groups at local levels, depending on the nature of the parties, but mostly from religious minorities, Harijans, tribals, urban businessmen, the urban working class, and low and middle groups in terms of education and income.[27] These support bases can, therefore, be identified, at least in broad outline. They provide a fairly 'hard core' of support for the various parties, but they may change over time. When such changes do occur they may be evidences of temporary fluctuations in support of particular parties or significant indicators and products of underlying changes in the political and social system.

Politicization and the Social Environment

Elections and political parties are major agencies for the increasing politicization of Indian life and society, one of the most conspicuous phenomena in post-independence India. This phenomenon is central to Indian political development, and it takes many forms. It is evidenced by the growing role of politics and government in India generally, by the increasing involvement in political life of individuals and groups which in the past have been quite inactive in the political arena, by the pervasive nature of politics in almost all aspects of Indian life, and by the obsession with politics which seems to characterize the news media and other avenues and agencies of public expression.

This phenomenon of politicization in India has some baffling and anomalous aspects. India is, as Rajni Kothari and many others have pointed out and as past history has demonstrated, essentially an apolitical society, with the masses of the people almost isolated from political life, except as the victims or the beneficiaries of the political rulers and the bureaucracy. Yet it is increasingly becoming a highly politicized society. These countervailing trends account for much of the apparent cross-pressures in Indian life.

Politicization seems to be an inescapable concomitant of modern or modernizing programs and policies. Indeed, Rajni Kothari calls it the 'driving force' of 'modernization.'[28] Possibly, therefore, India is becoming more highly politicized because it is becoming more modern, or at least more modernized. Whether such a high degree of politicization as actually exists, or at least seems to exist, is a necessary price to pay for modernization, or whether it is on the whole desirable or undesirable, can be debated endlessly, without any possibility of empirical resolution.

The paradox of a highly politicized and yet apolitical society must be borne in mind in any analysis of current trends and developments. 'The process of politicisation, however,' as D. L. Sheth has noted, 'is "adaptive" rather than "transformative".' In explaining this thesis Sheth writes:

> The traditional categories of social belonging are transferred to political and civic life introduced by modern political institutions. But these traditional categories do not remain immutable in the face of the demands made by modern democratic institutions. . . . In this process of adaptation, the ritualistic and religious aspects of group living are undermined in favour of political articulation of group interests, including even the more primordial group interests. This is sought through identification with larger collectivities like political parties and pressure groups.[29]

One outstanding example of this adaptive aspect is the so-called politicization of caste. Caste, an all-pervasive, rather rigid but still changing social institution, is clearly an important factor in Indian politics, but in the process of politicization it has taken on new dimensions and sometimes seems to operate as an agency of modernization as well as at other times as a social barrier to modernization.[30]

Thus, on the one hand, it seems impossible to exaggerate the degree of politicization of Indian life, and, on the other, one is inclined to wonder whether the apparently pervasive politicization is not in reality a surface phenomenon, confined largely to the polity and not affecting significantly the wider societal environment. By focusing on elections and the electoral process, which are by their very nature highly politicized phenomena, one may easily get an exaggerated and distorted idea of the extent of politicization in the society generally. Rajni Kothari, who has often referred to politicization as a central theme in Indian politics, has also issued this caveat: 'Politicization of the larger society and the people at large is left to the electoral process only; there has been very little effort at generating a sustained process of political awakening through the involvement of the people in the developmental process.'[31]

Trends in the Indian Political System: Electoral Analysis

In considering the role of elections in India's political development, two important general propositions or conclusions should be borne in mind. The first is that India's extensive experience with democratic elections has had a cumulative impact. Each general election has had distinctive features and has posed distinctive political questions, but each has had a great effect, both tangible and intangible, on subsequent elections, on the total electoral process, and on the evolution of the Indian political system.[32] The second is that the elections, and the total electoral experience, have not only been profoundly affected by the basic nature of the Indian political system and the overall political process, and have thus been significant dependent variables, but they have also affected the nature of the system and the process, and have thus also been important independent and intervening variables. This latter aspect of the role of elections in India has not yet been adequately explored, or even recognized, but it is an aspect that is emerging increasingly as a basic factor in the evolving political system.

A vast amount of aggregate data, supplemented by many case studies based on participant observation and increasingly on survey research and interview techniques, is available for the study of India's general elections and their place and meaning in the Indian context. A major source of aggregate data is the reports of the Election Commission of India. Sophisticated and in-depth electoral research on India's elections by Indian and foreign scholars was quite limited for the first three elections, but it was quite extensive for the fourth general elections in 1967, although many of the results of this more extensive and more sophisticated and more methodologically significant research were not made available for many years. In the meantime other important elections – the mid-term elections in four major States in 1969, the fifth general elections in 1971, and the State Assembly elections in 1972 – were held, and the mass of unassimilated data on Indian elections pyramided. More importantly, the Indian political scene changed a great deal after 1967 – partly, but only partly, as a consequence of the rather sensational trends revealed in the election results – and even detailed and sophisticated studies of the 1967 elections, while welcome, seemed to have lost some of their savor after an overly long gestation period.

Psephologists are painfully aware of the almost impossible task they face in making adequate use of vast amounts of data and other information in countries like India where elections are a normal, central, and accepted part of the political process. In India the task of analyzing the available data, and supplementing the aggregate data with field studies and micro-analysis, was made particularly difficult by the lack of scholarly preparation for the task of electoral research and the difficulties in organizing and funding large-scale collaborative research projects.

Five General Elections: Distinctive Aspects

A detailed analysis, using various methodological techniques, of the results of the five nationwide general elections in India, spanning a period of twenty years, would reveal many significant trends in the Indian political system, and would suggest many avenues of both macro and micro explanation. Each nationwide election should be studied in both macro- and micro-terms. The behavior and activity of voters, candidates, and parties at constituency, district, and state levels provide fascinating insights into the working of the electoral process at the basic levels. The overall results highlight and shape broad trends in the political system.

Each general election has distinctive aspects, especially when considered against the general social and political background. Three of the five general elections were held in the Nehru era, and were in effect what Angus Campbell has called 'maintaining' elections.[33] The first general elections, in 1951–2, had the excitement and the uncertainties of a new experience. The second, in 1957, came at the height of Nehru's influence and power, and before various economic, political, and internal troubles became critical. The third, in 1962, came after the abrupt change for the worse in Indo-Chinese relations (but before the border war with China at the end of the year), and at a time of mounting economic difficulties. The post-Nehru elections took on a different character, if only because the great leader was no longer at the helm of affairs. The results of the fourth general elections, in 1967, were obviously affected by the apparent lack of strong leadership at the Center, the humiliating defeat in the border war with China in 1962 and the frustrations in Indo-Chinese relations, two inconclusive conflicts with Pakistan in 1965, the Tashkent agreement of January 1966, which provoked mixed reactions in India, two unusually bad seasons and the accompanying human misery, a most unpopular devaluation, and other difficulties. The fifth general elections, in 1971,

Table 2.i

RESULTS OF GENERAL ELECTIONS IN INDIA, 1951–1971
House of the People (Lok Sabha)

Parties	*1951–2*		*1957*		*1962*		*1967*		*1971*	
	Number of seats won	*Per cent valid votes polled*	*Number of seats won*	*Per cent valid votes polled*	*Number of seats won*	*Per cent valid votes polled*	*Number of seats won*	*Per cent valid votes polled*	*Number of seats won*	*Per cent valid votes polled*
Congress Party	364	45.0	371	47.78	361	44.72	283	40.73	–	–
Congress (R)	–	–	–	–	–	–	–	–	350	43.64
Congress (O)	–	–	–	–	–	–	–	–	16	, 10.56
Jana Sangh	3	3.1	4	5.93	14	6.44	35	9.41	22	7.48
Swatantra	–	–	–	–	18	7.89	44	8.68	8	3.08
Communist Party of India	16	3.3	27	8.92	29	9.96	23	5.19	23	4.89
Communist Party of India (Marxist)	–	–	–	–	–	–	19	4.21	25	4.97
Kisan Mazdoor Praja Party	9	5.8	–	–	–	–	–	–	–	–
Praja Socialist Party	–	–	19	10.41	12	6.84	13	3.06	2	0.98
Socialist Party	12	10.6	–	–	–	–	–	–	–	–
Socialist Party of India	–	–	–	–	6	2.49	–	–	–	–
Samyukta Socialist Party	–	–	–	–	–	–	23	4.92	3	2.43
Dravida Munnetra Kazhagam	–	–	–	–	7	2.02	25	3.90	23	3.80
Other Parties	44	16.4	34	7.57	30	7.37	20	6.15	30	9.84
Independents	41	15.8	39	19.39	20	12.27	35	13.75	13	8.33
Total	489	100.0	494	100.0	497	100.0	520	100.0	515	100.0

Source: Adapted from reports of the Election Commission, Government of India found India in a very different mood. The Congress Party had split in late 1969, and the faction led by Mrs. Gandhi had clearly emerged as the strongest and most popular wing, and Mrs. Gandhi herself had developed a popular image as a strong, determined, leader, truly dedicated to socialism and social change and to the interests of the nation and the welfare of the masses of the people. The economic picture had brightened – thanks in part to the first impact of the 'green revolution.' The need was apparent for a strong government to give 'stability through peace and progress,' especially in view of the continuing problems at home and the developments in Pakistan which shortly after the Indian general elections led to bloody civil war and placed added burdens on India and added strains on Indo-Pakistan relations.[34]

Through all of these developments, over a period of 20 years, the Congress Party maintained its overwhelming predominance in the Lok Sabha, and in most of the States, except in certain ones, notably Kerala and Madras (Tamil Nadu), and in several states during the period 1967–71. At no time, except in 1967, did it win fewer than 68 per cent of the seats in the Lok Sabha, and even in 1967 it won 279 of the 521 seats, while the temporarily leading opposition party won only 44.

The loss of nearly 80 seats as a result of the 1967 election was widely heralded as marking the end of the era of one-party dominance, and the formation of non-Congress governments in many of the States (at one time as many as eight), the results of the mid-term elections in four major States in 1969, the controversy over the election of a President of the Congress in the late summer of the same year, and the split in the Congress a few weeks later all seemed to confirm this thesis. But the situation was soon reversed dramatically by Mrs. Gandhi and the 'new' Congress. After the elections of 1971 and 1972 and her handling of the crisis with Pakistan and the emergence of Bangladesh, Mrs. Gandhi dominated the political scene in a way that even her father, at the height of his power, did not equal.

Thus the general elections of 1967, which seemed to usher in 'the second Indian revolution' and to be, in V. O. Key's terms, a 'critical' election,[35] turned out, in retrospect, to be more of a 'deviating' election, or an aberration from the long-time electoral trends. The rather startling results of the 1967 elections were caused by sharp realignments within the electorate; but these realignments did not lead to a reversal in the prevailing political patterns and, above all, they did not prove to be durable.

Election Swings and One Party Dominance

Rajni Kothari and other astute analysts of the Indian political scene have developed the concepts of 'the Congress system' and the system of one-party dominance in India, especially during the Nehru era and since

1971. The general elections of 1967 seemed to bring an end to the system of one-party dominance, and several events in the period from 1967 to 1971 seemed to confirm this trend. Some observers even thought that it would lead inevitably to various forms of coalition government at the Center, as it did in nearly one-half of the States following the 1967 elections. Even Kothari referred to the change from the one party dominant system to a system of 'competitive dominance.'[36] But the 1971 elections – reaffirmed by the State Assembly elections of 1972 – seemed to restore the one-dominant-party system, in a somewhat different but in some respects even stronger form. These broad trends are indicated by the aggregate election data, especially if analyzed on national, State, and constituency levels; but more sophisticated analysis of political trends in India would of course call for the use of other kinds of information and other methods of interpretation.

Almost any study of aggregate electoral data would highlight the relative and varying fortunes of the major political parties.

The dominance of the Congress Party at the national level, and in most of the States in most elections, is clearly revealed in the election statistics. The aggregate data also reveal the marked discrepancy between seats won and votes polled, for the Congress, with its continued and usually overwhelming predominance in the Lok Sabha, has never received 50 per cent of the votes, and in 1967 its percentage of the total valid votes polled was only 40.73 per cent. Yet even in the latter election it won 68 per cent of the seats in the Lok Sabha. In the States its fortunes have varied considerably in some and have remained fairly constant in others. It has consistently had a majority of the Lok Sabha seats in Assam, Bihar, Himachal Pradesh, Madhya Pradesh, Mysore, the Punjab, and Uttar Pradesh, and, with a single exception in each case, Andhra Pradesh and Maharashtra. On the other hand, it has never won more than seven of the nineteen Lok Sabha seats from Kerala; in 1967 it was able to get only three of the thirty-nine seats from Madras; and in the elections of 1967 and 1971, when its overall fortunes fluctuated greatly, it made a consistently bad showing in West Bengal, winning only fourteen and thirteen seats, respectively.[37] These aggregate figures call attention to the need for special investigation of such aberrations, and obvious pockets of weakness, in the 'Congress system.' The reasons for these aberrations can usually be easily ascertained by historical research and first-hand investigation of a micro-political nature.

A study of the general elections will reveal certain broad swings, especially in the fortunes of the opposition parties. The Swatantra Party emerged on the national scene by winning eighteen seats in the Lok Sabha in 1962. It increased its strength substantially in 1967, becoming the largest opposition party in the Parliament, with forty-four seats, but in 1971 it was able to win only eight seats, and virtually ceased to exist as a national party. The socialist parties, in spite of internal divisions, had some strength until 1971, when they collapsed spectacularly. The Communist Party of India increased its strength in the second and third general elections. In 1964 it split into two parties. In 1967 the two Communist parties together won more seats than the CPI had ever won and in 1971, when most opposition parties suffered severe reverses, the CPI won as many seats as it did in 1967 and the CPI(M) gained six seats. Only one regional party, the Dravida Munnetra Kazhagam (DMK), has had any substantial representation in the Lok Sabha (in 1967 the DMK won all of the twenty-five Lok Sabha seats from Madras which it contested, and became the second largest opposition party in the national Parliament).

The sad state and varying fortunes of the opposition parties are clearly delineated in the aggregate election data. These fluctuations in political fortunes are interesting to plot, and are often suggestive of underlying trends; but the opposition parties have been too weak and too divided to play much of a role on the national political scene. In fact, all of the so-called national parties, except the Congress, seem to have lost whatever claims to national status they might have had. There is in effect no significant organized political opposition to the Congress on the national level, although in various ways, of course, opposition exists, for the opposition parties seem to be playing a far more influential role than their individual and collective weakness would suggest, and a great deal of opposition is provided within the heterogeneous framework of the Congress Party and by certain interest groups, of an ascriptive or 'modern' type, in Indian society. The nature and strength of 'the process of opposition' in India is a topic of intriguing interest. Such opposition is certainly not confined to the officially recognized opposition parties, whose role in the political system is in fact both more and less than would be expected from their character, objectives, and limited popular support.[38]

Electoral analysis reveals that all opposition parties in India today, not excepting the Communist parties, are really not national parties at all, but are in fact confined to a relatively few States and to certain constituencies in a few States. This localization of strength was dramatically revealed by the results of the State Assembly elections in 1972. The Jana Sangh got seventy-three of its 104 seats in the Legislative Assemblies of Bihar and Madhya Paradesh, the Congress (O) eighty-two of its eighty-eight seats in Bihar, Gujarat, Haryana, and Mysore, the Socialists thirty-three of their fifty-seven seats in Bihar, Swatantra eleven of its sixteen seats in Rajasthan, and the CPI(M) thirty of its thirty-four seats in Tripura and West Bengal. The CPI won seats in more States, but it got ninety of its 112 seats in those States where it was in alliance with the Congress – Bihar, Madhya Pradesh, the Punjab, Rajasthan, West Bengal, and also the Union Territory of Delhi. One could employ similar analysis to identify the pockets of strength of opposition parties on a constituency by constituency basis. The next step would then be to attempt to ascertain the reasons for localized opposition strength by a detailed micro-analysis of the situation in the identified constituencies.

Electoral analysis would also seem to support the hypothesis of the striking regularity of electoral performance in India, despite certain broad electoral swings and dramatic changes in certain constituencies and sometimes in some States. This regularity is revealed mainly in percentages of votes polled by various parties, and in degrees of support of the various parties by different groups in the electorate.

This kind of analysis does not indicate any dramatic shifts of an ideological nature, such as from left to right, or vice versa. Certainly no long-range ideological swings can be detected by concentrating on the relative fortunes of the opposition parties. No opposition parties, on the national level, have done well enough to point to any such swings. It would obviously be possible to characterize some parties – i.e., Swatantra – as more 'rightist' than others – i.e., the Communists. In the first and second general elections the nationally recognized 'leftist' non-Congress parties won thirty-seven and forty-two seats, respectively, and the Jana Sangh, which is often labelled, perhaps wrongly, as 'rightist' won only three in 1951–2 and four in 1957. In 1962 the Jana Sangh and the new Swatantra Party got thirty-two seats and the Socialists and Communists fifty-seven. In a sense, therefore, 1962 witnessed the emergence of the 'rightist' parties, but at the same time the 'leftist' parties also gained in strength. In 1967 the 'leftists' and 'rightists' got almost the same number of seats – seventy-eight and seventy-nine, respectively – thus increasing their representation substantially at the expense of the Congress. In the Congress landslide of 1971 all opposition parties except the Communists suffered badly, with the Swatantra – a 'rightist' party – and the SSP and PSP – 'leftist' parties – suffering routs so serious as to virtually eliminate them from the national scene.

If India has moved politically in a steadily leftward direction, as many observers have maintained, this shift has been reflected in the changing orientation within the Congress Party, rather than in the varying fortunes of the opposition parties to the left and right of the Congress. As has often been pointed out, the terms 'left' and 'right' seem to have little meaning within the Indian context.

On the State level ideological considerations may have affected, and been reflected in, election results. There seems to be a considerable correlation between the more radically inclined States and the showing of the Communist parties in national and State elections. It is hardly coincidental that the left Communists have fared best in West Bengal and Kerala, and to a lesser extent in Andhra Pradesh. But many other factors operate at the State level, and some of the parties that have done best in particular States, notably the Dravida Munnetra Kazhagam in Madras (now Tamil Nadu) are regional or State based parties with no pronounced ideological orientation of a generally recognized type.

A more accurate and more perceptive conclusion would be that Indian politics have become more radicalized without becoming more ideological, and that they have also become more secularized and more localized. But these significant trends are not clearly revealed in aggregate electoral data – thus illustrating the limitations of such data – and they have taken place mainly as a result of trends within the Congress and not in the opposition parties.

The 'Peculiar Arithmetic' of Indian Elections

A striking feature of Indian elections has been a high degree of regularity in the voting, despite considerable changes in the results. The way the people have voted has been much more consistent than 'the peculiar arithmetic' of Indian elections would suggest. Significant swings and changes have taken place in the elections results, especially at state levels, without significant changes in party support. This is a common feature of plurality and majority systems, which, A. J. Milnor has pointed out, 'are able to change the composition of the parliamentary majority without appreciably changing the percentages of the popular vote.'[39] But it is particularly notable in India, especially at state levels.

One broad illustration of 'the peculiar arithmetic' of Indian elections is the fact that in general elections the Congress has never obtained a majority of the popular vote, but it has consistently won more than half, and in every general election except the fourth 68 per cent or more of the seats in the Lok Sabha. Thus one could say that in a so-called one-dominant-party system the dominant party does not even command the support of half of the Indian electorate. It has, however, benefited greatly from the fragmented nature of the opposition, and usually from what E. P. da Costa of the Indian Institute of Public Opinion has called the Multiplier – the relation of seats won to votes cast. When the Multiplier has not worked in favor of the Congress – as in many States in the fourth general elections – Congress has lost heavily in seats as well as in votes, and election forecasts have been particularly inaccurate.[40]

Another factor which has been useful in predicting elections' outcomes, when it works as it usually does, is what da Costa has called the Splinter Factor, that is, the effect of the number of candidates in a constituency on the prospects of the Congress candidate. Generally speaking, in all of the first four general elections the Congress had greater success in straight fights – that is, where only one opposition candidate was contesting – than in multiple candidacy contests; and by and large the success of Congress candidates was inversely related to the number of candidates in a constituency, at least up to about six. This Splinter Factor seemed to have stood the test of time, and it proved to be a useful device in the election forecasts of the IIPO.; but in the fifth general elections in 1971 it worked precisely opposite to its usual behavior. In other words, on the whole the Congress did better in multiple-candidate contests than in straight fights, and better rather than worse when the number of candidates increased, up to the same figure of six or so. This peculiar behavior of the Splinter Factor, which is illustrated in the accompanying chart and which da Costa has not yet

Table 2.ii.

LOK SABHA: THE CONGRESS PERCENTAGE OF 'VALID' VOTES RELATED TO NUMBER OF CONTESTANTS: 1962, 1967 AND 1971

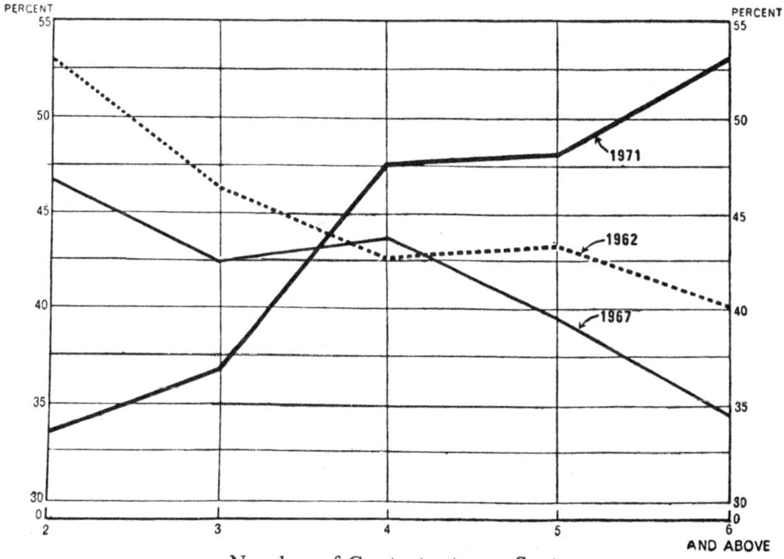

Number of Contestants per Seat

Source: Monthly Public Opinion Surveys of the Indian Institute of Public Opinion, XVI (December 1970, January, February 1971), 9.

satisfactorily figured out, accounts to a considerable degree for some remarkably poor performances by the IIPO in some contests in the 1971 general election, just as the erratic behavior of the Multiplier led to larger errors than usual in forecasting the 1976 elections.[41]

At State levels, as has been indicated, 'the peculiar arithmetic' of Indian elections is even more evident. A few statistics from West Bengal and Kerala, two States where the opposition to the Congress, mainly from the Communists, has been particularly strong, may be cited by way of illustration. In West Bengal in the fourth general elections the Congress won 62.30 per cent of the seats in the State Assembly with 47.29 per cent of the votes, whereas in the mid-term elections of 1969 it won only 19.64 per cent of the seats with 40.24 per cent of the votes. In the 1969 elections the CPI(M) won 15.36 per cent of the seats with 18.20 per cent of the votes. In the 1972 State Assembly elections the CPI(M) got only fifteen seats with 3.659 million votes, while the CPI got thirty-five seats with 1.110 million votes and the Congress 217 seats with 6.542 million votes. Thus whereas the Congress got less than twice the number of votes as the CPI(M), it got fourteen times as many seats in the Assembly. With a very small change in the percentage of the popular vote the fortunes of the Congress and the CPI(M) in some districts were sharply reversed. In Burdwan district, for example, a long-time left Communist stronghold, the CPI(M) won twenty-three seats and the Congress only one in the 1971 elections, but in the State Assembly elections a year later the CPI(M) won only two seats whereas the Congress garnered twenty-one.

In Kerala some of the discrepancies between votes cast and seats won were equally striking. In 1965, for example, the Congress Party, with 33.58 per cent of the votes, won thirty-six seats in the State Legislative Assembly, but in 1967, when its percentage of the popular vote rose to 35.42, it won only nine seats. In other words, with an increase in its popular vote it won only one-fourth as many seats. In the same elections the CPI(M) got 19.88 and 23.98 per cent of the votes, and forty and fifty-two seats. The differences in Congress and CPI(M) votes and seats in 1967 is particularly extraordinary, for the CPI(M) got fifty-two seats with 23.98 per cent of the votes, whereas the Congress was able to win only nine seats with 35.42 per cent of the votes.

Such discrepancies, which could be documented extensively, have led some observers of the Indian electoral system, including practicing politicians and leading Indian analysts, to recommend fundamental changes in the system. Many changes have been made in the techniques and methods of conducting elections, under the supervision of the Election Commission, but in all probability the basic character of the electoral system will be preserved as long as present system of parliamentary democracy endures.

Changing Character of Political Leadership: The Fourth and Fifth Lok Sabhas

Some indication of the changing character of political leadership in India can be gained from an analysis of the socio-economic characteristics and other background data of members of the Lok Sabha and the State Legislative Assemblies over a period of time. Election data can provide the starting point for such an analysis, which can then be pursued by other methods. In the Lok Sabha, for example, the turnover of members seems to be accelerating, and the character of the membership also seems to be changing somewhat. This point can be brought out by reference to changes in membership in the fourth and fifth Lok Sabhas, and to studies of the socio-economic background and characteristics of members of these two Lok Sabhas.

In the fifth Lok Sabha, elected in 1971, only 221 of the 520 elected members of the fourth Lok Sabha retained their seats. Since between thirty and forty newly-elected members had sat in previous Lok Sabhas, the number of real newcomers was about 50 per cent. Studies carried out by Ratna Dutta of the members of the fourth Lok Sabha and by correspondents of *The Times of India* of members of the fifth Lok Sabha make possible a comparison of the members of these two Lok Sabhas on the basis of age, education, occupation, and previous legislative experience.[42] Some of the more significant results may be summarized here.

Just over a third of the members of the fourth Lok Sabha were less than 45 years of age, while more than half of the new entrants to the fifth Lok Sabha belonged to the younger age group. Three out of five members of the previous Lok Sabha were university graduates, as compared to 68 per cent of the new members of the fifth Lok Sabha. Thus the new members in 1971 were both younger and better educated than the members of the previous Lok Sabha.

The most notable apparent changes in occupation were a sharp decrease in the numbers of M.P.'s who labeled themselves as 'agriculturists' (from 31 to 18 per cent), and a sharp increase in 'political, social and trade union workers' (from 21 to 32 per cent) and in 'journalists and teachers' (from 11 to 16 per cent). These figures may be somewhat misleading, for 'many people who derive a good part of their income from land are non-cultivating owners who have other occupations,'[43] and some of these may have preferred to list themselves as 'political, social and trade union workers.' The decline in number of 'agriculturists' seems particularly suspect in a country where three-fourths of the electorate live in rural areas. Until 1971 the proportion of M.P.'s who described themselves as agriculturists had increased with every election – from 22.4 per cent in 1952 to 29.1 per cent in 1957 and 31.1 per cent in 1967. The increase in the number of journalists and teachers may reflect the higher level of education of the new Lok Sabha members in 1971.

In at least one respect, namely previous legislative experience, each successive Lok Sabha seems to have been a less experienced body than its predecessor. The new members of the fifth Lok Sabha were clearly less experienced than the members of the previous body: 48 per cent of them had had no previous legislative experience, whereas the comparable figure for members of the fourth Lok Sabha was only 38 per cent. These figures call for careful analysis, for 'in an election that has taken the form of a vast spring-cleaning operation, it is only natural that many entrants to Parliament are totally new to politics.'[44] Moreover, further analysis will reveal the increasing importance of political experience in various forms at district and local levels, thus confirming the evidences of the emergence of new political elites in India, elites that are more localized and provincial in outlook and experience and are therefore more representative of their constituents and more attuned to underlying trends in Indian politics and society. The fact 'that more than half the new entrants have had legislative experience at the State and district levels shows to what extent this has become a prerequisite for entering national politics. . . . And even among those with no legislative experience, many had been involved for several years with their respective parties and held important elective organisational posts within it [*sic*]. One of the main functions of all democracies is to provide a ladder for the ascent of a new elite to the seats of power in the country. These figures confirm that the ladder to New Delhi starts in the treadmill of district politics.'[45]

The Meaning of the Vote in India

Enough evidence has been afforded by the Indian experience with elections over a period of nearly twenty-five years to demonstrate conclusively that 'elections in India do play a meaningful role in [the] allocation and exercise of power within the society, the classic purpose of any political system.'[46] But it is more difficult to determine what the vote means to the individual voter in India. As T. E. Smith has observed, 'more research is required . . . before any general pronouncements can be made regarding the interpretation of the meaning of elections by large groups of illiterate and materially backward voters – particularly in respect of central as opposed to local government elections.'[47] India provides the greatest and most significant laboratory for examining this question.

Obviously the vote may have different meanings in different social and political systems. In India it seems to mean very little to many eligible voters, or to have more social than political significance. On the whole the Indian people have exercised their voting rights with a remarkable degree of participation and apparent sophistication, but all election studies conducted on a survey research and interview basis have revealed the mixed motivations of the Indian voter and the rather idiosyncratic nature of the vote in India. It seems to be much less closely related to other acts of participation than in so-called developed political systems. In fact, participation as a value is given a much lower rating in India than in almost any other country where elections are an integral part of the democratic political process.[48] Moreover, the Indian voter seems to have less of a feeling of psychological involvement, which in most other political systems is closely related to voting. One comparative study of 'democratic participation' seemed to reveal a 'sharp difference between the meaning of the vote in India and elsewhere.' India and the United States, for example, were found to be 'similar in campaign activity and different in voting. The large group in India that votes . . . is brought to the polls by a different social mechanism than that which brings the U.S. citizen to the polls . . . voting in the U.S. seems to be more a part of a general voluntaristic set of activities. In India, it reflects less motivation on the citizen's part.'[49]

This difference may be less sharp if India is compared with other developing countries where competitive democratic elections have been carried on for a limited period of time, in basically illiterate societies, within the framework of a social system which emphasizes group or collective rather than individualistic behavior. It may also be less sharp in any kind of Asian political system, developed or underdeveloped, where democratic elections are meaningful. This is suggested by the some election studies in Japan, which has a highly developed economy, a highly literate citizenry, and a social structure that is still fairly rigid and that emphasizes the group or the collectivity.[50]

One should not underemphasize the meaning of the vote in India. Even in the first general elections, in 1951–2, when the turnout was lower than in subsequent elections, when most voters who cast their ballots were doing so for the first time, when many did not vote at all because of social or other inhibitions, and when many voted with great diffidence and uncertainty, it was quite clear that for most voters voting was a meaningful act. In fact, for some it seemed to have an almost mystical or religious significance, and for many it was apparently a rather heady experience. A report on the election of 1952 in a remote constituency in the remote Union Territory of Himachal Pradesh contained a poignant personal note: 'The number of people who did understand what they were doing – however vaguely – was impressive. They realized that in some way their vote did count. Why else would anyone be wooing them? Even a twenty-eight year old woman understood that her slip of paper would help send the Raja "to see after our troubles." She and her bent old mother had walked two miles to vote, and both of them were carrying a pink card which bore the Raja's symbol. The headman had given it to her so that she could remember for whom she was to vote. For a day, at least, she knew she was important. Even that is a beginning.'[51]

Increasing Maturity of the Indian Voter?

From such an impressive, if shaky, beginning the Indian voters have voted in increasing numbers in each general election, except for a decline in 1971, and they have shown increasing confidence and sophistication with each electoral experience. After the fourth general elections, in 1967, Pran Chopra, a well-known Indian journalist, declared: 'Even those who were left unconvinced by the first three elections have little reason to doubt now that the Indian voter votes with discrimination and without fear, that his interest in the democratic process is rising, not falling, and that the influence of the local factor upon him, especially of caste, though still strong, is also falling.'[52] In commenting on the same general elections, and on electoral development in India during the five years following these elections, Rajni Kothari perceived a significant 'shift from politics of manipulation of the voters by party organisational machines to a type of politics in which the direct appeal of parties and political personalities, the election campaign, and the issues at stake will play a major role.'[53] Writing in 1972, in a further development of these same themes, Kothari concluded that India's experience with elections has 'produced a mature and demanding electorate,' and that 'there has taken place a growing awareness of issues among the people, an inclination to punish parties and leaders that are unable to deliver the goods, a breakdown of community based loyalties and voting patterns, the growth of secular identities and allegiances, and accelerating processes of political interest, information, evaluation and hard bargaining on the basis of party commitments and their ability to translate them into reality.'[54] Kothari has developed these important theses in several of his recent writings. He feels that the Indian voter has come of age, that he is becoming increasingly influenced by the growing secularization of Indian political life, that his voting behavior is less shaped by ascriptive factors and by local bosses, and that he is increasingly using the test of performance in judging the parties and the candidates.

Almost all observers of Indian elections will agree that the Indian voter is showing a greater degree of maturity and sophistication, but many will have reservations about the relative influence of various motivational factors and the relative extent of the voters' concern with issues and performance. They will also be well aware of some of the limitations that still prevail as far as the political development of the Indian voter is concerned. This obvious point is documented in many electoral studies, including several conducted by the Center for the Study of Developing Societies, of which Kothari is the Director. In an analysis of the 'Dimensions of Voter Development,' based on comprehensive data from the 1967 elections, D. L. Sheth found that the Indian voter showed a moderate amount of party identification, a medium amount of political understanding, a high degree of issue orientation, a relatively high degree of political awareness, and a very low level of participation.[55]

'These responses,' in Sheth's opinion, 'reveal that a very large proportion of Indian citizens have a general trust in the effectivity of democratic institutions and view them as desirable in Indian conditions. The proportions compare well with those of other democratic societies.'[56] Several State studies of the 1967 elections seem to confirm this general interpretation, although one such study, conducted in Gujarat, found that urban voters are much more alienated from the system than rural voters. All of these studies, however, suggested that the degree of alienation from the total system was not great, that in general the commitment of the Indian voter to the political system is surprisingly high.[57]

Other studies, however, indicate a higher degree of alienation, especially in the volatile States of Bihar and West Bengal, and especially among young voters. In a sample survey of 700 voters in a parliamentary constituency in Bihar in 1971, 78.40 per cent of respondents favored democracy over dictatorship, but 71.40 per cent felt that the present electoral system was not protecting democracy, and 70 per cent felt that the future of India was dark.[58] A pre-poll survey in both rural and urban areas in West Bengal in 1971 found that only 34 per cent of the respondents gave an affirmative answer to the question: 'Do you believe that the elections can being about the desired change in our social, economic, and political structure peacefully?' It is significant that 59.2 per cent of respondents under thirty years of age answered this question affirmatively, which would seem to indicate that, contrary to the usual assumptions, older people are more disillusioned with the political system than are the younger ones. One commentator on this pre-poll survey saw in the replies an 'alarming trend toward a total disenchantment with the electoral system,' but he hastened to add that 'this overall negative, withdrawing attitude should not be mistaken for a radical, extremist outlook of a section of people who are positively against the parliamentary system.'[59]

A general judgment, which would be questioned by some students of Indian affairs, would be that elections have contributed to the political development of both the individual voter and the political system. In his overall commentary on *Politics in India* Rajni Kothari took as his central thesis 'that the politics of adult franchise and participation, and diffusion and decentralization of political power that it entails, would lead to a more responsible and a more integrated polity.'[60] His analysis is another reminder of the crucial importance of the electoral process in India's political development.

Because of their special importance with reference to the relation of elections to the overall process of political development and to the shaping of the political system, the following topics will be discussed in separate chapters: (1) the functions of elections, for the voter and for the political system; (2) the electoral process in India, with special attention to the selection of candidates, the campaign, and the actual voting experience; (3) the South Asian experience with elections, with particular attention to India's very extensive experience; (4) a profile of the Indian electorate, who the voters are, their demographic, social, economic, and political background, and their political behavior; (5) the determinants of voting behavior in India with emphasis on socio-economic determinants and such intervening variables as candidate-, issue-, and party identification or orientation.

3

THE FUNCTIONS OF ELECTIONS: POLITICAL CHOICE AND POLITICAL PARTICIPATION

In *The Dramas of Politics* James N. Rosenau identifies four broad functions which 'must be performed in order for a political system to persist and achieve its goals.' These are: 'the *normative* function whereby basic attitudes and loyalties are developed and sustained; the *sovereignty* function whereby the final decisions are made; the *bureaucratic* function whereby action is taken and final decisions are implemented; and the *support building* function whereby pre-existing norms are activated and consensuses are fashioned around proposed or decided courses of action.'[1] As Rosenau points out, the support-building function is institutionalized mainly through party and electoral systems. Thus in a broad sense one might say that the main function of elections, at least from a systemic point of view, is support-building, which may also be identified with a major function developed by the structural-functionalists, namely that of system maintenance. But it may be more useful to suggest that elections perform many functions, some of which are the same in all systems where they exist at all, and some of which differ in many systems.

Multiple Functions of Elections

Because of the possible multiplicity of functions, with great differences in different political systems, it is impossible to draw up a definitive list of the functions that elections presumably perform. Except in a very general sense, there is in fact no overall agreement on the functions of elections even in those countries where elections have long been central instrumentalities in the political system and where they have been studied extensively, as in Great Britain and the United States. One of the leading British psephologists, Professor W. J. M. Mackenzie, confessed quite frankly that 'We are not very certain of the functions of elections in our own society.'[2] Obviously it would be much more difficult for British or American or any other student of elections to agree on the functions of elections in other political systems, under different conditions and in a different social setting. Professor Mackenzie himself had some wise observations on this subject in a famous article on 'The Export of Electoral Systems.'[3]

The path of caution, and of wisdom, therefore is to begin with the assumption, which seems to be justified both by historical experience and by extensive empirical investigation, that elections perform many functions, and that these functions vary in number and significance in different political systems. Another important background consideration to bear in mind is that the functions of elections – or at least the relative significance of various functions – are different for the individual voter and for the political system. For the individual voter elections may be regarded as a means of political participation and to some extent of policy-influencing and policy choice, although for many voters, even in democratic societies, elections may be hardly more than customary acts to which little significance is attached. For the political system elections are important devices for assuring legitimacy and allegiance, and for system maintenance and support-building.

Exchange theory may be useful in this connection. The electoral system may be regarded as playing a role in the performance of exchange, of instrumental exchange, mainly between the voter and the party, and of systemic exchange, mainly between the voter and the polity. This suggests that there are obvious linkages between the functions of elections for individual voters and for the political system, with policy makers chosen by the voters and responsible to them for the maintenance and development of the political system in a central linkage role. 'At the level of exchange emphasis shifts from one in which the debate is about the outlines of policy . . . to one in which the system itself is in question. Instrumental exchange declines in favor of system exchanges. The immediate result is a weakening of the policy branches, particularly party and legislature, that seem initially concerned with aggregation, and a strengthening of those branches, such as the executive, that serve as symbols of system continuity. In short, insofar as the electoral system encourages the development of conditions under which system exchange is more prevalent than instrumental exchange, the policy process is subordinated to the defense of the existing political system.'[4]

This brief application of exchange theory suggests that while the functions of elections may be different from the point of view of the individual voter and the political system, these functions overlap and there are important linkages between the voter and the system. Elections, indeed, call for both micro- and macro-political analysis, and for a study of the linkages between micro and macro phenomena. This point was emphasized in a detailed study of the 1967 general elections in Gujarat, carried out by a group of political scientists at Gujarat

University. This intensive micro-study produced a significant macro-conclusion: 'Any voting behaviour study, by its very nature, has to concentrate on the micro-level of politics. . . . However, individual actors do not act in a vacuum. They operate within the confines of the broad framework established by the macro-level political system. It is the interaction between the actors and the system that constitutes the core of politics.' The study of elections provides an excellent opportunity to examine 'the inter-action between the actors and the system.'[5]

It is obviously impossible even to present a comprehensive list of the functions of elections, or to group these functions in any neat or discrete categories. In this chapter, and the following one, simply for purposes of convenience, electoral functions will be considered under four broad categories, with particular reference to the electoral experience of the countries of South Asia: (1) political choice, and the influencing of policy decisions; (2) political participation; (3) support-building and system maintenance; and (4) linkage patterns and functions.

Political Choice

Elections and Political Choice: General. To state that a main function of elections is that of political choice is to record one of the standard premises – or clichés – of modern democratic theory. This function is stated in innumerable ways, all, however, centering around political choice and the influencing of political decisions. The purpose of elections is to determine 'the will of the people.' Elections, as an Indian social scientist observed, 'compute public opinion.'[6] They may be used, or interpreted, as a plebiscite, a referendum, or a mandate. They are the means for choosing leaders, for determining who shall govern. They are also a means for influencing the elected leaders and the policy decisions of the elected government. They help to insure the responsiveness of leaders to the people as a whole. 'The election,' in the opinion of Robert Dahl, 'is the central technique for insuring that governmental leaders will be relatively responsible to non-leaders.'[7] Elections are devices for controlling political leaders; indeed, in the opinion of a British psephologist, this is 'their most important function.'[8] And the control of leaders presumably involves also some degree of control of governmental choices and policies.

Both kinds of control – over leaders and over policies – may be exercised in a very indirect way, but even this may be fairly effective. In the last analysis the political leader knows that sooner or later he has to face his constituents, and in a sense to give an acccount of his stewardship. 'The law of anticipated reactions,' which two prominent

American psephologists found to operate in elections for the U.S. House of Representatives, may also operate to some degree in other political systems, under other circumstances.[9] Hence, 'belief by future candidates in the possibility that voters may reject them at the next election because of their policies may lead them to anticipate public feeling, thus allowing indirect influence of elections upon policy formation.[10]

Elections provide the means for the peaceful and orderly transfer of power, for dealing with the vexing problem of succession, for 'the routinization of political change,' to use Michael Brecher's words.[11] 'Elections become a non-violent way of solving a difficulty common to all political systems – how to organize the succession from one group of men holding authority to another.'[12] This function is a particularly important one in developing countries, few of which have been able to solve the problem of peaceful succession and to develop satisfactory and acceptable procedures for the peaceful transfer of power.

The function of political choice is therefore a central function of elections in any genuinely representative political system. It is not only enshrined in the theory of modern democracy, but is also embodied in its practice as well. In no democratic system, however, is this central function performed in the manner and to the extent that democratic theory suggests. Elections are in fact blunt and rather inadequate instruments and devices for political choice. Even under conditions of complete freedom the choice that can be expressed is a limited and general one. It is at best a choice among political parties and leaders, usually on the basis of inadequate understanding of the real issues involved or of the real nature of the choice that has to be made.

Thus while this dual function of controlling, or at least influencing, both leaders and policies is always performed, even in well-established democracies it may be performed in only a nominal or routine or symbolic way. Empirical studies in many democratic systems have confirmed what general observation and experience have suggested, that even in successfully functioning democracies voters are often so limited in their opportunities for meaningful political choice that this function is by no means as important as it seems to be, except in a negative way, that they exercise very little real political control over their elected leaders, and that they have very little control over governmental policies.

Elections, like political parties, are agencies for interest aggregation, which inevitably means that the choice for the voter when he enters the booth on election day is a limited one. Moreover, it is usually made more or less in a *pro forma* manner, without much conviction or insight. In highly developed democracies, where elections have become routine and usually rather undramatic events, the choice that is exercised is circumscribed by the factors that have determined the nature of the vote and by the limitations of the choice. Under such circumstances, as Professor Mackenzie has observed, the kind of choice that is made in an election is hardly more than a 'ritual of choice.'[13] Indeed, as Rose and Mossawir have pointed out, 'For most individuals voting is not registering a fresh choice but reaffirming an allegiance.'[15]

In countries where democratic systems are less deeply rooted and less well developed and genuinely accepted, elections may serve rather to endorse and give legitimacy to regimes which are in reality not responsible to the popular will. Under such conditions the function of political choice is also primarily a ritual one, although in a very different sense from the ritualistic aspects of political choice in elections in mature democratic systems.

These generalizations would seem to be supported by the electoral experience of the countries of South Asia. One of the most important functions that elections in these countries has performed, at least in a formal sense, has been the choice of political leaders and ruling parties. Thus one could argue that Indian voters, in national elections, have shown a clear and consistent preference for the Congress Party, even though this has not been the case in some constituencies and States in some elections; that voters in Ceylon have consciously chosen between parties, and therefore between leaders, favoring the UNP up to 1956 and between 1965 and 1970, and the SLFP (and the United Front which it has headed) in the intervening years; that the voters of what was then East Pakistan, in the only direct, nationwide election in which they had a chance to participate, expressed an overwhelming preference for the Awami League and Sheikh Mujibur Rahman, and the voters of the main provinces of West Pakistan, the Punjab and Sind, in the same election gave a clear mandate to the Pakistan People's Party and Zulfikar Ali Bhutto; that the preference for the Awami League and Sheikh Mujibur Rahman was reaffirmed, in a less decisive way, in the first general election in Bangladesh, in March 1973; and that the voters of Nepal, in the only direct general election in which they have been allowed to participate, showed a distinct preference for the Nepali Congress and B. P. Koirala.

Elections and Political Choice in South Asia. It would be an exaggeration to say that the function of political choice has been a really central function of elections in any South Asian country, especially if political choice is linked, as it often is, with the influencing of policy decisions and the control of political leaders. Only in Ceylon has any party system emerged that has given the voters a meaningful choice between two parties capable of governing on the national level. One could justly say that since the general elections of 1956 the

Ceylonese voter has had a real choice between parties, with different composition, orientation, and policies. In India there has been little choice between parties in national elections for national offices, and even though the ruling Congress Party was given a scare in the fourth general elections in 1967 and was rent asunder by internal divisions in 1969, it has had no real rival on the national scene. The situation has been different in some States, where opposition parties or coalitions have had some spectacular successes (usually short-lived). In the general elections in Pakistan in December 1970, the voters in both wings of the country expressed clear – and different – choices as far as political parties and leaders are concerned, and these choices had a major effect on the course of subsequent events; but real political choice was certainly circumscribed, and the degree of actual control over subsequent political decisions or over the elected leaders was a very limited one. The Nepalese general election of 1959 indicated a clear choice between contending parties and leaders, but the efforts of the Nepali Congress Party under B. P. Koirala to establish a representative and democratic government were soon cut short by royal decree. Certainly political choice has been very restricted in Nepal, both before and after the short-lived experiment in parliamentary democracy in 1959–60.

In India, Pakistan, and Ceylon, but not in Nepal, general elections have served in some instances as a plebiscite, or referendum, or mandate for particular parties and leaders seeking popular support on the basis of general faith and particular policies. The general elections in these three countries in 1970–1, which, as has been noted; had quite different systemic impact, may be interpreted in this light. In a sense the leaders who scored overwhelming electoral victories – Mrs. Indira Gandhi, Sheikh Mujibur Rahman, Z. A. Bhutto, and Mrs. Sirimavo Bandaranaike – turned the elections into national referenda or plebiscites, and appealed quite successfully to the voters to give them a 'mandate' to carry out their radical election promises. In all three elections the outcome was determined more by personalities than by issues, and the choice that most voters made was apparently largely determined by their response to the leaders who dominated the election campaigns. Thus in a way these elections, and all other general elections in South Asia, were reasonably effective and reasonably peaceful institutionalized means of choosing leaders, and thereby of determining who should govern. They gave the elected leaders the political mandate and popular support that these leaders were seeking, but they served only in a minimal and formal way in influencing policy decisions or in ensuring the responsiveness of the leaders to the popular will. That will was too inchoate and too dimly perceived to be more than a general conditioning factor, and possibly also a kind of continuing pressure, in the eyes of the elected leaders.

Elections and Political Succession in South Asia. In India and Ceylon general elections have performed a major function in providing the procedures for determining political succession. On five different occasions in Ceylon since 1956 governments have changed from one party to another as a result of the verdict of the electorate, a record unmatched in any other developing country. In the last years of Nehru's life, with a dominant leader in a one-dominant-party system, many people in India and outside were asking the questions: 'After Nehru, who?' and 'After Nehru, what?,' and some were fearful that the Indian political system would not survive the test of political succession, for no arrangements for the succession to Nehru seemed to have been worked out. Yet when the great leader died, in May 1964, the question of succession was speedily resolved, with some tensions within the ruling Congress party but with no strain at all on the political system. When Lal Bahadur Shastri, Nehru's chosen successor as Prime Minister, died suddenly at Tashkent in January 1966, again the problem of succession was resolved within the top ranks of the Congress Party without much difficulty or delay, even though the Congress leaders were by no means agreed on Mr. Shastri's successor. Mrs. Gandhi's selection came as a surprise to many Indians, and as a shock to some. She made a rather rocky start, and was in a weak political position, which was not enhanced by Congress reverses in the fourth general elections in 1967, the mid-term general elections in four major states in 1969, the fight within the Congress Party over the selection of a President of India in the summer of 1969, and the split in the party the following November. But the fifth general elections in 1971, confirmed by the State Assembly elections in 1972, gave Mrs. Gandhi an overwhelming majority in the Lok Sabha, and the political mandate she was seeking. After the 1971 general elections she was again chosen as leader of the Congress Party and of the government, in what has been called the third succession since Nehru's death, and thereafter her commanding position in Indian political life was assured.

In India and Ceylon, therefore, the problem of succession, that has been so worrisome to most developing countries, has been successfully resolved and political change has been routinized. The electoral system has had a role in this vital area, and has thereby helped to strengthen the political system of both countries; but it has not always been able to accomodate certain dissatisfied elements in the society, who have already posed serious threats to the political system, as well as to particular governments in power.

Pakistan has never been able to handle the problem of succession in a peaceful and routinized way, and elections have played a very minor role in the process of succession. The 1970 general elections seemingly dictated the accession to power of Sheikh Mujibur Rahman in Pakistan;

but post-election negotiations to bring this about broke down in bloody repression and civil war in what was then East Pakistan. Yahya Khan continued to rule until the defeat of Pakistan in the war with India in December 1971. Only then was he forced to step down, to be succeeded, almost by default, by Z. A. Bhutto. One could argue that the 1970 general elections had clearly pointed to Bhutto as the popular choice for leader in West Pakistan, and that Bhutto's accession to power a year later was a logical, if deferred, consequence of the 1970 elections. It is also possible that the new political order in what is left of Pakistan, as institutionalized in the Constitution of 1973, provides a procedure for elections and for political succession within a democratic framework; but the new Constitution seems to give Mr. Bhutto almost unlimited power. It remains to be seen whether elections, when held, will have any significant function in providing Pakistan, at long last, with an accepted and orderly procedure for political succession.

The accession to power in Bangladesh, formerly East Pakistan, by Sheikh Mijibur Rahman in January 1972, as soon as he was released from custody in West Pakistan, was a logical consequence of the overwhelming mandate which he and his party, the Awami League, received in the 1970 elections in East Pakistan. The March 1973 general elections in Bangladesh confirmed his overwhelming mandate. Hence the elections of 1970 in Pakistan and of 1973 in Bangladesh did resolve, at least temporarily, the problem of succession in Bangladesh, and the procedures for succession, in which the electoral process seems to be central, are laid down in the new Constitution of 1972.

In Nepal the procedures for succession are determined by traditional and monarchical and not by democractic means, and will continue to be determined in this way as long as the present political system remains. The 1959 elections might have marked a new departure in Nepali politics, leading to a new kind of political system in which succession would be determined by normal parliamentary means; but King Mahendra soon ended this short-lived experiment, and again resumed complete political control.

A careful investigation of the circumstances surrounding each particular election and of the political situation in each South Asian country, therefore, would suggest that the area of political choice for the voters was in fact quite circumscribed. Such an investigation would indicate that even the voters of India and Ceylon, where nationwide direct elections have for many years been remarkably frequent and free, have had very little actual control over the elected leaders, except in the negative sense that the 'law of anticipated reactions' and the necessity of facing the voters in periodic elections have served as controlling mechanisms. Control over governmental policies by the electorate has been even more limited. In general, voters have tended to endorse and thereby help to give legitimacy to political leaders rather than to exercise much real control over them or the policies that they champion. Possible exceptions might be the popular support of, and perhaps even the demand for, more leftist-oriented policies on the part of the elected leaders and ruling parties in India and Ceylon. In general, however, in South Asia, as elsewhere, 'voting is often more of a "comment" on what the parties have done ... than an expression about performance.'[15]

Political Participation

A second major function of elections is to provide opportunities and channels for political participation. Since some degree of political participation is essential in any real democratic system, this function of elections is clearly a central one. Indeed, elections provide one of the most effective means of political participation, although by no means the only one. Such participation presumably strengthens the democratic system, although, as has been noted, it may be much more limited in fact than it appears to be and under certain circumstances a high degree of participation may impose serious strains on the system.[16]

Forms of Political Participation. Since political participation takes so many forms and varies so greatly, both in form and in spirit, in differing kinds of political systems, it is difficult – and perhaps unnecessary – to attempt to provide a precise definition. In general, as Sidney Verba and many others have pointed out, it refers to 'acts by those not formally empowered to make decisions – the acts being intended to influence the behavior of those who have such decisional power.'[17] Presumably it is intended to influence the behavior and actions of political decision-makers, and it embraces various activities designed to achieve this end, regardless of their degree of effectiveness; but of course, as Verba notes, 'successful participation refers to those acts that have (at least in part) the intended effects.'[18]

In conventional analysis political participation has generally been confined to those activities designed to influence decision-making which are carried on within the framework of the particular political system, which are considered to be legitimate, and usually which are not of a violent character. More recently, both because of an enlargement of the approach of scholars and more particularly because of an increase in acts of violence designed both to alter political systems rather fundamentally or to overthrow the systems, violent as well as non-violent, illegitimate as well as legitimate, anti-systemic as well as systemic activities have often been considered to be forms of political participation. For this reason perhaps a broader 'definition' of political participation is needed, such as that used by Myron Weiner: 'I shall use the concept of political participation to refer to any voluntary action, successful or unsuccessful, organized or unorganized, episodic or continuous, employing legitimate or illegitimate methods intended to influence the choice of public policies, the administration of public affairs, or the choice of political leaders at any level of government, local or national.'[19] This broader interpretation will be particularly useful in examining forms and consequences of political participation in South Asia. It will not be developed in this chapter, where we are concerned with political participation and the electoral process; but it should not be forgotten, for it provides the larger setting in which the drama of elections unfolds.

Voting is by far the most common and the most widely discussed form of political participation that is related to the electoral process, but there are many other forms, including various kinds of campaign activity, which are encompassed within the electoral process. That process, it should be recalled, involves the totality of operations that make elections such significant institutions in most political systems. Voting is only one of the aspects of the total electoral process, although it is a particularly distinctive one.

Before we focus on elections, however, some further comments should be made on the general nature of political participation. It is one of the 'crises of political development' which have been singled out and examined in great detail by the members of the Committee on Comparative Politics of the Social Science Research Council in the United States. It is obviously related to the other 'crises' or 'sequences' of political development that have been identified by these scholars, namely those of identity, legitimacy, penetration, integration, and distribution. Also worthy of examination are its relationships to such important concepts as political stability, economic development, and social mobilization.

Many of the commonly designed forms of political participation, including voting and other acts associated with the electoral process, are found in most political systems; but the same forms may serve very different purposes, function in very different ways, and have a very different place in different political systems. Broadly speaking, political participation is greater in a 'modern' society than in a more traditional one – or, stated in another way, it is greater in a developed than in a developing polity – and in a more open democratic system than in a more closed and authoritarian one. But obviously, while these widely accepted generalizations are probably generally accurate, one can immediately think of many exceptions and qualifications.

Some 'modern' systems, especially those of an authoritarian nature, may deliberately limit the forms and opportunities for political participation, while such participation may be more common than the uninformed observer would suspect in 'traditional' or 'transitional' societies, especially where a variety of ascriptive groups and associations exist and where these groups and associations are subject to a high degree of politicization. In more closed, authoritarian systems political participation may seem to be greater than in some more open, democratic systems. For example, voting turnouts may be higher, participation in various organizations greater, and the apparent degree of politicization higher. This may, of course, be more image than reality, more form than substance. A more closed, authoritarian system will seek to use political participation as a means of mobilizing the masses in support of the governing groups, usually very narrow élites, and certainly not as a means of effective participation in the sense of genuinely influencing decision-making and decision-makers. Many forms of political participation, such as voting and various kinds of group activity, will be in effect compulsory. Hence a turnout of 98 per cent or higher in an election, usually for a single slate of candidates, can hardly be called a significant act of political participation, and perhaps should not even be considered to be more than a formal or ritualistic act, whereas a turnout of 60 per cent in a genuinely free and competitive election in a more open, democratic system may be a significant indicator of extensive political participation.

As Myron Weiner has pointed out, 'most governing élites in the developing areas have chosen to restrict rather than enlarge political participation. . . . Most of the authoritarian élites governing the developing areas seek active rather than passive support and view some forms of political "participation" as desirable. Such governing élites often try to find new forms of political "participation" of the sort that will encourage or even mobilize citizens to support the regime and its goals without allowing them to make any demands upon it.'[20] South Asia provides two of the most interesting and most extensive examples or experiments of this kind, namely the systems of 'Basic Democracies' in Pakistan during the Ayub Khan era and of 'Panchayat Democracy' in Nepal, dating from the early 1960s. These systems were remarkable political experiments,[21] and seemed to work rather well for some time; but like other systems of 'guided' or 'controlled' democracy they rested on limited and narrow authoritarian and centralized bases and they were not able to prevent the citizens who were mobilized through them to support the ruling elites from using these systems to make increasing demands and exert increasing pressures upon their political masters.

Huntington's Models. Samuel Huntington has suggested three broad assumptions – or models, in a loose sense of the word – relating to political participation.[22] The first, and the most prevalent, is the normative concept that political participation is a 'good thing,' a desirable value or norm, an important 'political good.' This is indeed an assumption that is widely held and that is often simply taken for granted. It is seldom challenged or tested. It is almost an article of faith on the part of those who are dedicated to the democratic way, and it is a central concept of democratic political theory.

Political participation, according to this approach, is beneficial both for the individual and for the social and political system. It enables the individual to play various effective roles in the system, and to influence as well as support it. Within such a system individuals have a wide area of useful activity. As Sidney Verba has stated: 'Individuals may act as individuals; they may act individually but as part of an aggregate of individuals engaging in a participatory act (voting is the best example); they may act as members of either informal or formally organized groups.'[23] But whether considered from the systemic or the individualistic point of view, political participation is posited as a 'good,' indeed as an essential prerequisite for a genuinely democratic system. From this it follows that the higher the rate and the more varied the forms of political participation the healthier is the democratic system.

This normative assumption is an article of faith that is not only enshrined in theory but that also seems to be confirmed in practice. Seymour Martin Lipset has summarized this belief in more specific terms: 'Nevertheless, a situation which results in high participation by members of a group normally has a higher potential for democracy – that is, for the maintenance of an effective opposition – than one where few people show interest or participate in the political process. ... And conversely, a society in which a large proportion of the population is outside the political arena is potentially more explosive than one in which most citizens are *regularly* involved in activities which give them some sense of participation in decisions which affect their lives.'[24]

While recognizing the pervasiveness of this normative assumption, or model, especially in democratic political theory and to some extent in the professed norms of almost all political systems, it is necessary to enter certain qualifications and caveats. Political participation is not always considered a 'good' in some systems. It may be regarded as undesirable both by ruling élites and the masses of the people – by the ruling elites because they fear the consequences for their position and continuance in power, by the masses because they are apprehensive that political participation will make them more conspicuous targets of oppression and punishment and will involve them in processes beyond their understanding and areas of concern.

It has often been pointed out that a rapid rate of political participation may have adverse systemic effects; it may have unfortunate consequences as far as political stability is concerned, and it may create a 'crisis situation' for a political system. Too much political participation may be more dangerous than too little, for it will impose increasing demands and strains on a political system that may be incapable of meeting such demands and enduring such strains, even under more enlightened and effective leaders. It may lead to repression and reprisals by the ruling elites, or to violent and destructive activities on the part of the frustrated would-be participants. It can thus weaken as well as strengthen a political system, and hence would be considered as desirable by those who would like to weaken or even destroy the system and as highly undesirable by those who would strengthen and preserve it.[25]

The second assumption or model suggested by Huntington is a developmental one. Political participation may be regarded not only as one of the 'crises of development' but also as a necessary concomitant of political, economic, and social development. On the whole, moreover, a more developed society is a more participant one. Since development must be conceived as a total process, political development has to be considered in relation to other forms of development, and political participation, as one of the aspects of political development, has to be evaluated in relation to social, economic, and other forms of the development syndrome.

One intriguing question in this connection is the relationship between political development and socio-economic development. A great deal of research has been carried out on this question, including some significant research in South Asia. In general, there seems to be some significant and positive correlation between political development and socio-economic development, especially between certain forms of political development and socio-economic development, but there are many exceptions to this generalization. Moreover, it is obviously very difficult to develop satisfactory indicators for these various forms of development, and to isolate them so that they can be usefully measured and compared and used as a basis for general conclusions.

A third model, which according to Huntington may be called a status model, is relevant to all systems, especially so to developing societies, and is related to socio-economic as well as to political development. Generally speaking, there seems to be a significant and positive correlation in almost all political systems between political participation and socio-economic status, measured by such indicators as class or caste identification, income levels, occupation, education and levels of literacy, and the like. This phenomenon is also related to organizational involvement and a sense of civic obligation and personal efficacy. Again generally speaking, persons who are active in various organizations have a high sense of civic obligation and personal efficacy, and they are relatively more numerous in high than in low status groups.

Hierarchy of Political Involvement: General. It is necessary to bear in mind these larger dimensions of political participation as we focus on its role and significance in the electoral process. In the broader sense, as Myron Weiner's definition indicates, it embraces a variety of acts of an organized and unorganized nature, legitimate or illegitimate, violent or non-violent, within or outside a political system. In a more conventional and narrower sense it still embraces many actions not directly related to the electoral process, although there are some obvious forms of indirect relations. This is suggested in Table 3.i, taken from one of the most suggestive studies on political participation:[26]

This Table suggests a wide variety of acts of political participation within a political system, even though it may not indicate the wider dimensions of participatory acts. It also groups acts of political participation within the electoral process under the two main headings of voting and campaign activity. It may be useful to break these down into further categories, and to give a clearer notion of the political spectrum that is embraced by political participation in the electoral process. This ranges from exposure to political stimuli to a high degree of campaign activity, and spills over into party membership, contacting government officials, and the holding of party or public office. A 'hierarchy of political involvement', focused on the electoral process, is given in Table 3.ii, taken from a standard work on political participation.[27]

This 'hierarchy of political involvement' may be more suitable for the analysis of elections and political participation in some political systems than in others, but a similar hierarchy, with minor adaptations, has been usefully and easily employed in electoral studies in both developed and developing political systems.[28] In ascending order it starts with the most common and the easiest forms of political participation and ends with the least common and the most demanding. It is subdivided into different types of political activities, from spectator to gladiatorial, with the 'apathetics' listed below and outside the hierarchy. It presents one way to group participatory acts connected with elections. Sometimes these acts are described as various levels of political participation, roughly corresponding to the four classifications in this Table – Apathetics, Spectator Activities, Transitional Activities, and Gladiatorial Activities.

A study of recruitment patterns among local party officials in the United States, for example, listed four levels of political participation.[29] The first level consisted of 'Apathetics,' the same term as found in Table 3.ii. This includes those members of a society who never participate in politics and for whom politics is not a part of their lives. They may be exposed to some extent to political stimuli – it would be hard to avoid these in almost any polity – but they do not respond in

Table 3.i

THE FOUR MODES OF PARTICIPATION AND THE DIMENSIONS OF PARTICIPATION

	Modes of activity	*Conflict dimension*	*Cooperative dimension*	*Political outcome*	*Initiative required*
Electoral activity	Voting	Conflictual	Act alone	Collective outcome	Little
	Campaign activity	Conflictual	Act with others	Collective outcome	Some
Non-electoral activity	Cooperative activity	Nonconflictual	Act with others	Collective outcome	Some or a lot
	Citizen-initiated contacts	Nonconflictual	Act alone	Collective or particularized outcome	A lot

Source: Sidney Verba, Norman H. Nie, and Jae-on Kim, *The Modes of Democratic Participation: A Cross-National Comparison* (Beverly Hills, Calif.: Sage Publications, 1971), p. 17.

any significant ways. They do not even vote, or show any interest in voting. This, of course, calls attention to the phenomenon of non-voting, a subject that has been studied in many political systems for a long time.[30] These studies show that non-voting arises from many causes, and has many different implications for the political system. In general, it is a form of non-participation, but in some cases it may be in fact a participatory act, an act of protest or in effect a negative decision, rather than an indication of indifference or ignorance or apathy. Virtually all 'Apathetics' will be non-voters, but not all non-voters are 'Apathetics.'

Table 3.ii

HIERARCHY OF POLITICAL INVOLVEMENT

Holding public or party office	*Gladiatorial Activities*
Being a candidate for office	
Soliciting political funds	
Attending a caucus or a strategy meeting	
Becoming an active member in a political party	
Contributing time in a political campaign	
Attending a political meeting or rally	*Transitional Activities*
Making a monetary contribution to a party or candidate	
Contacting a public official or a political leader	
Wearing a button or putting a sticker on a car	*Spectator Activities*
Attempting to talk another into voting a certain way	
Initiating a political discussion	
Voting	
Exposing oneself to political stimuli	
	Apathetics

Source: Lester W. Milbrath, *Political Participation* (Chicago: Rand McNally & Co., 1965), p. 18.

The second level is formed by those members of a political system who correspond to what Angus Campbell has called the 'peripheral voters.' They may have some interest in politics, have some knowledge about it, be exposed to various forms of political stimuli, and they may even vote, intermittently and usually on a party basis or as a matter of habit. They seldom take part in any other acts of political participation beyond the voting level. They are not very actively identified with the system, but they do support it to some degree.

A third group, constituting the third level of political participation, is composed of citizens who are distinguished from the second group mainly by more interested, more regular, and more active participation in the voting process, and also by some limited types of participatory acts in addition to the voting act, including various forms of campaign activities.

A final level or group, and a very limited one in terms of numbers, is composed of those political activists who take the most active part in the total electoral process, and who often hold official positions in a party or in the government, at various levels. These persons comprise the political élite in most political systems, although in more authoritarian political systems they may be of hardly more than symbolic significance, or, if they are not, they may derive their real status in the system from other than electoral or representative sources. But usually they are real influentials, and they provide a major linkage between the political system and the masses of the people.

Hierarchy of Political Involvement: India. Fortunately a significant Indian study, based on extensive interviewing and statistical and other forms of analysis, is available for testing the applicability to India of the 'hierarchy of political involvement' and levels of political participation in the electoral process, as drawn from Western studies.[31] The author of this study, and those who worked with him in conducting the interviews and making the calculations and analysis, were thoroughly familiar with the Western studies, which they were consciously trying to test in the Indian experience. To do this they interviewed over 1,900 respondents in various parts of the country, as a part of a major project which was conducted in all parts of India in 1966, in connection with the forthcoming general elections, under the auspices of the Centre for the Study of Developing Socities in Delhi. Their research and analysis indicated that the approach used in Western studies of elections and political participation could usefully be applied in India and that, with some significant exceptions, their own findings paralleled those in the Western studies.

The Indian study analyzed the political stratification of the Indian electorate on essentially the same basis as did the American scholars who studied recruitment patterns among local party officials in the United States. The first, second, and fourth groups in the American study were also used in the Indian project, under almost exactly the same names – Apathetics, Peripherals, and High Politists (i.e., Activists). The third group was divided into two, labelled Spectators and Auxiliaries. The former were described as 'Those who only vote and have some interest *and* information, along with a few who with moderate levels of motivation, vote and engage in one other activity.' The latter embraced 'Those who vote and engage in one or two other activities with medium levels of interest and information.'[32] The distribution of the sample according to these classifications or categories is indicated in the following Table.

Table 3.iii

DISTRIBUTION OF THE ELECTORATE BY DIFFERENT POLITICAL STRATA
(*per cent*)

Strata					
LOW				*HIGH*	
1 *Apathetics*	*2* *Peripherals*	*3* *Spectators*	*4* *Auxiliaries*	*5* *Politists*	*Total*
20.8	20.0	29.8	17.6	11.8	100
N 401	385	573	340	227	1926

Source: Bashiruddin Ahmed, 'Political Stratification of the Indian Electorate,' *Economic and Political Weekly*, VI (Annual Number, January 1971), 252.

Except for the High Politists, these figures would not be surprising in almost any electoral study in almost any genuinely functioning democracy. It is difficult to believe, however, that nearly 12 per cent of the Indian electorate, as these findings suggest, are really High Politists, in the sense of being real political activists. The American scholars who conducted the study of recruitment patterns of local party officials in the United States stated that only about one per cent of the population could be considered as political activists.

The difference is largely resolved on the basis of different definitions of this particular group, and not on the basis of fundamental differences in voting behavior and participation. The American scholars included in their group of political activists only those who are the most active, mainly those who held office in a party or in the government, whereas the Indian scholars included in their fifth category of High Politists 'Those who vote and engage in two activities with high levels of interest and information, and all those who engage in three or more activities with medium or high levels of interest and information.' Apparently this included holders of party and/or governmental office, but it is obviously not mainly restricted to such persons.

The Indian scholars considered the Auxiliaries to the real actors, as well as the High Politists, the real actors, as the groups in the electorate to which 'special attention will have to be given. . . . it is these two groups, constituting about 29 per cent of the electorate, who together shape and influence political outcomes.'[33] One wonders whether this is not too catholic an interpretation, for the real political actors or

Table 3.iv

PER CENT OF THE ELECTORATE ENGAGING IN ACTS OF PARTICIPATION

	Act	*Per cent*
(1)	Canvassing for candidates	9.0
(2)	Getting out the vote	6.8
(3)	Raising money	2.4
(4)	Organising meetings and rallies	5.9
(5)	Participating in processions and demonstrations	5.4
(6)	Distributing campaign literature	6.8
(7)	Other types of campaign activity	3.5
(8)	Involvement in campaign through associations and groups	7.2
(9)	Attending public meetings and rallies	25.4
(10)	Member of a political party	7.8
(11)	Contacting party leaders for help in solving problems	9.0
(12)	Contacting government officials for help in solving problems	19.6
(13)	Voted in 1967 at both Parliamentary and Assembly levels	78.8

Source, Ahmed, 'Political Stratification of the Indian Electorate,' p. 252.

In order to show the ascending order of frequency, to parallel Milbrath's listing, this Table could be rearranged as follows:

Table 3.v

HIERARCHY OF POLITICAL INVOLVEMENT (INDIA)

Raising money
Other types of campaign activity
Participating in processions and demonstrations
Organising meetings and rallies
Getting out the vote
Distributing campaign literature
Involvement in campaign through associations and groups
Member of a political party
Canvassing for candidates
Contacting party leaders for help in solving problems
Contacting government officials for help in solving problems
Attending political meetings and rallies
Voting

Apathetics

activists who have the major voice in shaping and influencing political outcomes, in India as in every other democratic system, would probably constitute a much smaller percentage of the electorate.

The Indian study also presents a 'hierarchy of political involvement' (not so called) which is quite similar to the hierarchy that has been taken from Lester Milbrath's well-known work on political participation, which is simply a repetition of a very familiar listing. The Indian hierarchy of involvement is particularly valuable because it includes percentages of the respondents who engaged in each of the acts of participation that are listed.[34]

This listing cannot easily be subdivided into the four categories used by Milbrath – Gladiatorial Activities, Transitional Activities, Spectator Activities, and Apathetics – but it seems to contain more activities that would be regarded as Gladiatorial Activities, and fewer Transitional and Spectator Activities. On the whole, it indicates a higher degree of political participation on the part of Indians than is generally assumed to exist.

In India, as elsewhere, voting 'far outstrips all other types of activities;' but the table indicates a surprisingly high degree of participation in the electoral process. '84 per cent of the electorate engages in one or more political acts including voting'; and 'almost half of the Indian electorate participates in politics in one or more ways other than voting. But the number of acts in which this part of the electorate participate is not very evenly distributed. Nearly 27 per cent engages in one activity, approximately 12 per cent in two activities, and the remaining 8 per cent in three or more activities.' The number of respondents who stated that they had attended public meetings and rallies was impressively high – more than 25 per cent; but it should be borne in mind that in India attending meetings of almost any kind is fairly common, as a means of diversion or entertainment in a country where many other forms of entertainment that are popular in more developed countries are scarce or non-existent, where television did not exist in 1967, and where even the radio was not used for election purposes, except to give certain instructions to the voters from official sources. Another surprising figure is the number of persons – nearly 20 per cent of the sample – who said they had contacted government officials for help in solving problems. 'With the exception of two activities – contacting government officials and attending rallies – only a small part of the electorate . . . engages in any of the other acts of political participation outside voting.'[35]

One interesting deviation in Indian from the usual pattern was found in the relative absence of a 'cumulative structure' of participation. As Robert Lane has pointed out, 'there is a "latent structure" pattern in most populations such that those who perform certain less frequent political acts are almost certain to perform all the more frequent acts.'[36] The Indian findings do not support this generalization. Using 'getting out the vote' as a measure of involvement in electioneering, the study found that in only one more frequently practiced activity, outside of voting, did more than 42 per cent of those involved in 'getting out the vote' participate. This is brought out in the following table:

Table 3.vi

PER CENT ACTIVE IN GETTING OUT THE VOTE WHO ENGAGE IN OTHER MORE FREQUENT ACTIVITIES

	Involvement in Campaign Through Groups (7.2)	*Party Member-ship (7.8)*	*Contacting Party Leaders (9)*	*Canvas-sing (9)*	*Contacting Government Officials (19.6)*	*Attending Rallies (25.4)*	*Voting (78.8)*
Getting out the Vote (6.8)	29.8	41.5	24.4	62.4	39.3	20.2	93.1

Note: Percentages in parentheses are rates of performance of each activity.
Source: Ahmed, 'Political Stratification of the Indian Electorate,' p. 253.

These figures indicate that 'There is, apparently, a certain degree of randomness in the way people engage in different participatory acts. A closer look at the data, however, suggests that if there is a clustering effect it probably occurs more within a set of participatory activities that are similar in form rather than across the full range of participatory acts, whatever be the frequency of their performance. Support for this view comes from the difference in the extent of overlap between getting out the vote and canvassing, which are rather similar activities, and getting out the vote and contacting government officials, which have not much in common.'[37] The correlation among the twelve acts of political participation (not including voting) that are being considered is suggested in Table 3.vii, using Pearson's coefficient.[38]

This Table indicates that the correlation between the first seven activities, which are 'similar in form,' is quite substantial, 'with an average co-efficient of .521. It goes down to .402 when the next two electoral activities are included and drops to .291 when the three remaining non-electoral activities are added.' One may question the characterization of the last three activities as non-electoral. Milbrath follows the more usual practice of including them as participatory acts within, or closely related to, the electoral process; but the more refined

Table 3.vii

CORRELATIONS AMONG TWELVE ACTS OF PARTICIPATION
(PEARSON'S R)

	1	*2*	*3*	*4*	*5*	*6*	*7*	*8*	*9*	*10*	*11*	*12*
(1) Canvassing	–	.692	.461	.658	.615	.710	.425	.201	.368	.366	.139	.112
(2) Getting out the vote			.471	.624	.568	.629	.339	.182	.318	.329	.132	.126
(3) Raising money				.512	.464	.513	.340	.150	.176	.271	.071	.052
(4) Organising meetings					.657	.626	.322	.207	.329	.356	.119	.092
(5) Participating in processions						.615	.303	.222	.300	.342	.079	.091
(6) Distributing campaign literature							.396	.168	.316	.354	.113	.083
(7) Other types of campaign activity								.145	.213	.242	.050	.049
(8) Involvement in campaign through associations and groups									.127	.102	.086	.064
(9) Attending public meetings and rallies										.254	.135	.091
(10) Party membership											.143	.108
(11) Contacting party leaders for solving problems												.291
(12) Contacting government officials for solving problems												

Source: Ahmed, 'Political Stratification of the Indian Electorate', p. 253.

analysis that this Table summarizes gives further evidence of the non-cumulative and cluster stratification of the Indian electorate and suggests that 'there is a much wider distribution and a greater amount of participation in the Indian electorate than the simple frequencies in Table 1 (Table 3.iv in this chapter) would lead one to expect.'[39]

This last finding is a highly significant one. If it is really true, it does indeed, as Bashiruddin Ahmed maintains, support the conclusion that 'the structure of participation that emerges from our study is different from the one suggested by existing literature.'[40] The validity of this broad conclusion has still to be demonstrated, especially since it seems to run counter to other findings and assumptions about the generally non-participant nature of Indian society and of Indian politics, outside of voting, a 'spectator' activity. It is possible that the sample used in the study was not really a representative one. Apparently it was unintentionally weighted in favor of respondents who were more activist or at least more participant than the general run of Indian citizens. This is suggested by the fact that 78.8 per cent of the respondents in the sample stated that they had voted in both the Parliamentary and Assembly elections in 1967, whereas the average for the Indian electorate as a whole was nearly 20 percentage points lower than this figure.

Voting and Political Participation. Since a vast amount of data on elections results in many countries is available, and since 'voting is the single act of political participation undertaken by a majority of adults in a majority of the nations in the world today,'[41] it is quite understandable why voting is by far the most widely discussed form of political participation and why voting turnout is usually considered as a – indeed often *the* – main indicator of political participation. This approach has been widely adopted, at least since the publication of the seminal work on *Political Behavior* by Herbert Tingsten in 1937,[42] and it has been facilitated by quantitative and statistical analyses of election statistics and other voting data.

It is apparent, as Seymour Martin Lipset pointed out in a famous summarization, that 'Patterns of voting participation are strikingly the same in various countries. . . . Men vote more than women; the better educated, more than the less educated; urban residents more than rural; those between thirty-five and fifty-five, more than younger or older voters; married persons more than unmarried; higher-status persons more than lower; members of organizations, more than nonmembers. These differences are, however, narrowing in many countries.'[43] The validity of these generalizations has been tested, and with some exceptions generally demonstrated, by empirical studies in many countries. They seem to be generally valid in non-Western as well as Western, and in developing as well as developed, political systems, where genuinely free direct elections on the basis of universal adult suffrage are central features of the systems.

In this respect India and Ceylon, the two South Asian countries that have had an extensive electoral experience, are no overall exceptions, even though some specific exceptions and qualifications should be noted. In almost all elections in almost all parts of the two countries men have voted more often than women, especially in rural areas and among low caste groups. This would be particularly expected in India, where social conventions and taboos, as well as relative levels of literacy, have tended to keep women more aloof from public activities. In the first general elections the percentage of eligible women who actually voted was very low; but it has been gradually improving. The same is true with members of Scheduled Castes and Scheduled Tribes.

The better educated have usually voted more often than the less educated (possibly the higher average turnout in national elections in Ceylon than in India may be to some extent related to the higher levels of literacy); but it would not be difficult to find exceptions to this conclusion. Urban residents generally vote more frequently than those in rural areas; but, as Myron Weiner has pointed out, 'It should be noted . . . that the higher voting turnout is not simply a function of urbanization since the rural areas of the highly participant states have a higher voting turnout than the urban areas of the low participant states.'[44] In some elections, in some constituencies, rural voters have turned out in larger numbers than urban voters.

Since registration in India and Ceylon is carried out by the Government, and is not dependent on the initiative of the eligible voter, these countries are not faced with the problem of a high rate of non-registration of younger voters, as is the United States; but they do experience the same phenomenon of relatively low turnout by the younger voters. This is a particularly serious problem in countries where the majority of eligible voters are under 35 years of age. Perhaps the problem of more non-voting by unmarried than by married voters is not as serious in countries like India and Ceylon, where most adults are married, as it is in more atomistic societies like those of the Western world. As in most other countries higher status persons tend to vote more frequently than those of lower social status, but the voting behavior of different social groups, such as castes in India, varies greatly, and not simply along a vertical continuum. In India and Ceylon members of organizations, especially if political parties are included in this category, tend to vote more often than those who take little or no part in organizations, but the numbers of Indians and Ceylonese who are members of organizations which are oriented toward political participation, including parties, are quite low.

The relationship of voting turnout in India to two important variables that have been considered, namely literacy and urbanization, is suggested in the following table, presented by Myron Weiner and based on electoral and census data of the late 1950s and early 1960s:

Table 3.viii

POLITICAL PARTICIPATION: VOTING, LITERACY, AND URBANIZATION

Ranked according to highest per cent of electorate voting	*Per cent of electorate voting for state assembly 1962*	*Per cent literate population*	*Per cent urbanization*
Kerala	84.4[a]	46.2	15.0
Kashmir	72.9	10.7	16.8
Madras	70.7	30.2	26.7
Punjab	65.5	23.7	20.1
Andhra Pradesh	64.0	20.8	17.4
Maharashtra	60.5	29.9	27.1
Mysore	59.0	25.3	22.0
Gujarat	58.0	18.4	26.0
West Bengal	55.6	29.1	23.2
Assam	52.8	25.8	7.5
Rajasthan	52.4	14.7	16.0
Uttar Pradesh	51.4	17.5	12.8
Bihar	49.0	18.2	8.4
Madhya Pradesh	44.5	16.9	14.3
Orissa	35.6[b]	21.5	6.3
India	56.3	24.0	18.0

(*a*) Assembly elections held in 1960.
(*b*) Assembly elections held in 1957.
Sources: Election data from Election Commission, Government of India, *Report on the Third General Elections in India, 1962*, Vol. II (Statistical) (Delhi: Manager of Publications, Government of India, 1963); literacy and urbanization data from *Census of India*, Paper No. 1 of 1962 (1961 Census).

This Table confirms the general validity of the generalizations regarding the relationship of voting turnout to literacy and urbanization; but it also indicates that even on the macro-level there are many exceptions to these generalizations. Most of the highly participant States, as measured by voting turnout, are also high in literacy and urbanization; but the pattern is by no means uniform. Further complications are obviously created in the case of States where literacy is relatively high but urbanization relatively low, as in the case of Orissa and Assam, or *vice versa*, as in the case of Gujarat. Kashmir, with the lowest rate of literacy in all of India and also rather low in urbanization, but with the second highest voting turnout in 1962, is an obvious deviant. Its high level of turnout could probably be explained by special conditions and circumstances, which, as this case illustrates, may completely reverse the normal patterns of participation.

The Table also gives evidence of another obvious but important fact, namely that voting turnout varies greatly from State to State in India. It also varies greatly from constituency, even in the same State, and from election to election. The variations in voting turnout in the States, over a period of twenty years, are more clearly delineated in the following Table:

Table 3.ix

VOTER PARTICIPATION IN LOK SABHA ELECTIONS, BY STATES, 1952–1971

States	*Per cent turnout*
Madras	71.82
Kerala	69.68
Haryana	64.30
West Bengal	63.29
Maharashtra	59.90
Andhra Pradesh	59.40
Punjab	58.80
Jammu and Kashmir	57.53
Gujarat	55.60
Mysore	55.00
Rajasthan	54.04
Assam	50.37
Bihar	48.83
Madhya Pradesh	48.03
Uttar Pradesh	46.15
Orissa	43.20

Source: Adapted from Table IV in *Seminar*, No. 144 (August 1971), p. 15.

In general, turnout has been relatively high in such relatively more developed States as Madras, Haryana, West Bengal, and Maharashtra, and relatively low in such relatively underdeveloped States as Orissa, Uttar Pradesh, Madhya Pradesh, and Bihar. Kerala is to some extent *sui generis.* It has consistently had one of the highest turnouts of any Indian State, even though it is by no means one of the most economically developed States. The explanation is to be found in the highest degree of literacy in India, an unusual degree of political activity and interest, the active participation in politics of such important caste associations as the Nair Service Society and the Shri Narayan Dharma Paripalam Yogam (the SNDP, an association for the uplift of the low-caste but politically active Ezhava community), and various Christian and Muslim groups, and other indigenous factors.

For an underdeveloped country, with a population consisting mostly of illiterates with little political experience and in a generally non-participant society, the turnout in the nation-wide general elections has been reasonably good, if not highly impressive. The turnout in the first general elections was slightly more than 50 per cent of the eligible voters, and in the second it was only 47.54 per cent, but since then it has been well over 50 per cent, and in 1967 it reached a high of over 60 per cent. These figures are slightly lower than turnout in American Presidential elections in recent years. They are, of course, markedly lower than the turnout in general elections in several European democracies, as in England and the Federal Republic of Germany.[45]

In Ceylon the voting turnout has been substantially higher than in India, and indeed than in the United States. In fact, it compares favorably with turnout in almost any other democratic state. It was only 55.9 per cent in 1947, but since then it has ranged from 69 per cent in 1956 to 85.2 per cent in 1970. The turnout in Pakistan's first – and only – general election was an impressive 60 per cent, and in Nepal's only general election it was only 43 per cent.

Although voting turnout is probably used more frequently as an indicator of political participation than any other variable in the 'participant syndrome,' it is in many ways a most unsatisfactory indicator. Data on voting turnout are available for many elections in many political systems, and hence are often used for comparative purposes. A high turnout is not necessarily an indicator of a genuinely democratic system. Obviously the highest turnouts are to be found in totalitarian or authoritarian systems where elections may be used to demonstrate support for one-party regimes and where the citizens are virtually compelled to vote. They are also abnormally high, of course, in the few democratic states where voting is compulsory. They tend to be higher in more developed democracies, with a longer and better established tradition and a more routinized procedure of elections, than in new democracies in the developing world.[47] If turnout is based on percentage of adult males who vote, rather than, as is more usual, on percentage of eligible voters who exercise the franchise in particular elections, some genuinely democratic states, such as Switzerland until 1971, when it finally granted the franchise to women, and some

Table 3.x

TURNOUT IN GENERAL ELECTIONS[46]
(percentages)

India		*Ceylon*		*Pakistan*		*Nepal*	
1951–2	51.55	1947	55.9	1970	60	1959	43
1957	47.54	1952	70.7				
1962	54.80	1956	69.0				
1967	57.93	1960 (March)	77.6				
1971	54.81	1960 (July)	75.9				
		1965	82.1				
		1970	85.2				

United Kingdom		*United States*	
1955	76.8	1948	51.5
1959	78.7	1952	62.0
1964	77.1	1956	60.1
1966	75.8	1960	63.2
1970	72.0	1964	62.1
		1968	60.2

Source: Adapted from *Report on the Seventh Parliamentary General Election in Ceylon, 27 May 1970*, Ceylon Sessional Paper No. VII – 1971, p. 54 (Table X).

professedly democratic states which confine most democratic rights, including voting, to a privileged few (South Africa is the most notable example) have very low voting turnout.

As recent voting studies have demonstrated quite convincingly, voting is perhaps the least demanding, as well as the most common, of all the participant acts connected with the electoral process. The act of voting may be an act of extreme commitment and involvement, but usually it is not. 'Voting requires the least initiative and may, therefore, be engaged in with little internal motivation.'[48] Moreover, 'unlike campaign activity, voting differs in its meaning for the individual elector from nation to nation.' In some countries, especially the United States, voting is clearly an integral part of the 'participant syndrome,' and has a strong relationship to political commitment and psychological involvement. 'On the other hand, in those countries . . . where voting bears little or no relationship to general propensity for political activity, there is little or no relationship to psychological involvement. Where voting is part of a participant syndrome, it appears to be associated with concern about public life. In other nations, . . . it is related to such orientations and associated with partisan attachment.'[49]

India appears to be an example *par excellence* of a political system where the act of voting is not an integral part of the 'participant syndrome,' reflects little psychological involvement, motivation, or concern about public life, and is closely associated with partisan attachment. This is due to peculiarities in political culture, political experience, and value systems. It is a convincing proof that the act of voting, while often quite similar in form and purpose, may have quite different meanings and significance in different political systems. It is a reminder that, for example, 'in India voting is sharply different from voting in the United States in terms of the kinds of people who vote, the attitudes associated with voting, and the processes that bring people to the polls.'[50] This does not mean, however, that voting turnout and the voting act generally in India cannot be compared with similar phenomena in other political systems. The problem here is clearly a common one in political science, especially in cross-cultural and cross-national research, namely the problem of equivalence, that is of finding measures of comparison that are '*equivalent enough* so that it is meaningful to ask further questions.'[51] But it does suggest that in India, even more than in most other political systems, voting turnout may be a particularly unsatisfactory indicator of meaningful political participation.

Political Interest, Efficacy, and Sense of Civic Obligation. This discussion raises a number of related points. Political participation will obviously be greater among individuals who are interested in politics. 'The more interested an individual is in politics, the more likely he is to participate.'[52] Interest in politics has been shown to be related to the various factors, such as age, sex, literacy, social status, degree of urbanization, and organizational connections, which affect voter turnout; but since turnout is a poor indicator of real political interest, especially in India, other tests of interest should be applied.

Political participation is also closely related to the sense of political efficacy, a concept first well developed by election analysts at the Survey Research Center at the University of Michigan, in the form of a scale of political efficacy, and subsequently applied in electoral research in many countries.[53] Surveys conducted in India along these lines indicate that Indian voters generally have a noticeably lesser sense of political efficacy than voters in Western democracies or in Japan. A survey carried out in the four major Indian States that held mid-term elections in 1969 – Bihar, the Punjab, Uttar Pradesh, and West Bengal – showed that in India as in all other countries there is a close relationship between socio-economic status and the strength of a sense of efficacy and that there are wide variations in this sense of efficacy in different parts of the country (for reasons that should be examined carefully); but it was also plain that in India the sense of political efficacy is quite low.[54] Evidently most Indian voters do not have much confidence in their political efficaciousness, that is, in themselves as citizens.

Presumably in highly-participant polities a large number of citizens will have a strong sense of civic obligation. This is, however, not necessarily true. Even in the most highly-participant polities the sense of civic obligation is surprisingly low, especially if a sense of civic obligation is measured by the standard of the acceptance of the obligation to participate actively in public affairs, rather than merely in a passive sense, such as to vote without any particular sense of commitment. The authors of *The Civic Culture* report that the percentages of respondents who thought that the ordinary man should be active in his community were 51 per cent in the United States, 39 per cent in England, 26 per cent in Mexico, 22 per cent in Germany, and only 10 per cent in Italy.[55]

In India scattered studies seem to confirm what most observers would suspect, namely that few citizens have a strong sense of civic obligation. Few think that the ordinary citizen should be active in his community's political affairs, and few are in fact active, except in the rather passive form of activity represented by the casting of a vote in various kinds of elections.

This lack of a strong sense of civic obligation is not surprising, and does not distinguish India from a number of other democratic states. What does seem to distinguish India, however, is what appears to be a remarkably low evaluation of political participation as a value, or as a desirable norm. In few other successfully functioning democracies – France may be another example – is political participation rated so low in the scale of normative values. This is brought out in the most elaborate cross-national study of values in politics that has yet been made, which fortunately included India.[56]

Elections and Political Participation in South Asia. Further testing will be needed before the validity of the finding that participation as a value has a low rating among Indians can be established. It would seem to fit into the thesis that India is an essentially non-participant society. To the extent that it is true, it makes the extent of actual political participation in India even more impressive than the actual record, which is also rather impressive, would indicate. Much of this participation centers around the electoral process; and there are encouraging signs that this kind of participation is increasing, and is having a positive effect on India's political development. In all South Asian countries one may entertain greater doubts about the effects of other forms of political participation outside the electoral process, especially those which challenge and threaten the political system itself.

In India and Ceylon elections have clearly been a major channel of political participation, which has been impressive in extent and in operation. It is hard to say, however, how meaningful this participation has been, either for individuals or for the political system. Indians have participated in many ways in 'the world's largest democratic elections'; but for the most part their participation has been confined to fairly passive activities, such as attending election meetings and voting. Moreover, as has been pointed out, in India political participation is rated very low as a 'value' – apparently about as low as in any democratic country in the world. In Ceylon participation seems to have been greater, as reflected in more widespread activity during the electoral campaigns and in a higher voting turnout than in India; but in recent years support for the political system, including the institution of elections, seems to have declined markedly. In fact, substantial elements of the population – notably the younger people, in a country where the majority of the population are young – have turned to more activist and agitational forms of political participation that have presented serious challenges not only to the institution of elections but apparently even to the political system itself. Obviously, in Pakistan and Nepal political participation has been much more limited, indirect, and peripheral. In Bangladesh it is patently more extensive than in the days when the area was a part of Pakistan, but there seems to be considerable doubt as to the extent to which it will be expressed constructively within the electoral and political system and the extent to which it will be expressed destructively in agitational challenges to the existing system.

4

THE FUNCTIONS OF ELECTIONS: SUPPORT-BUILDING AND LINKAGE PATTERNS

In the previous chapter we explored two major functions of elections – political choice and political participation. These functions are of central importance in all democratic polities, and, at least in a symbolic way, are performed in all political systems where elections, however peripheral, are a part of the institutionalized political process. But it is important to bear in mind that elections serve many other, if somewhat related functions, which cumulatively may be of equal or greater significance. This chapter will consider some of these other functions, grouped under the two general headings of support-building or system maintenance functions, and linkage patterns and functions. The broad scope of the functions has been suggested by James Rosenau in an interesting section of his book, *The Dramas of Politics*. The section is entitled 'The Delights of Unintended Consequence.' While it refers to American presidential elections, it gives a comprehensive view of the functions of elections in general:

> An especially gratifying analytic insight is the discernment of systemic or subsystemic consequences of an action or event that were not intended or perhaps not even recognized by the actors involved. Whether or not the intended outcome of the action has occurred, the student discerns repercussions which, although not immediately relevant to the action, seem likely to have long-range consequences for the integrative or adaptive capabilities of the system in which they occur. Consider, for example, a presidential election. Most eyes are on the candidates and the voters, on the promises of the former to the latter and the reactions of the latter to the former. Election night excitement builds as the outcome nears and the next day there is considerable speculation about the implications for domestic and foreign policy in the next few years. The student of politics shares the involvement leading up to and immediately following election day. His training as well as his

curiosity, however, will lead him along additional paths. He is likely to approach the campaign and election with the assumption that they serve other functions besides providing the personnel and general policy orientations that will guide the nation for the next four years. And the more he wonders about other functional consequences, the greater might be his delight in finding a wide range of possible results that are not readily discernible. He may see the election campaign, for example, as a mechanism for political education and for recruiting and training leaders. Neither the Constitution nor the candidates intended it, but the promises and charges that fill every day of the campaign expose the young to the institutions and values of the society and teach the voters about the nature of the system and the problems of the world. People are learning about ecology and economics, about farming and financing, about civil rights and public responsibilities, about alliances and diplomacy, and about various possible orderings of the importance of these problems. They have an opportunity to learn how controversies evolve and how they are restrained, how political institutions frame issues and how they process them, how commitments are made and how they endure, how bargains are made and how promises are kept (or broken), how the future might be structured and how the past can be interpreted. As the student of politics observes these processes of socialization and education, his training and orientation incline him to look even further and to ask about the potential consequences of these processes for the system's legitimacy and for its ability to confront problems. Indeed, if he is insistent in his effort to discover unintended consequences at all levels, he will try to understand the function of the election for the training and recruitment of future political leaders. From such a perspective, the election is not simply an instance of 'winner take all.' Those who lose may remain part of the leadership pool for the future, thus enlivening an investigation of whether the way in which they conducted their campaigns enriched or diminished the reservoir of political talent available in the years ahead.[1]

A number of important functions of elections emerge from this reflective commentary. These include providing political leaders and general policy orientation, the recruitment and training of leaders, political education, political socialization, strengthening a system's legitimacy and capability, and providing a 'reservoir of political talent,' with 'unintended consequences at all levels.' These functions are performed in varying degrees by elections in all democratic political systems, including elections in the political systems of South Asia.

Support-Building and System Maintenance Functions

As has been noted, Rosenau lists support-building as one of the four main functions of a political system, and he points out that this function is institutionalized through party and electoral systems. In the sense in which Rosenau uses the term, support-building might be considered as the all-embracing function of elections, and hence all other functions could be subsumed under it. This might be particularly true if support-building were linked with system maintenance, certainly a major function of elections. In some ways the two terms may be regarded as synonymous, at least in the vocabulary of political science. In some respects support-building is more comprehensive than system maintenance, in that it is designed to help a political system achieve a variety of goals. No doubt system maintenance is a primary, and an indispensable, survival goal, but once that goal is achieved there are many other goals that a political system must seek to promote. In other respects system maintenance is more comprehensive than support-building, for it could be said to subsume all of the four functions of a political system that Rosenau lists and to relate these functions to basic systemic foundations.

A great many functions of elections could be included under the general captions of support-building and system maintenance. Among these are legitimacy, political stability, integration, identification, assimilation, involvement, commitment, allegiance-maintaining and allegiance re-affirming, and mobilization.

Legitimacy. Professor W. J. M. Mackenzie has referred to 'the immense strength of the tradition that elections confer legitimacy.'[2] Elections may help to confer or to establish, or to maintain or re-affirm, or to refute or weaken or destroy the legitimacy of a regime or even of a political system. Presumably by their participation in the electoral process citizens of a country indicate their basic support of the political system, and by their non-participation in elections they may reflect a lack of support or a high degree of disillusionment or even alienation. By their support or non-support they can also indicate their verdict on the legitimacy of the regime. A regime that is strongly endorsed at the polls in genuinely free direct elections has a claim to legitimacy that few other regimes can have; but it must be remembered that while massive electoral participation may help to ensure the legitimacy of a political system, it may not necessarily ensure long-term support of even an apparently highly popular government. Moreover, as Rose and Mossawir have pointed out, 'The significance of elections in building legitimacy is also difficult to measure. . . . History shows sufficient cases of regimes with electoral systems failing to achieve legitimacy, so that elections are a contributing rather than a controlling factor in legitimacy.'[3]

In South Asia elections have been used as a device for establishing or maintaining legitimacy, but in very different ways and to varying degrees. They have clearly been a major instrument of legitimacy in India and Ceylon, where ever since independence elections have been a central institution of the political systems, and the governments in power have had wide electoral support. These governments could claim to have legitimacy by virtue of 'the will of the people,' as evidenced by electoral results. In Pakistan and Nepal legitimacy of regimes has generally been based on other grounds. To be sure, Pakistan would not have been created and the Muslim League would not have come to power after independence if it had not demonstrated through elections (on the basis of limited suffrage) that it had the support of the majority of the Muslims of the subcontinent, and especially of the Muslims in the areas that became Pakistan; and Prime Minister Bhutto can maintain with some justification that the legitimacy of his regime rests upon the electoral success which his Pakistan People's Party scored in the ill-fated general elections in Pakistan in December 1970. But regardless of the validity of these claims, no national government in Pakistan from the death of Mohammad Ali Jinnah in 1948 to the electoral victory of Z. A. Bhutto in West Pakistan in 1970 could base its claim to legitimacy on electoral grounds. No national elections at all were held during the period of so-called parliamentary government up to 1958, and during the Ayub Khan era the only so-called national elections were held on a very indirect and limited basis, with 80,000 – and eventually 120,000 – 'Basic Democrats' serving as an electoral college, more to re-affirm the legitimacy of a regime whose real claims to legitimacy rested on other grounds than to demonstrate a solid basis of popular support. In Nepal, since the overthrow of the Ranas in 1950–1, legitimacy has clearly rested in the King, and has been based on traditional, ascriptive, and symbolic grounds, and certainly not on electoral support. In Bangladesh Sheikh Mujibur Rahman can justifiably claim that the legitimacy of his regime rests basically upon the will of the people as evidenced by the overwhelming support which they gave to the Awami League in direct general elections in December 1970 and March 1973.

Political Stability. A considerable degree of political stability is essential for the maintenance of all political systems, but it may be achieved in a variety of ways. In traditional and authoritarian systems it is often achieved, at least temporarily, without elections or other means of popular participation; but in democratic systems it is usually related more directly to the electoral process.

Political stability does not necessarily imply a regime dedicated to the maintenance of the status quo. In many societies, especially in the developing countries, it may in the short run be maintained by regimes following status quo policies, but in the long run it may be possible to maintain only by fairly radical and sweeping political, economic, and social change.

Political stability is one of the functions or goals of elections, but the contribution of elections to political stability in different countries and circumstances is a mixed one. Clearly elections may have both stabilizing and destabilizing effects on political systems. This is well illustrated in the electoral experience of the countries of South Asia.[4] Most of the elections in India and Ceylon had stabilizing effects, but the 1967 general election in India, which greatly reduced the majority of the Congress Party in the Lok Sabha and gave it a minority position in several key States, and the sixth general election in Ceylon in 1970, which seemed to have stabilizing effects but which was soon followed by internal challenges to the government that had been elected by an overwhelming mandate and to the political system itself, may be said to have had at least partially destabilizing effects. The failure to hold direct nationwide general elections for many years in Pakistan and Nepal raised doubts about the legitimacy of the systems in these countries and led to demands for greater popular participation, with consequence destabilizing effects; but the single experiment in national elections on the basis of universal suffrage in each country did not have happy results, and led to the disruption of Pakistan and to the resumption of rule from 'the Palace' in Nepal, with some trappings of 'Panchayat Democracy.'

Thus elections in South Asia have contributed both to political stability and to political instability. It might be more accurate to observe that the political instability that sometimes seemed to follow elections was a surface phenomenon that was necessary in societies undergoing increasing pressures and rapid change, and that the instability would have been much greater if elections had not been held and much less if the verdict of the elections had been accepted by ruling elites and had been carried out more fully and in greater good faith.

For in South Asia the demands for change are certain to increase, and it is doubtful that the more important changes that are needed in the economic and social spheres can be effected without a broadening of the political base. This in turn calls for a greater measure of popular participation and support, which will be difficult enough to achieve without genuinely free and direct elections and almost impossible to achieve in the long run without them.

The problems of political stability and political change will continue to vex the countries of South Asia. 'All of the major elections in South Asia in recent years gave overwhelming mandates to parties and leaders dedicated both to political stability and to radical economic, political, and social change. . . . But while the mandate is clear in each country, the prospects of fulfilling it are much less so. The achievement of greater political stability along with radical economic and social change is a difficult task under the best of circumstances, and it is particularly difficult in the South Asian political, economic, and social environment.'[5]

Integration, Identification, Assimilation, Involvement. These are all important functions of elections, especially since they bring individual citizens into closer relation to the political system. Elections may have significant integrative effects. As A. J. Milnor has observed, 'the act of voting itself integrates the voter into the political system. By playing a part in the political system which he conceives of as meaningful and useful, he is in a very real sense affirming his role in the system.'[6] It also tends to give the voter a feeling that he has a stake in the system. It involves him in ways that he can understand and gives him a sense of participation, meaningful or otherwise. 'Casting a ballot is more than a choice between parties. It is a direct involvement of the individual in the political system, in the process of government; and for any state – particularly one in the beginning stages of development – that is a very important achievement.'[7]

Elections have performed all of these functions in India and Ceylon, but not extensively in Pakistan and Nepal. 'Probably no features of India's evolving political system have contributed more to its political development or to the political education of its people, or to the forging of links between people and government, than these massive general elections.'[8] Conversely, the absence of direct nationwide elections has retarded the political development of Pakistan, and probably also of Nepal, although in Nepal the prerequisites for successful general elections were noticeably lacking.

Access, Allegiance-Maintaining, Allegiance-Re-affirming, Commitment, and Mobilization. As we have seen, many of the major types of political participation, including voting and campaign activity, are integral parts of the electoral process. To a degree unparalleled by any other political institution, elections are important avenues of access to a political system. If these avenues are relatively open to all citizens, elections will also serve as agencies for securing the commitment of the citizenry to the system, for they will feel that they are a part of it and that they have ways and means of making their wants known and of promoting their interests. They can choose their leaders, and hold these leaders accountable for their acts and policies.

Elections, furthermore, are instruments for maintaining allegiance to a political system, for re-enforcing 'traditional orientations of allegiance,' and for re-affirming allegiance. Indeed, as Rose and Mossawir have stated, 'for most individuals the function of voting at a given general election is not that of . . . registering a fresh choice, but rather re-affirming an allegiance established long ago.'[9]

As a function of elections, mobilization may be interpreted in at least two different ways. In the first place, it may be interpreted as mobilization of citizens into the political system in ways that will give them a greater stake and voice in the system than they would otherwise enjoy. In this sense it is associated with genuine political participation. Presumably this is the meaning of mobilization through the electoral process in democratic and relatively open systems. But mobilization may also be interpreted as a means of insuring the support of, and indeed of controlling, the mass of the people in the system. This is obviously the function of elections in 'mobilization systems,' including those of a highly authoritarian and even totalitarian nature. One could say that all of the general elections in India and Ceylon, and the single national elections in Pakistan and Nepal, have served mobilization functions, according to the first interpretation of the term, whereas the elections to the different tiers of political institutions under the Basic Democracies system in Pakistan during the Ayub Khan era and under the Panchayat Democracy system in Nepal since the early 1960s, all of which were on the basis of a very limited franchise and, except for the elections of members of the basic units, were by indirect vote, were deliberately designed to serve mobilization functions in the second sense of the term.

Unlike the functions of political choice, whether of leaders or of policies or of both, and of political participation, support-building functions of elections seem to be mainly designed to give support to political systems and regimes rather than to the people who constitute the electorate. They may benefit, and offer rewards to, the masses of the people, but the flow is mainly from the bottom upward, with those in control of the political system giving hardly more than lip service to their 'masters', the voters. Hence support-building may be characterized as an important but somewhat hazardous function, which needs to be watched closely in a 'reconciliation' system such as exists in India, whereas it may be characterized as perhaps the most important function in a mobilization system, of an authoritarian or totalitarian type.

Linkage Patterns and Functions

As has already been noted, elections serve important functions both for the individual citizen and for the political system, and provide important channels of interaction between a citizen and the government. In the broadest sense, as Gerald M. Pomper has observed, 'elections provide the linkage between the behavior of the voter and the actions of government.'[10] Hence elections serve very significant linkage functions.

Protection. One of these linkage functions is that of protection, meaning chiefly the protection of the citizens by giving them a voice in their own affairs and a check, however indirect and inadequate, on those whom they elevate to power and whom they support with their votes. According to democratic theory, 'Elections would give the voters a means of protection, a method of intervention in politics when their vital interests are being threatened. By their very existence, they would act as a restraint on government and tend to bring representatives to further the needs and wants of their constituents.'[11] Obviously elections serve this protective function quite inadequately in many political systems, but it is an important function nonetheless for the citizens of a country, and one that few political leaders can ignore. In contrast to the support-building and system maintenance functions, which, as the terms suggest, are mainly designed to support the system and their regimes in power, the protective function is mainly designed to safeguard the interests and role of the individual citizen against the system and the ruling regime. It is meaningful and real in some political systems, and rather meaningless in others.

In South Asia the protective function of elections is quite significant in those countries, namely India and Ceylon, where free, direct elections have for some time been an integral and central part of the political systems, and rather meaningless in those countries where such elections have been rarities and where they have been peripheral to the various political systems that have been tried. The value and reality of this function may become apparent in the new nation of Bangladesh, which has held only one nationwide general election to date (although it came into existence in part as a result of the first such election in undivided Pakistan in December 1970), and it is possible, but less likely, that elections will serve as a protection to the voters in Pakistan, under the hybrid political system that was adopted after the loss of its eastern wing as a result of civil war and India's military intervention in 1971. The Pakistan Constitution of 1973 seems to lack some of the normal democratic safeguards and protective features, including free and full scope for the electoral process. The same observation might be made of the new Constitution of Sri Lanka, which went into effect in May 1972.

Education. In Rosenau's interesting commentary on the functions of elections, which was quoted at the beginning of this chapter, the educative function of elections was given special stress. This function, as Rosenau sees it, is a very broad as well as a very important one. It has innumerable aspects and ramifications. In Rosenau's view, elections 'expose the young' – and he might have embraced all voters in his comments – 'to the institutions and values of the society and teach the voters about the nature of the system and the problems of the world.'[12] They also serve less exalted, but nevertheless significant, educative functions.

In his *Considerations on Representative Government* John Stuart Mill wrote: 'Among the foremost benefits of free government is that education of the intelligence and of the sentiments which is carried down to the very lowest ranks of the people when they are called to take part in acts which directly affect the great interests of the country.'[13] Elections are among the most significant and most pervasive of these acts, and they undoubtedly contribute to the 'education of the intelligence and of the sentiments' of those who participate, which in direct elections means people of all social strata and backgrounds.

Elections are training grounds for people in the arts of government. For those who are not accustomed to them, massive national direct elections are a novel and a somewhat frightening and bewildering experience. As people become more accustomed to the electoral process, the cumulative educational effect of elections becomes increasingly apparent. As elections become a normal, routinized, and regular feature of the political process, voters have little difficulty in performing their electoral roles. The danger then is that they may become rather bored with the whole process.

All of these educative effects of elections are quite apparent in the electoral experience of the countries of South Asia. The early educative effects will emerge from a study of the first general elections in any of these countries. No one who has observed at first hand the first general elections in India, in 1951–2, will forget the mixture of excitement, curiosity, confidence, and apprehension with which millions of Indians who had never before cast a vote in a massive general election participated in the campaign and cast their ballots. These mixed feelings lingered on in subsequent elections, but with each election confidence increased and the apprehension, and also to some extent the curiosity and the excitement, decreased, even among first-time voters. And as elections became a frequent and routinized part of their experience, as well as of the political process, Indian voters showed an impressive degree of maturity, along with some signs of apathy and boredom. One of the remarkable political phenomena of the twentieth century is the way in which millions of politically inexperienced Indians, most of whom were illiterate and socially very conservative, took quite naturally to the process of democratic elections, one of the most sophisticated aspects of modern political systems, and participated in 'the world's largest democratic elections' in an impressive and meaningful way.

The people of Ceylon, too, showed an equal or even greater degree of political maturity in their electoral participation, and turned out in even larger numbers, percentage-wise. Their performance was impressive, but less so than the Indian performance, because their elections were on a much smaller scale, because they had held elections on the basis of universal adult franchise for a longer period than the Indians, and because they had a far higher degree of literacy than the Indian voters.

For Pakistanis and Nepalese, also, their first and only nationwide elections were educational experiences, in which they participated with a surprising degree of assurance and maturity; but they have had no opportunity to benefit from the cumulative impact of national elections, which have been aberrations and not normal features in their political experience. There can be little doubt that the Bangalees of Bangladesh were able to conduct their first national election after independence, in March 1973, quite successfully, in spite of the unsettled state of the country, in part because of their participation in the national elections in Pakistan in December 1970, when they turned out in large numbers to give overwhelming support to the Awami League and their charismatic leader, Sheikh Mujibur Rahman.

Recruitment and Training. Elections serve important functions in the area of recruitment and training, which are essential in any political system. They serve as agencies for recruitment and training of at least four different key groups: voters generally, party members, party activists, and political leaders.

Elections recruit voters, and involve masses of people in activities ranging from simply the act of voting to active participation in the campaign in innumerable ways, usually through participation in the activities of political parties and through partisan identification. Through participation in party and campaign activities, in the actual voting on election day, and in other ways voters are not only recruited into politics but they are also trained as citizens and participants. This double function is a particularly important one in developing political systems, where channels of recruitment and training are somewhat limited.

Because parties are particularly active during elections, the electoral process serves as a major recruitment and training institution for political parties. It provides an incentive for people to enrol as party members, and it trains them in the kinds of political activities for which parties mainly exist. It also helps parties to recruit and train those who will play more active roles than ordinary members, including leaders of all kinds. Elections provide many opportunities for party activists to gain experience and to show their capabilities and effectiveness.

Political parties are of course the main recruiting agencies and support bases for political leaders, but such leaders may emerge through the electoral process in or outside of parties. These leaders usually come up through the ranks, rising from party posts and lesser political offices to higher roles, but in any event they usually emerge from the electoral process and are ultimately dependent on the voters for support. In genuinely democratic systems elections will be meaningful instruments for indicating this support, whereas in more controlled systems they may serve the same purpose, but in a less meaningful way.

In countries such as Pakistan and Nepal, with little experience in direct, nationwide elections, the degree of support of political leaders, who may claim legitimacy and position on other bases or who may also claim widespread public support without having tested that alleged support in popular elections, may be very difficult to determine. The 1959 general elections in Nepal, for example, for the first time revealed the relative degree of popular support that various contending parties really enjoyed, and gave the Nepali Congress a clear popular mandate. The 1970 elections in Pakistan showed that the Awami League and Sheikh Mujibur Rahman had even greater popular support than was generally imagined, although the refusal of the National Awami Party and Maulana Bhashani to participate in the elections was partly responsible for the Awami League's almost complete electoral sweep of National Assembly seats from East Pakistan. These elections also showed that Z. A. Bhutto and his Pakistan People's Party had greater support, especially in the Punjab, than was generally expected, and gave Bhutto and his party a political base which after the defeat of Pakistan in the war with India of December 1971, brought Bhutto to power in Pakistan.

Socialization. As many empirical and psychological studies have shown, political socialization is a product of the total societal environment; it begins practically from the birth of a human being, and continues throughout one's life; it is profoundly conditioned by such basic institutions as the family, the school, and the community, as well as by the prevailing value systems and currents of thought and action in the social order.[14] Since a political system is part of a larger and more comprehensive social system, and since politics is conditioned by the societal environment, it is hardly surprising that one's political attitudes and behavior are a reflection of the political socialization process, which antedates any active participation in politics and is quite different from the degree of any active participation, although the two phenomena are clearly related.

Elections are usually not the most influential agencies of political socialization, but they do serve to a greater or lesser degree in this way. They help to bridge the gaps, if any, between the polity and the society, and between an individual's social and political world. 'The politics of mass society,' to use Kornhauser's term, are deeply rooted in the social order, and involve in politics large numbers of people whose interests, activities, and orientations are much more social (in the societal sense) than political. This kind of politics brings the masses into the political arena to an unprecedented degree, and involves them in many procedures, such as elections, that are rather unfamiliar to them but that are major institutions in most modern political systems.

In the South Asian countries, in particular, elections are important agencies of political socialization. They serve as links between the society and the polity, in countries where the society is still largely based on ascriptive and traditional institutions and values, and where the polity at the national level is essentially non-ascriptive and 'modern,' or at least 'transitional' to a far greater extent than is the society. Thus elections are of key importance in any consideration of the nature and influence of 'tradition' and 'modernity' in the South Asian scene.

This is one of the most widely discussed themes in most studies of developing societies and political systems, and one of the most baffling and elusive.[15] Students of both social and political development speak of the 'modernity of tradition' and the 'traditionalism of modernity.' They can easily show that many of the apparently traditional aspects of the social order are changing under the impact of 'modern' trends, and that the most seemingly modern aspects of the polity are by no means devoid of traditional influences. This is one of the reasons why 'modern' institutions do not always operate in developing countries as they do in more politically developed countries. Hence to a Western observer much that seems familiar in form does not work in familiar ways, and much that seems exotic and incomprehensible may not operate in wholly unfamiliar ways. Perhaps a partial explanation is that different social and political systems may serve some of the same basic functions, even though they seem to operate in very different ways. By helping to bridge the gap between the polity and the society, political socialization serves both social and political purposes, and performs important linkage functions.

Elections may play a larger role in the political socialization process in developing countries than they do in more developed countries. This would seem to be particularly true in the countries of South Asia, where both social and political systems are quite complex and are at various stages of social and political development, and where the themes of tradition and modernity are central to any political discussion, as well as to any societal analysis. Anyone who has observed, or even simply studied, elections in South Asia will have been fascinated, and at times bewildered, by the mixture of the familiar and the unfamiliar in the way elections are staged and in the curious mixture of the traditional and the modern in the conduct of one of the most modern of major political institutions, at least in scale and in centrality in the political system.

Communication. Elections are also important agencies of political communication, not only between the polity and the society, in the political socialization sense, but also between the people and their government, in the sense of political linkages. They provide an opportunity for the people to have more direct contact with their leaders, or would-be leaders, than they have at any other time, and for the political leaders or would-be leaders to communicate more directly with the people than they do either before or after the election periods.

South Asian elections offer fascinating opportunities for study from the point of view either of communication theory or of the techniques of mass communication. For the parties and the candidates for office the elections are massive efforts at communication, and all kinds of approaches and channels are used. There are, however, two great exceptions. Since television does not exist, except in a few South Asian cities and mostly on a limited and experimental basis, it plays almost no role in South Asian elections. Parties and candidates are not allowed to use TV for campaign purposes. Nor does the radio, which in all South Asian countries is strictly controlled by the government, figure prominently in election campaigns. Party spokesmen are sometimes alloted one or two brief periods to appeal for support – but in India even this has seldom been done, mainly because the parties could not agree on the allocation of time – and party manifestoes are sometimes summarized in radio broadcasts; but for the most part the radio is used only to instruct the voters in election procedures and regulations, and to appeal to them to exercise their voting privileges. Newspapers carry quite full reports of party activities, campaign proceedings and speeches, and election trends and prospects, and they sometimes print advertisements prepared by the central or State Election Commissions, but they seldom publish party advertisements. Parties and candidates rely mainly on public meetings, house-to-house and other forms of face-to-face canvassing, posters, banners, signs on walls and fences, campaign literature, processions, and forms of entertainment that appeal to local tastes and habits. For weeks the Indian voters are subject to a massive communication campaign.

Their own methods of communications differ greatly in different parts of the area. They may communicate their views by participation in party and campaign activities or by contacting party spokesmen and candidates; or they may communicate more passively by attendance at public meetings or by listening to candidates and party workers in house-to-house canvassing or small group sessions. In the final analysis they communicate most effectively through their votes. This is a method of communication which all political organizations and candidates heed; it is in effect the end product of the communication process during the entire electoral campaign.

After the voting is over there is far less communication between the voters and the parties and political leaders, but even in the long periods between the elections much of the communication that does take place is prompted by the knowledge on all sides that elections will come again. This is an aspect of the influence of anticipatory reactions, to which students of elections frequently call attention.[16]

Politicization. The extent of the politicization of a society is very difficult to ascertain, or to measure. The United States, for example, is often characterized as a highly politicized society. Certainly politics is a subject of absorbing interest and attention in America, and the extent of political participation, except for voting turnout, is higher than in most other democratic polities. Yet even in the United States very few citizens are active participants, and politics does not form a significant part of the world of most of its citizens. In less developed countries, with briefer political experience and with essentially non-participant societies, politics is even more remote from the little worlds of the majority of the people, who live mostly in rural areas, who are influenced by ascriptive ties and institutions, who seldom participate in any political activities, and who are largely illiterate.

In South Asian countries these conditions exist to an extreme degree; but the extent of political politicization seems to vary greatly, both in consonance with these generalizations and in some cases in apparent contradiction of them. All of the societies of South Asia are essentially non-participant societies, at least as far as more 'modern' forms of participation are concerned. Low degrees of politicization seem to characterize Nepal, West Pakistan, and some parts of India; but one could make a case for considering Ceylon and India, at least, as highly politicized societies. Ever since independence, and to some extent even before, the people of these two countries have been involved in politics in numerous ways, including participation in frequent elections, the pervasive role of the government in almost all aspects of their life, and the increasing emphasis on national planning and the expansion of public sector activities and enterprises.

If one wanted to offer support to the thesis that India and Ceylon are highly politicized societies, he could point to the recurrent phenomena of nationwide elections and to the ways in which these elections seem to dominate the national scene for many weeks before the voting takes place. Many foreign observers who have been in these countries while election campaigns were in progress have been surprised with the almost total obsession with politics during these periods.

In some respects, therefore, India and Ceylon are highly politicized societies and elections contribute significantly to the politicization process; but in other, and perhaps more significant, respects, related to the nature of the social order and to the basic life styles and interests of the masses of the people, these two countries are still basically non-participant and non-politicized societies, in spite of the deceptive appearances of high politicization during election campaigns and in spite of the apparently high interest in politics on the part of the newspapers and the relatively few educated people and political activists. But whatever the actual degree or impact, elections certainly serve as agencies of politicization, if only in an intermittent and limited way.

Secularization. Elections are secular processes, usually conducted in secular political systems dedicated to secular political goals; but in some countries, both in the West and in the developing world, the secular systems, goals, and processes exist in basically non-secular societies, which condition the psychological environment in which elections are held and the voting behavior of the electorate. Moreover, religious parties, such as the Catholic parties of the Catholic-majority countries of Western Europe and Latin America and the Muslim parties of the Muslim states of North Africa and the Middle East, or most of the parties of Israel, often play a major and sometimes a decisive role in the political system. There are other political groupings, such as the Komeito Party in Japan, which have not had much success in the political arena but which are much more important than their electoral support would suggest, mainly because they are associated with influential non-political or at most semi-political movements (such as the Soka Gakkai in the case of the Komeito Party) and reflect deep-seated forces of a religious nature in the social milieu.[17] Some Catholic-oriented parties are more independent and more secular in nature than others, and these include most of those, like the Christian Democratic Union in West Germany or the Christian Democratic parties in several Latin American states, which are of major significance in several political systems. But even religiously-based parties must function, as parties, in a secular political order, and many of them seem indeed to be growing increasingly secular in the process. Elections, as has been indicated, are agencies of political secularization, which help to bridge the gap between the society, which may be religiously-impregnated, and the polity, which is often much more secular in nature.

The societies of South Asia are among the most religiously-impregnated social orders known to man, and the religious aspects of society inevitably affect the style and nature of the political systems. In such a setting it may seem absurd to speak of secularization. Quite clearly, Pakistan and Bangladesh are Muslim states, India is a Hindu state (with a large Muslim minority), Ceylon is a Buddhist state (with a dissatisfied Hindu – mainly Tamil – minority), and Nepal is a Hindu state (with a strong Buddhist minority). Pakistan is a self-proclaimed Islamic Republic, and Nepal is a Hindu kingdom, with a 'god-king' who presumably derives his legitimacy from his religious sanctity and traditional roots. Ceylon is a secular state, but Buddhism, the religion of the majority, like the Sinhala language, the language of most Buddhists, is given special recognition in the 1972 Constitution, which brought the Republic of Sri Lanka into being. India and Bangladesh are secular states, and secularism is one of the central goals of national policy, even though both are religiously-impregnated societies, as has been stated, with one religious group – the Hindus in India and the Muslims in Bangladesh – in a clearly dominant position. Some parties with deep religious roots exist in both countries, but the ruling parties – the Congress Party in India and the Awami League in Bangladesh – are strongly secular, as are most of the major opposition parties. There are less secular elements and leaders in both the Congress and the Awami League, but these elements have never been able to prevail, except perhaps on certain specific issues, such as the Hindu Code Bill in India.[18]

Secularism was almost an article of faith to Jawaharlal Nehru, who was himself an agnostic, although a Hindu (and a Brahmin) by origin. Unlike Mahatma Gandhi, who wrote in an oft-quoted phrase that he knew 'no politics apart from religion,' Nehru sought, with considerable success, to keep religion out of politics as much as possible. His successors as Prime Minister, Lal Bahadur Shastri, who was an orthodox and conservative Hindu in his social life and behavior, and Mrs. Indira Gandhi, who is as areligious as her father ever was, have jealously preserved the secular aspect of the Indian polity.

A striking feature of politics in South Asia, even in countries which are not dedicated to secularism, is that almost all of the top political leaders have been, as Keith Callard wrote of the leaders of Pakistan in the first decade after independence, 'men of politics rather than . . . men of religion.'[19] Exceptions to this generalization at the highest level, such as Nazimuddin, who was both Governor General and later Prime Minister of Pakistan, and the Kings of Nepal, have been very few, and except in Nepal, of little political significance. Many examples of religiously-minded political leaders, such as Purshottamdas Tandon, who was Congress President in 1950–1, and who resigned after an historic disagreement with Nehru, could be cited among the second and lower echelons of ruling parties in South Asian countries, and of course among the top leaders of the religiously-oriented and religiously-based parties, which have existed in all of the South Asian states; but these leaders have had little influence on national policy. At sub-national levels the influence of religiously-minded leaders and groups has undoubtedly been much greater.

This leads to another generalization that would seem to be supported by experience, namely that the polities of the South Asian states (with the exception of Nepal, and also of the smaller states of Bhutan and the Maldive Republic, where such a generalization is meaningless) become increasingly secular as one moves from local, and especially rural, levels to urban areas, districts, states or provinces, and the national level. Another and related generalization would be that whereas the societies of South Asia are religiously-impregnated at all levels, in varying degrees, the polities are more religiously-impregnated and less secular at their base and much more secular than religious at the apex of the political pyramid.

These generalizations would be supported by a careful study of election experiences and results. On the whole, as has been noted, elections in South Asia, as in most other parts of the world, are secular exercises, associated with essentially secular political systems. But at lower levels, especially in rural areas, the secular aspects are sometimes colored significantly, and in a few instances even overshadowed, by their function as linkages between the society and the polity, between religious and ascriptive groups and practices and secular political institutions and behavior. At these levels, also, religion and politics seem to mix, and often are almost indistinguishable. Candidates of even the most secular parties, such as the Congress or the Communist parties in India, are usually selected from dominant caste or communal groups (with increasing exceptions as economic factors and mobility become more apparent), and the appeals to the religiously-minded voters (the vast majority) often reflect the vocabulary and flavor of religious beliefs.

Even candidates for the Lok Sabha will be mainly drawn from such groupings, and base their campaigns as much on religious as on secular appeals. With time this will become less true, and, as has been noted, the secular tone of politics increases as one moves up the political hierarchy from rural to sub-national and national levels. But, to use a characterization of the 'idioms of Indian politics' popularized by Professor Morris-Jones, much of politics in India at local levels is carried on in the 'traditional' idiom, and at times even in the 'saintly' idiom, while at the national level the 'modern' idiom prevails.[20] But it is important to remember that all three idioms can be found, in varying degrees of intensity and influence, at all levels of Indian politics, that all three often overlap, and that the particular language or idiom of Indian politics does not necessarily indicate the real nature of the politics that is being practiced, let alone really believed.

Doubtless part of the explanation for what seems to be a remarkable degree of secularization in Indian politics may be ascribed to the fact that the secularization is often more apparent than real. But this is no means the whole story. The conscious dedication of the leaders of India (and now Bangladesh) to secularism is an important and impressive political fact, which has helped to shape the political evolution of independent India and which has seemed to demonstrate that it is possible to have a basically secular polity in a basically religious society. In this process elections have played a major role.

Consensus and Conflict Resolution. In free societies elections presumably express 'the will of the people'; they decide who shall govern. They do not produce a consensus, except perhaps on the basic framework of governance, but they do determine the wishes of the majority of those who take the trouble to cast their votes. In a sense, they are divisive forces, for decisions are made by majority vote and not by consensus. Hence 'the will of the people' is really the will of the majority. This principle is widely accepted in Western democratic theory, although some of the most astute students of Western democracy, notably John Stuart Mill, have warned against 'the tyranny of the majority.'

Elections are also conceived of as a means of conflict resolution. Decisions are made, and controversies settled, by 'ballots, not bullets.' Conflicts exist in all political systems. In totalitarian and authoritarian systems they are sublimated and suppressed, and the fiction of consensus is preserved. Even elections are used as instruments for indicating consensus, as the nearly unanimous votes in favor of a single slate of candidates are alleged to attest. In some non-totalitarian, but at least usually partially authoritarian, systems elections also are alleged to be agencies for achieving consensus, and not simply for indicating the will of the majority. In such systems the conflict that in fact exists is either sublimated or resolved through agreement among caste, communal, group, tribe, or other ascriptive leaders, and the vote becomes merely a means of affirming the consensus that has been reached by sublimating or papering over the underlying conflicts.

In South Asian societies, and especially among Hindus and Buddhists, a strong tradition of consensus rather than conflict exists, and is deeply rooted and enshrined by religious and other traditional sanctions. In caste, communal, and other ascriptive groups, and in local panchayats and other bodies, every effort is made to reach agreement by consensus, rather than to resort to such divisive steps as voting, which would reveal existing disagreements and divisions.[21] Some Indian states, for example, have offered monetary and other rewards to panchayats and other units of the Panchayati Raj system which reached decisions by consensus, rather than by majority and minority voting. There is a strong underlying opposition in India to parties and elections, not so much because they are alien and Western institutions as because they tend to divide and to force people to take sides and to reveal areas of disagreement. Some prominent Indian leaders, including Western educated leaders, most notably Jayaprakash Narayan, have been strong champions of 'partyless democracy,' which would establish a very different kind of political system in India, based on 'democratic decentralization' with a rural and traditional base and an emphasis on decision by consensus, at all political levels.[22]

In South Asia, as elsewhere, elections are not effective agencies for achieving consensus, unless the will of the majority, as indicated by popular votes, is taken as an indication of consensus (an interpretation which would be rejected in Hindu and Buddhist circles, at least). They are more effective agencies for conflict resolution, however, and in fact this may be one of their major functions in political systems that are superimposed on plural societies, with many internal divisions and fissiparous tendencies. To the extent that they help to achieve conflict resolution within rather than outside the political system, they contribute greatly to the preservation and legitimacy of the system itself.

Elections as Plebiscites, Referenda, Mandates. The view that elections express 'the will of the people' assumes that elections serve as plebiscites or referenda. Obviously certain elections are specifically designed for this purpose. A standard dictionary definition of a plebiscite is 'a vote by which the people of an entire country or district express an opinion for or against a proposal.' This may be on a fairly specific or limited proposal, or it may be on a proposal of great significance, such as the use of a plebiscite to determine whether a people wish to remain in one country or join another. When a nationwide general election is interpreted as a plebiscite, this usually implies that the election is an expression of the people's choice of a government or an expression of confidence or lack of confidence in a ruler. A referendum, again according to a dictionary definition, is 'the principle or practice of submitting to popular vote a measure passed upon or proposed by a legislative body or by popular initiative.' In this technical sense the use of a referendum is provided for in the constitutions of a number of political systems. In the more general sense a national election may also be viewed as a referendum, not so much on a specific proposal or proposals of the government or ruler as on the overall record and degree of popular confidence in the government or ruler.

The dictionary definitions are less of a starting point for a discussion of elections as mandates, for a mandate has many meanings, most of which are not directly relevant to the electoral process. But at least one standard definition is relevant, namely of a mandate as 'an authorization to act given to a representative.' A general election may be interpreted in this light. It may be viewed as an 'authorization' to the political leader or leaders to move forward with their broader programs, perhaps as outlined in their campaign pledges and party platforms or manifestoes. Certainly successful politicians often interpret electoral successes in this way, and they may use the will of the people, as expressed in an election, as a 'mandate' to carry out programs of greater or lesser importance. Sometimes a political leader will seek re-election on such a basis, in which case he may be said to use the election as a plebiscite, a referendum, and a mandate.

The electoral experience of South Asian countries, especially of India and Ceylon, provides some outstanding illustrations of the use of elections in these ways. The elections in India, Ceylon, and Pakistan in 1970–1, which are described at some length in Chapter 7, could be so characterized.

In the fourth general elections in 1967, the first to be held since she became Prime Minister, Mrs. Gandhi and the Congress Party suffered serious reverses, both on national and especially on State levels. Before the fifth general elections in 1971 she forced a showdown within the Congress Party which led to its split in late 1969, and she was able to obtain the support of the majority of Congressmen and of Congress supporters in most parts of the country for the wing of the divided Congress that she headed. Thereupon she moved her party more to the left, and was successful in creating a new and much more favorable image for her party and for herself. She then had the Lok Sabha dissolved a year before its normal five-year term, and appealed to the people in the fifth general elections to provide her a broader base of public support, to endorse her socialist programs and pledges, and to give her a popular mandate so that she could implement her programs and pledges in spite of opposition from more 'reactionary' interests. Thus the 1971 elections in India were a plebiscite, a referendum, and a mandate, and in these elections the Indian people gave Mrs. Gandhi an overwhelming majority in the Lok Sabha.[23] Since elections to only three State Legislative Assemblies were held in connection with the 1971 general elections – and these were in States where the Congress Party was not in a very strong position – the State Assembly elections a year later became another test of Mrs. Gandhi's popularity and strength. By appealing to the people for 'another mandate – this time from the States' she scored another overwhelming electoral victory.[24]

Mrs. Bandaranaike and her United Front used the 1970 elections in Ceylon in the same way. These elections became a plebiscite on the programs of the ruling United National Party regime and the United Front, a referendum on the policies of the UNP, and a mandate to Mrs. Bandaranaike, whose United Front won by an impressive margin.[25]

The Pakistan general elections of December 1970 were also in effect turned into a plebiscite on the respective pledges of the contending parties in both wings of the country, a referendum on the past regimes, especially that of Yahya Khan, who had ruled under martial law for the two previous years but who was not a candidate in the elections, and, as the results proved, an almost unanimous mandate to Sheikh Mujibur Rahman and his Awami League Party in East Pakistan. Z. A. Bhutto interpreted the surprisingly powerful showing of his Pakistan People's Party in West Pakistan as a mandate, which a year later brought him to the head of a truncated Pakistan. Sheikh Mujib became Prime Minister of the new state of Bangladesh which emerged after the traumas of the cyclone tragedy of November 1970, the general elections in the following month, the civil war of 1971, and the Indo-Pakistan war of December 1971. Both Bhutto and Sheikh Mujib could, and did, base their claims to legitimacy and to popular support on the results of the 1970 elections; and Sheikh Mujib's 'mandate' was reconfirmed, although less impressively, in the general elections in Bangladesh in March 1973.[26]

Ritualistic and Symbolic Functions. 'Elections,' in the words of Gerald Pomper, 'are the great public ceremonies of American life.'[27] This is even more true in developing countries, where other sources of entertainment are not so numerous, and where elections are newer and often more exciting experiences. Anyone who has observed election campaigns and/or the actual voting in any developing country must have been impressed with the ritualistic and symbolic aspects of the electoral process. In India, for example, an election is a great *tamasha*, or festival. It is good entertainment, as well as exciting politics. It provides entertainment for virtually the entire population, young and old, even though only those of a certain age (twenty-one years in India and Pakistan, eighteen in Sri Lanka and Bangladesh) and above are allowed to vote. It has been said of India that, 'If there is a genuine national festival, it is the General Elections.'[28] Thus an election has great symbolic as well as practical significance, for the individual voters, for the population at large, for the candidates for office, for the national leadership, and for the political system as a whole.

This broader ritualistic and symbolic significance is well explained in Murray Edelman's well-known work, *The Symbolic Use of Politics*. The 'prime function of elections,' according to Edelman, is to serve as 'a symbolic reassurance' that serves to 'quiet resentment and doubts about particular political acts, reaffirm belief in the fundamental rationality and democratic character of the system, and thus fix conforming habits of future behavior.'[29] Moreover, as Albinski and Pettit have stated, 'elections can acquire a sacramental or commemorative aspect. The election becomes a conspicuous symbol of nationhood and social purpose.'[30]

Voting as an End in Itself. For the individual voter, campaign participation and voting may have little more than ritualistic or symbolic significance, even though these acts will serve larger national purposes. As Rose and Mossawir suggest, 'The voter's support for the electoral process on grounds that appear to be more symbolic and expressive than instrumental suggests the possibility that voting may be an end in itself, providing emotional gratifications for those who participate in elections.'[31] In developing countries, in particular, where the masses of the people are unfamiliar with the procedures and purposes of national elections, voting may indeed be considered as mainly an end in itself, a culmination of a novel and rather intriguing but somewhat baffling experience. Because it will also be the only act of political participation in which the majority of the citizens will be engaged, it will be all the more likely to appear in their minds as a rather unique and isolated event, rather than as a part of a larger political process. They may be aware that they are participants in a national decision-making exercise, but they will hardly consider their limited measure of participation as likely to have an impact on the choice of rulers or of policies.

Voting as a Passive Response. Most voters, in fact, may go through the process of voting more as a passive response to social pressures, because it is 'the thing to do,' the thing that seems to be expected of them, than as an active and voluntary measure of political participation. The reasons for this are clear. 'Voting is not so much behavior freely undertaken by an individual solely to initiate or advance interests, but rather a more-or-less passive response by an individual to continuing social pressures, whether the demands are manifested overtly by mobilization through a single party or transmitted more subtly through a diffuse process of socialization.'[32] Because this is a major reason for voting in many countries, especially in developing countries, the act of voting often has a low salience and significance, even though it is by far the most common and most widely discussed form of political participation.

Voting as a Duty. In many political systems large numbers of people vote not so much because they feel that they will have some real impact on the policies or personalities of their government but simply because they feel that it is their 'duty' to vote. As Rose and Mossawir have pointed out, 'The low emotional effect of elections suggests that for most voters the gratification obtained from voting is a result of having done a necessary but not particularly desirable duty.'[33]

Many empirical studies have confirmed the prevailing impression that 'the duty to vote ranks high among all of the civic obligations recognized by Americans.'[34] Similar empirical studies in many other countries, including England, France, Germany, Italy, and Mexico, have reached the same conclusion.[35] The duty to vote is given a higher rating in the United States than in many other democracies, including several in which the voting turnout rates are significantly higher than in the United States. In all these states, however, a feeling that one has a duty to vote seems to result from the process of political socialization and to be reinforced by societal norms and conventions. This is less true in developing countries, where processes of political socialization have not been brought to bear very intensively on electoral participation and where the duty to vote is not so closely associated with basic norms and values.

In the countries of South Asia the turnout of voters in national elections, especially in Ceylon, has compared favorably with the turnout in most Western democracies, but in all probability the duty to vote is not so generally recognized, or accepted, as a primary civic obligation. Such a generalization is made more on the basis of observation of the political process in these countries and of study of the underlying cultural and societal environment than on the basis of empirical studies; but the few studies of such themes that have been made seem to provide confirmation of this generalization. A cross-national survey study of participation in five nations – Austria, India, Japan, Nigeria, and the United States – for example, concluded that there was 'a sharp difference between the meaning of the vote in India and elsewhere,'[36] partially because there was almost no relationship in India between voting and psychological involvement. Since a sense of civic obligation is usually related to the degree of psychological involvement of a voter, a logical assumption would be that the former variable is not given as high a rating as in many other democratic systems. Further research is needed before definitive conclusions can be reached on this interesting point.

Elections and Alienation. Elections may not only serve the function of producing a greater degree of involvement in and commitment to a political system. They may also produce evidence of a considerable degree of systemic disaffection and alienation. India and Ceylon provide interesting laboratories for a study of this phenomenon. Some extremely radical groups in these two countries, such as most Naxalites in India and a few of the more radical groups of young people in Ceylon, are so alienated from the existing system that they will not participate in elections. Instead, they seek to destroy the system by extra-constitutional and often violent means. Other radical groups, such as the Communist parties, may operate within or outside the system, in accordance with the prevailing party line and the prevailing assessment of the existing situation and the relative opportunities that are afforded by working for agreed-upon ends – i.e., to destroy the existing system – within or outside the system. If they participate in elections, which presumably are designed to serve support-building and system-maintenance functions, they will seek to achieve precisely opposite ends.

In India a survey research study carried out in four important states – Bihar, the Punjab, Uttar Pradesh, and West Bengal – in connection with the 1969 mid-term elections in these States showed that the great majority of the respondents felt that the present system of government was worth keeping 'even if it delays actions'.[37] Between 7 and 22 per cent of the respondents gave an unfavorable evaluation of the system. As would be expected by anyone who is familiar with the situation in these States, the alienation from the system was least in U.P. and the Punjab and highest in Bihar and especially West Bengal. It was especially marked among the young voters. This is particularly important in India, where the majority of the voters are under thirty-five years of age. The reasons for a greater degree of alienation of the young are suggested by Ramashray Roy:

> . . . stability in political preferences in India is a function of accumulated experience through the adult life of voters and 'settling down' in the political sense occurs only when a voter has participated in three or more elections. It is true that in other democracies young voters are usually socialised in political norms at an [*sic*] young age through their interaction in the family setting

with their parents and peer groups. . . . this occurs in the case of only about 16 per cent of voters in India. This means that a large number of voters are initiated into the political world only in their adult life, and largely through electoral participation. . . . The preponderance of young voters, a marked tendency on their part to be unstable in their partisan choice, the continuing fragmentation of opposition parties, the widespread feeling of political ineffectiveness – all these factors taken together are likely not only to bring about unstable electoral outcomes but also to strengthen tendency towards anomic political behavior.[38]

In Ceylon large numbers of dissatisfied and radically-inclined young people worked within the system by supporting Mrs. Bandaranaike and her United Front in the general elections of May 1970; but many of these became alienated from her and her government shortly after her electoral victory, and resorted to agitational and violent means, apparently designed not only to overthrow her government but also the political system itself.[39] This still seems to be the object of many young Ceylonese. Their disaffection and alienation are major threats to the political system that not long ago seemed to be so solidly entrenched.

The Functions of Elections: A Summing-up

In these two chapters on the functions of elections, we have considered a great variety of functions under the broad headings of political choice, political participation, support-building and system maintenance, and linkage patterns and functions. Elections, as we have seen, may bring masses of citizens into active participant and even decision-making roles in the political system, or they may serve system maintenance or linkage functions, without much active participation or decision-making influence. They may have destabilizing as well as stabilizing effects, as our studies of the 1967 general elections in India and of the general elections in Pakistan and Ceylon in 1970 have shown. They may even make more for alienation from than commitment to and identification with the system.

In South Asian countries, as in other political systems where elections are held, national elections serve many functions, of a passive and active, positive and negative, nature. On the whole, in spite of frequently expressed reservations about their effectiveness or even desirability, they have served useful purposes. They have indeed been indispensable to the preservation of the political systems that have evolved in India and Ceylon. They have been peripheral rather than central to the political systems of Pakistan and Nepal. They may become more significant in the new political order in Pakistan, as they almost certainly will in Bangladesh.

Elections are usually resorted to even in closed political systems. In those that are in any significant degree open they are virtually indispensable for systemic preservation and development. They are multi-functional institutions, serving both specific and general purposes. As John Plamenatz has observed, 'It is because there are elections from time to time that the precise demands made on the people's behalf are always listened to. Elections are most important not only for what happens at them but for what happens because of them'[40] – or, he might have added, for what might happen without them.

5

THE ELECTORAL PROCESS IN INDIA

Elections are a part of the electoral system, which embraces 'all those means whereby a person becomes a member of an elected assembly.'[1] Thus they are a part of a larger political process, of which nominating procedures, campaigning, and the actual voting are only parts – although the most conspicuous, and culminating, parts.

Electoral Systems and the Electoral Process

Electoral systems, moreover, must be viewed as a part of the larger political system, and this, in turn, must be considered as a part of the even more comprehensive and more important social system. 'Of electoral systems in general we may say that their real meaning depends upon their ultimate governmental effectiveness, their relationship to other political institutions and the social system within which they operate.'[2] It is within this larger framework that one of the most fascinating aspects of elections, namely that they often operate very differently and serve different functions even when they seem to be similar in form and conduct, can be at least partially explained.

The electoral process, therefore, has to be viewed as much more than a series of discrete elections conducted along certain lines, under certain constitutional and legal provisions, supervised by legally authorized agencies, and involving the activities of certain political parties and other recognized political groupings directed toward the wooing of the masses of the electorate in certain accepted and identifiable ways. The process is much broader and much more coordinated than this, and it serves much broader purposes. 'Although we think of the electoral process as one which spans a limited period of time at regular intervals, it should actually be conceived as a continuing process which may change form in the interval, but whose purpose for any given party is the legitimation of its goals (for society) and, toward that end, the accommodation of interests, views or values. As such it is a process in which the aspiring decision-maker is continuously involved, with greater or lesser intensity over time.' And it serves much larger political and social goals as well. 'The whole electoral process, in fact, is one of societal goal legitimation and accommodation of interest. The "electoral" goal of the aspiring decision-maker is an instrumental one, vis-a-vis the primary societal goal.'[3] Nor should one overlook the cumulative effect of elections, especially if they are conducted successfully and regularly over a period of time. They thereby become agencies for both political stability and legitimacy, and also for peaceful but potentially substantial – even revolutionary – change.

In developing societies, in particular, this dual function of regular democratic elections should not be underestimated, although it is frequently overlooked. As Imtiaz Ahmed has noted, 'The ability of the electoral process itself to provide change in political behaviour has been less readily recognized.'[4] This factor is obviously of no great significance in developing societies which do not have regular democratic elections. Since the great majority of the newly emerging countries fall into this category, the role of elections in these countries is obviously limited and largely symbolic, and the electoral process itself lacks both continuity and centrality.

W. J. Mackenzie has laid down four conditions for the successful functioning of an electoral system: 'There are, first, an independent judiciary to interpret electoral law; (secondly) an honest, competent, non-partisan administration to run elections; (thirdly) a developed system of political parties, well enough organized to put their policies, traditions and teams of candidates before the electors as alternatives between which to choose; (fourthly) a general acceptance throughout the political community of certain rather vague rules of the game, which limit the struggle for power because of some unspoken sentiment that if the rules are not observed more or less faithfully the game itself will disappear amid the wreckage of the whole system.'[5]

These conditions do not fully exist in any developing country; but perhaps India comes closer to meeting them than any of the others. In spite of some claims to the contrary, it may be said to have an independent judiciary and a non-partisan election administration. It certainly does not have 'a developed system of political parties,' perhaps not even a party system at all, but it does have a large number of political parties, including a few that are recognized as national parties, operating within the framework of a system of one-party dominance. In spite of limited time and limited experience, 'a general acceptance . . . of certain rather vague rules of the game' seems to be developing, which in time may give deeper roots to the electoral, and indeed to the democratic, system. But it is still too early to do more than speculate on the chances of the survival of the existing political system, in which the electoral process has a central role.

In discussing the electoral process in India we should bear in mind these broader aspects and conditioning factors. We should also bear in mind the basic nature of the political and electoral system. India is a federal polity, with a parliamentary system that is clearly modeled after British patterns but which functions in very different ways from the Westminster model. For its major elections of members of the Lok Sabha and the State Legislative Assemblies, India uses a plurality or simple majority system of voting in single-member constituencies, on the basis of universal adult suffrage. The same system is also used in elections of members of many, but by no means all, local elective bodies. Considerable dissatisfaction has been expressed with this system, and some demands have been voiced for the adoption of some form of proportional representation, especially for the adoption of the list system of voting;[6] but, 'realistically speaking, there is no chance of its being adopted.'[7] Another form of proportional representation, namely the single transferable vote system, 'is already in vogue . . . in smaller elections to the offices of Rajya Sabha and in elections to the Legislative Councils of the States having such Councils.'[8] Moreover, not all members of all representative bodies are directly elected; some are nominated or appointed (even the Rajya Sabha may have up to twelve such members), and some are chosen by various procedures of indirect elections, as is the case with most members of the *zilla parishads* and *panchayats* in the Panchayati Raj system (except in Maharashtra and Gujarat).

In this chapter we shall concentrate on four major aspects of the electoral process: (1) preparations for the elections; (2) the selection of candidates by the political parties and the nominating process; (3) the campaign; and (4) the actual voting. We shall be concerned almost exclusively with national elections, that is with the major types of elections that are held in India. During the first four nationwide elections, voters cast ballots both for members of the Lok Sabha and the Legislative Assembly of the State in which they lived. The fifth general elections, in 1971, were held for members of the Lok Sabha and for members of the Legislative Assembly in only three States. Thus for the first time national and State elections were largely de-linked. In 1969 elections of members of the Legislative Assemblies of four major States were held during the same period, and in 1972 members of the Legislative Assemblies of all Indian States except those which had chosen Assembly members during the 1971 general elections were chosen in what amounted to a national election, even though it did not involve the selection of members of the Lok Sabha.

Preparations for the Elections

Part XV (Articles 324–9) of the Indian Constitution lays down the basic provisions regarding elections. Article 326 provides that 'The elections to the House of the People and to the Legislative Assembly of every State shall be on the basis of adult suffrage.' This was the provision which determined the basic character of the electoral system. It was, as the Election Commission stated, an 'act of faith,' a bold move that some regarded as a desperate gamble that was likely to fail and others as convincing proof that all citizens would be given the opportunity to shape their own political destiny and that the system of parliamentary democracy based on free elections in which all adults of 21 years of age and over were eligible to participate would be more than a façade and a sham. This basic and historic decision did much to shape the character of the electoral system and to plant that system solidly at the center of the political system.

The Constitution also contained provisions for the size of the Lok Sabha and the various State Legislative Assemblies, for the delimitation of constituencies, and for the reservation of seats for Scheduled Castes and Scheduled Tribes. These provisions have been changed by Constitutional amendments, mainly to take into account India's expanding population, changes in State boundaries, and improvements in the conditions of certain underprivileged groups, and they have been spelled out in greater detail in various acts, orders, and rules. Among these are the Representation of the People Acts of 1950 and 1951, the States Reorganization Act of 1956, and the Conduct of Election Rules of 1961.

Delimitation of Constituencies. The delimitation of constituencies, a delicate and important task, is entrusted to a Delimitation Commission, set up under the Delimitation Commission Act of 1952. 'For purposes of election, the states are divided into territorial constituenceis in such manner that the ratio between the population of each constituency and the number of seats alloted to it is, so far as practicable, the same throughout the state. The allocation of Lok Sabha seats to the States as well as the Assembly seats, and the division of each State into territorial constituencies is readjusted after every census. The delimitation of constituencies was done under the Delimitation Commission Act, 1952, which *inter alia* allocated the Lok Sabha seats to the States and also established the number of seats in the State Legislative Assemblies. In every case, one parliamentary constituency is constituted by a combination of Assembly constituencies.'[9] Because of population growth the number of elected seats in the Lok Sabha has increased from 489 in the first general election to 520 in the fifth; and in 1973 the Parliament, giving consideration to the population figures obtained in the 1971 census, passed the Constitution (Thirty-first Amendment) Bill which increased the upper limit for membership in the Lok Sabha to 545. It is perhaps appropriate – or at any rate inescapable – that the world's largest democracy should have one of the largest national legislative bodies.

All of the constituencies for the Lok Sabha and State Legislative Assemblies are now single-member constituencies; but this was not always the case. 'In the first General Election, the 489 seats of the Lok Sabha were arranged into 314 single-member constituencies, 86 double-member constituences, and 1 three member constituency; the 3,373 State Assembly seats were arranged in 2,124 single-member constituencies, 578 double-member constituencies, and 1 three-member constituency. . . . In the second General Election the 494 elective seats of the Lok Sabha were arranged into 312 single-member constituencies, and 91 double-member constituencies. . . . The 2,906 State Assembly seats were arranged in about 2,480 constituencies including double-member constituencies.'[10] This arrangement was changed in the Two-Member Constitution (Abolition) Act of 1961; hence in the third and subsequent general elections all seats for the Lok Sabha and the State Legislative Assemblies have been from single-member constituencies. The reservation of seats for Scheduled Castes and Scheduled Tribes, which was provided for in the Constitution and which was one of the main reasons for double-member constituencies, continued with the elimination of such constituencies. In 1952–7 seventy-two seats in the Lok Sabha and 477 seats in State Legislative Assemblies were reserved for Scheduled Castes; the comparable figures for Scheduled Tribes were twenty-six and 192.[11] This special reservation of seats for the two major underprivileged groups in India was to cease as of 26 January 1970; but it has been extended because of the continuing need for special measures to ensure sufficient representation of these two groups.

The Election Commission. According to the Seventh Schedule of the Constitution (Item 72 on the Union List) responsibility for 'Elections to Parliament, to the Legislatures of States and to the offices of President and Vice-President" is vested exclusively in the Central Government. Thus India has a centrally controlled electoral system. Responsibility for the conduct of all major elections is vested in an Election Commission, which, according to Article 324 of the Constitution, is charged with 'The superintendence, direction and control of the preparation of the electoral rolls for, and the conduct of, all elections to Parliament and to the Legislature of every State and of elections to the offices of President and Vice-President held under this Constitution, including the appointment of election tribunals for the decision of doubts and disputes arising out of or in connection with elections to Parliament and to the Legislatures of States.' The Election Commission is headed by the Chief Election Commissioner, who is appointed by the President of India and who has an independent status (for example, he 'shall not be removed from his office except in like manner and on the like grounds as a Judge of the Supreme Court'). Thus far, in fact, since no additional Election Commissioners have been appointed, the Chief Election Commissioner has also been institutionalized as the Election Commission. Two able persons, Sukumar Sen and S. P. Sen Varma, occupied the post of Chief Election Commissioner for a period of some twenty years. Under the leadership of Sukumar Sen the Election Commission and all affiliated agencies and individuals gained an enviable reputation for probity and efficiency; the same tradition was carried on by Mr. Sen Varma, although toward the end of his long period of service there were increasing complaints that the Election Commission was becoming politicized and was not maintaining the expected standards of political integrity and neutrality.

The Election Commission discharges a number of very important functions, including the preparation of the electoral rolls, the appointment of a Chief Electoral Officer (always a State government official) for each State, and Electoral Registration Officers and Returning Officers and Assistant Returning Officers for each Assembly and Parliamentary constituency, and the receiving of election petitions and the appointment of Election Tribunals to pass on such petitions.

As T. E. Smith has observed, 'The successful management of a modern election with electors numbering several millions is an administrative undertaking of considerable size, involving a series of operations, the organisation and timing of which must be carefully planned and supervised. For those involved in electoral administration, there are periods of very heavy work and also periods of comparative inactivity; this is true not only of registration officers, who will be busy with electoral duties at the time of the registration of electors, and of returning officers, who will be busy during the period of an actual election, but also, to some extent, of the "top management" of elections which issues the necessary instructions to registration officers, returning officers and other subordinate authorities. In the development of a genuine electoral administration, then, what is required is an administrative machine, capable of conducting an election with impartiality and without confusion, consisting of a small permanent nucleus and large reinforcements who can be seconded for electoral duties from other work at periods of peak activity.'[12] This is almost a precise description of the way elections are managed in India. For this adherence to such high standards those in charge of the preparation and conduct of elections, from the Chief Election Commissioner to the polling officers, deserve special commendation and recognition.

Preparation of Electoral Rolls. Article 325 of the Constitution provides that 'There shall be one general electoral roll for every territorial constituency for election to either House of Parliament or to the House or either House of the Legislature of a State and no person shall be ineligible for inclusion in any such roll or claim to be included in any special roll for any such constituency on grounds of religion, race, caste, sex or any of them.' The preparation of the electoral rolls is one of the major tasks entrusted to the Election Commission. Unlike the practice in some democratic polities, such as the United States, the registration of voters is not a responsibility of the individual voters but of the central government, and specifically of the Election Commission. This is obviously an enormous and enormously difficult task.

Before the first general elections could be held in 1951–2 – the first general elections ever held in India on the basis of direct and universal adult suffrage – more than 173 million eligible voters had to be registered, mainly by house-to-house canvas throughout the country, and the electoral rolls had to be prepared. This involved an army of specially recruited officials, and constant checking and rechecking to ensure that all eligible persons got on the electoral rolls, that their names were accurately recorded, and that no ineligible or 'bogus' voters were listed. Special difficulties arose because of the magnitude of the operation, extending to all parts of a vast country, and the limitations of time and circumstances. Enumerators often were not sufficiently qualified to undertake the task of registration, and their problems were accentuated by the differences in language and dialects, the illiteracy and often the suspicions of the vast majority of the eligible voters, and the refusal of thousands of women, especially in rural areas, to give their full names (apparently they felt that by so doing they would be disloyal to their husbands, who alone had the right to know), which of course meant that these women could not be registered, and therefore could not vote. Some 2.8 million women refused to give the registrars their proper names, and accordingly their names could not be included in the electoral rolls. 'There were special problems arising from linguistic complications, the difficulty of obtaining accurate names in a country where varying practices are followed in this respect and where many people are known by the same designation, the ambiguous status of hundreds of thousands of refugees from Pakistan, and the virtual impossibility of obtaining reliable information in "backward" areas.'[13] Once the basic electoral rolls were prepared, scrutinized, and posted, official notification of the first general election could be made.

The electoral rolls have been in a virtually continuous state of revision, to correct errors, add the names of new voters as they reached the minimum age of twenty-one, delete the names of those who were deceased or who became ineligible to vote, and in general to keep the rolls accurate and up to date. On the whole this task was performed with reasonable efficiency, although there were frequent complaints and unduly long delays in registering new voters and cutting deceased voters from the rolls.

The sheer numbers of persons who were registered were staggering. The list of eligible voters numbered approximately 173 million for the first general elections, 193 million for the second, 218 million for the third, 250 million for the fourth, and 273 million for the fifth. From the numerical point of view, at least, the Indians could rightly boast of holding 'the world's largest democratic elections.'

The Nominating Process. 'The electoral process is formally set into motion by the Presidential announcement calling upon electors in all parliamentary constituencies to elect their representatives to the Lok Sabha. Similarly, the Governors of the States issue notifications calling upon electors to elect their representatives for the Legislative Assemblies.' At the same time the Election Commission issues 'notifications specifying the time table for nominations, scrutiny, withdrawals, and polling.'[14] Candidates must meet the requirements laid down in the Constitution and in the Representation of the People Acts of 1950 and 1951. They are usually selected by the recognized political parties, and they may also contest as independents. 'There is no requirement for local residence in the constituency. . . . The electoral law only requires that the candidate must be a registered voter in some constituency or the other of the legislature to which he is seeking election.'[15] Before he can file a nomination paper, he must pay a deposit, which he forfeits if he fails to poll more than one-sixth of the total number of valid votes cast in his constituency. The deposit is about twice as large for candidates for the Lok Sabha as for the Legislative Assembly, but the exact amount of the deposit required of candidates to Legislative Assemblies varies from State to State.

Shortly after the deadline for the filing of nomination papers has passed, the papers are scrutinized by the Returning Officers, who reject those which are invalid and draw up a list of the validly nominated candidates in each constituency, 'arranging their names alphabetically according to the script of the regional language in the list.'[16] The final list of candidates is determined only after the last date for withdrawals, usually a few days after the final date for nominations. The number of withdrawals is often very considerable.

Normally about three weeks elapse between the last date for withdrawals and the actual polling date or dates. During this time the electioneering gathers momentum, and the parties and candidates vie with each other in their appeals to the millions of eligible voters, who are courted and wooed by all the devices that ingenuity can devise and election laws will permit. During this time the vast army of electoral officials – numbering over a million – is busy with the final preparations for the voting, under the general supervision of the Chief Election Commissioner and the Chief Electoral Officer of each State. These officers are concerned that everything will be in readiness for the gigantic exercise that is looming ahead. They have to be sure that all polling stations and polling officers will be ready, that a sufficient number of ballot papers and ballot boxes is available, and that the voters are adequately informed about their rights and about the procedures for voting.

Recognition of Parties. The Election Commission determines what political parties will be recognized, on both national and State levels, and what symbols will be assigned to each party.

Even though the Congress Party has been so dominant in national life that India is often said to have a one dominant party system, there have always been several other parties that have claimed, with somewhat questionable justification, also to be national parties and that have been recognized as such by the Election Commission. At the State level the number of parties has been even greater, and in some States the Congress has consistently been in a minority position as far as popular votes have been concerned. Sometimes it has not had enough support to control the governments of some States.

No fewer than seventy-seven so-called political parties took part in the first general elections in 1951–2. Of these fourteen were recognized by the Election Commission as national parties, and fifty-nine were recognized as State parties. Of the fifty-one parties which put up candidates for the Lok Sabha (then known as the House of the People), only 20 won one or more seats and only four won nine or more seats. In fact, the largest number of opposition seats was won by the Communist Party of India, but it got only sixteen seats whereas the ruling Congress Party got 364!

After the first general elections the Election Commission established a rule that has been in effect ever since, namely that only those parties which polled at least three per cent of the total valid vote in the previous general election would be recognized as national parties. This reduced the number of recognized national parties to four for the second general elections (two of the parties that had each polled more than 3 per cent of the total votes in 1951–2 merged shortly after the first general elections), to four for the third general elections, to five for the fourth general elections, and to eight for the fifth general elections.

The first general elections were held over a period of many weeks, from late October 1951 to late March 1952. Most of the voting took place in January 1952. The second general elections were conducted in a little less than three weeks. Balloting in the last three general elections has taken no more than ten days, with most of the votes being cast within a week.

Selection of Candidates

The selection of candidates is obviously of central importance for political parties. It is also a major aspect of the electoral process, and it serves key functions in the political system as a whole. 'Among all the procedures that make up the final electoral process,' Ramashray Roy has observed, 'the selection of candidates is by far the most important.'[17] As Gunnar Sjöblom has pointed out, 'The proposal of candidates to various political positions by the parties is one of the methods by which the recruitment function in the Polity is fulfilled.'[18] These broader functions have been spelled out more specifically by W. H. Morris-Jones, who has made intensive investigations of the selection process in India:

> To underline the central significance of candidate selection for the internal health of the party is not of course to imply that this is its only importance. From the point of view of the party as a contestant against other parties, the decision as to candidates may make the difference between victory and defeat, and it should be a matter of nice calculation to assess which applicant for a ticket has the resources – of personality, energy, finance, and, above all, connexions or influence – which will win the day. From the point of view of party as combatant in the arena of the representative assembly, candidate selection determines the quality of the forces available for battle in the public forum. Again, this process has to be seen as the one which determines the quality of the reservoir from which talent will be filtered through to Governmental level. Finally, from the standpoint of the individual applicants, here is a critical moment in the shaping of a political career.[19]

Thus the selection process has a considerable bearing on the quality of leaders to be chosen for political positions, on the fortunes of political parties as well as of individuals, on the nature of the electoral process, and on the character of the leadership and the orientation of the political system. It is a difficult and time-consuming process which often becomes 'the focal point of group conflict,'[20] and may create bitterness and divisions within parties. The nature of the process, and its effects, vary from country to country, from party to party, and frequently within the same party at different periods of time.

In view of its central importance at various levels of a polity, the nomination and selection of candidates has received surprisingly little detailed study in most democractic systems. This has certainly been true in India, where the selection process is particularly complicated and particularly important. As in most other democratic systems this process varies considerably in the different political parties and often within the same party. Since the Congress Party has been the dominant party in India, and since no other political party has been able to offer effective opposition at the national level, it is quite logical that most scholars who have studied the selection of candidates in India have concentrated on selection procedures within the Congress Party.

Patterns of Candidate Selection. No uniform policies or patterns of candidate selection have been followed by the Congress Party. Two major aspects which have varied greatly have been the relative roles and influence of selection agencies of the Party at sub-district, district, State, and national levels, and the roles and influence of certain State and national leaders, such as the Chief Ministers or the Presidents of the Pradesh Congress Committees at the State level, and certain members of the Central Election Committee or the Working Committee or the Prime Ministers at the national level.

The patterns of selection have varied from general election to general election. In the first general elections Prime Minister Jawaharlal Nehru, who had just won a battle for internal control of the Party which had led to the resignation of Purshottamdas Tandon as President of the Party, gave firm directions that the emphasis should be placed on the selection of really good candidates; but the main responsibility for the selection of these candidates was given to the bodies that have normally been the first to prepare lists of recommended candidates, namely the District Congress Committees and the Pradesh Congress Committees. In the second general elections 'an attempt was made to strike a balance between the district and state levels, and provision was also made for an elaborate system of checks by A.I.C.C. observers.'[21] The C.E.C. issued 'detailed instructions to the PECs as to how they were to receive suggestions from the DCCs, how these were to be examined in the districts by PEC representatives, and how panels of names thus compiled were to be considered by the PECs in the presence of CEC representatives.'[22] In the third general elections the Mandal Congress Committees and to some extent the new *panchayat samitis* played significant roles in the selection process. Applications were sent to the DCCs with the recommendations of the Mandal Congress Committees, and to the PECs with the recommendations of the DCCs. After individual interviews with candidates who seemed to be most suitable, the PEC forwarded recommended lists to the CEC, which, as usual, made the final selections, at least in a formal sense. In the fourth general elections greater responsibility was vested in the PECs. Candidates were instructed to apply directly to the PECs. Although the

PECs were instructed to consult with district leaders and DCCs, the actual manner and extent of the consultations were left to the PECs. As a result some PECs were assiduous in such consultation, while others paid little attention to lower committees and party leaders. In the fifth general elections the CEC played an even more central role than in previous elections, especially in the selection of candidates in States where the PECs were ridden with factionalism or other internal divisions and were unable to reach agreement on candidates in many constituencies. In some instances a representative of the Congress High Command was designated to sit with the members of a PEC in a State where the Congress leadership was divided or the Congress position weak and assist in the selection of candidates or recommend changes in the lists prepared by the PEC.

The role of individual Congress leaders in the States and at the Centre has often been quite significant. Outstanding among these have been strong Chief Ministers, special observers sent out by the CEC to States where the local leaders and PECs were for one reason or another divided or weak, and the Prime Minister. Until 1971 the Congress Chief Ministers, in States where the Congress Party was firmly entrenched and where the Chief Ministers were strong and effective leaders, had a major role in the selection of candidates for both State and national offices. The PECs would usually accept his suggestions, and sometimes did little more than give formal approval to the list which he prepared; and the CEC generally accepted the list sent from his State, with few changes or objections. In the fifth general elections, however, the Chief Ministers had little say in candidate selection, although in some States the majority of candidates were their supporters. The final decision was usually made by the CEC, or by Mrs. Gandhi herself, and sometimes involved major changes in the list of recommended candidates forwarded by the PEC. Chief Ministers in two States were forced to resign, against their will, just before the general elections, because of pressure from Mrs. Gandhi, and most of the other Congress Chief Ministers were largely ignored or played only minor roles in the selection of candidates. After the voting, when Mrs. Gandhi's Congress Party had scored an overwhelming victory, the Prime Minister herself hand-picked the new Chief Ministers in several States, often by-passing the major candidates for the post, and often naming someone of no great standing in the State who was not directly involved in the factional in-fighting in the State Congress Party and who, above all, was loyal to Mrs. Gandhi.

An intriguing aspect of candidate selection within the Congress Party is the role of special observers sent by the High Command to States where factionalism and other divisions exist within the Congress leadership and where the Congress position is threatened. Sometimes these persons act simply as observers, or as advisers; but often they play much more decisive roles, and their recommendations to the CEC and the Congress High Command may be decisive in determining the final list of candidates and sometimes even the future of some of the State leaders.

An interesting example of the role of such an observer was provided by the mission of Morarji Desai, then a major leader of the undivided Congress, in the second general elections, in the troubled State of Bihar. 'Factionalism in Bihar was one of the most persistent problems facing the Central Election Committee. In 1957, when Morarji Desai was sent to Bihar to supervise the selection of candidates, there were 4,000 applicants for the 318 assembly seats and the fifty-five Lok Sabha seats. Upon arrival in Patna, Desai was presented with an agreed list of candidates drawn up jointly by the competing factions. Upon reviewing the list, he is reported to have interviewed all 4,000 applicants. This gave him some idea of the state of Congress politics in Bihar. Then, using as an excuse the Working Committee's broad guidelines for the selection of candidates . . . he proceeded to revise the entire list. In the process he dropped 40 per cent of the sitting members of the state assembly, including some party stalwarts against whom there was documentary proof of corruption. Morarji's list was further revised by the Central Election Committee.'[23]

In 1971 top party leaders sent to various States by Mrs. Gandhi, notably Uma Shankar Dixit and D. P. Mishra, played a major role in the selection of candidates and in decisions regarding party leadership in several States.

In some general elections, notably the second and the third, individual members of the CEC have played major roles in the selection of candidates, especially in States where the PECs have not been able to forward unanimously approved lists. Lal Bahadur Shastri played such a role in the 1957 elections, and he and Mrs. Indira Gandhi played the same role in the 1962 elections. Undoubtedly the reputation that these two people gained as tough, effective, and impartial arbitrators in the selection process was a factor in the later selection of each as Prime Minister of India. 'One of the striking features of the selection process for 1967, another consequence of the divisions among the central leadership, was the failure of the necessary, widely trusted arbitrators to emerge. As a result, selection disputes had to be settled by bargaining and horse trading on an unprecedented scale.'[24] Four years later the Prime Minister herself had a direct hand in resolving selection disputes and in determining who should get the party tickets.

Jawaharlal Nehru seldom intervened directly in the selection of Congress candidates. In the first general elections, as has been noted, he exhorted his top subordinates in the party, in the States and at the Center, to select candidates of outstanding integrity, but he devoted little time or attention to the actual selection process, and he expressed disappointment with the outcome of the process. In the second and third general elections he took an even more detached role in the selection of candidates and in the campaigning. Lal Bahadur Shastri, his successor as Prime Minister, did not hold that office during a general election. His successor, Mrs. Gandhi, after showing seemingly great indecision and ineffective leadership in the fourth general elections, when the Congress Party which she led suffered the most severe reverses in the history of independent India, staged a remarkable political recovery thereafter. In 1969 she played a major role in the events leading to a split in the Congress, and her wing of the divided party soon gained a commanding position, even more impressive than that of the undivided Congress in the Nehru era. In the fifth general elections in 1971, which gave her an overwhelming mandate, and in the nationwide State Assembly elections in 1972, which decisively extended her mandate to most of the States, Mrs. Gandhi had a direct role in the selection of candidates, and in several particularly controversial situations she made the final decisions. After her decisive electoral victory, she also hand-picked the Chief Ministers in several States where the party was divided and where various Congress leaders were jockeying for power. Both in candidate selection and in the choice of Chief Ministers she often ruthlessly ignored, by-passed, or even forced the resignation of some Chief Ministers and many party bosses at State, district, and local levels, thus cleverly 'outfoxing' those who were generally regarded as indispensable brokers and controllers of needed 'vote banks'.

Criteria of Candidate Selection. From the first general elections Jawaharlal Nehru urged his party to select candidates of outstanding merit and character. 'The test must be integrity first, integrity second and integrity third, integrity and ability,' he declared.[25] In other statements he repeated this message, but with certain more practical modifications. 'We want men of integrity,' he said, 'but they must accept our election manifesto and our general programme.'[26] A great deal of attention also must be given to 'local choice.' In a communication to all PECs he wrote: 'We must choose persons who can represent worthily Congress principles and ideals, who are men and women of proved integrity, and who have the ability to discharge the responsibilities of membership of the legislatures.' Moreover, 'candidates chosen by us should not only possess integrity but be known to do so. . . . Any person whose past record is considered to be bad from the Congress point of view should not be selected, even though he might be considered locally to have chances of winning the election.' He also stipulated that Congress candidates should 'represent fully the non-communal character and approach of the Congress,' and should have 'a progressive social outlook.' He urged that a special effort should be made to nominate candidates from minority groups, especially Muslims, and to select a number of women candidates.[27] The candidates who were selected by the Congress to contest the first general elections often fell far short of these high standards. In October 1951 Nehru frankly remarked: 'I am greatly disappointed that, in spite of my efforts, the result is so poor.'[28] In the second general elections he took a much less active part in the selection of candidates and in the campaign. Immediately after the elections he expressed his distress that 'the elections have brought up not only this business of caste again, but provincialism and linguism.'[29]

Case by case studies of candidates selected by the Congress in all three general elections that were held in Nehru's lifetime – and in all subsequent general elections – would show that most of his party's candidates fell far short of the standards he had prescribed. More practical criteria were laid down by the CEC for the guidance of the PECs in preparing their lists of candidates. By 1967 these criteria, which were 'to be taken into account generally,' laid down eight qualifications for a candidate: (1) he should be an elected party member; (2) if he is a sitting member, he should have submitted a statement of his assets, income, and expenditures; (3) he should have a good record of political, economic, and social work; (4) he should be in agreement with the basic policies of the Party, 'particularly those relating to communal harmony, untouchability, prohibition, land reforms, co-operatives, and social and economic justice'; (5) he should have participated actively in constructive work and developmental activities; (6) his record of experience in legislative or local bodies, if any, should be considered; (7) if he is a sitting member, his contacts with his constituency, his record in the legislature, and his performance in paying contributions to the Party should be examined; and (8) his observance of party discipline should be taken into consideration.[30]

Obviously the actual criteria in the selection of candidates may be a considerable departure from the criteria laid down by the CEC. 'Not even such an elaboration of detail could ensure a uniform selection process, for it must be remembered that what are perhaps the most important criteria for selection are never formally proclaimed by Congress leaders. These factors, which quite naturally dominate the selection process, are usually articulated only by implication in the consideration of the candidate's "ability to win." In fact, however, it is under this rubric that the really dominant factors in individual candidate selection at both state and national levels become apparent, for, in considering a candidate's ability to win an election, it is necessary to take into account caste, community, minority, regional, and traditional loyalties. All political parties are forced to make equivalent calculations, and it is obvious that in a societv of the sort found in India such considerations must inevitably play a role. Although the Congress leadership never makes them explicit, preferring to speak publicly in more general terms, observers regularly analyze the nomination and election process in communal and caste terms.'[31]

One perceptive Indian political scientist has suggested a rather different list of criteria of candidate selection from that suggested by the CEC. His list also contains eight criteria: (1) money contribution; (2) dominant group, caste, or faction; (3) perception of advantages; (4) ability to win; (5) locality of the candidate; (6) the candidate's role in post-election ministry-making; (7) patronage of the central leadership; and (8) the value of the candidate in the legislature.[32]

Examination of Congress Party records with reference to the selection of candidates in two general elections provides convincing evidence that 'ability to win' was often the decisive criterion, sometimes leading to nominations of candidates who clearly did not meet other suggested criteria. This criterion, however, was not a major consideration in most constituencies in the 1971 general elections. Because of the 'Indira wave' nomination in most constituencies was tantamount to assured election; hence factors other than ability to win could be given special prominence, and the most important of these seemed to be loyalty to the Prime Minister. Mrs. Gandhi herself professed to be concerned primarily with such factors as the social outlook and orientation of the candidates, the elimination of office holders whose records were unsavory, the need for new faces and younger, more dynamic candidates and for more adequate representation to lower castes, minority groups, and women, and in general for a new image for her Party, which was contesting a general election for the first time since the Congress split in 1969.

In seeking 'another mandate – this time from the States' in the State Assembly elections in March 1972, Mrs. Gandhi played an even more decisive role in candidate selection than in the general election of the previous year.[33] In the months and weeks prior to the State elections she had virtually forced the ouster of several Congress Chief Ministers who, in her opinion, would be a handicap to her in her efforts to give a new image and a new orientation to her party, even though in some cases these Chief Ministers still had the support of the majority of the Congress M.L.A.s in their respective States. She also by-passed, and in some cases dissolved, the regular PECs, and directed the appointment of *ad hoc* PECs in their place. At the local levels her party's organization was generally very weak and in disarray, due in part to the consequences of the split in the Congress in 1969 but also to Mrs.

Gandhi's tactics of working through new and usually untried and inexperienced local leaders rather than through the regular local party bosses who had cast their lot with her wing of the party. This flaunting of the usual political conventions naturally caused a great deal of bitterness, division, and dissatisfaction, which were accentuated by the selection process, always a source of division. As a result many local leaders and others who were prominent in her party either seceded from the party and openly supported opposition candidates or stood as candidates themselves on an Independent or opposition party ticket, or, more commonly, worked behind the scenes to secure the defeat of the regular Congress candidates.

Many observers thought that the obvious weaknesses in party organization, the disgruntlement of many party leaders, and widespread defections, amounting almost to rebellion in a few States, would seriously and adversely affect the election results. In fact, they seldom did, and on the whole they appeared to strengthen rather than weaken the new Congress which won an even more impressive victory in 1972 than in 1971. One could argue that this decisive victory in both elections was due mainly to the 'Indira wave,' to the prestige and image of the Prime Minister rather than the Party, and that when and if Mrs. Gandhi's image became tarnished and her hold on the masses of the people diminished, the weaknesses in party organization and the internal divisions would then become more apparent, and would in all probability have disastrous effects; but there can be little doubt that, paradoxically, the Congress benefited from the purges or by-passing of long-established party leaders and seemed to suffer very little from organizational weaknesses and divisions at the local level.

In early February 1972 a correspondent of *The Hindu* reported that the Congress High Command 'has thrown the party organisation all over the country into a flux in the process of screening the applicants and prescribing the norms for their selection. . . . Almost all the Pradesh Congress Committees and the ad hoc committees have proved to be divided houses. The Chief Ministers have been down-graded to such an extent that quite often the party chief feels obliged to differ with him if only to avoid being identified with him. . . . The system of screening – and the canvassing and influence-peddling that go with it – has made many of the candidates pocket their pride or compromise their self-respect in chasing the mirage.'[34]

Almost invariably the scramble for Congress tickets led to New Delhi. Thousands of office-seekers and their supporters flocked to the capital, and besieged the Congress offices and, whenever possible, tried to present their case to members of the CEC, to other top Congress leaders, and in a few cases where access could be achieved, to the Prime Minister herself. About 3,000 persons came to New Delhi on such missions from both Andhra Pradesh and Madhya Pradesh, where the party was particularly divided. 'The Congress (R) headquarters, in Delhi,' reported *The Hindu* correspondent, 'presents a sad spectacle these days with thousands of applicants milling around the premises, either pleading their own cases or making representations against their rivals in the race for the party tickets. It has the appearance of a district court with road-side typists typing out petitions, which are collected at a special counter and processed by trusted party workers, enjoying the confidence of the leaders entrusted with the screening work.'[35]

A study of the process of selection of candidates on a State by State basis would throw additional light on the rather chaotic and less than uniform basis of the selection process, the application of varying and often ill-defined criteria in the selection of candidates, the lack of organization and the in-fighting within Congress ranks, and the decisive role of the CEC and Mrs. Gandhi.

A few examples may be cited by way of illustration. In Andhra Pradesh, where the Congress was particularly divided, dissatisfaction with the final list of nominations was so great that some 500 members of the party, including some who had held prominent positions in the party or the State government, filed nominations against the regular Congress candidates (about one-half withdrew later, and very few were eventually successful). Nearly one-half of the candidates chosen were new faces. Between 55 and 60 per cent of the nominations went to women, members of the backward classes, young people, and laborers. The PEC had great difficulty in agreeing on a list of candidates, and this was done only after repeated trips to New Delhi by PEC members and some 3,000 applicants for tickets and their supporters, and after repeated visits to the State by representatives of the Congress High Command. Even when the list was finally prepared, forty-six changes in it were made by the CEC, in several instances on the instructions of Mrs. Gandhi.

In Assam tickets were denied to all former members of the cabinet of Mohendra Mohan Choudhury, who had been forced out as Chief Minister shortly before the campaign began, even though he still commanded the support of the majority of the Congress members in the Legislative Assembly. In Bihar the problem was to work out some sort of compromise between warring factions in the Congress Party, where at least four fairly equally balanced groups were centrally involved. Even a panel headed by K. C. Pant, sent to Bihar on the instructions of Mrs. Gandhi to scrutinize the lists of candidates and to attempt to bring the competing factions into a workable compromise, had little success, except to provide Mrs Gandhi with a direct report on the sad state of her party in Bihar. Eventually the PEC, unable to agree on a list of recommended candidates, decided to refer the entire list to Mrs. Gandhi, without any indications of preference. Seven former Chief Ministers received tickets.

In Haryana the Chief Minister, Bansi Lal, and some members of his cabinet were accused of corruption, and some Congress leaders in the State attempted to persuade the CEC and Mrs. Gandhi to repudiate these persons and name a 'clean slate'; but in the end Bansi Lal, most of his ministers, and candidates recommended by him were chosen. In Madhya Pradesh the Chief Minister, S. C. Shukla, was ousted shortly before the elections, as a result of pressure from the Centre, even though he still had majority support in the Legislative Assembly; and tickets were denied to large numbers of his followers. This led to many defections and a great deal of in-fighting, which did not seem to be reflected in the electoral results.

In Maharashtra a bitter battle was being waged within the State Congress Party between followers of the Chief Minister, V. P. Naik, known to be Y. B. Chavan's man (Chavan was the long-time boss in Maharashtra and a minister in the central government who was thought to have ambitions to become Prime Minister some day), and a rival faction led by a State cabinet minister, Shankarrao Chavan. At one time it seemed that Naik was about to lose out, mainly because it was thought that Mrs. Gandhi did not want to further strengthen the political base of Y. B. Chavan. The original list recommended by the P.E.C. contained a large number of followers of Shankarrao Chavan. This list was scrutinised by D. P. Mishra, representing the CEC, and was substantially altered. The final list contained a majority of supporters of Naik, but seven members of his cabinet were refused Congress tickets. It was widely rumored that Naik had been forced to pledge loyalty to Mrs. Gandhi, and not to Y. B. Chavan, as the price for his continued political survival.

In Mysore many new candidates were named, and the number of candidates from the two caste groups that had long dominated the politics of that State – the Lingayats and the Vokkaligas – was drastically reduced. The CEC made some forty changes in the list submitted by the PEC. Most of the approved candidates were supporters of Devraj Urs, the President of the Mysore Pradesh Congress Committee, who was not himself a candidate but who, shortly after the elections, was selected by Mrs. Gandhi as the new Chief Minister of the State.[36]

When the final lists of Congress candidates were known, it was clear that they constituted 'a mixed bag,' with an unusually large number of new candidates, and representatives of the young, women, and minority groups. The main criteria for selection seemed to have been loyalty to Mrs. Gandhi and a generally left-of-center orientation and a willingness to assist the Prime Minister in giving the Congress a new and more radical image. A columnist in *The Statesman*, writing when the nomination process was in its final stages, drew four broad conclusions regarding the selection process: (1) it was clear that 'no uniform criteria were applied and the norms of selection varied from State to State;' (2) 'the selection of candidates has only perpetuated groupist conflicts;' (3) 'the induction of young blood or fresh talent has not materialized to the extent anticipated;' (4) 'caste considerations have continued to predominate;' and (5) 'the process of elimination and selection has been chaotic, hasty and, in several instances, arbitrary.' The columnist made these observations regarding the type of candidates chosen: '... broadly speaking, the new lists do not differ materially in character and composition from the lists which used to be approved by the united Congress in previous elections. There is nothing in the 1972 lists which reflects the purpose of the Congress leadership or the new direction in which the leadership wants to orient the party.'[37] A correspondent of *The Hindu* was also not impressed with the methods or results of the selection process, although he did indicate that large numbers of new candidates had been selected: 'The old-timers with established local influence have, no doubt, been uprooted and humiliated in the course of this shock treatment. But the new-comers are by and large political light-weights, a generally unknown quantity with no special achievements to their credit in a positive context other than a nominal identification with the party's radicalism.' He also referred to 'the train of bitterness left behind by the arbitrary methods of selection.'[38]

However arbitrary the methods of selection, however disorganized the Congress Party was at local and State levels, however far short the candidates selected fell from the standards which Mrs. Gandhi presumably had in mind, and however great the bitterness and dissatisfaction of would-be candidates and party leaders who were by-passed and ignored, the election results indicated that all of these factors were of little weight in the face of the 'Indira wave.' The majority of India's voters were quite willing to give Mrs. Gandhi a vote of confidence, almost a 'blank check,' and they seem to pay little attention to the candidates who were standing on her party's ticket. They were voting for her, more than for particular candidates, and they gave her the second mandate that she sought.

The Campaign

A political campaign is always an interesting happening in the political life of a nation. It attracts a great deal of attention inside a country, and often outside as well. It brings to the surface many aspects of the political process; it provides insights into the inner workings of the political system and into the basic motivating forces in politics and society. Generally speaking, it involves larger numbers of people in the political process than any other event, even though the participation of most people may be limited largely to a spectator role culminating in the not very active act of voting.

Campaign Functions and Strategies. A 'campaign fulfils many functions in the political process. First, campaign arouses voters' curiosity; identifies issues of debate and spreads information. . . . Secondly, campaign mobilizes voters and helps in their politicisation and integration into the system. Thirdly, it makes the voters' choice easy by posing alternative policies and programmes as well as by debating their merits and demerits. In a broader sense, campaign acts as a catalyst; it sets the ball rolling.'[39] For days, or even weeks, it may be an all-absorbing activity on the part of candidates, party workers, many government officials, and thousands of citizens. For a time it may attract more attention of more people than any other event, even including sports, local developments, personal problems, and other matters which normally occupy a person's interest. While the campaign is in progress thousands of citizens are temporarily brought out of their own little worlds and areas of concern into the broader world of national life and national concerns. Seldom do they take a more active interest in national affairs or become a more active part of a larger political community.

In India a political campaign is an unusually fascinating spectacle, a kind of national festival or *tamasha* that extends from the remotest village to the centers of power in New Delhi. It involves larger numbers of people than any other national activity. It is featured by all the color of traditional methods adapted to modern political purposes. Almost every Indian is in some way exposed to a political campaign, although in many instances the exposure may be surprisingly limited and ineffective. Almost every Indian must be aware during a campaign that something unusual is going on, even though his own interest and participation may be minimal. Empirical evidence seems to confirm these generalizations. A detailed study of the 1967 general election in Gujarat, for example, indicated that 29.3 per cent of the people of that State, based on a sample survey, had a high degree of exposure to the campaign, 36.9 per cent a medium degree, and 35.2 per cent a low degree.[40]

In India, as elsewhere, a voter is exposed to multiple pressures, which are often conflicting, and which may create a great deal of uncertainty and confusion in his mind. The phenomenon of conflicting multiple pressures, often referred to as 'cross-pressures,' has been extensively studied in many Western political systems, especially since the concept of 'cross-pressures' was first developed and systematically studied by some of the early American students of voting behavior using more sophisticated analytical and methodological techniques.[41] In India it has been less extensively studied, but it is equally obvious. Because of it, the problem of trying to determine the factors that influence voting behavior – the so-called voting determinants – is always a difficult task which cannot lead to very definitive conclusions.

The Gujarat 1967 study indicated that the subject of 'cross-pressures' on the Indian voters would indeed be a fruitful area of analysis. It advanced some tentative findings under this heading, such as that the degree of 'cross-pressures' was higher in urban than in rural areas, among young voters than among those of middle or later years, among women than among men, and that it tended to decrease with an increase in literacy and in income.[42]

Even though the political campaign is the most time-consuming, most costly, and usually most spectacular aspect of the electoral process (one could argue that in the United States a nominating convention was more exciting, and that in most countries the actual act of voting was the real dramatic climax to the whole process), it is hard to determine precisely what effect it may have in determining the way a citizen will vote. One of the early empirically-based studies of a British general election by a prominent psephologist of the Nuffield College group pointed out 'how little the behaviour of the voter seems to be determined by ordinary campaign activities and arguments;'[43] and this theme is recurring in all the Nuffield electoral studies. The same point is brought out again and again in voting behavior studies in the United States and in various European countries. Butler and Stokes suggest that the British general election of 1970 'provided one of the rare examples of an election that may have been finally decided by what happened during the campaign.'[44] Possibly the American presidential election of 1948 – and perhaps also that of 1960, if we may accept the contention that the Nixon-Kennedy television debates may have been a decisive factor in Mr. Kennedy's narrow victory – may be further examples of deviations from the normal rule.

The general conclusion seems to be that a political campaign, for all the effort, expense, and attention devoted to it, has far less influence in determining the decision of a voter than one would normally expect. Studies of the timing of the voting decision indicate that substantial numbers of voters have already made up their mind about the way they will vote before the campaign begins. Another fairly large group will state that they made the decision only in the last few days, or even hours, before they went to the polling stations. These last-minute decisions may have been a delayed reaction to the campaign, or they may have been due to other and more immediate factors, such as the influence of family, or friends, or groups of a non-political nature, or personal inclinations and preferences.

From the point of view of the parties and the candidates the major aims of any election campaign may be said to be three-fold: (1) 'to strengthen party supporters into their loyalty; (2) to win over as many undecided voters as possible; and (3) to convert or demoralise supporters of rival parties.'[45] From the point of view of the individual voters the purpose of a campaign should be to provide them with the kind of information and understanding that they need in order to reach a voting decision in accord with their own preferences and interests, hopefully within the framework of the national interests, and to give them an opportunity to evaluate the relative merits of the various parties, candidates, and issues. From the point of view of the political system a campaign is a necessary part of the electoral process and is a vehicle for political participation in and identification with the system, leading to a genuine political choice.

Campaign strategies have to be evolved with all of these points of view in mind. Even though the parties and candidates are primarily concerned with conducting a winning campaign, in order to do so they must show, or at least convince a sufficient number of voters that they are showing, a proper concern for the interests of the individual voters and of the political system as a whole. 'In essence, campaign strategies should provide information on (i) the political system; (ii) the contending ideologies; and (iii) the contending candidates. Effectiveness of the strategy, judged in terms of percentage of votes polled, will perhaps partly depend upon the selection of channels and media to communicate the above three types of information to the electorate. It will also partly depend upon the "style" that is, on "How it is said".'[46]

The Role of Issues. Throughout a campaign candidates and their supporters constantly talk about the issues, which are sometimes defined in very general and sometimes in quite specific terms. One wonders why so much emphasis is given to the issues, when there is overwhelming evidence that on the whole most voters pay little attention to issues and seldom make their final voting decision on the basis of the position of candidates and parties on general or specific issues. Most electoral studies have tended to confirm the assertion of Polsby and Wildavsky, that 'All but major public issues are ... eliminated for most people.'[47] In India, as has been noted, issues seem not to be decisive factors in voting determination. Voters seem to be more interested in parties or in candidates than in issues, and they are often more influenced by socio-economic factors and local circumstances than by more obviously political considerations. There is some evidence, however, of a growing awareness of, and a growing concern with, issues on the part of the Indian voter. In any event, party spokesmen and candidates talk a great deal about them.

In India, with the possible exception of the fourth general election in 1967 – the only general election held after Nehru's death and before Mrs. Gandhi had consolidated her power – the voters have responded more to national than to regional, or local, or international issues. In the Nehru and Indira Gandhi eras, furthermore, they seem to have been influenced more by national than by local considerations. There are of course many exceptions to this, but on the whole it would seem to be valid. Yogesh Atal found that even in the three small communities, at district and sub-district levels, in which he conducted his investigations in the 1967 elections the voters were primarily concerned with national issues, only secondarily with local issues, and almost not at all with international issues.[49] Both Jawaharlal Nehru and Indira Gandhi invariably stressed national issues and considerations in their appeals to the voters, even when they were campaigning in remote villages and other rural areas. Congress candidates for the Assembly, as well as for the Lok Sabha, usually have solicited support mainly on the grounds that their elections would strengthen the position of the national party and the dominant leaders, rather than on their own merits or their position of local issues. Opposition parties and candidates, of course, have taken a different course. Sometimes they have concentrated on local issues and have depended on the appeals of particularly popular candidates; but they have also tried to discredit the national leadership and policies of the ruling Congress Party, and have claimed that local Congress candidates are simply stooges of top Congress leaders and are therefore not acceptable representatives of the people in the constituencies.

Election Manifestoes and Slogans. One main channel through which the issues are presumably identified and a party's position on them explained is the election manifesto. Every major party and sometimes even Independent candidates have issued election manifestoes in the course of every general election. A great deal of effort, and often debate, is involved in the preparation of these manifestoes. Theoretically they are very important documents, for they put the parties and candidates on record on various issues and they provide a check list which voters can use in comparing the positions of different parties and candidates. After the election they serve as an instrument of accountability in checking on the performance of the winning parties and candidates, as compared with their campaign pledges. 'What the manifestoes do provide is a perspective on some of the major public policy issues for the country at the time of the election, as perceived by those political party elites involved in drafting these documents.'[49]

Election manifestoes are given a considerable amount of attention at the time of their release. They are easily available to anyone who wishes to read them, and they are often referred to by candidates and others in the course of the campaign. But they seem to be more statements 'for the record' than actual guidelines for the campaign, or for political performance. They are prepared mainly by the élite groups within the parties, and they have little impact even on elite groups among the voters. Since the vast majority of the Indian voters cannot read, they obviously are not directly affected by election manifestoes, even though they may hear about them at second hand. In any event, they pay little attention to them.

Slogans are more effective than manifestoes in political campaigning. 'Characterised by brevity, rhyme, and rhythm, these highly telegraphic statements' are 'like weapons in the war.'[50] They are couched in a language and a form that appeal particularly to illiterate voters; they are easy to remember and they are often quoted. They stir up interest in the campaign, often by appealing to the selfish concerns or the prejudices of the voters. They contribute little to enlightenment, but they do keep the campaign from becoming dull.

In his study of the 1967 campaign in three small communities in Uttar Pradesh, Yogesh Atal made a careful study of the slogans used by the contending parties and Independent candidates. He found it useful to analyze these slogans under two main headings: slogans used by the Congress Party, and those used by rival parties and Independent candidates. The Congress slogans were mainly designed to attack and discredit other parties, to appeal for support of the Congress on grounds of national security and national interest – 'in the interests of the Country's security,' or 'for the freedom of the Country' – and to assert the inevitability of a Congress victory. The slogans of other parties fell into three main types: those denouncing the Congress Party, those attacking other rival parties, and those serving a self-advocating function.[51]

One of the most successful slogans used in Indian or any other national elections was the famous appeal which Mrs. Gandhi and other Congress spokesmen and candidates made during the fifth general elections and the 1972 State Assembly elections. This slogan, *Garibi hatao*! ('Abolish poverty!'), had an electrifying effect on the Indian masses, who knew all too well what poverty was and what it meant. The opposition parties were never able to counteract the impact of this slogan. While they too would have been happy to make the same pledge, Mrs. Gandhi and her Congress Party had beaten them to it. When they tried to convince voters that they could do a better job in abolishing poverty, or that Mrs. Gandhi could not possibly fulfill this pledge and was therefore deceiving the voters, and above all when they raised the counter-slogan, *Indira hatao*! (or 'Indira must go!'), their efforts were unproductive and in fact often boomeranged.

It would be difficult to assess the role of the slogan, *Garibi hatao*!, in Mrs. Gandhi's overwhelming electoral victories in 1971 and 1972, but it was certainly a great help to her. To some extent this slogan has returned to haunt her in the post-election months, especially when the euphoria created by her electoral successes and her firm and successful leadership of the country in its crisis with Pakistan in 1971 and the handling of the Bengali refugees had somewhat evaporated and when rising prices, drought conditions, and economic hardships generally led many Indians to criticize the Prime Minister for her failure to implement her election pledges.

Campaign Techniques. Many ingenious campaign techniques have been used in Indian elections. These techniques have been geared to the nature of the Indian electorate, including their mass illiteracy and social attitudes and values, and to the problems of communication in a vast nation where channels of communication are still quite limited. On the whole, emphasis was given to such techniques as meetings, processions, banners, flags, and other visible and rather spectacular demonstrations rather than to the written word, although numerous pamphlets and leaflets were distributed and posters and slogans on walls and fences were used everywhere.

Two of the most effective media of electioneering in most Western democracies, namely television and the radio, have played almost no part in Indian elections. Television was not available in India until recent years, and even now it is confined to a few metropolitan areas. Even in these areas TV sets are few, and programs are put on for only a few hours a day. All-India Radio, the only radio available in India, is run by the Government, and it has never been used by political parties in elections. From time to time the Government – i.e., the ruling Congress Party – has offered to allot a very limited period of time to representatives of each party during campaign, but the parties have never been able to agree on the allocation of time.

Nor have Indian newspapers, either the English or Indian language press, been used on any large scale for advertising by parties or candidates. In recent elections some opposition parties, notably the Jana Sangh and Swatantra, have done some newspaper advertising, but this has been quite limited and relatively ineffective. Naturally party newspapers, which are quite numerous, have been used as vehicles of campaign propaganda. The regular newspapers report election news and proceedings at great length, and they carry frequent editorial comments and articles by columnists on elections. Certainly a general election in India is a well-reported event. Indeed, while a campaign is under way it tends to overshadow almost all other news. One is reminded of the way in which the New York *Herald*, in the days of Horace Greeley, reported American political news, especially Presidential elections.

The numerous and varied campaign techniques may be summarized under the three main headings that Yogesh Atal used in analyzing these techniques in the three small communities in Uttar Pradesh in 1967.[52]

In his categorization the campaign strategies and techniques were grouped according to the methods which they tried to exploit.

The first method emphasized visibility-observability, and included the use of the following types of material 'to give a face-lift to the community': (1) Wall paintings. These appeared in great profusion on almost every available space. Generally they showed some sense of the artistic and the dramatic, and were often painted with the use of stencils 'to facilitate quick duplication.' Usually they were simple signs, giving prominence to the election symbol and the name of the candidate. (2) Posters and big leaflets. These too were numerous, and were designed mainly for visibility and general effect, rather than for any detailed message. They were posted in prominent places, often with large photographs or other appropriate pictures. (3) Flags. Party flags were on display not only in party offices but also in shops, homes, vehicles, and elsewhere. In some places parties and candidates seemed to vie with each other in promoting such displays, and sometimes in preventing rival parties from displaying their flags. In Kerala in one election an interesting variation of the contests over the display of flags was the rivalry of two competing coalitions in seeing which group could fly its flags at the greatest height. (4) Arches and gates. These were constructed across roads, and were usually decorated with huge photos of national and local leaders and candidates and streamers, buntings, posters, etc. (5) Banners. These were usually also hung across roads and streets, or from houses and offices. 'These banners contained the request to vote, the election symbol, and the names of party and candidates were indicated in the message.'[53] (6) Visible indicators on persons, including caps (many supporters of the Congress wore khaki caps, of the Jana Sangh yellow or saffron caps, of the Akali Dal in the Punjab blue turbans, and of the Republican party – formerly the Scheduled Caste Federation – blue caps), badges, and metal and plastic buttons.

The second major technique emphasized reading-hearing. These included: (1) Propaganda on loud speakers, which were mounted on vehicles, in party offices, and sometimes in shops. Loud speakers were of course also used extensively at public meetings. Few persons who have observed an Indian general election will forget the constant blaring of loud speakers, from which there seemed to be no escape. (2) Cinema slides and documentaries. Slides bearing election appeals were frequently shown in cinema houses all over the country. The Swatantra Party was the most active and effective in producing documentary films for campaign purposes. (3) Gramophone records. These were used by various parties, and were quite popular, since gramaphones were widely available in India. 'Known poets and singers were commissioned . . . to compose and sing songs,'[54] which included propaganda for particular parties and candidates in some ingenious ways. (4) Written material. Much of this kind of material was of a non-party nature, and was available in local and national newspapers, in English and Indian languages, and in government publications and releases. Some regular newspapers openly supported particular candidates and parties, and of course the party newspapers were major agencies for the distribution of election news and appeals. Parties also made extensive use of posters and leaflets containing a considerable amount of printed material as distinguished from large posters and leaflets that appealed mainly to the visibility-observability objective, slips containing such useful information as the identification of a voter's name on the electoral roll and the election symbol of the party issuing them (these were often delivered to voters at their homes, and were carried by them to the polling stations on the day of voting), pamphlets in great abundance and variety, printed letters, and election manifestoes (usually these were not distributed widely, but they were available in party offices, they were reprinted in many newspapers, and some of their key points were printed in party pamphlets).

The third method emphasized the personal-informal approach – an approach that was especially effective in India. Under this heading came such important techniques as the following: (1) Door-to-door canvassing, by candidates, party workers, and other campaigners. This was 'perhaps the most distinguishing feature' of the campaigning in the three communities that Dr. Atal surveyed, and indeed of most of the election campaigns in India, including national elections. (2) Processions, which were often of vast length and size, with many colorful features. For a foreign observer these great processions were among the most interesting and colorful features of Indian political campaigns. (3) Dance-parties. 'Professional dancers specially hired for the purpose went out in the market, and in the villages, and performed dances to attract people.'[55] A variation on this was the use of folk-singers and ballad singers, such as *kirtan* singers, to entertain the people, and to tell familiar stories based on classical themes through the medium of song, often with the insertion of political propaganda in the course of the recitals. The Communists and some of the more traditional parties were quite adept in this technique. (4) Meetings. In early general elections public meetings seemed to be the most popular and the most frequent method of electioneering. In recent elections these mass meetings have still been frequently held, but not as often as in the past. There seems to be a growing feeling that such meetings, while spectacular shows, are not as effective vote-getting devices as was at first thought.

Nehru was at his best in vast public meetings, and through them he was able to address and be seen by large numbers of his countrymen. No other technique, especially since the use of the radio was denied, could have exposed him to so many people, or exposed so many Indians to their greatest leader. In a country where the personal factor is so important, and where the *darshan* – obtained simply by being in the presence – of a great leader is so valued, public meetings have a very special role in electioneering and other aspects of public life.

Mrs. Gandhi has also used public meetings in the same way as her father did. In the first general elections in which she participated after she became Prime Minister – the fourth elections in 1967 – she seemed ineffective and ill at ease on the public platform; but in the 1971 general elections and the 1972 State Assembly elections she addressed large numbers of hugely attended public meetings with great confidence and skill. By this time she had achieved a far greater hold on her job and on the people of her country, so that she would capitalize on her new and stronger image and her great personal appeal.

Atal found that most of these election techniques were used in the COC, but that there was much less exposure to them in the LC and very little indeed in the SC. This is a useful reminder that even a general election penetrates to small communities only to a limited degree. But in describing the impact of these techniques in the COC Atal caught some of the atmosphere and flavor and excitement of an Indian election campaign at a high point:

> COC was exposed to a wide variety of propaganda and also for a comparatively longer period. From the date of the official clearance of the nomination, parties began their campaign exercises in COC. Each subsequent day had an added emphasis: campaign activities went on mounting high and high, becoming more colorful, vigourous, varied, and noisy. While the parties were busy spreading the message, the awakened electorate also got spurt [*sic*] and started discussing informally – in peer groups, at restaurants, betel-shops, and public places – the election politics. Election themes provided the main talking points. Rumours had their wings. Personality exaltation and character assassination became matters of routine. A deepening involvement of the masses was visible as the days passed by. The atmosphere of the town was rented [*sic*] with election politics.[56]

Electoral Arrangements and Alliances. Since opposition parties in India have been so weak, one would expect that some of them would frequently join together in electoral arrangements or alliances for the purpose of defeating Congress candidates. Such alliances have been made in every national election, but they have generally been very loose electoral arrangements of 'heterogeneous elements whose only apparent bond of unity was the desire to defeat Congress candidates.'[57] They have generally been confined to particular States, and they have generally been quite ineffective and ephemeral.

One immediately effective electoral alliance was the Samyukhta Maharashtra Samiti, a coalition of almost all major opposition parties from right-wing and locally-based parties to the Communists, which in 1957 had considerable electoral success in the Maharashtra section of what was then the undivided State of Bombay over the linguistic issue and the demand for the creation of a separate State of Maharashtra, which was granted three years later. After the 1957 elections the Samiti continued to exist, but gradually it lost the support of some of its constituent parties and became hardly more than a weak front for the CPI. A looser and less inclusive anti-Congress electoral alliance in the Gujarat region of Bombay State, called the Mahagujarat Janata Parishad, also had some success in 1957, and it also continued to exist for some years thereafter, in weakened form.

In West Bengal, during the 1957 elections, there were no fewer than three separate electoral arrangements, each consisting of several parties and dissident Congressmen.[58] In the fifth general elections in 1971 four of the major opposition parties – the Congress (O), the Jana Sangh, Swatantra, and the SSP – joined in a unique electoral arrangement which seemed to present a formidable combined opposition to the ruling Congress Party; but this so-called 'Grand Alliance' proved to be anything but grand. Its constituent parties did not cooperate in all States and constituencies where they were contesting, and they would probably have done better on their own than in association with parties with which they had such basic differences.

The undivided Congress Party seldom entered into any kind of electoral arrangements with any other parties, especially with extremely right-wing or left-wing parties. The two parties that have emerged from the undivided Congress of the Nehru era have occasionally agreed to electoral arrangements. The outstanding example of this policy by the Congress (O) has already been cited, namely its association with three other opposition parties in the 'Grand Alliance' in 1971. In fact, it took a leading role in the formation of this alliance. The New Congress led by Mrs. Gandhi has generally not been forced to consider electoral arrangements, but it has made such arrangements, or at least understandings, in several States, as in West Bengal, Tamil Nadu, and Kerala. In Tamil Nadu its electoral understanding with the DMK was short-lived. In Kerala, for the first time, it entered into an understanding with a united front in which the CPI was a leading member and it supported a coalition government headed by a CPI Chief Minister.

On the whole, however, the ruling Congress Party has seldom entered into electoral arrangements of any kind. Opposition parties have resorted to them more frequently, with some success at local levels but with almost none at national levels. These alliances, or attempts at alliances, have been interesting features of election campaigns. They have, for the most part, been loose alliances of convenience. They have added greatly to the color and to the complexity of election campaigns without achieving any very significant long-range results. In view of the weakness of opposition parties, except in some States and constituencies, and in view of the generally unbalanced nature of the Indian party system and the generally disorganized state of most so-called parties, the ineffectiveness and relative infrequency of electoral alliances may be less surprising than one might at first assume.

The Voting – and After

Timing of Voting Decision. The question of the timing of the voting decision has fascinated students of voting behavior for many years, and a great deal of empirical evidence has been gathered on this subject. Obviously the timing of the voting decision may give some indication of other aspects of the electoral process and voter motivations, such as the degree of 'primordial' or other loyalties, including loyalty to a party, the influence of the election campaign on the voters, and the *ad hoc* or long-range nature of voting behavior. In most democratic states a large number of voters make up their mind how they will vote before the campaign starts; few change their minds during or as a result of the campaign, but another large number seem to make their voting decision very shortly before the polling day, or even on the day itself. The same pattern apparently prevails in India, although it obviously varies considerably from State to State.

No nation-wide empirical survey of this question has yet been made in India, but several State-wide studies, and at least one four-State study, are available. The four-State study was made in 1969, at the time of the mid-term elections in the four major States of Bihar, the Punjab, Uttar Pradesh, and West Bengal. The results are shown in Table 5.i.[59]

The variations among these four States are quite striking. 62 per cent of the respondents in Bihar and 49 per cent in West Bengal indicated that they had made up their minds about voting only in the closing days of the campaign or on the actual day of polling, whereas the comparable figures for U.P. and the Punjab are 40 per cent and 29.4 per cent. In contrast, nearly 60 per cent of the Punjab respondents and more than 41 per cent of those in U.P. indicated that they had made up their minds about voting before the campaign started, whereas only 33 per cent of the respondents in West Bengal and 21 per cent of those in Bihar made the decision so early. These results confirm what other kinds of analyses have indicated, and in fact what is generally known

Table 5.i

TIMING OF VOTING DECISION, BY STATES

	(Per cent)			
When Decided to Vote	*Bihar*	*Punjab*	*UP*	*West Bengal*
On polling day	77 24.06	17 5.88	65 16.46	44 18.41
A few days before the poll	122 38.13	68 23.53	93 23.54	73 30.54
Just after the campaign started	54 16.88	33 11.41	74 18.73	43 17.99
Before the campaign started	67 20.93	171 59.17	163 41.27	79 33.06
Total	320 100.00	289 100.00	395 100.00	239 100.00

about the politics of these four States, namely that there is a fairly high degree of partisan stability in U.P. and especially in the Punjab, and a low degree in the volatile State of West Bengal and the very chaotic State, politically speaking, of Bihar.

An empirical study of the 1967 election in Gujarat suggests that that once highly stable State was roughly comparable to West Bengal with respect to the timing of voting decisions.[60] The respondents indicated the timing of their voting decision as follows:

	Per cent
Four weeks or more before the election	39.6
Very day of elections	36.1
One week before the election	12.7
Two to three weeks before the election	4.2

A higher percentage of respondents said that they had made up their minds before the campaign started than in the case of the West Bengal respondents, but about the same percentage made their decisions in the last stages of the campaign or on the day of voting. In the case of Gujarat, a surprisingly large number stated that they had in fact made their decision on the polling day itself, indicating a degree of voter volatility that was not formerly associated with Gujarat.

Preparations for Voting. The conduct of a general election is obviously a massive operation. The numbers of Indians who have participated in the general elections, as has been stated, have varied from 173 million to more than 270 million. Millions of ballot papers have to be printed, more than 2.5 million ballot boxes have to be obtained and distributed, between 200,000 and 300,000 polling stations have to be set up, and about a million persons have to be mobilized for the actual supervision and conduct of a general election.

The cost to the central and State governments, as well as to the political parties and candidates, is very great. While these costs do not approach those incurred in the United States, especially since the advent of television, there are frequent and well-justified complaints that election expenses, public and private, are much too high; and as in the United States and almost every democratic state the money spent on elections by parties and candidates far exceeds the legally authorized limits. In most States a candidate for the Lok Sabha, for example, is permitted to spend no more than Rs. 25,000 for campaign expenses to promote his candidacy, but the actual expenses actually incurred by or in support of a Lok Sabha candidate is generally reported to be well over Rs. 100,000, and in some cases at least four or five times that figure.[61]

The Election Commission has made every possible effort, through the radio, printed matter, and other channels of communication, to instruct the voters on the proper voting procedures, and the political parties and candidates (numbering 17,500 for 489 seats in the House of the People and 3,300 seats in the State Legislative Assemblies in the first general elections) have also been quite helpful, although neither parties nor candidates have contributed as much as would be expected to voter education.

In the first two general elections the multiple ballot box system of voting was employed. A voter would find inside a polling booth as many ballot boxes as there were candidates, with the symbol of the party or candidate (if an Independent) on the outside of each box. He voted simply by inserting the ballot paper in a slot in the box containing the symbol of the party or candidate he wished to support. This system had the merit of simplicity and intelligibility – very important considerations since most of the voters were illiterate and were unaccustomed to the exercise of the franchise; but it also had major defects, being cumbersome, expensive, and open to such abuses as the stuffing of ballot boxes, the transfer of ballot papers from one box to another, and the removal or destruction of ballot papers.

Beginning in the third general elections a different system, the more conventional marking system, was employed. A voter is given a ballot paper containing the names and symbols of each candidate. Using an inked rubber stamp which is handed to him by a polling officer, he enters a polling booth and stamps the ballot paper between the lines containing the name and symbol of the party and candidate of his choice. He then deposits the folded ballot paper in a ballot box, in the presence of polling officials and often representatives of the various parties and candidates as well.[62]

This is a more efficient system, but it too has defects. Chief among these are the suspicion, sometimes apparently well founded, that the secret ballot has ceased to be secret, for each ballot paper has a number, which is recorded by a polling officer against the name of the voter. 'The voter's electoral choice can be identified if the Government could check the name of the person casting the vote.' To be sure, this can legally be done only under an order from a competent court or tribunal, or the Election Commission may 'order the production and inspection of election papers while in the custody of the returning officers,' if electoral fraud or irregularity is suspected. But 'the whole procedure is open to exploitation, particularly when the vast number of [the] electorate is illiterate.' Illiterate voters are often warned that they will be punished if they do not vote for a certain parties or candidates, and they believe that their votes will be checked and will become known to those who have no legal right to know how they voted.[63]

Another objection to the marking system is that it has produced a higher percentage of invalid votes than the multiple ballot box system. Quite understandably, there are many invalid votes because of the ignorance and inexperience of the voters; but on the whole the percentage of invalid votes has been surprisingly low. It did increase somewhat, but not alarmingly, when the marking system was substituted for the multiple ballot box system, and it has been declining again with each general election. In the third general elections, in which the marking system of voting was used for the first time in a national election, the percentage of invalid votes was around 5 per cent, but it declined to 4.65 per cent in 1967 and to 3.25 per cent in 1971. These figures compare favorably with percentages of invalid votes in most other political systems.

Electioneering ceases forty-eight hours before the closing hour of polling in each constituency. Or perhaps it would be more accurate to say that the campaign is then formally over, and legally no more campaign activities can be carried on. Behind the scenes a great deal of activity continues and last-minute efforts are made to persuade or coerce the voters, through private pressures and appeals and often through the distribution of money, liquor, and other forms of bribery and corruption.

Voting Procedures. Voting in each constituency is almost invariably held on one day, from early in the morning to late afternoon. Parties and candidates often send agents to get people to come to the polls, and often provide transportation for voters from whom they expect support, even though this practice is illegal under election laws.

The process of voting itself is a fascinating spectacle, as millions of people in all parts of the country go to the polling stations, which are set up within easy access for most voters (although in remote and geographically difficult areas this is a real problem). Voting is the supreme act of an Indian citizen, often his only significant act of political participation, and it is of course the culmination of a political campaign, the end product of the entire electoral process. For that day, at least, the citizen is 'sovereign,' in a symbolic and to some extent in a real sense.[64]

The procedure of voting in India is relatively simple. A voter usually first stops at the table or tent, set up at a certain prescribed distance from the polling station, which is manned by representatives of the party which he wishes to support. Here his name is checked against the electoral rolls (copies are made available to parties and candidates) and he is given final instructions.

> On the voter entering the polling station, the first polling officer locates his name in the roll, enters therein against his name the number of the assembly ballot paper to be issued to him, and passes on the ballot paper to the second polling officer. The latter similarly enters against the voter's name in his copy of this roll the number of the parliamentary ballot paper to be issued to him. He then passes on both the ballot papers to the third polling officer who marks the voter's left forefinger with indelible ink and hands over both the ballot papers to him. . . . After receiving the ballot papers, the voter goes to the fourth polling officer who takes both the ballot papers from the voter, explains to him how to record his vote, hands over the assembly ballot paper and an inked rubber stamp to him and passes on the parliamentary ballot paper to the fifth polling officer who sits opposite to him at the same table. The voter then proceeds to the first voting compartment, records his vote on the assembly ballot paper, comes out and drops the folded ballot paper into the ballot box kept on the table in front of the fifth polling officer. The latter then hands over the parliamentary ballot paper and an inked rubber stamp to the voter who proceeds to the second voting compartment, records his vote on the parliamentary ballot paper, brings it back and drops it in the same ballot box and quits the polling station.[65]

This procedure has been followed in the third, fourth, and fifth general elections, with the exception that in the fifth elections the voters in all but three States cast ballots only for candidates for the Lok Sabha – since the national and State elections were de-linked for the first time. In the State Assembly elections of 1972 – the first de-linked State elections on a nearly nationwide scale – the voters of course cast ballots only for candidates for State Assemblies.

When the hours set aside for voting come to a close, the ballot boxes are sealed and taken under police and other supervision to a safe place of storage. Shortly thereafter the actual counting of the ballots is done, by accredited election officials in the presence of candidates or their authorized representatives. The results are usually announced within two or three days after the voting ends in all parts of the country. At first the results were announced as soon as they were available, even though voting had not yet taken place in many constituencies in different parts of the country; but this practice was abandoned in the face of protests that the premature announcement of some results might influence the voting decisions of citizens who had not yet gone to the polls.

The Aftermath. Once the votes have been cast, and counted, and the results announced, most of the parties, candidates, and election officials can relax and enjoy a surcease from their strenuous duties. But the task of the Election Commission and high election officials continues. After every election the Commission is flooded with complaints of irregular practices or other abuses, including electoral frauds and the rigging of certain elections. Formerly these complaints came 'in thousands and thousands, so much so that they had to be kept in gunny bags. But at the time of the Lok Sabha elections in 1971, the total number of complaints from the entire country was 2,092 only and at the time of the assembly elections in 1972 the total number was still less – it was only 1,433.'[66] After each election also a number of election petitions, alleging various kinds of irregularities and injustices, have been filed. The numbers of such petitions have not been large – respectively thirty-nine, fifty-nine, forty-six, fifty-one and fifty-eight; but, as the Chief Election Commissioner has often pointed out, this number, while small, compares unfavorably with the experience in Britain, where no election petition charging corrupt practices has been filed since 1911.[67] These petitions are considered by election tribunals, and in some cases the elections have been invalidated, often after months of delay, on grounds of corrupt practices.

Charges of 'rigging' of elections have been made, usually by defeated candidates and opposition parties, after every election. They were particularly numerous after the fifth general elections, when a new technique of rigging was alleged, namely the use of 'chemical treatment of ballot papers and marking on the same the voting marks with magic invisible ink in effectuation of a pre-planned design hatched for the purpose.'[68] Various allegations charging this kind of rigging were filed in the High Courts of several States, but they were turned down in every case as not proved.

On the whole, the great national elections in India have been impressive and successful demonstrations of the democratic process in operation. The electoral campaigns have been marked by some violence, especially in certain States, but the actual voting has usually proceeded in a peaceful manner and voting has seldom had to be suspended and new elections held as a result of acts of violence on polling day. In spite of many general allegations of fraud and corruption, the number of cases of elections being declared invalid as a result of corrupt practices has been remarkably small. The broad conclusion emerges that the Indian general elections have been generally fair and free. This is a major achievement indeed, which contrasts sharply with the electoral experience in most other developing countries. It raises the question whether India will in time go the same way as most other states of the Third World or whether the Indian example, by its sheer magnitude and success, may in time influence other developing countries to return to more democratic practices and to make them more meaningful in fact as well as in form.

6

INDIA'S ELECTORAL EXPERIENCE

India has had the most extensive experience with democratic elections of any so-called developing country. A few of the new states of Asia, notably Ceylon and the Philippines, have had even more general elections than India. Ceylon (now Sri Lanka) has had the additional distinction of having introduced universal adult suffrage twenty years before India and of having changed governments from one party to another as a result of the electoral process – an experience that is exceedingly rare in the new states of the Third World and that is quite unique in South Asia. But no developing country has held elections on the vast scale of India's general elections. Indeed, India rightly boasts of the fact that it has held 'the world's largest democratic elections.'[1]

On five different occasions – in 1951–2, 1957, 1962, 1967, and 1971 – between 105 and 145 million people in India have gone to the polls to cast their votes in nationwide general elections. In 1969 nearly 60 million Indians participated in elections to the Legislative Assemblies in five major States, in 1972 some 105 million voted for members of the Legislative Assemblies in sixteen States and two Union Territories, and in 1974 elections were held in four States and one Union Territory, involving about one-fifth of the population of India and an electorate of 50 million. In addition to these massive exercises in free, competitive elections, India has witnessed several other State elections, many by-elections, *panchayat* elections (especially since the inauguration of the system of Panchayati Raj in 1959), municipal elections, and other elections of central importance to the political system.

All of these elections have been direct elections on the basis of universal adult franchise. Various kinds of indirect elections have also been of considerable importance, including the rather complicated systems of proportional representation through which elected members of the Rajya Sabha (the upper House of the Indian Parliament) and the President and Vice President of the Indian Republic are chosen, and also the indirect elections that are provided for in most States for the *panchayat samitis* and *zilla parishads* (sometimes called by different names) in the Panchayati Raj system.

Elections have become such a commonplace feature of the Indian political scene that some observers have suggested that the Indian voter, having grown accustomed to what a generation ago was a novel experience, is now rather election-weary, and may therefore be rather blasé about the whole election process. The people of Kerala have participated in seven national and State elections since the formation of the State in 1956. Within the space of twelve months in 1971–2 most of the Indian people were involved in a general election and in separate State elections. During this period the citizens of two of India's major cities, Calcutta and Delhi-New Delhi, also participated in important elections to the governing municipal corporations. Hence elections have come frequently in independent India and talk of elections is heard almost all the time. Undoubtedly this has contributed to the high degree of politicization which seems to characterize the Indian scene, with both beneficial and deleterious consequences for the political system.

Because of this extensive electoral experience, as an astute Indian journalist has pointed out, 'free elections tend to be taken for granted in India, although few other developing countries have been able to institutionalize the system.'[2] This statement calls attention to a danger – that free elections will be taken for granted – and to a significant fact about elections in India – namely that they seem to have become institutionalized as an integral feature of the Indian political system. India is indeed the outstanding example of the institutionalization of elections among the developing countries, and is one of a very small number of states – numbering hardly more than twenty-five in the entire world, including the highly developed democratic states of the Western world – where people regularly exercise the rights of free, direct, competitive elections on a mass franchise basis. The existence of this phenomenon, but also its rarity and its fragile roots in the political culture, should be noted by those who are concerned with the future of the Indian political system, especially as far as the prospects for continuing and strengthening the democratic system are concerned.

Electoral Experience Prior to 1947

Although elections, as Professor Morris-Jones has observed, are one of the things that Indians do well,[3] only those who have been twenty-one years of age or over since 1951 have had any extensive electoral experience, or indeed in most cases any experience at all. No elections on the basis of universal adult suffrage were held in India prior to 1951. However, India did have some electoral experience prior to 1947, especially in two elections, in the decade prior to independence, in 1937 and 1945–6, which profoundly affected the political destinies of the people of the entire subcontinent and helped to determine the bases of political power in the two states that emerged at the end of British rule.[4]

From Indian Councils Act of 1892 to Government of India Act of 1935. The principle of representation, and in an indirect way of elections, was first incorporated in the Indian Councils Act of 1892, which enlarged the councils of the Governor-General and of the Provisional Governors, and which provided that some of the additional non-official members should be elected by an indirect process by certain corporate bodies, such as municipal councils and chambers of commerce. 'By conceding the principle of elections and by giving the Legislative Councils some control over the Executive, the Indian Councils Act of 1892 paved the way for further reforms in India.'[5]

In the Government of India Act of 1909, embodying the Morley-Minto reforms, the elective principle was further recognized and extended, although still on a limited and indirect basis. The Imperial Legislative Council was enlarged from twenty-five to sixty members, and twenty-seven of these were to be elected by various indirect means, by a broader group of constituencies than was provided for in the Indian Councils Act of 1892. This Act opened the door to communal representation by creating six constituencies for Muslim landholders, in response to the petition of the delegation of Muslims to the Governor-General, led by the Agha Khan, which claimed that Muslims were under-represented in the imperial and legislative councils. Once conceded, the principle of communal representation – the so-called 'separate electorates' – was incorporated in all subsequent electoral arrangements during the British period, even though Gandhi and other leaders of the Indian National Congress were strongly opposed to it. It has been largely abandoned in independent India, except for a few small minority groups and for the large numbers of members of the Scheduled Castes, Scheduled Tribes, and other 'backward classes'; and special representation for these underprivileged groups is provided for not by creating separate constituencies for them exclusively but by designating certain constituencies as 'reserved' constituencies where candidates must belong to one of the 'backward' groups but where voting is on a universal and not on a restricted communal basis.

A major step toward broader representation through the elective process was heralded in the famous pledge of Edwin Montagu, the Secretary of State for India, on 20 August 1917, during the course of the First World War, that 'the policy of His Majesty's Government . . . is that of the increasing association of Indians in every branch of the administration and the gradual development of self-governing institutions with a view to the progressive realisation of responsible government in India as an integral part of the British Empire.'[6] This pledge took concrete, if disappointingly limited form in the Government of India Act of 1919. The old Imperial Legislative Council was replaced by a bicameral body, consisting of a Council of State of sixty-one members elected on the basis of a highly restrictive franchise (about 67,000 eligible voters), and a Legislative Assembly of 146 members, 106 of whom were to be elected directly from general and Muslim constituencies on the basis of a considerably broadened franchise of some 5,000,000 voters, still tied mainly to land-holding. In the provinces – then eight, but soon to be eleven – the Governors' legislative councils were also enlarged, and made directly elected within the framework of a broadened but still limited franchise. It is worthy of note that shortly after the Act of 1919 was implemented, women received the right to vote on the same basis as men. 'Thus India came to have for the first time in her history an elected parliament with powers to influence largely her administration.'[7]

The broader significance of these concessions, which at the time seemed to Indian leaders to be so limited and to Britishers so bold, should not be overlooked. 'Apart from anything else, the councils provided, over the next twenty-six years, an effective school of public life. It was their existence, together with the background of general Western education and Indian employment in the services, which provided India with the 'know-how' of government when independence came, and saved her from the embarrassments and troubles which beset Indonesia in a similar situation.'[8]

As the Indian independence movement gained momentum in the Gandhian era, the demands for a greater voice by Indians in their own affairs mounted, and the divergent courses of the Indian National Congress and the Muslim League became more apparent. The Congress claimed to represent all Indians, whatever their ethnic, caste, or religious affiliation might be, whereas the League professed to speak for the large Muslim minority in British India and the Princely states. Significant steps were taken in the 1920s and 1930s which brought India closer to the goal of greater autonomy, which gradually came to mean complete independence. Landmarks were the report of the Indian Statutory Commission (the Simon Commission) in 1930; the report of the All-Parties Conference in 1928, which under the chairmanship of Motilal Nehru, Jawaharlal's father, laid down basic principles for a Constitution of India; the report of the Indian Statutory Commission (the Simon Commission) in 1930 which, while largely ignored and criticized at the time of its release, contained recommendations which were later incorporated in the Government of India Act of 1935 and which paved the way for provincial autonomy and a federal constitution; the report of the Franchise Committee, under the chairmanship of Lord Lothian, the Parliamentary Under-Secretary of State for India, which resulted in a five-fold increase in the electorate, to include about 35 million voters; the three Round Table Conferences of 1930–2 which, although apparently unproductive and frustrating, did lead to a new round of concessions and proposals; the Gandhi-Irwin Pact of March, 1931, in which Gandhi won certain concessions in return for calling off a civil disobedience campaign; Gandhi's most famous fast in 1932 against a proposal by the British Government to create separate electorates for the 'untouchables'; and, above all, the Government of India Act of 1935, the last and most important of the great landmarks along the road from limited representation of Indians to self-government and eventual independence.

This Act, one of the most thoroughly and hotly debated pieces of legislation in the history of the British Parliament, laid down the framework of a federal state in India, to consist of both the eleven provinces of British India and the many Princely states, with the members of the federal legislature of two houses – the Council of States and the House of Assembly – representing British India to be mostly elected. A great deal of autonomy was given to the provinces, six of which were to have bicameral legislatures and the rest a single chamber to be known as the Legislative Assembly. The Legislative Assemblies were to have 1,585 seats, chosen by an electorate numbering some 35 million people; 959 of these were general seats (including 151 reserved for representatives of Scheduled Castes and Scheduled Tribes), 482 were Muslim seats, and the rest were reserved for other class and communal and special groups.

The 1937 Elections and After. While the federal provisions of the Government of India Act of 1935 never went into effect, because of the resistance of the Indian princes, the new arrangements for the provinces were soon implemented. Both the Indian National Congress and the Muslim League decided to participate in the elections for members of the Legislative Assemblies for all eleven provinces, and for members of the Legislative Councils in six of them. The elections were held in January and February 1937, with 54.5 per cent of the some 35 million eligible voters participating. The Congress won 716 of the 1585 seats in the provincial Assemblies, or about 45 per cent of all the seats, but it won only 5.4 per cent of the Muslim seats. The Muslim League, which was not well organized to contest this election, won only 109 of the 482 Muslim seats; it did not win a majority in any of the four Muslim-majority provinces. The Congress won a clear majority in six of the eleven provinces – Bihar, Bombay, the Central Provinces, Madras, Orissa, and the United Provinces – and it became the largest single party in three others.[9] The elections showed that the Congress could rightly claim to represent Hindu India, but that its hold on the Muslims of the subcontinent was quite negligible. They also showed that the Muslim League was not yet accepted by a majority of Muslims in any province.

Having won a fairly impressive electoral victory, the Congress leaders then became involved in an historic debate over the question of acceptance of office in those provinces where it had a majority in the Legislative Assemblies. On 18 March 1937, the All-India Congress Committee decided to permit 'the acceptance of office in provinces where the Congress commands a majority in the legislatures, provided . . . the leader of the Congress party in the legislature is satisfied and is able to state publicly that the Governor will not use his special powers of interference or set aside the advice of ministers in regard to their constitutional activities.'[10] Not until 21 June 1937 did the British Government, through the Viceroy, Lord Linlithgow, issue an assurance on this point that the Congress leaders regarded as satisfactory. In July Congress ministries were formed in the six provinces where the Congress had won a majority of the seats in the Legislative Assemblies. Later in the year the Congress formed a ministry in the North West Frontier Province, and in March 1938 in Assam.

In forming these ministries the Congress took special care to include some Muslims, but it refused to enter into coalition ministries with the Muslim League and it admitted only Muslims who were not members of the League. This policy was severely criticized at the time, and in later years some observers have insisted that it was a tragic mistake because it created an unbridgeable gulf between the Congress and the Muslim League and made partition almost inevitable. Even today the debate continues, but it seems likely that the decision, which, however regrettable, was understandable in the light of the conditions that existed in 1937, was not such a decisive turning point in Hindu–Muslim, and Congress–Muslim League relations, as many observers have suggested.[11] In the context of the time it would have required a far-seeing act of statesmanship and forbearance for the Congress, on the morrow of a rather decisive electoral victory, to have joined hands with the Muslim League, whose showing in the elections seemed to refute its claim to represent the Muslims of the subcontinent.

On the whole, the Congress ministries in most of the provinces worked quite satisfactorily, and serious conflicts between them and the Governors, representing the British raj, were avoided. But these ministries did not long remain in office; they resigned in the fall of 1939, in protest against the action of the British Government in declaring India at war with the fascist powers. During the war the Congress was out of office, and after the famous 'Quit India' resolution of August 1942, most of its top leaders were in jail. The Muslim League, however, generally cooperated with the British in the war effort, and as a result was in a much stronger position when the war ended. This was reflected in the even more adamant position taken by Mohammed Ali Jinnah, such as his insistence at the Simla Conference in the summer of 1945 (25 June to 15 July), where twenty-one political leaders of India were called together by the Governor-General to suggest names for his Executive Council, that all Muslims to be considered for positions on the Council must belong to the Muslim League.

Elections of 1945–6. Shortly after the abortive Simla Conference Churchill and the Conservative Party were defeated in the 1945 elections in England. The new Labor Government, with Clement Attlee as Prime Minister, was much more sympathetic than was Mr. Churchill to the demands for self-government in the Indian subcontinent. One of the first concrete steps in this direction was taken on 19 September, when Mr. Attlee in London and the Viceroy Lord Wavell in New Delhi simultaneously announced that elections to the Central and provincial legislatures, long delayed because of the war, would be held during the coming winter. Preparations were immediately begun to revise the electoral rolls, although the size of the electorate was not substantially increased, in spite of Congress demands. The campaign soon resolved itself into a direct contest between the Congress and the Muslim League, with minor parties and Independents playing only a minor role.

The election results strengthened the position of both of the contending parties, and highlighted the increasingly unbridgeable gulf between them. In the elections to the Central legislature the Congress got 91 per cent of the votes cast for the 'general' seats, and all fifty-seven of these seats; while the Muslim League got 86 per cent of the votes in the Muslim constituencies and all of the thirty Muslim seats. In the elections to the provincial assemblies the Congress won 925 seats, gaining an absolute majority in eight provinces and constituting the largest single party in the remaining three. The Muslim League won 446 of the 495 Muslim seats, and formed ministries in two provinces, Bengal and Sind. In March ministries responsible to the newly elected provincial assemblies were formed in all the provinces.[12]

In March 1946, the British Government sent a Cabinet Mission to India, to assist the Viceroy 'in setting up in India the machinery by which Indians can devise their own constitution,' and to mediate between the Congress and the Muslim League. Two months later it released its plan to begin the constitution-making process, by constituting a Constituent Assembly by elections by the members of the newly-elected provincial assemblies, with seats allocated to three communal communities, namely Muslim, Sikh, and general, and to the Princely states, on a population basis. 'The most satisfactory method,' the Cabinet Mission stated, 'obviously would be by election based on adult franchise, but any attempt to introduce such a step would lead to a wholly unacceptable delay in the formulation of the new Constitution.'[13] Later ninety-three members would be selected to represent the Princely states, by methods to be agreed upon between the Assembly and the rulers of the states.

After detailed negotiations both the Congress and the Muslim League accepted the Cabinet Mission Plan, in spite of many reservations, and they participated in the elections to the Constituent Assembly, in July 1946. In the elections the Muslim League won all but seven of the seats reserved for Muslims. The Congress won 203 of the 212 general seats, and a total of 208 of the 296 seats in the Assembly. 'Although indirectly elected and therefore not responsible to the mass of Indians, the Constituent Assembly was a highly representative body.'[14] Almost immediately after the elections, Mohammed Ali Jinnah withdrew his support of the newly-elected Constituent Assembly, and instructed the representatives of the League to boycott it. Thus, while the elections in late 1945 and 1946 led to the establishment of new governments in the provinces of British India and to a Constituent Assembly for the purpose of framing a Constitution for a presumably united and independent India, they did not succeed in healing the rift between the Congress and the Muslim League, which eventually led to the partition of the subcontinent and the emergence of two independent states, instead of one.

Late in 1946, after a great deal of jockeying and extensive negotiations, with British representatives acting as intermediaries, a central cabinet, headed by Jawaharlal Nehru, with which the Muslim League refused to cooperate, assumed office, and on 9 December the Constituent Assembly, also without the participation of the Muslim League members, began to function. Not long after the League decided to cooperate in the new ministry (but not the Constituent Assembly) Mr. Attlee made the famous announcement that the British Government would withdraw from India by June 1948. On 3 June 1947, the new Viceroy, Lord Mountbatten, announced that the time-table for independence would be moved up to 15 August 1947, and that two states, not one, would be created in what had been British India and the India of the Princely states (to the extent that the Princely rulers would accede to one or the other of the new states).

Thus the stage was set for the partition of the subcontinent, with all its momentous consequences, and for the emergence of the new states of India and Pakistan. In the long and complicated story leading to this dénouement, the two principal actors were the British Government and the Indian National Congress, with the Muslim League gradually emerging as the spokesman of the majority of the Muslims of the subcontinent, a claim which it was really able to substantiate only after the Second World War. Elections, though on a limited scale, played a part in this story, being of hardly more than symbolic significance when first introduced in the Indian Councils Act of 1892 and somewhat extended in the Government of India Acts of 1901 and 1919; but the elections of 1937 and 1945–6, with a greatly enlarged though still limited electorate, are of central importance in the final pages of the story, leading to the transfer of power and to partition and independence.

The Constituent Assembly and Elections

Shortly after the historic British announcement of 3 June 1947, which decreed that partition was a necessary price of independence and which advanced the date of independence to mid-August, only ten weeks away, two committees of the Constituent Assembly made a basic decision which profoundly affected the nature of the electoral system, and therefore the political system, that free India would adopt. On 9 June the Union Constitution Committee agreed to recommend to the Constituent Assembly that elections to the lower House of the central legislature should be 'direct, on the basis of territorial constituencies, and by adult suffrage,' and at about the same time the Provincial Constitution Committee made a similar recommendation for elections to the lower Houses of the provincial legislatures.[15] These recommendations were revolutionary, in the context of the Indian political and social environment. They envisioned an electoral system that would be quite different from any that had prevailed before. During the last years of British rule, elections were conducted on a limited scale, with a restricted franchise, based mainly on property-holding and education, and with separate electorates and constituencies for certain minority groups, especially Muslims.

However revolutionary they were, these recommendations were in keeping with long-standing demands of the Indian National Congress. As early as 1931 the Congress adopted a resolution drafted by Jawaharlal Nehru, affirming that "The franchise shall be on the basis of universal adult franchise.' Again and again Nehru expressed his faith in a democratic system with a government chosen by the people on the basis of universal, direct suffrage, with no communal electorates.[16] In *The Discovery of India*, written during the Second World War, Nehru wrote: 'I am a convinced believer in adult franchise, for men and women; and though I realize the difficulties in the way, I am sure that the objections raised to its adoption in India have no great force and are based on the fears of privileged classes and interests.'[17] The Congress reluctantly agreed to waive its claims for the selection of members of a

Constituent Assembly on the basis of universal adult suffrage, because insistence on this would indefinitely delay the elections to such an Assembly, but it was determined that when India obtained its independence the principle of adult suffrage would be instituted immediately. Hence the recommendation of the Constitution Committees was both an affirmation of a long-held Congress position and a bold 'act of faith,' as the Election Commission described it in its report on the first nationwide general elections in 1951–2.[18]

When the members of the Constituent Assembly considered the legislative provisions of the Draft Constitution, from January to May 1949, they agreed quickly on the desirability of electing members of the lower house of the central legislature by direct, universal suffrage, by a single vote system and mainly in single-member constituencies. Thus a major decision was made with remarkably little opposition.[19] K. M. Panikkar, a member of the Assembly, later called adult suffrage the most striking feature of the Constitution.[20] The question of the reservation of seats for communal minorities was debated at greater length, and eventually it was agreed that separate electorates for communal groups, which had existed ever since 1909, should be abolished. Special provisions were made for Scheduled Castes, Scheduled Tribes, certain other 'backward classes' and minority groups, but not on the basis of separate electorates which give communalism statutory recognition. There was little support for the election of members of the lower House by proportional representation, as advocated by some members of the Assembly, but rather complicated forms of this rather complicated system were adopted for the election of members of the Council of States (the upper House of the national Parliament) and the Legislative Councils in those States which were to have an upper House, and also of the President and Vice President of India.

On 26 November 1949, the Constituent Assembly gave its final approval to the new Constitution of India, which had been drafted and debated with such scrupulous attention over a period of many months during the final stages of British rule and the early months of India's experience as an independent state. The Constitution entered into effect on 26 January 1950. On that day the Republic of India was born. Ever since, 26 January has been celebrated as India's Republic Day. Dr. Rajendra Prasad, who had presided over the Constituent Assembly, was sworn in as India's first President, Jawaharlal Nehru continued as the Prime Minister, and while the Constituent Assembly, having fulfilled its mission, ceased to exist, its members continued to function in their other capacity as members of the interim Parliament of the country, until a regular Parliament could be chosen in the first general elections. Preparations were immediately begun to hold these elections, but they were not held until some two years later, in late 1951 and early 1952.

Thus India entered upon its independent existence, first as a Dominion in the Commonwealth, with a Governor General, a Prime Minister, and an interim Parliament, and then as a Republic, still in the Commonwealth, with a President, a Prime Minister, and in due course a Parliament with a lower House chosen on the basis of direct, universal suffrage. From the beginning India's dedication to parliamentary democracy was a genuine and fundamental one, and in this democratic system nationwide elections played a central role.

India's General Elections

The five nationwide general elections in India between 1951 and 1971 were major events in the political history of independent India. They were impressive because of their massive scale, the relatively peaceful and efficient way in which they were conducted, and their consequences for the political system. Each election had interesting and distinctive characteristics, and each merits very special study and analysis. The cumulative impact of the elections should also be borne in mind, for collectively they have contributed to India's growing political maturity and development. Indeed, the routinization of the electoral process has been one of the most significant of India's political achievements.

The First General Elections, 1951–2. Quite naturally, the first general elections, in 1951–2, were attended by greater excitement and uncertainty than any of the following elections. They were an unfamiliar experience for both most of the voters and for the political parties. Never before had nationwide elections on the basis of universal suffrage been held in India; never before, in any country, had so many people participated in democratic elections; never before had so many illiterate people participated in direct national elections.

The first Indian general elections attracted worldwide interest, both because of their magnitude and uniqueness, and because they might provide some indication of the prospects for democracy in politically inexperienced, economically underdeveloped, and socially conservative developing countries. In its report on the first general elections the Election Commission of India observed that it was 'a great and fateful experiment unique in the world in its stupendousness and complexities. The carrying out of this unprecedented experiment attracted worldwide attention and journalists, politicians and other observers came from numerous foreign countries to study its working at first hand. . . . In fact, every country desiring to adopt parliamentary elections on adult franchise but . . . faced with difficulties in the shape of illiteracy, ignorance and undeveloped communications evinced the utmost interest in the Indian elections. . . . It appears probable that the main features of our system of elections will be adopted in future years by many of these countries.'[21]

Nehru and other Indian political leaders were well aware of the importance of the first general elections in setting standards for the future and as indicators of the strength – or weakness – of India's fledgling democracy. 'Nehru pointed out that it was the first election in India on a colossal scale and the standards set up would set a precedent and influence future elections and coming generations.'[22] The campaign preceding the voting was as much a massive effort to educate the voters as it was to win their allegiance to particular parties and candidates. Nehru himself was particularly active and effective in this respect.

The campaign was fought out more on the basis of parties and personalities than on issues. In a sense there were no real national issues, except the issue of support for or opposition to the ruling Congress Party and its charismatic leader, Jawaharlal Nehru. To put it in another way, Nehru himself was the issue, and his personality – as a famous cartoon by India's leading political cartoonist, Laxman of *The Times of India*, indicated – dominated the campaign and the elections. In elections to the State Assemblies local issues and grievances were important determinants of voting behavior, but even here many voters cast their ballots on the basis of their support for or opposition to Nehru and the Congress Party.

'Because of shortage of election officials and some special problems of geography and climate, the voting was scheduled at different times in different places, extending over a period of some four months, from 25 October 1951 to 21 February 1952, although most of the voters went to the polls in January 1952.'[23] On the whole, the elections went off well, in spite of some confusion because of ignorance and inexperience. The turnout varied greatly in different parts of the country. Altogether slightly more than half the eligible voters actually voted, a figure that has been surpassed in all but one of the subsequent general elections.

The election results revealed certain patterns and trends that have generally characterized the Indian political scene since independence, with some variations in the relative showing of the Congress and various opposition parties and with a more mixed and uncertain picture in the States. The elections confirmed the dominance of the Congress Party, and the weakness and fragmentation of the opposition parties. In the House of the People and in the State Assemblies the Congress won more than 70 per cent of all the seats, even though it received only about 45 per cent of the popular vote. In the House of the People it

'Burden of Personality' (R. K. Laxman in *The Times of India*).

won 364 of the 489 seats, whereas the most successful opposition parties – the Socialist Party, with 10.6 per cent of the votes, and the Communist Party of India, with 3.3 per cent – were able to get only twelve and sixteen seats, respectively. The Congress won a clear majority in all the twenty-two Part 'A', 'B' and 'C' States except Orissa, where a local conservative party, the Ganatantra Parishad, won almost as many seats, PEPSU (Patiala and East Punjab States Union), where it won only twenty-six out of sixty seats, Travancore-Cochin, where it got only 41 of 108 seats, and Madras, where the Communists in the Andhra area and pro-Dravidian groups in Tamilnad proved to be quite strong. In most subsequent elections in these States (except in PEPSU which was merged into the Punjab), the Congress has been unable to win a majority of seats in the Legislative Assemblies. They have been problem States for the Congress, as they were in 1951–2.

In its report on the first general elections the Election Commission stated: 'The successful completion of the general elections in India can be said to constitute an important land-mark in the history of democracy. Never before has such a vast electorate gone to the polls. The future of the democractic way to life in India depended very largely on the success of the experiment as also on the extent to which these elections would evoke public enthusiasm and satisfaction.'[24] Most observers seemed to be convinced that India's 'act of faith,' its 'tremendous experiment' in democracy, had paid off, and had demonstrated the soundness of the decision of the Constitution-makers to adopt the system of universal adult franchise immediately.

To some, however, the elections had raised doubts about the wisdom of this decision. Among these, strangely enough, appears to have been Jawaharlal Nehru, who had been one of the strongest champions of the basic decision in favor of universal adult suffrage and direct, secret elections. During the election campaign he had warned repeatedly against communalism and provincialism, and he had insisted that the candidates should be persons of integrity and quality. In an address at a UNESCO symposium in New Delhi on 20 December 1951, while the elections were under way, Nehru confessed that he was 'a little doubtful' whether the masses of the people were likely to select the right leaders through the electoral process. 'The quality of the men who are selected by these modern methods of adult franchise,' he said, 'gradually deteriorates because of lack of thinking and the noise of propaganda. . . . He [the voter] reacts to sound and to the din, he reacts to repetition and he produces either a dictator or a dumb politician who is insensitive.'[25] A few days later, he indicated to some journalists who were accompanying him on a campaign tour that he favored a combination of direct and indirect elections for India. 'In a country like ours,' he reasoned, 'with such large numbers, there should be some sort of indirect elections in the higher stages and direct elections in the lower stages. Direct election for such a vast number is a complicated problem and the candidate may never come in touch with the electorate and the whole thing becomes distant.'[26]

There is some evidence that Nehru continued to hold such views. In June 1956, for example, he was reported to have told a convention of Congress workers that 'The system of direct elections on a large scale had become very expensive and had created undesirable conditions in our political life,' and he suggested that 'elections should be direct at the base and indirect from there onwards.'[27] But in all probability these were theoretical musings, which Nehru seldom voiced publicly. Whatever his reservations about the desirability of direct elections on the basis of universal suffrage for his country, and whatever his fears about the effects of these elections in stirring up communal and other deep-rooted evils in Indian society, Nehru certainly made no effort to change the electoral system or to reverse the basic decision that had been made in 1947–9, with his enthusiastic support.

The Second General Elections, 1957. Between the first and second general elections, a number of important developments occurred in India that had a considerable bearing on the course of Indian politics and the evolution of the political system. In three States where the Congress had fared rather badly in the first general elections – in PEPSU, Travancore-Cochin and Andhra Pradesh (created a separate State in October 1953) – new State elections were held because of the unstable political situation, which led to the imposition of President's rule (direct rule by the central government) in PEPSU and the new State of Andhra Pradesh. In PEPSU the Congress won a clear majority. In Andhra Pradesh the Congress and its allies routed the Communists, gaining a decisive majority in the Legislative Assembly. In Travancore-Cochin, however, the Congress won only forty-five of the 117 seats and supported a minority government headed by the PSP until the spring of 1956, when President's rule was again imposed.[28] In January 1955, at its annual session at Avadi, the Congress passed its historic resolution which declared that its goal was 'the establishment of a socialistic pattern of society,' a goal to which it has adhered ever since.

On 1 November 1956, only a few weeks before the second general elections were held, when the election campaign was about to get under way, the political map of India was re-drawn by the reorganization of the Indian States, reducing their number from twenty-nine to fourteen, and abolishing the classification of the States into Part 'A', Part 'B', and Part 'C' States. Except in undivided Bombay State and to a lesser degree in the Punjab, the reorganization helped to satisfy the linguistic groups in each of the newly created States, so that for some time, at least, linguistic issues were not as important as they had appeared to be prior to the reorganization. As later developments showed, however, linguism is one of the deep-seated and emotionally-loaded issues in Indian society and it has kept reappearing in politics, as in Indian life generally.

The second general elections were held during a period of three weeks, from 24 February to 14 March 1957. Preparation for these elections was an easier task than for the first general elections, even though the electorate had increased by nearly 20,000,000, for much of the basic work had been done and many of the basic decisions had been made in preparing for the 1951–2 elections. 'Even more than in 1951–2 the second general election was an election without issues, as far as national politics were concerned.'[29] On State and local levels, however, a number of issues did exist, especially in undivided Bombay, where nearly all the opposition parties in the Maharashtra area joined in a united front called the Samyukhta Maharashtra Samiti to press the demand for a separate State of Maharashtra, and where many of the opposition parties in the Gujarat area formed a looser arrangement called the Mahagujarat Janata Parishad to champion the demand for a separate state of Gujarat.

In addition to electoral alliances and arrangements in several other states, some influential local parties were active in particular States, notably the Ganatantra Parishad in Orissa, the Dravida Munnetra Kazhagam in Madras, and the Akali Dal in the Punjab. The CPI showed signs of greater strength and activity in several States, mainly Kerala and West Bengal. In Andhra Pradesh it was still trying to recover from the route which it experienced at the hands of the Congress in the State elections of 1955.

Except in a few States the campaign was far less exciting and meaningful than it had been in 1951–2. Nehru himself, who had devoted weeks to tireless campaigning in the earlier period, was much less active in electioneering in 1956–7. Apparently he also took much less interest in the outcome of the elections, perhaps because he was fairly sure this time of an overwhelming Congress victory, but also possibly because he was rather disappointed with the electoral experience of five years before. On one occasion during the campaign he said, 'With all our strength I am sure we can win. But I really do not care much if we win or lose.'[30]

'In 1957 the Indian people voted with more confidence and, presumably, with greater understanding and judgment than they had in 1951–2. Many of the fears and suspicions which had kept thousands of eligible voters from registering properly, or from casting valid ballots, were removed by 1957.'[31] But only 47.54 per cent of the 193 million eligible voters actually cast their ballots, an even lower turnout than in 1951–2. The results of the elections did not change the basic political complexion of India, at either national or State levels. The Congress got 47.66 per cent of the popular vote, and 371 of the 489 seats in the House of the People (the Lok Sabha). It lost between 300 and 400 seats in State Legislative Assemblies, but it still retained a clear majority in the Assemblies of every State except Kerala and Orissa. In several other states, such as Bombay, Bihar, Uttar Pradesh, and West Bengal, its losses were significant, but they were not great enough to challenge the Congress hold on these States.[32] What they did do was to put pressure on the Congress to redress the grievances that had led to appreciable attrition in Congress support.

One result of the 1957 elections attracted particular attention, not only in India but throughout the world. In Kerala the CPI, with a popular vote less than that of the Congress, won sixty seats in the

(R. K. Laxman in *The Times of India*)

Legislative Assembly, as compared to forty-three for the Congress, and with the help of five Independents whom it had supported it was able to form a government in that State. The Communist Government in Kerala lasted for only two years. In 1959 it was dismissed abruptly by the central Government of India, amid charges and counter-charges of the most extreme kind:[33] But it attracted widespread attention because it was the first Communist government to be formed in any unit of any democratic state, and its performance was therefore watched with particularly close attention. Was it to prove to be the wave of the future, or a colossal fiasco, or a warning of the consequences of permitting Communists to come into power in a democracy, even in a limited part of the nation through the normal democratic process of a free election?

On the whole, there was a general feeling that Indian democracy was stronger after the second general elections, that the successful conduct of its second mass experiment in democracy had confirmed the positive impact of the first. In its report on the second general elections the Election Commission of India declared: 'If the first general elections served to teach the vast number of uneducated voters what the vote means, the second general elections familiarized them with the exercise thereof with discrimination and understanding.'[34] Some observers, however, held a more critical view. To them the second elections had revealed some alarming trends in the Indian political system. Typical of this school of thought was a commentary in the Royist journal, *The Radical Humanist*:

> First, the prestige and strength of the Congress is steadily declining. It has lost its hold in urban–industry areas, and more particularly over the middle class. . . . Secondly, there is no powerful democratic alternative to the Congress. . . . The 'shift in the mass mood toward radicalisation' will continue, and the CPI with its militant organization, effective techniques of manipulating mass-psychology and an alluring radical programme appears . . . as the most potent threat to democracy and freedom. . . . If the elections have any lesson to offer, it is that the future of democracy in this country is dark, because appreciation of its values is lamentably lacking.[35]

The Third General Elections, 1962. Between the second and third general elections an important State election was held in Kerala in 1960. After the Communist Government in that State had been dismissed in July 1959, President's rule was imposed and new elections were called. The results were very different from those in 1957, largely because the Congress formed an electoral alliance with the PSP and the Muslim League, and because the policies and actions of the Communist Government from 1957 to 1959 had alienated many voters. Although the Communists increased their share of the popular vote, and in fact received more votes than the Congress, their membership in the Assembly dropped from sixty to twenty-six, while the Congress won sixty-three seats, the PSP twenty and the Muslim League thirteen.[36]

On the national scene a new and uncertain factor was introduced by the abrupt change in India's relations with China in 1959 and thereafter, as a result of the ruthless Chinese suppression of the revolt in Tibet, the flight of the Dalai Lama to India, clashes between Indian and Chinese troops along the northern borders, the revelation for the first time of long-standing difficulties with China, China's refusal to accept the McMahon Line as the border between India and China in the North East Frontier Agency area, the building of a road by China across the Aksai Chin region of Ladakh and the stationing of Chinese troops in that area, which India claimed to be a part of its territory.

The effects of these traumatic events on the elections seemed uncertain. On the one hand, they might lead the Indian voters to rally even more strongly to the support of Nehru and the Congress Government; on the other, they might lead many voters to turn against leaders who had concealed the facts of the deteriorating relations with

China and who seemed impotent to stem the Chinese advances. At any rate, the new and mounting crisis with China was a grim backdrop for the third general elections. At home there seemed to be other reasons for sober reassessment, such as the rather unsatisfactory results of the Second Five Year Plan (1956–61) and the greater prominence of caste factors in the selection of candidates and in the election campaign.

(R. K. Laxman in *The Times of India*)

All of these considerations seemed to have little effect on the election results, which were substantially similar to those in the two previous elections.[37] The Congress lost over ten seats in the Lok Sabha, and its percentage of the popular vote declined by about three points. It won a clear majority in all the States except Madhya Pradesh.

Some observers fancied that they saw evidences of a swing to the right in the election results, for the new conservative Swatantra Party won twenty-two seats in the Lok Sabha and the rightist Jana Sangh increased its membership from four to fourteen, whereas the PSP lost seven seats. The CPI, however, increased its membership by two seats, and remained the leading opposition party in the Lok Sabha. All of these opposition parties had such insignificant representation as compared with the Congress that changes in seats held could make little difference in the ideological coloration of Indian politics.

Later elections certainly refuted the thesis of a rightist trend in India. In 1967 the Swatantra and Jana Sangh scored further electoral successes, but so did most other opposition parties; and in 1971 all major opposition parties except the Communists (both wings) suffered severe reverses. In general there seems to have been a trend toward the left and an increasing radicalisation in Indian politics, but this trend is revealed more by changes in the balance of forces within the Congress Party and by the increasing radicalisation of the Indian voters as a result of many deep-seated factors than by any shifts or swings in the representation of the major opposition parties in the Lok Sabha.

The Fourth General Elections, 1967. 'The 1962 elections were the last of the Nehru era, the last to conceal the changes which were taking place in Indian politics – changes which were leading to the slow erosion of Congress strength without a corresponding increase in strength in any other parties of national importance. These changes became more evident only after the traumatic events of the following years, notably the Chinese attack of late 1962 and the Indian reverses, the death of Nehru [in May 1964], the war with Pakistan in 1965, and the bad seasons and economic setbacks of the mid-1960s; and they were dramatically highlighted in the fourth general elections in 1967.'[38]

'The campaign preceding the elections was held in an atmosphere of despondency, frustration, and almost continuous agitation.'[39] So bad did the law and order situation appear to be that some observers believed that the elections would have to be postponed, or possibly could not be held at all. Even when it was apparent that they would be held as scheduled, the gloomy predictions continued. The South Asian correspondent of *The Times* caused a minor sensation by his flat assertion that these would be 'surely the last' elections to be held in India.[40]

In the fourth general elections the main issues were economic and psychological. Almost everyone complained of the food shortage and rising prices, and many deplored the Government's decision, in the summer of 1966, allegedly under foreign pressure, to devalue the rupee, which seemed to have negative effects in India. Psychologically, the swing away from the Congress, which had been under way for some time, became a major factor in the campaign. Whereas in the past a Congress candidate had a distinct advantage, and could count on a kind of plus factor – or on what the Indian Institute of Public Opinion labeled a 'Multiplier' effect – in many States, in the fourth general elections anti-Congress sentiment was so strong that Congress candidates labored under a special psychological handicap. Even Mrs. Gandhi, Nehru's daughter, who had become Prime Minister on the sudden death of Lal Bahadur Shastri in January 1966, could do little to stem the anti-Congress tide. The contrast between her relative political ineffectiveness in 1967 and her amazing success four years later is truly remarkable.

(R. K. Laxman in *The Times of India*)

Because of the trend away from the Congress, the hitherto dominant party suffered severe losses at both local and national levels. Its share of the popular vote fell by some five percentage points; its representation in the Lok Sabha fell from 361 to 283 seats; and it failed to win a majority of the seats in the Assemblies of eight States, containing two-fifths of the population of the country. It suffered particularly severe reverses in Bihar, Kerala, Madras, the Punjab, and West Bengal. In Kerala it was able to keep only one Lok Sabha seat, and in the State Assembly it won only nine of the 133 seats, making it even ineligible for recognition as an opposition party. Many of its top political leaders, including the President of the Congress, nine Union Ministers, and four Chief Ministers, were defeated. The two major conservative parties, Swatantra and Jana Sangh, significantly increased their membership in the Lok Sabha – Swatantra from eighteen to forty-four and Jana Sangh from fourteen to thirty-five – and became the two leading opposition parties in the Lok Sabha. The leftist opposition parties fared almost as well. The SSP membership rose from six to twenty-three, the PSP from twelve to thirteen, and while the CPI lost six seats the new Communist Party of India (Marxist) won nineteen, thus increasing the Communist representation in the Lok Sabha from twenty-nine to forty-two. One State party – the DMK of Madras – won twenty-five seats in the Lok Sabha, making it the third largest opposition party on a national scale, an ironic situation for a party that at one time had espoused strongly secessionist goals.[41]

Except in Madras, the sharp Congress reverses were occasioned as much by unusually effective opposition electoral alliances as by the anti-Congress swing in the country. No national pattern could be discerned in these alliances, for they differed in every State where they were formed, and, as the experience of various kinds of coalition governments in several States was soon to demonstrate, none had any real cohesion or more than temporary popular support.

The election results seemed to confirm the reality of swing away from the Congress, and the loss by the Congress of the support of some key groups which in the past had faithfully supported it. This change was summarized shortly after the fourth general elections by E. P. W. da Costa, managing director of the Indian Institute of Public Opinion: 'The Indian electorate, believed inert and incapable of independent dramatic choice between sophisticated political alternatives, has exhibited marks of revolutionary change. The young, . . . the less educated, . . . the minorities, particularly the Muslims and the Sikhs and perhaps at last the lowest income groups whose patience is wearing thin are rewriting their basic loyalties.'[42] To this extent, as has been noted, the fourth general elections seemed to have been a 'critical' election, to borrow Professor V. O. Key's phrase again, for it seemed to lead to basic realignments in the Indian political system; but events were soon to prove that the realignments were only temporary, and that the elections could more properly be described as 'deviating' than as 'critical' or 'realigning'.

Certainly the Indian political scene was changed dramatically as a result of the fourth general elections. They seemed to mark the end of the long period of one-party dominance, and to usher in a period of 'competitive dominance,' to use Rajni Kothari's term, characterized by weak, coalition governments, shifting political alignments, and an increasing degree of political instability and confusion. In the year following the elections 'one out of every seven legislators in the States . . . changed his political affiliation at least once,'[43] and some changed several times. 'In the same period there were fourteen changes of governments in the States, four of them in a single State (Bihar). In 1967–9 six of the Indian States were under President's Rule for varying lengths of time. At one time nine of the seventeen States had non-Congress governments. All but one (Madras) were coalition governments of many different complexions. With few exceptions the coalition regimes proved to be quite unstable, and many of them soon fell, giving way to Congress governments, to other coalitions, or to President's Rule, which after February 1967 was a recurrent phenomenon in Indian political life.'[44]

Mid-Term Elections, 1969, and Congress Split. In May 1968, President's Rule was ended in Haryana through a mid-term election, which gave the Congress a majority of the seats in the Legislative Assembly and enabled it to form a government. In February 1969, mid-term elections were held in four more States – Bihar, the Punjab, Uttar Pradesh, and West Bengal – and the Union Territory of Pondicherry, all of which had been under President's Rule, and in Nagaland. These mid-term elections, involving two-fifths of the entire Indian electorate and a major part of the Hindi 'heartland', did little to clarify the political situation in the States where elections were held or to revive the Congress fortunes.[45] They led to a weak Congress government, which was short-lived, in Bihar, and to anti-Congress governments, most of which soon experienced political difficulties, in the Punjab, U. P., and West Bengal.

In the latter State the Congress was virtually routed in the mid-term election. Even though its popular vote did not decline precipitously, its strength in the Legislative Assembly fell from 127 to fifty-five, whereas that of the CIP(M) increased from forty-three to eighty, of the CPI from sixteen to thirty, and of the Forward Bloc from thirteen to twenty-one. A United Front consisting of fourteen parties, headed by the CPI(M) and including the CPI, engineered the electoral debacle of the Congress, and formed a government which for a year gave West Bengal a strong dose of political radicalism, mixed with infiltration of the civil service and the police and a high degree of terrorism in both rural and urban areas.[46] In this case elections, used by the Communists to achieve their revolutionary goals in a democratic society, seemed to be instrumental in contributing not to political development but to political decay.

The mid-term elections of 1969 seemed to confirm the trends toward coalition governments and political instability. There was even considerable speculation about the possibility of a coalition government at the Center. This speculation increased as a result of the sensational split in the ruling Congress Party a few months after the 1969 mid-term elections. The long simmering differences between the 'old guard' of the Party, led by the so-called 'Syndicate' (a group of long-time Congress bosses), and the group led by Prime Minister Indira Gandhi came out into the open in the summer of 1969 in the selection of the next President of India (to succeed Dr. Zakir Husain, who died in May of that year). At the last moment Mrs. Gandhi threw her support to Dr. V. V. Giri, the Vice President, who had been denied the Congress nomination, against the official Congress candidate, Sanjiva Reddy. Dr. Giri was elected by a narrow margin. This led to an open break. In early November Mrs. Gandhi and her followers were expelled from the Congress Party by a divided High Command. She promptly formed her own Congress Party, which became variously known as the Congress (R), the 'R' standing for Requisitionist, the 'New Congress,' or in common parlance as the Congi (the Indira Congress), whereas the other wing of the party became known as the Congress (O), with the 'O' standing for Organization, or the 'Old Congress,' or the Congo (the Old or Organization Congress). As a result of these developments the Indian National Congress, in the form in which it had evolved from its founding in 1885 to the Gandhi and Nehru era and beyond, ceased to exist, and in its place two bitterly hostile parties, each claiming to be the real Congress Party, the real heirs of Gandhi and Nehru, came into existence.

It soon became apparent that Mrs. Gandhi's wing of the divided Congress had greater popular support by far than the Organization Congress; but even though she had the support of most of the Congress members of the Lok Sabha, her party did not have a majority of the Lok Sabha seats, and her overall political position was uncertain. In various ways, including the championing of such popular measures as the nationalization of banks and the abolition of the privy purses for the former ruling princes and astute political maneuvering, she was able to develop a very positive image for herself and her party, while the Organization Congress found itself increasingly labeled as a conservative, boss-ridden remnant, out of touch with the people, the needs of the country, and the spirit of the times.

The Fifth General Elections, 1971. In late December 1970, Mrs. Gandhi decided to hold general elections about a year before the scheduled date, and to appeal to the people for a 'fresh mandate' to ensure the 'proper and effective implementation of our secularist socialist policies and programs through democratic processes.' Thus she put her own prestige and political future on the line. In a sense she was herself the only real issue, for the election was fought on the basis of support for or opposition to her and her program. The political spotlight was focussed even more sharply on her because she towered so far above any other leaders in her party, and because the major opposition to her – a misnamed 'Grand Alliance' of the Congress (O), Swatantra, the Jana Sangh, and the SSP – tried to counteract her very appealing slogan of *Garibi hatao*! (Abolish poverty) by the slogan *Indira hatao*! (Remove Indira, or Indira must go). She took an active role in the selection of candidates, often by-passing leaders of her own party at various levels who presumably controlled the 'vote banks' and the party machinery, and she personally directed the strategy of the campaign and took a very active part in it.

The campaign was marked by a higher incidence of violence than any previous campaign. Since the fifth general elections were the first to be held since the Congress split, the first before the expiration of the normal five year term of the Lok Sabha, and the first to 'de-link' the national and State elections (only three States – Orissa, Tamil Nadu, and West Bengal – held State elections concurrently with the national election), and since it was difficult to estimate the intangible effects of the 'Indira wave,' there was more than the usual uncertainty about the election results.

Contrary to most predictions, Mrs. Gandhi scored a sweeping victory in the elections. Her party increased its representation in the Lok Sabha by 130 seats, giving it nearly three fourths of all the Lok Sabha seats. Only in Gujarat, Kerala, Nagaland, Tamil Nadu, and West Bengal did it fail to get more than half of the Lok Sabha seats. All major opposition parties except the CPI(M), whose strength was limited mainly to West Bengal, and the CPI, which won no more than five seats in any State, lost heavily. In the three State elections the New Congress greatly increased its representation in West Bengal, but it still won fewer seats than the CPI(M), and the political uncertainty in that State continued; it won fifty-one seats in Orissa, but two opposition parties, the Utkal Congress and Swatantra, won sixty-eight seats between them; and in Tamil Nadu it did not contest the State election, in return for DMK support for some of its Lok Sabha candidates.[47]

The fifth general elections clearly gave Mrs. Gandhi the 'fresh mandate' that she had sought. It gave her a virtually impregnable position in the Indian political scene, thus ending the period of minority government and political uncertainty, and in a sense marking the return of a system of one-party dominance, but in a different form from that enjoyed by the undivided Congress in the Nehru era. Because of the crisis with Pakistan which became acute immediately after the fifth general elections – with the beginning of the ruthless actions of the Pakistani troops in East Bengal – she had a temporary reprieve from the task of implementing her sweeping pledge to abolish poverty; and her firm leadership in dealing with the many problems created by the crisis with Pakistan, including the presence of millions of refugees from East Bengal in India and the war with Pakistan in December 1971, gave her even greater popular support and power.

Many Indian commentators have pointed out that the 1971 elections

(R. K. Laxman in *The Times of India*)

gave India the political stability and the strength that it needed to meet the crisis of 1971. Typical of this interpretation is the year-end observation of the editor of *The Times of India*:

> The year which is drawing to a close has been a year of decision for India. Never since 1947 has it been swept by so strong a gale of change. The political system has proved its strength in the gravest crisis the country has had to face in the 24 years of its independence. It was lucky for it that it had held a general election on the very eve of the great tragedy in Bangla Desh. Without the massive backing at the polls, the Government wouldn't have had the grit to liberate it in the teeth of opposition from China and the U.S.[48]

State Assembly Elections, 1972, and Aftermath. In the aftermath of military victory and in the resulting atmosphere of euphoria, elections were held in 16 Indian States and two Union Territories in March, 1972. As in the general elections of 1971 the 'Indira wave' proved again to be irresistible. Again Mrs. Gandhi had a major hand in the selection of Congress candidates and in the conduct of the campaign. Again she dominated the campaign. She appealed to the Indian voters for 'a fresh mandate – this time from the States,' and again the people responded to her appeal. The Congress won more than 70 per cent of the 2,727 Assembly seats – a gain of 544 – and a clear majority of seats in all the major States and the Union Territory of Delhi (where it had previously been in a minority position). The 1972 elections 'seemed to confirm what the 1971 elections had indicated, that in some States, notably Gujarat, Mysore, the Punjab, and West Bengal, a basic political change, amounting almost to a political revolution and a shift in basic political loyalties, had occurred.'[49]

As in all general elections, the Congress won its impressive showing in legislative representation with less than a majority of the popular vote; but no opposition party received even 9 per cent of the vote. Indeed, all opposition parties were left with only localized pockets of strength, and were highly fragmented. Thanks to electoral alliances with the Congress the CPI made a respectable showing in Bihar and West Bengal; the CPI(M) got thirty of its thirty-five seats in Tripura and West Bengal; the limited Congress (O) support was confined mainly to Bihar, Gujarat, Mysore, and U.P., and the Jana Sangh support mainly to Bihar, M.P., and U.P.; Swatantra got eleven of its eighteen seats in Rajasthan; and the Socialists made a respectable showing only in Bihar. Thus the 1972 State Assembly elections confirmed the results of the 1971 elections, highlighting the preeminence of the Congress and the weakness and regional character of the major opposition parties at State as well as national levels.[50]

(R. K. Laxman in *The Times of India*)

With the crisis with Pakistan successfully resolved, and with her new electoral mandate, Mrs. Gandhi was in a strong position to turn to the problems of political and economic development that still faced her. 'Among these problems were those of dealing with the factionalism, and dissension within several Congress State parties, notably Andhra Pradesh and Gujarat, and of assuring adequate cooperation and support from the States for the radical measures which were called for to implement the party's election pledges. Clearly the test of performance could not be long delayed.'[51] In her message to the nation on the occasion of the 25th anniversary of India's independence, on 15 August 1972, Mrs. Gandhi stressed the economic problems rather than the political achievements. 'Democracy,' she said, 'has come to stay and has proved itself. But economic freedom in the shape of economic self-reliance of the nation and also improvement in the daily lives of our common people has yet to be achieved.'[52]

Because of the continuing economic problems Indians celebrated the 25th anniversary of independence in a mood of austerity; but there could be no mistaking the spirit of renewed self-confidence and expectation, the product of the developments of the past year and a half. Some Indians wondered about the effects of these heady developments upon the democratic system; but most seemed to agree with the editor of *The Times of India* that 'Mrs. Gandhi has given the political system a new lease of life and a new vigour.'[53]

State Assembly Elections, 1974. Having reached the commanding heights of political power, as reflected in her electoral triumphs in 1971 and 1972, Mrs. Gandhi was soon faced with new challenges and new problems. Her efforts to implement her electoral pledges seemed limited and ineffective. Her party was held together largely by her leadership and charisma, and it was bedeviled by internal divisions, factional and personal rivalries, inept leadership at most levels, and widespread corruption. A real 'crisis of confidence' again set in on the political front, and the economic situation further deteriorated.

By late 1973 and early 1974 the country seemed to be in the throes of both an economic and a political crisis, featured by growing economic distress, caused by droughts, shortages of basic foodgrains, and serious inflation (aggravated by the adverse consequences of the oil embargo in the fall of 1973 and higher prices for oil and other vital products), by growing criticisms of the government in power, centering on failures to live up to election pledges and charges of widespread corruption, and by growing frustration and unrest, often taking the form of violence and other threats to the existing system.

Mrs. Gandhi and the Congress Party were therefore in a considerably weakened position as they prepared for 'mini-general elections' in the latter half of February 1974 in four States, including the most populous of all the Indian States and the home State of Mrs. Gandhi, Uttar Pradesh, and one Union Territory, with a total electorate of almost 50 million people. In early 1974 the Congress suffered a series of reverses in by-elections to the Lok Sabha and to Legislative Assemblies in several States, notably Maharashtra and Gujarat. In Gujarat, once one of the most stable of Indian States, large-scale food riots and violence led to many deaths, the fall of the Congress government headed by a Chief Minister who had been hand-picked by Mrs. Gandhi, the dissolution of the Legislative Assembly, and the imposition of President's Rule.

In Uttar Pradesh the Congress Chief Minister was replaced shortly before the February elections, in a last-minute move by Mrs. Gandhi to give her party a more favorable image in her own State. Even this step seemed unlikely to prevent a Congress debacle in India's largest State. But as the date of the elections approached, a number of factors helped to brighten the prospects of the Congress. In addition to the appointment of a new and more popular Chief Minister, these included

Mrs. Gandhi's indefatigible campaigning in all parts of the State, featuring the inauguration of many development projects and other visible material benefits, a Congress alliance with the CPI, the weakness of the opposition parties and their failure to work out any effective anti-Congress alliances, and Mrs. Gandhi's successful appeals to depressed and minority groups, notably the Scheduled Castes and the Muslims. As a result the Congress was able to maintain a slim majority in the U.P. Legislative Assembly, even though it lost nearly sixty seats and its popular vote declined by one-third, as compared to 1971. It still won twice as many seats as its chief rival, the BKD (an anti-Congress coalition which at one time had been able to form a government in U.P.), and no other party got more than sixteen seats in an Assembly of 425 members.

In Orissa, which had been under President's Rule, the results were also more favorable to the Congress than had been anticipated. While the Congress fell five seats short of a majority in the Assembly, its sixty-nine seats were more than twice the combined totals of its leading opponents, the Utkal Congress and the Swatantra Party, and it received 37 per cent of the popular vote, an increase of 9 per cent over 1971. With the support of the seven CPI members, a Congress ministry was formed after the elections.

In Nagaland the Nagaland Nationalist Organization, which had been continuously in power since the State was formed in 1963, and which had generally cooperated with the Congress Government in India, was narrowly defeated by the United Democratic Front, which had links with the underground 'federal government' and which with the support of several Independents was able to form a government. In Manipur a united front of the two leading local parties defeated a Congress-CPI alliance. In Pondicherry the DMK, which had broken away from the ruling DMK in Tamil Nadu, won twelve of the thirty Assembly seats, the Congress and the Congress (O), which cooperated for the first time anywhere in India, won seven and five seats respectively, and the DMK got only two seats.

Thus the fortunes of the Congress and Mrs. Gandhi changed considerably between 1972 and 1974. In spite of many evidences of growing disillusionment and frustration with its performance, the Congress fared better in the 'mini-general elections' in 1974 than most observers had predicted. This outcome was certainly no enthusiastic endorsement of Mrs. Gandhi and the Congress, as the elections of 1971 and 1972 had been, but rather was an indication of the solid support base of the Congress and of the absence of any viable and credible alternative in most States. The election results of 1974 left the Congress in a somewhat weaker position, but they did not reflect the extent of the unrest and distress in the country.[54] Perhaps, as one perceptive

Indian journalist observed, 'The voters had given perhaps the last chance to the Congress to retrieve its position between now and 1976.'[55]

Reflections on India's Electoral Experience

India's electoral experience has been by no means confined to five huge nationwide general elections, and three major mid-term State elections; but these have been the most conspicuous and important electoral exercises in India, or indeed in any other developing country.

Elections have clearly been central to the Indian political system. Their routinization has solidified their importance and role in the system, although it has also lessened the excitement of the electoral experience. Some of the excitement has remained, for the novelty has not really worn off, especially as large numbers of new voters enter the political system. Moreover, elections in India have always been more than just important political events; they have been a kind of national festival, or *tamasha*, a source of entertainment, education, and excitement for countless millions of people.

In a rather unfavorable social environment, the bold 'act of faith' of giving the franchise to all citizens of India and holding regular direct secret elections on the basis of adult suffrage has apparently paid off, especially when one compares India's experience with free, democratic, and direct elections with that of other developing countries that have tried all kinds of more limited and more indirect forms of popular participation or that have experimented tentatively with general elections without accepting the will of the people as expressed through the ballot box and without making elections central and routinized institutions of the political system. In India today there are few influential groups or individuals who are openly opposed to free direct, democratic elections, whatever their reservations about them. It seems likely that they are now so entrenched in the Indian political system that they cannot be abandoned, or even made less central to the system, without weakening the system itself. Few would deny that they are central to the Indian political process, or that they have contributed to the political development of India in many tangible and intangible ways.

This optimistic assessment must be qualified by a recognition of growing doubts and fears. By 1974 many concerned observers were calling attention to the growing anomie and alienation in the country. Disillusion with Mrs. Gandhi and the Congress and desperate economic circumstances gave rise to doubts about the efficacy and desirability of the political system itself. Demands for reform in the electoral system were voiced more frequently than ever before.[56] A prominent Indian journalist observed after the 1974 elections: 'The people may not have lost faith . . . in the electoral process. But it has been shaken rather rudely.'[57] A more basic question was whether people were losing faith in the democratic system. Another leading Indian journalist, in the post-election period of reflection and reassessment in 1974, reported that 'doubts about the country being able to overcome its mounting difficulties under the present system of parliamentary government are spreading. More and more people are coming to feel that the system is too corrupt, too divisive, too undisciplined, to lead anywhere but downhill. The sceptic has plenty of evidence to support this view.' But, asked this seasoned observer, 'is that the entire picture? The question is vital because the achievements of the system are apt to be overshadowed, if not completely overlooked, especially at such times.'[58]

7

THE ELECTORAL EXPERIENCE OF PAKISTAN, CEYLON, AND NEPAL

The varied electoral experience in the other countries of South Asia provides interesting comparisons and contrasts with the Indian experience. A brief analysis of this experience, in the heartland of the Third World, should suggest some broader perspectives for the comparative study of elections and political development in more general and more conceptual terms.

Variations in Electoral Experience in South Asia

Pakistan's electoral experience has been quite different from India's. This is hardly surprising in view of the very different political systems that have evolved in the two countries. India has retained the same political system since independence, and in spite of some gloomy prophets that system seems to be firmly established and likely to endure. Secret elections on the basis of universal adult suffrage – and especially direct, nationwide general elections – have been central mechanisms of the political system; as a result of extensive and successful experience they have become routinized features of the political order.

Pakistan, on the other hand, has experimented with three different kinds of political systems, and it is now embarked on a fourth political experiment. All of the past systems seemed to work for a time, but eventually broke down. In none of them did elections play a central role. In the first political experiment, under a distorted version of parliamentary democracy, elections were held only on a provincial basis, for provincial Assemblies. Nearly a decade passed before independent Pakistan got a new Constitution; and while this Constitution provided for free, democratic elections on the basis of universal adult franchise, these elections were never held.

The October 1958 'revolution' ended the first political experiment and ushered in the second, a decade of martial law and 'guided democracy' under Ayub Khan. Under the ingenious system of 'Basic Democracy', which Ayub instituted, the Basic Democrats – members of the basic units of the BD system, numbering originally 80,000 and eventually 120,000 in both wings of the country – were directly elected on a universal suffrage basis, but they were then used as an 'electoral college' to choose the members of the provincial Assemblies, the National Assembly, and the President of Pakistan. The most interesting and eventful election under the BD system was the presidential election of 1965, which had some novel and rather surprising features; but this had little impact on the controlled political system, and it was certainly not central to it.

For many years Ayub Khan seemed not only to control the instruments of power but also to have considerable popular support; but like many strong rulers, however benevolent and well-intentioned some of them may have been, he failed to give his strong rule a solid institutional base, and to provide for succession and continuity. In the end he was forced to step down. Instead of transferring power to more democratically inclined leaders, who admittedly were hard to find among the top leaders of Pakistan in 1969, he transferred power to another military man, Yahya Khan.

Yahya's short-lived political experiment began with the reimposition of martial law and with generally repressive tactics; but he gave increasing evidence that he was sincere in his pledge to be only an interim ruler and to take steps to give Pakistan a new and more genuinely democratic system. In his Legal Framework Order of 30 March 1970, he laid down the framework of that order, and the steps by which it would be brought into being. The first major step was a nationwide general election – the first free, direct, nationwide election in the history of Pakistan – with the franchise vested in all adult citizens. This election was held in December 1970, and seemed to be free, fair, and successful; but it tended further to polarize the politics of the country on a regional basis, and instead of leading to the further steps contemplated under the Legal Framework Order it was followed by a political impasse, bloody repression and civil war in East Pakistan, the break-up of the country, military defeat by India, and the emergence of the new nation of Bangladesh. In the aftermath of these tragic and traumatic events a new political experiment, under Zulfikar Ali Bhutto, began in the remaining part of Pakistan – formerly West Pakistan. The Constitution of 1973 provides for a parliamentary instead of a presidential system and the election of members of the National Assembly and of the provincial Assemblies on the basis of universal adult franchise. According to both the letter of the Constitution and the professions of Mr. Bhutto elections will have a central place in Pakistan's new political system.

Bangladesh began as a parliamentary system and then, on January 25, 1975, became a presidential system, by an amendment to the

Constitution of 1972. National elections on the basis of universal adult franchise were held successfully in March 1973. As long as the present Constitution is in effect and the present leaders are in power it seems fairly certain that free, direct elections will have a central place in the evolving political system of Bangladesh.

Universal adult suffrage and free, direct elections were introduced in Ceylon nearly twenty years before they were incorporated, for the first time, in the Indian Constitution of 1950. Ceylon (now Sri Lanka) has held more nation-wide elections since independence than has India, and, unlike India, some of these elections have led to the peaceful transfer of power through the electoral process from one party, or coalition, to another. But, of course, Ceylon's elections have been on nothing like the scale of India's mammoth general elections, and in spite of Ceylon's impressive record in staging frequent general elections successfully the general political, as well as economic and social, outlook is by no means bright, and the future of the present political system seems to be quite unclear.

Nepal presents a very different and more limited kind of electoral experience. Before the 'revolution' of 1950–1 and its partial emergence into the modern world it was a closed kingdom under the feudal rule of the Ranas, with politics being largely confined to the court intrigues and rivalries of various members of the Rana family, and without even the pretense of a popular base of support, except through controlled forms of support of the regime.

After the 'revolution' King Tribhuvan allowed political parties to function in a peculiarly Nepalese way, and some of his governments were presumably formed on an essentially party basis; but while he gave some hints of a willingness to consider the establishment of free institutions, including free, democratic elections, he never even approached the hour of fulfilment of his vaguely worded promises. His son and successor, King Mahendra, was presumably a more modern monarch, and in 1959 he permitted the first – and only – nationwide general election in Nepal's history. This led to a decisive victory for the Nepali Congress under B. P. Koirala, and to the establishment of a parliamentary system, at least in form, with a Nepali Congress government nominally responsible to the elected Parliament. But this experiment was too heady wine for King Mahendra, especially since he feared that the elected government headed by B. P. Koirala was really scheming to abolish the monarchy; and in December 1960, he abruptly and unceremoniously terminated the brief experiment in parliamentary democracy. Gradually the outlines of his alternative system of guided democracy, which he termed 'Panchayat democracy', emerged. This was a centrally controlled system, even though direct elections for members of the basic units of the system and indirect elections for higher bodies, up to the 'National Panchayat', were provided for. When King Mahendra died in 1972, his son Birendra carried on in the same way, retaining all effective power in his own hands.

Under the kind of political system – or systems – that Nepal has had, elections at first had no place whatever, and then only a minor place, mostly of a symbolic nature, supportive of the monarchy. The general elections of 1959 were an interesting but unique deviation from the prevailing pattern of control, and the parliamentary democracy that emerged from them had shallow roots and was soon uprooted. Elections under the system of 'Panchayat democracy' have been of greater symbolic than actual importance, and in general the Nepalese political system has continued to be far too centralized, and far too much under the control of the monarch, to permit elections to be of any great significance, except as a symbolic instrument and as one of several means – and by no means the most meaningful – of legitimizing the system under a Hindu 'god-king'.

Electoral Experience in Pakistan

The Muslim League and Elections. In the complicated events leading to the partition of the subcontinent and the emergence of Pakistan the Muslim League, under Mohammed Ali Jinnah, played a central role. Eventually its espousal of the 'two-nation theory' and its rigid insistence on a separate political status for the Muslim-majority areas of the sub-continent made partition virtually inevitable; but not until 1945–6 was its claim that it spoke on behalf of the majority of Muslims of British India and the Princely states given tangible confirmation, as a result of its showing in the elections of that period. From its formation in 1906 until the early 1940s it clearly represented only a minority of India's Muslims. In the elections of 1937 to the Legislative Assemblies of the eleven provinces of British India, held under arrangements stipulated in the Government of India Act of 1935, the League, as has been noted, was able to capture only 109 of the 482 Muslim seats, and it did not win a majority of the votes even in the four Muslim-majority provinces. During the next eight years, however, its political fortunes and strength markedly improved, as was demonstrated conclusively in the elections in 1945 and 1946 to a central legislature and to provincial assemblies. The League won all of the thirty Muslim seats in the central legislature, and 84 per cent of the Muslim seats in the provincial assemblies. It was able to form ministries in two provinces, Bengal and Sind, and its claims to be the voice of the majority of Indian Muslims could no longer be ignored or discounted.[1] Thus in the pre-partition years elections served both as a means of negating the claims of the League to represent the Muslims of India and then of confirming these claims.

In June 1946, an all-India Constituent Assembly was elected by communal groups in the provincial Assemblies, voting by proportional representation, and by the appointment of delegates from the Princely states. The Muslim League won all but seven of the Muslim seats. This Constituent Assembly first convened in December, 1946, but the Muslim League refused to allow its elected representatives to participate in it. After the British announcement, in June 1947, of the plan to partition the sub-continent, a separate Constituent Assembly for Pakistan was formed out of the Muslim members from those provinces which were to form the new state of Pakistan. Since the Punjab and Bengal were to be divided, representatives were chosen from West Punjab and East Bengal, which were to be associated with Pakistan.

Constitution-Making and Elections, 1947–1958. The Constituent Assembly of Pakistan met for the first time on 10 August 1947, four days before the formal creation of Pakistan. It was always a small body, with never more than seventy-five members and with an abnormally high rate of absenteeism, and it never was an effective institution, either as a federal legislature or as a Constitution-making body. In fact, it never was able to draft an acceptable constitution, even though it had apparently reached agreement on most of the provisions of a draft constitution before it was suddenly dissolved in 1954. An Objectives Resolution, adopted by the Assembly in March 1949, seemed to indicate that Pakistan's eventual political order would be a democratic state, parliamentary and federal in form, with guarantees of fundamental rights and social justice for all, and with representative national and provincial Assemblies elected by the people on the basis of adult suffrage. The same basic framework was suggested by the Interim Report of the Basic Principles Committee, submitted to the Assembly in September 1950, and in the final BPC Report, submitted to the Assembly in December 1952. The Report was finally adopted in September 1954, at the last session of the first Constituent Assembly, and a Drafting Committee, assisted by the renowned British constitutional expert, Sir Ivor Jennings, was created and instructed to prepare a draft Constitution, which was eventually printed but never made public or even discussed by the second Assembly.[2]

In October 1954 the Governor-General, in a move that created great surprise and continuing controversy and challenge, summarily dissolved the first Constituent Assembly, and in the following May he issued an order providing for the constitution of a new Constituent Assembly of eighty members, equally divided between East and West Pakistan, to be chosen by the provincial Assemblies by a system of proportional representation and by electoral colleges for Karachi and Baluchistan. It is worth noting that the member from Karachi was chosen by direct vote of the citizens of that city, on the basis of universal adult franchise – the first full exercise of the franchise by citizens of Pakistan in voting for national offices. The main elections to the second Assembly were held in June 1955. Only fourteen of the members of the first Assembly at the time of dissolution were returned.

In January 1956, abandoning previous drafts of a constitution, the Government presented its own draft to the second Assembly, and after considerable debate this draft, with a few amendments, was adopted in late February. It went into effect on 23 March 1956.

The first Constitution of Pakistan provided for a directly elected unicameral National Assembly of 300 members (with ten additional seats reserved for women), half of whom were to come from East and half from West Pakistan. A similar provision was included for unicameral provincial Assemblies. All citizens of Pakistan twenty-one years of age and older were eligible to vote for members of these Assemblies. The Constitution hedged on the touchy issue of joint versus separate electorates, which had caused so much controversy and debate in the electoral history of pre-partition days. Article 145 provided that 'Parliament may, after ascertaining the views of the Provincial Assemblies and taking them into consideration, by Act provide whether elections to the National Assembly and Provincial Assemblies shall be held on the principle of joint electorate or separate electorate. . . .' The Electorate Act of 1956 provided that for national and provincial elections East Pakistan should have a joint electorate whereas West Pakistan should have separate electorates, but in the following year an Electorate (Amendment) Act established joint electorates for both wings of the country.[3]

After the Constitution was adopted, an Election Commission was appointed and preparations for Pakistan's first nationwide general elections were begun; but before the elections could be held the political structure provided for in the Constitution, and the Constitution itself, were swept away, and in October 1958, Pakistan passed under military rule.

During the nearly a decade that was required for Pakistan to get its first Constitution the basic constitutional framework was determined by the Government of India Act of 1935 and the India Independence Act of 1947, as amended. The general framework of the Constitution of 1956, and the general nature of the political system that it established, were 'a logical continuation of the Government of India Act.'[4] Thus the political system of Pakistan from its creation until the military take-over of October 1958 was closely modeled on the British system of parliamentary democracy, as modified by the more highly centralized and restrictive provisions of the Government of India Act of 1935. It was further modified, and in fact distorted, by the decision of Jinnah to become Governor-General instead of Prime Minister, by the political instability of the first decade of independence, and above all by the peculiar circumstances, problems, and culture of the bifurcated country.

Although the National Assembly of Pakistan during this period was never chosen by direct popular vote, the members of the provincial Assemblies were. Elections of members of the provincial Assembly of the Punjab and the North West Frontier Province were held in 1951, and of Sind in 1953. In each case the Muslim League won more than two-thirds of the seats, although in the elections in the Punjab it got only 52 per cent of the Muslim seats. Moreover, there were recurrent charges that the elections were anything but free and fair. As the Electoral Reforms Commission observed: 'It was widely and persistently complained that these elections were a farce, a mockery and a fraud upon the electorate.'[5]

East Pakistan Elections of 1954. The East Pakistan elections of 1954 had very different results. They were a debacle from which the Muslim League never really recovered. For some time resentment against the dominant Muslim League had been building up in East Pakistan. When elections could no longer be postponed, the League was still unprepared to face the East Bengali voters, and the main opposition groups made its plight more serious by forming a United Front. In 1953 the veteran Bengali political leader, A. K. Fazlul Huq, went into opposition and formed a new Krishak Sramik (Peasants and Workers) Party. 'This party stood for the achievement of the degree of provincial autonomy envisaged by the Lahore Resolution of 1940.'[6] It had many similarities to the famous 9-Point program of the Awami League in the early 1970s, which was the basis of the successful electoral effort of the League, under Sheikh Mujibur Rahman, in the national elections in East Pakistan in December 1970, and which in a sense provided the ideological and political base for the new East Bengali state of Bangladesh. Thus in retrospect the birth of Bangladesh can be traced back to the very origins of Pakistan, and the conditions that eventually gave it birth were highlighted in the East Pakistan elections of 1954, and their startling and unexpected results. For the United Front, formed mainly by an agreement between Fazlul Huq's new political group, the KSP, and the Awami League, scored an amazing electoral victory, and the once dominant Muslim League was virtually wiped out – forever, as later became apparent – in East Pakistan. The United Front won 223 of the 237 Muslim seats, whereas the Muslim League won only ten. The United Front also won ten of the non-Muslim seats, and the Muslim League none.

The East Pakistan elections of 1954 had profound effects on the whole future of Pakistan, and, as has been suggested, in retrospect was a harbinger of the growing rift between the two wings that in 1971 led to the break-up of Pakistan in the form in which it had existed since independence. 'Such a massive defeat in a province containing more than half the national population inevitably undermined the position of the central government. Central and Bengal politics became intertwined, and neither can be understood in isolation.'[7] After 1954 Pakistan was never the same again. It had in fact received its mortal death-blow, although the full consequences were not apparent for many years. The elections certainly were a major factor in and impetus to the decline of the Muslim League, thus illustrating another major difference between the political evolution of India and Pakistan. Whereas India had the benefit of the continued leadership of a strong and charismatic leader for nearly twenty years after its independence, and of the continued domination of the party that had spearheaded the independence struggle throughout its career as an independent nation (with some temporary signs of weakness in the period 1967–71), Pakistan lost its Quaid-i-Azam, Mohammed Ali Jinnah, hardly a year after independence, and the East Pakistan elections of 1954 revealed weaknesses in the party of independence, the Muslim League, that within a short time led to major divisions within the League and to its virtual disappearance as a major force.

In these and other respects, then, the East Pakistan elections of 1954, even though only elections to a provincial Assembly, had important effects on and consequences for the political development of Pakistan.

Elections in the Ayub Khan Era, 1958–1969. General Ayub Khan, who took over control of Pakistan on 27 October 1958, after ousting General Iskander Mirza, felt that parliamentary democracy was unsuitable for Pakistan, and he declared that he wished to institute a form of democracy that would be more genuinely attuned to Pakistan's needs and conditions, one which would 'enlist the active participation of the ordinary citizen in the task of national reconstruction.'[8] In a widely-discussed article in the American journal, *Foreign Affairs*, in July 1960, he wrote: 'We must have democracy. The question then is: what kind of democracy? The answer need not be sought in the theories and practices of other people alone. On the contrary, it must be found within the book of Pakistan itself.'[9]

From his study of 'the book of Pakistan' Ayub came up with an ingenious scheme known as Basic Democracy, whose directly elected basic units – the union councils in rural areas and union and town committees in the towns and cities – were to serve not only as agencies of local government, administration, and development, but also as an electoral college to choose the President of Pakistan and the members of the provincial Assemblies and the National Assembly. In December 1959 and January 1960, the members of these basic units – then only 80,000 in number, equally divided between the two wings – were directly elected in small constituencies numbering between 800 and 1,600 voters.

On 14 February 1960, these 80,000 'Basic Democrats' were called upon to participate in a referendum 'to make known their confidence' in the President and to authorize him to formulate a constitution. 'Only 60 per cent of the eligible voters cast their votes. Nevertheless, it was an impressive achievement because it was only the first time that the nation as a whole went to the polls. . . . It was believed that an affirmative majority vote would be deemed to confirm President Ayub Khan as President for a first term of office under the prospective constitution. Nearly 96 per cent of the Councillors voted affirmatively and on 17 February 1960, Ayub Khan was sworn in as the first elected President of Pakistan.'[10]

Ayub immediately appointed a Constitution Commission, which worked hard for more than a year, during which it circulated an elaborate questionnaire and examined more than 550 witnesses. In its report, submitted to Ayub Khan on 29 April 1961, it recommended a strong presidential system of government, such as Ayub was known to favor, but it flatly rejected Ayub's favorite scheme of using the Basic Democrats as an electoral college and instead recommended that the President and members of the national and provincial Assemblies should be elected directly by a restricted franchise composed of citizens who had attained a certain standard of literacy and who held an unspecified amount of property.[11] It also recommended that elections should be held on the basis of separate electorates.

Not satisfied with this report, Ayub Khan appointed two committees to scrutinize and revise the recommendations of the Constitution Commission, and on 1 March 1962, he promulgated a Constitution – the second in Pakistan's history – which clearly reflected his own ideas and wishes. This Constitution provided for a strong presidential system, with the Basic Democrats retained as the electoral college. Ayub Khan was sworn in as the President of Pakistan under the new Constitution, and martial law, which had been in effect since October 1958, was brought to an end. The Basic Democrats elected 150 members of the National Assembly and then 300 members of provincial Assemblies. In June the National Assembly met, the Constitution was declared in force, and the ban on political parties was lifted.

Thus Pakistan entered upon another political experiment, under a new Constitution, with a new form of 'democracy' presumably more suited to its needs. It was obviously a limited and mostly indirect form, a type of guided or controlled democracy in which the President had virtually complete control. On the basis of hearings before a new Franchise Commission, and returns from questionnaires sent out by the Commission, it seemed clear that there was rather limited support for the new order and a continuing demand for a system of parliamentary democracy, with direct elections based on universal adult franchise. The Franchise Commission itself, in a report submitted in August 1963, recommended the retention of the presidential system, with the President to be elected by an electoral college (presumably the Basic Democrats), but with members of the national and provincial Assemblies to be chosen by universal and direct franchise. However, a Franchise Bill, introduced soon after the report was submitted, retained the indirect system of election for the nation's top representatives.[12]

Before the next Presidential election could be held, it was necessary to hold new elections to the basic units of the BD system. These were held in November 1964. The turnout was much greater than in 1959–60. Many persons who refrained from contesting in the first BD elections were candidates this time, and the interest in the elections was much keener. 'The new Basic Democrats were reported to be more mature, educated and affluent than their earlier counterparts.'[13]

In September 1964, some weeks before the new Basic Democrats were elected, the Presidential campaign got under way in earnest with the formation by five major opposition parties of a Combined Opposition Party, which nominated Miss Fatima Jinnah, sister and long-time hostess of the Quaid-i-Azam, Mohammed Ali Jinnah, as its Presidential candidate. This gave an entirely new twist to what might otherwise have been a dull campaign leading to a foregone conclusion. Miss Jinnah, who had hitherto taken no part in active politics, was a popular candidate, and she could and did invoke the name of her brother, the father of Pakistan, against the existing ruler of the country. She was a vigorous and outspoken critic of Ayub Khan, whom she called a dictator. She charged that his regime had created an 'atmosphere laden with fear and reeking with corruption.' She called for the abolition of Ayub's political system, and the substitution of a parliamentary system and direct adult franchise. This demand aroused widespread approval, especially among students, intellectuals, professional and labor groups, women, and others who opposed the Ayub system for a wide variety of reasons. She also promised to quit after she had given Pakistan a free parliamentary system, a promise which seemed rather quixotic but which 'eased to a great extent the debate over whether it was un-Islamic to have a woman head of a Muslim state.'[14]

Ayub Khan campaigned on his record, promising 'progress and stability.' He charged that Miss Jinnah lacked the capacity for the leadership of the nation, and he frequently stated his view that women are generally too emotional to head any state. While he did not directly enter the controversy over the appropriateness of a woman seeking to head a Muslim state, he obviously encouraged such a feeling; and the more othodox Muslim religious leaders openly declared that this would be contrary to the principles of Islam.

While the main target of the campaign was the 80,000 newly elected Basic Democrats, who alone would have the right to vote in the Presidential election, the campaign aroused nationwide interest. The two main candidates attracted huge crowds almost everywhere, especially in East Pakistan. Often Miss Jinnah was greeted by larger and more enthusiastic crowds than President Ayub himself, even though he obviously had many ways of exerting influence over the Basic Democrats who would decide between him and Miss Jinnah. After all, the system of Basic Democracy was his creation, and the Basic Democrats owed their office to him. If he were re-elected, they would continue to play a political role of considerable importance, whereas if Miss Jinnah were elected, they would lose their main political functions, and possibly the entire BD system would be abolished. They were somewhat bewildered by the larger dimensions of the campaign, and by the obvious popularity of Miss Jinnah. They were the special targets of attention of all the leading candidates, who participated in a series of ten 'projection meetings' at which they addressed groups of Basic Democrats and answered questions; and of course workers for these candidates assiduously sought their votes.[15] 'For the first time in Pakistan, a national election was held in which a lot of interest was taken by the people. But unfortunately like previous elections, there was also allegation of official interference.'[16] The Basic Democrats were subjected to all kinds of pressures by Ayub Khan's supporters, and their future depended on his re-election.

Under the circumstances, the results of the elections were rather surprising. Although Ayub Khan was re-elected, the election was surprisingly close in East Pakistan, where Ayub got only 53.1 per cent of the votes and Miss Jinnah 46.6 per cent, and where Miss Jinnah carried the main cities of Dacca and Chittagong. In West Pakistan, however, Ayub got 73.6 per cent of the votes, and Miss Jinnah only 26.1 per cent, although she carried the largest city of the western wing, Karachi. Overall Ayub got 63.3 per cent of the votes, and Miss Jinnah 36.4 per cent.

After this Presidential election, the subsequent elections of members of the National Assembly and the provincial Assemblies came as an anti-climax. Even in these elections, however, Ayub won only a bare majority of the popular votes in East Pakistan, even though the party which he headed, the Pakistan Muslim League, got 72 per cent of the seats from East Pakistan in the newly elected National Assembly. In the

East Pakistan Provincial Assembly his party won a bare majority of the seats as well as the votes. In West Pakistan it fared very well in the elections both to the National and to the Provincial Assembly. In that province the Combined Opposition Party could do no better than it did in the Presidential elections, gaining hardly more than 25 per cent of the votes.[17]

One can argue that even under the controlled system that Ayub Khan established, especially after the promulgation of the 1962 Constitution and the end of martial law, elections on a national and provincial level, although indirect and far from really free, contributed to Pakistan's political development, and may indeed have paved the way toward a different and probably more representative, if still limited, political system. One Pakistani political scientist has expressed the view that 'With the introduction of the 1962 Constitution, the stage was reached at which the people had begun to realise that they had some power. The Basic Democracies elections and the functioning of the various tiers of the system, the elections to the legislatures and the controversy over direct versus indirect elections all had gone a long way to extend popular awareness.'[18] Thus, inadvertently no doubt, forces had been unleashed at the height of Ayub Khan's power which in time were to end his rule and lead to another agonized period of searching for a suitable political order – a search which has extended through at least four different political experiments without really satisfactory results.

The elections of early 1965 confirmed, and to some extent gave additional legitimacy to, Ayub Khan's rule. At the same time they revealed an attrition of support for the regime, especially in East Pakistan and in major cities in both wings. In the remaining months of his rule Ayub Khan experienced a series of problems and pressures with which eventually he could no longer cope. These included his serious illness, dissatisfaction with the results of the September 1965 war with India, and with the Tashkent agreement that followed, growing demands for a greater measure of autonomy in East Pakistan, increasing complaints in that province of growing disparity between the two wings and favoritism to West Pakistan, unrest and disturbances among students, intellectuals, labor, and other groups, growing support for Zulfikar Ali Bhutto and for his concept of 'Islamic socialism' and his criticisms of the domestic and foreign policies of the Ayub regime. In the end Ayub was brought down by widespread political unrest, reflecting the growing sub-nationalism in East Pakistan and the growing radicalism in West Pakistan, and by the withdrawal of support by some of the top military commanders. In late 1968 he made a belated promise to give the country a parliamentary system of democracy, with free and direct elections on the basis of universal adult franchise; but the pledge came too late for him to implement, even if he really intended to do so. In March 1969, when the military leaders no longer stood behind him, he had no choice except to resign. Instead of turning the government over to civilian leaders, he resigned in favor of General Mohammed Yahya Khan, who immediately imposed martial law and sought to restore law and order.[19]

The Yahya Khan Era: First General Elections. During the first year of his rule Yahya Khan took a number of concrete steps to implement his promise to transfer power at the earliest possible date 'to the representatives of the people elected freely on the basis of adult franchise.'[20] The procedures to be followed were spelled out in greater detail in the Legal Framework Order, promulgated by Yahya Khan on 30 March 1970,[21] and in subsequent Presidential orders and ordinances. On 13 July Yahya confirmed the date of 5 October for elections to the new National Assembly and of 22 October for elections to the two provincial assemblies. About a month later, because of floods and other natural disasters in East Pakistan, he moved the dates up to 7 December and not later than 19 December. Thus the stage was set for the first direct nationwide general election in Pakistan's chequered history, which presumably was to be the first major step along the road to constitutional government and democracy.

Because of its unique character, and its hopes for the future, the Pakistan general elections of December 1970 attracted special interest and attention. Many people in Pakistan and elsewhere were doubtful that Yahya was really sincere in his pledges to turn the country over to civilian, democratic government; many more were convinced that the West Pakistani military, bureaucracy, and other members of the 'Establishment' would not permit Sheikh Mujibur Rahman, leader of the majority party in East Pakistan, the Awami League, to become Prime Minister of Pakistan even if, under the 'one man, one vote' arrangement, he won a majority of seats in the National Assembly.[22] But for the first time in Pakistan's history free, direct elections seemed to be central to the plans for the evolving political order and to offer a way out of the political morass in which the country had been foundering ever since the early days of its independence. Unfortunately, even though, contrary to many predictions, the elections were held successfully and were generally free and fair, they did not lead to the happier results which had been intended. This was not due to any failure in the electoral process, but to more deep-seated weaknesses and divisions in the Pakistani body politic.

In a sense the campaign of 1970 began on 1 January, when the resumption of full political activity was permitted. The two main political parties – the Awami League, led by Sheikh Mujibur Rahman, in East Pakistan, and the Pakistan People's Party, led by Zulfikar Ali Bhutto, in West Pakistan – campaigned actively throughout the year. Altogether twenty-four 'parties' were alloted election symbols, but only about half a dozen were of any real political significance, and one of these – the National Awami Party, led by the veteran pro-Chinese Communist Bengali leader, Maulana Bhashani – eventually refused to participate in the voting. The greatest national interest centered on the activities of the Awami League and the Pakistan People's Party. Certainly the leaders of these two parties, Sheikh Mujibur Rahman and Z. A. Bhutto, seemed to be the most colorful and the most influential personalities among the leaders of major parties, and they attracted the greatest attention and drew the biggest crowds. Unfortunately, each of them had strength in one wing of the country only, and the two men had a long record of mutual antipathy and distrust. Their prominence highlighted the sad fact that there was no really important party in the campaign that could be called a truly national party and no really important political leader who could be called a truly national leader. The course of the campaign, and more importantly the election results, further highlighted the split between the two wings of the country and the absence of a real national consensus. The elections did not create the fatal split, but they dramatized and accentuated it.

In November 1970, a natural disaster occurred in East Pakistan that profoundly affected the election results in that province. Hundreds of thousands of people in the delta areas and offshore islands of East Pakistan were killed or made homeless and reduced to subhuman conditions by a devastating cyclone and tidal wave. This natural disaster made it most difficult to hold the scheduled elections in the devastated areas; and elections were postponed in nine parliamentary constituencies in areas that had been hardest hit. More importantly, it widened the rift between East and West Pakistan, for the people of East Bengal felt that the response of the Government of Pakistan and of the West Pakistanis to their desperate need had been sluggish and inadequate. Sheikh Mujibur Rahman and the Awami League, in particular, capitalized on this feeling. Undoubtedly the amazing showing of the League in the elections was due in part to the cyclone disaster and the reactions to it in East Pakistan.

On 7 December more than 34 million citizens of Pakistan – about 60 per cent of the registered voters – went to the polls to elect 291 members of the National Assembly (elections for nine more members had been postponed to January 1971). The elections passed off quite peacefully in all parts of the country, and there was general agreement that they were held without fraud or intimidation and with relatively few election irregularities.

The results of the election heralded a new political situation in

Pakistan. In the Eastern wing the Awami League won all but two of the seats. In West Pakistan the Pakistan People's Party won eighty-three of the 138 seats, with a particularly impressive showing in the major provinces of the Punjab and Sind. The same general results emerged from the elections of members of the provincial Assemblies, held on 17 December.[23]

In general, the results of the December 1970 elections further polarized the politics of Pakistan, and left the destinies of the country mainly in the hands of three men of very different backgrounds and views: President Yahya Khan, Zulfikar Ali Bhutto, and Sheikh Mujibur Rahman. In the weeks that followed the three leaders failed to agree on many basic issues. Instead of moving from the elections to the convening of the National Assembly, the drafting and promulgation of a Constitution, and the transfer of power to civilian rule under a system of parliamentary democracy, the country was torn apart by bloody repression and civil war in East Pakistan, which before the end of the year led to the military defeat of Pakistan by India, the break-up of the country, and the emergence of Bangladesh as an independent nation.

The Bhutto Era: Constitution-Making and Elections. Immediately upon assuming the offices of President and Martial Law Administrator, on 20 December 1971, Bhutto promised to give Pakistan a new and more democratic political system, and he moved rapidly to implement his pledge. The system of Basic Democracy was replaced with a program known as People's Local Government, with all the basic units known as 'People's Local Councils.' Needless to say, the members of the new Councils had no role whatever as an electoral college, as the Basic Democrats in the Basic Democracy system had had. On 22 April 1972, an Interim Constitution, approved by the National Assembly acting as a Constituent Assembly, entered into effect and martial law was lifted. The Interim Constitution provided for a system of parliamentary government for the 'Islamic Republic of Pakistan,' with the National Assembly to continue for another five years, unless it was dissolved at an earlier date. Work was begun immediately on a permanent Constitution, and on 20 October 1972, an all-party constitutional agreement was announced. This indicated that Pakistan would become a federal parliamentary system, with the lower house of the National Assembly to consist of 200 members elected by direct adult franchise. (Ten more seats were reserved for women, 'to be elected by members of the National Assembly from their respective Provinces.')[24]

On 10 April 1973, a Constitution Bill was passed by the Assembly.[25] The new Constitution entered into effect at midnight on 13–14 August 1973, exactly 26 years after Pakistan became an independent state; and shortly after midnight Z. A. Bhutto ceased to be the President of Pakistan and took the oath of office as the Prime Minister. Thus Pakistan embarked on another major political experiment. A new and truncated Pakistan had emerged from the civil war and the Indo-Pakistan war of 1971. In August 1973, a new Pakistan emerged, from a legal and constitutional point of view. Presumably direct elections on the basis of universal adult franchise will be held in due course, and as in all genuinely parliamentary systems of democracy elections will be a central mechanism of the new political system. If they are not, the system itself will be a façade, thinly disguising another variation of authoritarianism.

Electoral Experience in Ceylon

The political development of Ceylon during the past half century has been admirably and concisely summarized by Professor S. Arasaratnam. It evolved 'from unrestricted Governor's rule, through representative government (1924) to semi-responsible government (1931) to responsibility and independence (1948). After independence it went through a decade of bourgeois-liberal rule, laissez-faire economic policies and élitist control of politics and administration. This lasted until the electoral revolution of 1956 brought in the second phase of cultural (or communal) nationalism. Communal politics gave way to politics based on economic and social philosophies.'[26] As this summary indicates, elections clearly played a central role in Ceylon's political development.

The story of Ceylon's electoral experience includes its introduction of universal adult suffrage much earlier than any other Asian state, and an election (1956) which is perhaps the outstanding example in all of Asia of a critical, or realigning, or ruralizing election, which not only led to a transfer of power by peaceful electoral means – an event all too rare in Asian experience – but also changed the basis of popular representation and support. Ceylon offers a prime example of what Professor Urmila Phadnis has called 'the decisive influence of the politics of the ballot box on the political system.'[27] It also, unfortunately, offers an example of a successfully functioning electoral system which has legitimized the political system but eventually, as Howard Wriggins has observed, has threatened 'the unity and stability of the institutions that make elections possible.'[28]

Electoral Experience Prior to Independence. Ceylon's electoral experience has been extraordinary – especially for an Asian state – in its duration and its variety. Direct elections to municipal councils on a universal male franchise were instituted more than a century ago. 'The election principle in island-wide affairs was accepted for the first time in 1912, when the franchise was opened to the Ceylonese who had received an education along European lines – roughly 4 per cent of the population.'[29] In 1928 the famous Donoughmore Commission recommended that the Legislative Council be replaced by a State Council, most of whose members should be elected on the basis of an 'unqualified franchise', with universal adult suffrage (men over twenty-one, women over thirty), and with communal electorates to be abolished and territorial constituencies to be created.[30]

In 1931 the so-called Donoughmore Constitution entered into effect, and elections to the new State Council, on the basis of universal adult suffrage (the Secretary of State, Lord Passfield, had revised the recommendation of the Donoughmore Commission to permit women over twenty-one to vote), were held. This was a landmark in the electoral history of Asian countries. 'For the first time an Asian country was to have universal suffrage without income, property, literacy, or sex qualifications.'[31] Fifteen years were to pass before any other Asian country introduced universal suffrage, and twenty more years before India conducted its first nationwide general election on the same franchise basis.

The elections of 1931 were important more for symbolic reasons than for their practical impact. About 100 candidates stood for forty-six seats in the State Council. Half of them contested under party labels, but parties existed only in embryonic form in this period and the election was fought more on the basis of personalities than on party lines and on local rather than national issues. The Donoughmore Constitution was intended to be a temporary one, paving the way for eventual self-government. Some eligible groups, including the Ceylon Tamils, boycotted the elections, and 'almost every candidate expressed his displeasure at the nature of the new system and promised his constituents that he would press for its revision if he were elected.'[32]

New elections to the State Council in 1936 were conducted along substantially the same lines, although this time the Ceylon Tamils and most other groups that had boycotted the 1931 elections participated, and the organization and conduct of the campaign were greatly improved.

The next national elections in Ceylon were not held until 1947, and they were of a very different nature. Because of the war elections to the State Council were postponed, and in the meantime many events transpired which moved Ceylon more rapidly along the path to independence. In September 1941, the British Government promised that 'the question of constitutional reform in Ceylon . . . will be taken up with the least possible delay after the war,' and in May 1943, it pledged that 'the post-war re-examination of the reform of the Ceylon Constitution . . . will be directed towards the grant to Ceylon . . . of full responsible government under the Crown in all matters of internal civil administration.'

In September 1945, a Commission headed by Lord Soulbury proposed a broader and more representative system of government, with a cabinet responsible to an elected legislature of two houses, a lower House of ninety-five elected members and six nominees, and an upper House of thirty members, half to be elected by members of the lower chamber by a system of proportional representation, and half to be nominated by the Governor-General.[33]

In accordance with the recommendations of the Soulbury Commission the first representative parliamentary elections were held in Ceylon in August–September 1947. By this time political parties were more numerous and more active, although no real party system had emerged. The contest was mainly between the newly formed United National Party (UNP) led by D. S. Senanayake, who became known as the Father of the Nation, and a group of opposition parties of disparate composition and objectives, plus many who stood as Independents. The UNP was an amalgamation of the Sinhala Maha Sabha (Buddhist), Ceylon Muslim League, Ceylon National Congress, and personal followers of D. S. Senanayake. In the elections it won forty-two seats in the lower house. Five opposition parties – the Lanka Sama Samaj Party (LSSP, a Trotskyite party founded in 1935), the Bolshevik-Leninist Party (which split from the LSSP in 1945), the Communist Party (formed by the Stalinist faction that was expelled from the LSSP in 1939), the Ceylon Tamil Congress (founded in 1944), and the Ceylon Indian Congress (founded in 1939) – won thirty-one seats, with ten going to candidates of the LSSP, and twenty-one Independent candidates were also successful.[34]

UNP Ascendancy, 1947–1956. By winning the support of most of the Independent and nominated members of the lower house, the UNP was able to form a government. This was the beginning of a decade of rule by the UNP. Shortly after its first government was formed, the British Government announced that Ceylon would be given 'fully responsible status within the British Commonwealth', and on 4 February 1948, Ceylon became an independent nation. In 1951 the UNP, which seemed to have no real rival, suffered a blow that later turned out to be a near-fatal one with the defection of S. W. R. D. Bandaranaike, Minister of Local Government and Health, a Western-educated Sinhalese Christian who rejected many of the ideas of the West, embraced Buddhism, became the spokesman of the majority Sinhalese population, and tried 'to infuse a Sinhala-consciousness' into Ceylonese nationalism.[35] Shortly after his defection Bandaranaike formed the Sri Lanka Freedom Party (SLFP), a move that proved to be 'a landmark in the growth of parliamentary democracy in Ceylon.'[36]

The death of D. A. Senanayake as a result of a riding accident in

March 1952 was a grievous blow to the ruling UNP; but in the general election of 1952 it was able to win 54 seats in the lower House, thus giving it a majority of the seats, even though it did not get a majority of the popular vote. Opposition parties were able to win only twenty-eight seats, including 9 each for the SLFP and the LSSP.[37] In view of the weak and fragmented opposition and the growing electoral strength of the UNP, Ceylon seemed to be moving to a one-dominant-party system, such as existed in India under the Indian National Congress and Jawaharlal Nehru. But even during the campaign there were signs of a growing dissatisfaction with the UNP, and with the élitist and Western-educated and Western-oriented group that led it. The beginnings of the emergence of a truly competitive party system, with two major political groups representing very different approaches, advocating very different policies at home and abroad, and drawing their main support from different strata of the society, can be dated from the early and middle 1950s. The undercurrents in Ceylonese politics that were undermining the UNP and shifting the base of political power erupted to the surface in the landmark election of 1956.

For nearly a decade, however, through two general elections, the UNP was able to command popular support, and to broaden the base of political participation in Ceylon. 'The continuing experience of exercising the vote gave even the most remote villager a sense of participation in this democratic process and strengthened his conviction in representative government as an institution relevant to his immediate needs. The governments that held office during these years were thus legitimized by the popular will and governed by popular consent.'[38] By the mid-1950s that popular support, but not faith in the democratic process, was eroded, and this fact was reflected in the electoral debacle of 1956.

The 'Critical' Election of 1956. The defection of S. W. R. D. Bandaranaike and the death of D. S. Senanayake had greatly weakened the UNP, although this weakness was not reflected in the election results in 1952. D. S. Senanayake's son, Dudley, had become Prime Minister after his father's death, but he seemed to have no taste for the job. In the fall of 1953 he gave way to Sir John Kotelawala, who soon became rather unpopular because of his élitish and pro-Western learnings.

In 1956, the UNP felt strong enough to call another general election, just after it had presumably neutralized the SLFP's pro-Sinhalese orientation by adopting a resolution in favor of Sinhala as the only official language of the country. But it had already so alienated the people in the Kandyan area, the Buddhists, and traditional elements generally that it could not hope to counteract the SLFP on grounds of language and religion. These issues 'provided Mr. Bandaranaike and his followers with a better channel to the mass of the voters than anything available to the U.N.P.'[39] Mr. Bandaranaike enhanced his electoral prospects by forming a coalition with a few minor parties known as the Mahajana Eksath Peramuna (MEP, the People's United Front), which appealed to communal and provincial emotions by such slogans as 'Sinhala only' and 'Buddhism in danger.' It was 'a coalition of resentment against the U.N.P.'[40]

As a champion of Sinhala nationalism and communalism, and of the Buddhists, Mr. Bandaranaike had a clear edge over the UNP leaders. For some time Buddhists had been entering the political arena, and by 1956 they had become a significant factor in politics – an extraordinary phenomenon that soon became evident in Vietnam and other Asian states.[41] Just before the 1956 elections the Sangha Sabhas or Buddhist Associations formed a political grouping, the Eksath Bhikku Peramuna, for the express purpose of helping the MEP defeat the UNP.

In spite of these developments, most observers expected the UNP to retain its dominant position, although with some reduction in strength. Few anticipated the magnitude of the ruling party's defeat or of the MEP's victory. When the results were in, it was evident that an electoral revolution had occurred. The popular vote for the UNP fell by nearly 300,000 votes, while that of the opposition rose by 450,000 votes. Because of the successful tactics of the SLFP in forming the MEP, the UNP lost more heavily in seats than in popular vote. Of its seventy-six candidates only eight were returned. The MEP got fifty-one seats, other opposition parties and groups thirty-six seats, and Independents eight seats.[42]

The 1956 general election in Ceylon was one of the most interesting and most significant elections to be held in any Asian state. In the language of American psephologists, it could be described as a critical, a realigning, and a ruralizing election.

It was a critical and a realigning election because it not only led to a change in government from one party or group to another, but it marked a shift in the base of political power and a realignment of political forces in Ceylon, and gave politics deeper roots in Ceylonese traditions, culture, and society. 'The 1956 election was a turning point in the history of Ceylon and wellnigh produced a social revolution. It resulted in the dethronement of the westernized élite, both professional and commercial, which had dominated the politics of Ceylon for over twenty-five years. In their place it enthroned the nationalist-minded élite and the Sinhalese-educated professional classes. It thus broadened the base of political power and in a sense made Ceylon's democracy more genuinely democratic. It altered the nature and content of politics and introduced new values and even a new terminology to the political scene.'[43] Of all the elections in South Asia 'it alone resulted in a marked transfer of power from one segment of the population to another. . . . It was not the elective confirmation of a *coup d'état*, but a genuine change in leadership effected by the cumulated choice of hundreds of thousands of individual voters.'[44]

It was also a ruralizing election; indeed, in the opinion of Samuel Huntington it 'may be termed the archetype of the "ruralizing election." '[45] In 1956, as Robert Kearney has noted, the rural lower middle class and lower class Sinhalese 'suddenly discovered their political strength and shattered the monopoly of political power previously held by a small, affluent, westernized élite.'[46] 'The election agitation . . . drew into political activity rural professional and middle-class groups which, with the aid of the priesthood, brought into question the traditional influence wielded in the countryside by landowners and rural notables. . . . This rejection by large numbers of the rural voters of the traditionally prominent was perhaps the most significant internal aspect of the election, moving the locus of popular representative power from the hands of the wealthy to the rural middle classes, from the English-educated to the Sinhalese educated.'[47]

In the Western, and especially the American press the debacle of the pro-Western UNP government and the overwhelming victory of a party and a coalition that had pledged to nationalize foreign-owned tea and rubber plantations, to expel the British from their air and naval bases in Ceylon, to make Ceylon a republic, probably outside the Commonwealth, and to move over to a type of neutralism that would give more satisfaction to Moscow than to Washington, were viewed with considerable alarm. But, as the South Asian correspondent of *The New York Times* observed, while the election would have 'large international repercussions,' it was fought largely on domestic issues. 'The real reason this country is repudiating Sir John Kotelawala's Government,' he reported from Colombo, 'is not because it is pro-Western but because Sir John and his party have become too cocky in their twenty-five years of power and have lost contact with the desires and the complaints of their own people.'[48]

Elections of 1960, 1965, and 1970. The transfer of power from the UNP to the SLFP-dominated coalition through the verdict of elections was a notable event, and one that has been far too rare in the electoral history of Asian countries. The new government seemed to be strongly entrenched in the majority ethnic, religious, and linguistic groups; but in consequence of its religious and linguistic policies it discriminated against minority groups and laid the basis for increased tensions. 'In the process,' as Howard Wriggins has observed, 'minority interests are ignored and intercommunal hostility reaches a new height. Accordingly, elections allow a peaceful change of leaders but one byproduct may be a noticeable increase in social conflict.'[49] The events of the next four years proved the wisdom of this observation.

Soon after forming a government, Mr. Bandaranaike began to have difficulty with his Marxist allies within and outside the MEP. In May 1957 the LSSP withdrew its support from the government. In May 1959 Mr. Bandaranaike announced that he had parted company with Marxist elements in the MEP and in the SLFP. In June the Communist Party withdrew its support. Communal tension and fighting became so prevalent that in May 1958 the Government proclaimed a state of emergency. This was lifted in March 1959 but in September of that year Mr. Bandaranaike himself became a victim of religious and communal tension, when he was assassinated by a Buddhist *bikkhu*.

The loss of its great leader, coming after loss of support from Marxist groups and increasing communal and religious tensions, forced the SLFP government, under a weaker leader, to call new elections, which were held in March 1960. The SLFP tried to capitalize on the popularity of its dead leader, and the opposition parties on the increasing tensions that had characterized the SLFP rule. Candidates of no fewer than twenty-three political parties and 162 Independents – 899 candidates in all – contested for the 151 seats in the House of Representatives. The results were indecisive, with the UNP, with fifty seats, gaining a four-seat margin over the SLFP.

A minority UNP government, with Dudley Senanayake as Prime Minister, was formed, but it was unable to govern effectively, and in a few weeks it called for another election in an effort to get a stronger base. In this campaign most of the minor parties disappeared, and the main opposition parties formed a united front against the UNP. They also found a new leader in Mrs. Sirimavo Bandaranaike, widow of S. W. R. D. Bandaranaike, who in May became President of the SLFP and who took an active part in the campaign. Because of the united front of the main opposition parties the UNP won only thirty seats, although it received a plurality of the votes. The SLFP got seventy-five seats and the LSSP twelve seats. The SLFP thereupon returned to power, with Mrs. Bandaranaike as Prime Minister – the first woman ever to hold such a position in any country.[50]

The new SLFP government was harassed by communal conflicts, by a coup attempt in January 1962 by leaders of the armed forces, and by disputes between the moderate and leftist forces within the government. In December 1964, Parliament was dissolved, and new elections were called for March 1965. Since 1960 the UNP had refurbished its image by adopting a program of 'democratic socialism', and it had broadened and strengthened its organizational base, especially among young voters. In the 1965 election campaign it was able to enter into electoral arrangements with several smaller parties. In the elections it got sixty-six seats and a plurality of the votes, while the SLFP got forty-one seats and the LSSP ten.[51]

A national government headed by Dudley Senanayake, with the support of a bloc of ninety-six seats in the House of Representatives, was formed. This government ran into a sea of troubles, mostly on the economic front. Its decision to cut down the rice ration from two subsidized measures to one free measure was particularly unpopular. During its period of rule unemployment, especially among the educated, and the cost of living increased alarmingly.

When fresh elections were due, in 1970, the UNP was in a weaker position, and it was faced with a United Front consisting of the three major opposition parties, the SLFP, the LSSP, and the Communist Party, headed by Mrs. Bandaranaike, who took a more radical stance. The UNP spokesmen warned that a victory for the United Front would mean 'the end of our democratic set-up.' These warnings seemed to fall on deaf ears. The UNP had again become quite unpopular, and apparently 'rice issues' were decisive in the minds of many voters, including some 800,000 new voters between the ages of eighteen and twenty-one, who voted for the first time.

In the elections of 27 May 1970, the UNP got a bare plurality of the votes, but its membership in the House of Representatives fell from sixty-six to seventeen. The SLFP won ninety-one seats itself, and its electoral allies, the LSSP and the Communist Party, won nineteen and six seats, respectively, thus giving the United Front a majority of more than two-thirds in the House.[52]

Mrs. Bandaranaike became Prime Minister for the second time, at the head of a large coalition government that included leaders of the LSSP and the Communist Party. She moved quickly to implement all of her sweeping electoral pledges. But the economic and financial difficulties continued, employment remained high, and some of the discontented young Ceylonese of more radical persuasion became speedily disillusioned with the Prime Minister and her government. In April 1971, this unrest among the youth erupted in a violent uprising that for a time threatened to bring down the government and perhaps even the political system. The armed challenge was soon contained. But the causes of the unrest and the grave economic difficulties and social tensions remain as constant reminders that even a government that was voted into power by an overwhelming margin cannot give real stability to a political system that is constantly beset by such subterranean pressures and forces.[53]

Sri Lanka and the New Constitution. By early 1972 the promised new Constitution was ready. After much debate this Constitution was approved by the Constituent Assembly, and on 22 May it formally entered into effect. On this day Ceylon became the Republic of Sri Lanka (the Sinhalese name for Ceylon).

Under the new Constitution a unicameral legislature, called the National State Assembly, was made the supreme instrument of the state, exercising executive and judicial, as well as legislative power in the name of 'the People.' A Constitutional Court was established, with limited powers to advise on the constitutionality of acts of the Assembly. Sri Lanka was described as a 'socialist democracy,' with Sinhalese as the official language (with some provisions for the use of Tamil in certain cases) and with Buddhism being given 'the foremost place' (but not accorded the status of the official religion). The chapter on 'Fundamental Rights and Freedoms' contained no provisions regarding freedom of the press or property rights.

Contrary to the usual practice in democratic states, no general elections were held after the adoption of the new Constitution. Instead, the Constitution provided that sitting members of the House of Representatives, elected in 1970, could keep their seats for another five years, which gave them, and the government of Mrs. Bandaranaike, a possible tenure of seven years (barring an early dissolution). It is constitutionally possible, therefore, that the next general elections in Ceylon will not be held until 1977. This will be the longest period without a general election since independence. More seriously, the question is a moot one whether the Asian country which has the longest record of free, direct elections on the basis of universal suffrage may not be moving toward a more controlled system of 'socialist democracy' in which not only elections but fundamental rights as well will be more severely restricted and curtailed. If this is not 'the wave of the future' in Sri Lanka, general elections, even if less frequently held, will continue to play a central role in the evolving political system.

Electoral Experience in Nepal

Nepal, like Pakistan, has held only one nationwide general election on the basis of universal adult suffrage. This was held eleven years before the Pakistani general election, but it had considerably less impact on the political system of the country than the election in Pakistan. Nepal's electoral experience, in fact, has been a very limited one, and elections have never been central to its political evolution, in spite of some lip service to the principle of popular representation by free and democratic elections.

During the Rana period, roughly from the mid-nineteenth century to the 'revolution' of 1950–1, Nepal was a closed country with a closed political system, and the only oppositional politics 'was the monopoly of the members of the traditional ruling order.'[54] During the period of transitional politics from 1951 to 1959 there was a great deal of talk about, and among the 'modernizing élite' a growing demand for, representative institutions based on democratic elections and a party system. A brief experiment with parliamentary democracy followed the general elections of 1959; but King Mahendra, like his father King Tribhuvan, had little faith in parliamentary or any other genuine form of democracy and he regarded political parties, and especially the Nepali Congress, with aversion and distrust. After his coup in December 1960, he gradually evolved a new political order, described as 'partyless Panchayat democracy,' in which elections played only a nominal role, except at local levels of the system. The young King Birendra, who acceded to the throne in January 1972, has shown no more interest in genuinely representative and democratic institutions than his father and grandfather did, although he is regarded as a more 'modern' ruler and is trying to evolve a more participatory system which will not threaten his ultimate control.

The Political System of the Ranas. The political system of the Ranas was 'accountable neither to the King nor to the people.'[55] A few very tentative and limited proposals to broaden the base of the system could be cited. The first Rana Prime Minister, after a visit to England and France in 1850–1, 'appointed a parliamentary office to prepare the foundations for the introduction of a parliamentary system,' and nearly seventy years later another Rana Prime Minister 'called a meeting of the most prominent members of the Rana family to discuss the introduction of constitutional change.'[56] But nothing came of these tentative efforts. Toward the end of the Rana regime a few more significant steps, presaging the shape of things to come, were taken.

In 1946 the Nepali National Congress was formed by a group of Nepali political exiles in India, for the avowed purpose of overthrowing the Ranas and instituting a constitutional democratic government under the leadership of the King. On 16 May 1947, Prime Minister Padma Shamsher, in a famous speech, announced that he wished 'to associate the people with the government to a greater degree than in the past,' and he mentioned the possibility of elections to such bodies as municipal and district boards. On 26 January 1948, he presented Nepal with its first constitution which, while reserving final power to the Rana Prime Minister, provided for a three-tiered electoral system, with direct elections to the primary panchayat units. In introducing this constitution Padma Shamsher used words and expressed views that were reminiscent of those which King Mahendra voiced two decades and more later. 'We have tried,' he said, 'to mould the elective system of the west to the Panchayat system, which is an essential part of our heritage. . . . It is the government's desire that all good, able and energetic elected representatives of the people should come to the centre, and co-operate with the government, but it would be very unfortunate if the introduction of political elections should lead to quarrels or disorder in the country.'[57]

The 1948 Constitution, however, was never put into effect. In November 1950, revolution broke out in Nepal, King Tribhuvan took refuge in the Indian embassy in Kathmandu and was then flown to India, and in February 1951 he returned to take control of the country. Thus 'the Rana regime and its constitutional system were discarded simultaneously.'[58]

Nepal's First General Elections. On 15 February 1948 King Tribhuvan issued an historic proclamation, promising to introduce a new political order 'based on a democratic constitution framed by elected representatives of the people.' In April 1951 an Interim Government of Nepal Act was promulgated, providing a framework of government until the promised Constituent Assembly could be elected and a new constitution drawn up. From November 1951 to August 1952 a cabinet headed by M. P. Koirala was in office, but it had very limited scope and the government remained firmly in the hands of the King. Elections were promised no later than April 1953, but they were never held. King Tribhuvan seemed to desire to establish some form of limited representative government, but he was obviously reluctant to yield any real power. 'Neither the political nor the economic infrastructure of a democratic system of politics existed in Nepal in 1951, and indeed the very concept and values of a democratic polity were as alien to the general populace as it was [*sic*] to most of the traditional élite. . . . In the critical transitional period from 1951 to 1959, there was no substantial popular support . . . for the few ill-conceived efforts to introduce and sustain democratic institutions and processes.'[59]

Shortly after he succeeded his father in 1955, King Mahendra announced that general elections would be held in October 1957. These elections were not held as scheduled, but in December 1957, the King set 18 February 1959 as the new date. This time there was no further postponement and stalling. A famous royal proclamation of 1 February 1958 announced that elections would be held for a regular Parliament, and not just a Constituent Assembly. A Public Representation Act in May of the same year provided that the country would be divided into 109 constituences and that all Nepalis twenty-one years of age and over would be given the franchise. In February 1959 the King promulgated a new Constitution, and announced that the elections would be held a week later. The Constitution provided for a Parliament of two houses, with the lower House to be elected directly on the basis of universal adult franchise.

The 1959 general elections were a new and thus far a unique experience in Nepal's political history. Although political parties had been functioning, after a fashion, since 1946, they had had little place in the transitional politics of the post-1951 period; and since no nationwide elections had been held, their relative strength and degree of popular support could not really be determined. In the 1959 elections candidates of seven so-called national parties and 268 Independents contested. The results showed that one party, the Nepali Congress, led by B. P. Koirala, was much stronger than any of the others. The Congress won 38 per cent of the popular vote and seventy-four of the 109 seats in the lower House, the Gorkha Parishad 17 per cent of the votes and nineteen seats. No other party got more than 10 per cent of the vote or more than five seats, and the Presidents of all of the parties except the Nepali Congress were defeated. Independents got 16 per cent of the total vote, but only four won seats in the lower House.[60]

As a result of the Constitution and the elections of 1959 Nepal embarked on its first – and last – experiment in parliamentary democracy. A Nepali Congress government, with B. P. Koirala as Prime Minister, was installed in May 1959, marking 'the end of the inchoate transitional politics and the introduction of a confident, vigorous political structure for the first time since 1951.'[61] But while the new government seemed to be doing well, and gave Nepal a greater degree of political stability and more representative institutions than it had previously enjoyed, it soon became a victim of deeply-rooted forces in Nepali society. Its activities and programs 'placed it directly in opposition to ali those elements which had dominated transitional politics from 1955 to 1959 and which had been routed nearly out of political existence in the general elections of 1959.'[62] It also found that it was being viewed with increasing disfavor, and suspicion, by the King himself.

Elections under 'Panchayat Democracy'. On 15 December 1960, in a sudden coup, the King brought the short-lived experiment in parliamentary democracy to an end. He abrogated the 1959 Constitution, dismissed the Parliament and the Cabinet, and again assumed direct control of the country. After some interim arrangements, he outlined a new political structure in the Constitution of 1962, to be known as Panchayat Raj, or 'partyless Panchayat democracy.' 'Parliamentary democracy,' he declared, 'has proved unsuitable because it lacks the Nepali qualities which are found in the panchayat system.' The new system was a four-tiered layer of panchayats, from the primary level of village and town panchayats through district panchayats to the top tier of the National (Rashtriya) Panchayat – 'the "parliament" under Panchayat Raj.'[63] Only members of the primary units were to be directly elected. These units were set up after local elections in 1962, and by April 1963 members of the higher panchayats had been indirectly elected and the new system was actively functioning.

It is an interesting and novel political experiment, a variation on previous panchayat-based structures in Nepal and on other forms of guided democracy, with strong and direct central control, that have at different times been tried, without much success, in Pakistan, Indonesia, and other Asian states. 'It is based on a teleological concept of democracy which assumes that the Nepali people are unprepared for autonomous political action except at the lowest levels of task complexity and that the constitutional authority – that is, the King – holds ultimate responsibility for the determination of the country's political system.'[64] This system worked reasonably well during the remaining years of Mahendra's reign, and it is being carried on, with some modifications which may in time change its nature or lead to its replacement, by Mahendra's son, King Birendra. It has given Nepal at least short-term stability, but at a low level of political achievement. It can work only as long as the King retains the ultimate power firmly in his own hands.

Reflections on South Asia's Electoral Experience

This review of the electoral experience in other South Asian states demonstrates that the electoral history of South Asia is by no means confined to India, although obviously the Indian experience is the most significant aspect of the story. Ceylon has had a longer and in some ways more intensive electoral experience than India, but it has of course not been on such a large scale. Pakistan and Nepal have had more electoral experience than is generally recognized, but each country has held only one nationwide general election on the basis of universal adult suffrage, and in each case the general election had generally destabilizing rather than stabilizing effects and the political arrangements that were envisioned after the elections either could not be implemented, as in Pakistan, or were soon discarded, as in Nepal.

Elections have clearly been more central to the political development of India and Ceylon, and apparently they will also be in the case of Bangladesh, than of Pakistan and Nepal; but since the political system of Ceylon, in spite of long experience with relatively stable governments and an impressive record in holding elections, now seems to be in jeopardy, and since the political future of Bangladesh is still very much in question, it would seem that elections in India have contributed to genuine political development in a way that no other South Asian state has experienced.

It is interesting to note that three nationwide general elections in three South Asian states, held within a period of less than a year of each other, produced overwhelming victories for a particular political party, but at the same time had very different results in terms of political development and stability. The reasons for this seeming paradox are worth examining in some detail.

8

THREE ELECTIONS: VARIATIONS IN SYSTEMIC IMPACT

In South Asia elections have had both stabilizing and destabilizing effects. Indeed, the electoral experience in South Asia offers fascinating case studies of the role of elections in political development and political decay, to use Huntington's words.[1] This is particularly true of the fifth general elections in India in March 1971, the first general elections in Pakistan in December 1970, and the seventh general elections in Ceylon in May 1970, all of which were held within a period of less than a year. All seemed to have many similarities, but they had very different effects in terms of immediate consequences and systemic stability.

Varying Effects of Three Elections on Political Development

It is interesting to contemplate the effect of these elections on the political development of India, Pakistan, and Ceylon. Before they were held the political situation in all three countries seemed to be growing increasingly unstable and uncertain, to such an extent that many gloomy statements were being made about their political future as united and integrated polities. Then came 'free and fair' general elections that were conducted with impressive efficiency and success and that, contrary to almost all predictions and expectations, resulted in overwhelming victories for particular political groups, giving them the capability of providing stable, popular-based governments. All of these elections seemed to provide a clear mandate for political, economic, and social change, as well as for political stability and development. All seemed to clarify the political situation in the three countries, and to link the governments that emerged more closely with the masses of the people and to identify politics more closely with the society. All seemed to indicate a clear choice with regard to political leadership (although in Pakistan the choice was clearly different in the eastern and western wings), and a strong desire for more radical political and economic policies and orientation. All seemed to presage a new order under political leaders who were clearly 'the people's choice.'

Yet the impact of these elections on each country was quite different. The fifth general elections in India gave Mrs. Indira Gandhi an overwhelming personal endorsement and gave the country a government capable of governing. It undoubtedly led to greater political stability in India, at a time when the country was faced with growing internal problems and a grave external crisis because of the civil war in East Pakistan and the tensions with Pakistan that culminated in the Indo-Pakistan war of December 1971. Without such enhanced political stability India would have been hard pressed to meet such serious internal and external challenges. The first nationwide elections in Pakistan, which were conducted with remarkable success, were the first major step in Yahya Khan's carefully worked out step-by-step plan for the restoration of democracy in Pakistan; but the plan broke down immediately after the first major step was successfully taken, and instead of contributing to the political development of Pakistan, the elections further polarized and highlighted the division between the two wings and led to results that soon proved disruptive to the unity of Pakistan. The seventh nationwide parliamentary elections in Ceylon brought Mrs. Sirimavo Bandaranaike back to power, with an overwhelming mandate, and seemed to give Ceylon a much greater degree of political stability and a strong and determined government. The new government moved speedily and forcefully to implement its many radical election pledges, but it was still unable to satisfy the demands of some of its more radical young supporters, or to cope with deep-seated economic and social problems. As a result, within less than a year after its overwhelming victory at the polls, the government was faced with an armed rebellion on the part of disgruntled youth, which threatened its existence and perhaps even the foundations of the political system and which created a politically explosive situation in the countryside, and also with a deteriorating economic situation with which it could not cope.

Thus the 1971 elections in India led to greater political stability, the 1970 elections in Pakistan to greater political instability and to the break-up of the country, and the 1970 elections in Ceylon to apparently greater political stability which in less than a year turned into greater instability so serious as to threaten the future of the political system as well as of the ruling government that had come to power with such an impressive mandate.

Why did free nationwide elections, on the basis of universal adult suffrage, held within a year of each other in the same part of the world, with many similar and many unexpected features, lead to such different results? The answer cannot be simply that India and Ceylon had had more experience with elections, although this certainly was a fact, for the elections in Ceylon had quite different long-term consequences from those in India. Nor can it be that Pakistan had had little experience in, and had shown little aptitude for, representative institutions, whereas in India and Ceylon a parliamentary system has been functioning ever since independence, although this too is an historical fact. Rather the answer must be sought at deeper levels of politics and society, in the different circumstances and different political experiences of the three countries.

In considering this phenomenon of variations in systemic impact under conditions that seem to have many similarities as well as differences, elections may be considered as independent, intervening, and dependent variables in a larger political process, involving basic trends in both the political and the overall social system.

The Fifth General Elections in India

Political Developments, 1967–1971. Before the fifth general elections the political prospects for India looked almost as grave as did those for Pakistan. Indeed, on the surface, before the December 1970 elections Pakistan, under the firm hand of Yahya Khan, seemed to be more stable politically than India under Mrs. Gandhi, who had the support of barely one-half of the members of the Lok Sabha. A number of events in 1967–70 had contributed to what a well-known Indian journalist called 'the increasing fragmentation of political life.'[2] The fourth general elections in 1967 had resulted in surprising reverses for the ruling Congress Party, led by Mrs. Gandhi, leaving it with a narrow majority in the Lok Sabha and in a minority position in many of the States.[3] These elections were widely heralded as marking the end of the one-dominant-party system that had existed since India's independence. They ushered in a period of growing political instability. Coalition politics, frequent political defections and 'floor-crossings,' and unstable and frequently shifting anti-Congress coalition ministries, with frequent periods of President's Rule, characterized the political scene in many States.[4] 'The politics of coalition and defection' seemed likely to spread to the Centre, as the Congress government, with its slim majority, was threatened by defections and dissensions and by an unfavorable climate of opinion in the country at large.

The fourth general elections, therefore, seemed to have destabilizing effects on the political system as well as on the Congress government. The mini-general elections in four major States – Bihar, the Punjab, Uttar Pradesh, and West Bengal – in 1969 re-emphasized this disturbing trend.[5] In all four States shaky coalition governments were formed soon after the elections, but none lasted for more than a few months, and 'the politics of coalition and defection' continued.

The political situation in the country and the future of the Congress Party seemed to become more precarious as a result of the internal feuds within the Congress Party which led to its break-up and disappearance in the form in which it had existed since its formation in 1885.[6] In the long run Mrs. Gandhi's bold gambles of 1969 paid off handsomely. The split in the Congress actually strengthened her hand, giving her greater freedom to recreate her Congress Party according to her own image and views, along more 'progressive' and more radical lines, and giving her a better opportunity to establish the base of her political support solidly among the masses of the Indian people. But while it was quickly apparent that the 'Indicate' was stronger than the 'Syndicate', and had much greater popular support, Mrs. Gandhi and her party were in a weak position, organizationally and politically. The political instability that had beset the country since 1967 continued; increasing food prices and unemployment were only partially offset by a mild economic recovery from the serious economic distress of 1967–9; and the incidence of violence was alarmingly high.

In the Lok Sabha Mrs. Gandhi's political position was not improved in 1970. In biennial elections of one-third of the elected members of the Rajya Sabha, in March, her party's strength in the upper house was reduced from 103 to eighty-eight. Changes in government occurred in five States, but the Congress was not able to form a government in any of them as a result, although in two – Bihar and Kerala – it supported the new coalition governments. But if her formal political position remained unsatisfactory, Mrs. Gandhi's popular support seemed to grow. Two of the measures which she sponsored in 1970 were particularly popular. One was the nationalization of fourteen major private banks, effected by Presidential ordinance in February after the Supreme Court had declared a bank nationalization law of 1969 unconstitutional. The other was a Presidential order in September abolishing the privy purses of the former Princely rulers, after a constitutional amendment to achieve this objective had failed to secure the approval of the Rajya Sabha. This order was declared illegal by the Supreme Court on 15 December, an action which caused a widespread public outcry and which was a factor in leading Mrs. Gandhi to make a momentous political decision.

Fifth General Elections: Novel Features and Prospects. On 27 December, at her request, President Giri dissolved the Lok Sabha and called for new general elections. In a broadcast to the nation Mrs. Gandhi said that 'In the present situation, we feel we cannot go ahead with our proclaimed program and keep our pledges to our people;' and she asked for a 'fresh mandate . . . to effectively implement socialist and secular programs and policies.'[7]

Again Mrs. Gandhi had decided upon a 'bold gamble' for very high stakes. Her decision, which had been predicted by only a minority of

Indian commentators, was generally applauded by her supporters and criticized by her opponents. Many foreign observers viewed the move as 'a desperate bid to reverse a tide of despair and anarchy that increasingly threatens Indian democracy,' to use the language of a *New York Times* editorial, and they shared the *Times*' assessment of the consequences of her failure or her success. 'If Mrs. Gandhi's gamble succeeds,' declared the *Times*, 'India could enter a new era of more mature political stability and more energetic development under a moderately leftist regime. If, however, the New Congress fails to gain a working majority in the coming election, the present trend toward fragmentation in India politics will probably be accelerated, with potentially disastrous consequences for the subcontinent.'[8]

The fifth general election in 1971 was notable and unique in many respects. It was the first general election to be held after the split in the Congress Party, and therefore the first real electoral test of the relative strength of the Old and the New Congress. It was the first general election to be held before the expiration of a regular term of the Lok Sabha (five years). It was called one year before it would normally have been held. It was the first general election to be 'delinked' from State elections. In all previous general elections candidates for most State Legislative Assemblies as well as for the Lok Sabha were contesting. This time State elections were held simultaneously with the Lok Sabha election in only three States – Orissa, Tamil Nadu, and West Bengal. This was the first election in which a Congress majority did not seem to be assured, and it was probably the hardest fought election in India's electoral history. It was also marred by a greater incidence of violence than any previous election. There were more than 200 political murders during the campaign period in West Bengal alone.

Another novel feature was that for the first time the main opposition non-Communist parties formed an electoral alliance against the Congress. The 'Grand Alliance' of the Old Congress, the Swatantra Party, the Jana Sangh, and the Samyukta Socialist Party, however, proved to be anything but 'grand'. It was a strange alliance of unlikely bedfellows; it never worked very well, and it never sparked much popular interest or support. It campaigned mainly on the slogan, *Indira hatao*! (Remove Indira), which gave Mrs. Gandhi an opportunity to appeal to popular sympathies and to take the higher ground of asking for support to implement her slogan of *Garibi hatao*! (Remove poverty).

Mrs. Gandhi was, in fact, the main issue in the campaign. As an Indian journalist observed in mid-February, 'it is Mrs. Gandhi's election – a referendum on her policies and her continuance in office.'[9] She moved about the country indefatigably, appealing to the people to combat reactionary forces and to give her a mandate to implement her socialist program and to abolish poverty. The response of the people, especially in the final stages of the campaign, was remarkably enthusiastic.

The prevalence of the 'Indira wave' was an interesting phenomenon of the elections. It had been demonstrated in State elections in Kerala in September 1970, which proved to be a prelude to the fifth general elections. In that State, where the Congress showing had been about as poor as in any part of the country, a united front led by the CPI and supported by the New Congress, won enough seats to form a government. The Congress (R) increased its representation from five to thirty-two seats, and a new enthusiasm for the party and for Mrs. Gandhi was very much in evidence.[10]

Throughout the campaign most informed observers failed to take adequately into account the intangible but profound impact of the 'Indira wave,' and thus made some monumentally wrong predictions. Most predicted a close result. Very few even suggested that Mrs. Gandhi's party might get a clear majority of the Lok Sabha seats. The Director of the Indian Institute of Public Opinion, one of the country's most astute political analysts, wrote in January that the fifth general elections would be different from previous elections 'in three vital respects': (1) 'In all the previous four the victors were all too clearly visible. This is the first election in which the betting can be truly even.' (2) 'This is the first election in which the posture of the electorate is deemed unpredictable.' He referred to 'the huge personal equation' as a particularly unpredictable factor. (3) Another new factor was 'the forging throughout India of an Opposition alliance which will virtually banish the standard patterns of multicornered contests of 1957, 1962, and 1967.' This analyst thereupon made this monumentally wrong prediction: 'With a high (possibly higher) popular vote, the new Congress will in all probability get fewer seats than the combined Congress did in 1967. . . . Neither the new Congress nor the Opposition alliance is . . . at all likely to strike a majority of [262] seats in a House of 523.'[11] Most other close students of the campaign expressed the same erroneous views. 'The current betting in Delhi,' wrote S. Nihal Singh on 13 February, 'is that the Congress (R) will obtain about 240 seats, denying Mrs. Gandhi an absolute majority.'[12] And on the eve of the voting the prestigious Southern newspaper, *The Hindu*, stated that 'it is an educated guess that the Congress (R) may deem itself lucky to retain in the new House even the 220-odd seats it held in the dissolved Lok Sabha.'[13]

Table 8.i

RESULTS OF FIFTH GENERAL ELECTIONS IN INDIA, MARCH 1971: LOK SABHA

State	*No. of seats*	*Congress (R)*	*Congress (O)*	*Jana Sangh*	*Swatantra*	*CPI*	*CPI (M)*	*SSP*	*PSP*	*Independents and other parties*
Assam	14	13								1
Andhra Pradesh	41	28				1	1			11
Bihar	53	39	3	2		5		2		2
Gujarat	24	11	11		2					
Haryana	9	7		1						1
Himachal Pradesh	4	3								
Jammu and Kashmir	6	4								1
Kerala	19	6				3	2			8
Madhya Pradesh	37	21		11				1		4
Maharashtra	45	42							1	1
Mysore	27	27								
Nagaland	1									1
Orissa	20	15			3	1				1
Punjab	13	10				2				1
Rajasthan	23	14		4	3					2
Tamil Nadu	39	9	1			4				25
Uttar Pradesh	85	73	1	4		4				3
West Bengal	40	13				3	20		1	3
Union Territories including Delhi	18	15					2			1
Total	518	350	16	22	8	23	25	3	2	66

Fifth General Elections: Results and Aftermath. Voting took place between 1 and 10 March. In spite of the response to Mrs. Gandhi's campaign and in spite of the stakes involved, only a few hundred thousand more persons voted this time than in 1967, even though 25 million more people were eligible to vote. The results came as a great surprise to almost everyone, and changed the Indian political picture greatly. Mrs. Gandhi's Congress Party, which had only some 220 seats in the Lok Sabha at the time of its dissolution, won 350 seats, giving it a two-thirds majority in the lower House and placing it in a commanding position in Indian political life. It won a majority of the Lok Sabha seats in all States except Gujarat, Kerala, Nagaland, Tamil Nadu and West Bengal. Among its major electoral coups were the capture of all twenty-seven of the twenty-seven Lok Sabha seats in Mysore, seventy-three of the eighty-five in Uttar Pradesh (where the undivided Congress had won only forty-five seats in 1967), all five of the Bombay seats, all seven of the Delhi–New Delhi seats (where the Jana Sangh had captured six in 1967); and it increased its strength from one to six seats in Kerala, from six to fifteen in Orissa, and from three to nine in Tamil Nadu.

All opposition parties, except the two Communist parties and the Dravida Munnetra Kazhagam, suffered heavy reverses. The CPI(M) gained six seats, but twenty of its twenty-five seats came from the single State of West Bengal. The CPI could win no more than five seats in any State, and in most States it had no successful candidates. The DMK, of course, elected all of its twenty-three members from the single State of Tamil Nadu. The 'Grand Alliance' could win only forty-five seats, whereas its constituent parties had elected 150 M.P.'s in 1967. The strength of the Congress (O) fell from sixty-five to sixteen, of the Swatantra from thirty-five to eight, of the Jana Sangh from thirty-three to twenty-two, and of the SSP from seventeen to three. In effect, all of these parties, with the possible exception of the Jana Sangh, were virtually eliminated as significant national parties.[14]

In the State Assembly elections in Tamil Nadu the ruling DMK increased its strength from 138 to 184 seats. Because of its electoral understanding with the DMK, the Congress Party did not contest this election. In Orissa it increased its Assembly membership from two to fifty-one, making it the largest single party in the State; but it was not able to form a government immediately, for the Swatantra Party and the Utkal Congress were able to obtain the support of some minor parties and Independents and form a ministry, which in 1972, however, gave way to a Congress regime. In West Bengal the Congress made a remarkable recovery, increasing its representation in the Assembly from thirty-eight to 105.[15] Although the CPI(M) also increased its strength from eighty to 112, the Congress entered into an alliance with other moderate and left-wing parties and formed a government. This government fell in June, under the pressure of continuing political instability and violence in India's most volatile State and the growing problem of millions of refugees from East Bengal, and President's Rule was again proclaimed. After the State Assembly elections in 1972, however, the Congress was able to form a stronger government which, with firm support from the Centre, was able to create better conditions and greater confidence in West Bengal.

The 1971 general elections ended, at least temporarily, the political instability and the prospect of coalition government at the Centre, and seemed to mark the return of a system of one-party dominance, such as had existed throughout the Nehru era and until 1967.[16] In some respects Mrs. Gandhi seemed to be a stronger leader than even her father was, even though she lacked her father's charisma and could never aspire to a position in national life comparable to that which Nehru occupied in his heyday. Certainly she was more ruthless, and less considerate of old associates, than her father was. She also showed less consideration for the niceties of constitutional and parliamentary government. She did not hesitate to cut down any political leaders, however strongly entrenched they seemed to be in certain States, or to appeal directly to the people for support over the heads of the party bosses and the controllers of 'vote banks' at all levels.

Having gained an overwhelming mandate, Mrs. Gandhi moved quickly to reconstitute her cabinet and to reorganize the Congress Party at national, State, and local levels. In several key States the regular Pradesh Congress Committees were replaced by *ad hoc* committees. Mrs. Gandhi forced the resignation of several prominent Chief Ministers (including Mohanlal Sukhadia, who had been Chief Minister of Rajasthan for seventeen years), PCC chiefs, and other party leaders. With a sufficient majority in the Lok Sabha, she pushed through three very controversial Constitutional amendments. The 24th amendment restored to Parliament the right to amend any part of the Constitution, a right that had been taken away by the Supreme Court in a much-debated decision in 1967. The 25th amendment, which was even more controversial and in the opinion of many conservative Indians even more dangerous, made drastic changes in Article 31 of the Constitution, relating to property rights; and the 26th abolished the privy purses and other privileges of the former Princely rulers, a step which had been thwarted in 1970, first by the lack of a sufficient majority in the Lok Sabha and then by a decision of the Supreme Court.

The Crisis with Pakistan, 1971. Mrs. Gandhi was in effect given a reprieve of about a year before she was faced with the problem of living up to popular expectations that had been aroused by her pledge to 'abolish poverty' and her other campaign promises. This reprieve came because of the civil war in East Pakistan and the crisis with Pakistan which faced India throughout the rest of 1971. India was fortunate to have a strong and stable government to deal with a crisis of this magnitude. Mrs. Gandhi and her government publicly condemned the Yahya Khan regime in Pakistan for its ruthless and bloody repression in East Pakistan after the breakdown of negotiations with Sheikh Mujibur Rahman in the weeks following the general elections of December 1970. They also publicly supported the 'freedom fighters' in East Bengal.

Indian sympathies were wholly on the side of the East Pakistanis. A few days after the commencement of the military repression in East Pakistan the Indian Parliament unanimously adopted a resolution, introduced by Mrs. Gandhi, expressing 'wholehearted sympathy and support' for the people of East Bengal, and calling on the government of Pakistan 'to put an end immediately to the systematic decimation of the people, which amounts to genocide.'

The spill-over effects of the tragic events in East Pakistan soon put grave new strains on the Indian political system, social structure, and economy. By the mid-summer of 1971 the number of refugees from East Bengal in India, mostly in the troubled State of West Bengal, was over five million, and by December it was perhaps double that figure. Refugee relief became an increasingly intolerable strain on India, amounting at the end to between two and three million dollars a day.

This was one of the many factors arising from the civil war in East Pakistan which led many Indians to demand that India intervene militarily in the Pakistani civil war.[17] Mrs. Gandhi held out against these demands for some months; but she was openly unneutral in thought and deed. She permitted the use of Indian soil by the Mukti Bahini and other 'freedom fighters' of East Bengal, and allowed the training of resistance forces in India and the supply of arms as well as food and equipment to them. After she received less than adequate assurances of concrete support during her visit to the United States and several countries of Western Europe in October–November 1971, she apparently concluded that she had no option except to force a military show-down with Pakistan.

The war that ensued in December lasted only fourteen days, and resulted in a decisive victory for India, ending any real threat from Pakistan and giving India a more dominant position in the subcontinent and an unparalleled degree of self-assurance and confidence. It also led to the break-up of Pakistan, the replacement of Yahya Khan by Z. A. Bhutto in what was left of Pakistan, and the emergence of Bangladesh as an independent nation under the leadership of Sheikh Mujibur Rahman, whom India has supported strongly, and the Awami League.

Mrs. Gandhi's obviously tough and unneutral position during the

1971 crisis with Pakistan was widely criticized abroad, but her firm and decisive leadership during the crisis, including the Indo-Pakistan war of December, further strengthened her already commanding political position in India.

Pakistan's First General Elections

The general elections in Pakistan in December 1970 – the first, and the last, nationwide general elections on the basis of universal and direct suffrage to be held in the history of Pakistan – certainly had destabilizing effects on the Pakistani political system. They polarized and widened the gulf between the eastern and western wings and were soon followed by the break-up of the country and very different patterns of political development and control in both what was left of Pakistan and in the newly emergent nation of Bangladesh. Thus they had very different, and indeed quite opposite, consequences, in terms of political stability and systemic impact, from the Indian general elections three months later. They provide further evidence of the truth of Howard Wriggins' observation that 'electoral politics . . . may threaten the unity and stability of the institutions that make elections possible.'[18] As events quickly proved, in Pakistan these supporting institutions were not sufficiently developed or supported to permit the new orientation and the new freedoms that seemed to be demanded by the voters through the electoral process.

The conspicuous novelty of the 1970 elections, as well as their unexpected results, heightened their destabilizing effects on Pakistan's political system. In fact, it would have been difficult, if not impossible, to adapt the political system in ways that seemed to be dictated by the popular mandate, even if the general political climate and circumstances were favorable; and Pakistan in 1969–70 was in the throes of a transition period and was experiencing special political and economic difficulties that, coupled with its consistent record of inexperience in genuinely free and democratic institutions, made the necessary systemic adaptations particularly difficult to effect.

Elections prior to 1970. All of the elections during the troubled first eleven years of parliamentary democracy were held on a provincial basis for members of provincial Assemblies only. Although these provincial elections were held on the basis of universal adult franchise, there was considerable basis for the verdict of the Electoral Reforms Commission that in general 'these elections were a farce, a mockery and a fraud upon the electorate.'[19] Free, direct general elections were provided for in the Constitution that was finally adopted in 1956, but before such elections could be held the Constitution was abrogated and Pakistan came under martial law and military rule.

During the Ayub Khan era elections played very little part in the controlled political system, either during the period of martial law from 1958 to 1962, or after the Constitution of 1962 was promulgated. The only direct elections were for members of the basic units of the Basic Democracies, in 1960 and 1964. All other elections, including those for the higher units of the BD system in 1960 and 1964, for the members of the National Assembly and the Provincial Assemblies in 1962 and 1965, and in the most significant election of the Ayub Khan era, the Presidential election of January 1965, were indirect and limited to a few voters, with the Basic Democrats serving as the electoral college. Ayub Khan developed an ingenious electoral system, but it was clearly designed to give the people the illusion but not the reality of participation and to provide legitimacy to Ayub's regime without in any way sharing power.

Toward the end of his rule Ayub Khan promised to permit nationwide elections on the basis of universal suffrage, but this offer was obviously a last desperate move to save his tottering regime and came too late to be implemented. When he had no choice except to step down, it is significant that he turned over power, not to civilian representatives but to another military ruler, in effect selected by the top military leaders who had finally turned against Ayub.

Elections in Yahya Khan's New Order. Immediately after he assumed control of Pakistan the new leader, General Yahya Khan, in a broadcast to the nation declared: 'I wish to make it absolutely clear to you that I have no ambition other than the creation of conditions conducive to the establishment of constitutional government. It is my firm belief that a sound, clean and honest administration is a prerequisite for safe and constructive political life and for the smooth transfer of power to the representatives of the people elected freely and impartially on the basis of adult franchise.'[20] Yahya let it be known that he intended to remain in power only long enough to supervise the process of holding free elections and the restoration of constitutional government; and although such a goal and such an act of self-abnegation are rare on the part of the many military strong men who have assumed control by non-democratic means and who have ruled in non-democratic ways in various developing countries, Yahya took many steps and gave many evidences that he really meant to do what he said he would do. In July 1969, Yahya announced that he had set a timetable of twelve to eighteen months for making arrangements for nationwide general elections. In October he let it be known that he would soon make public his proposals for providing a constitutional basis for holding free elections.

On 28 November in another broadcast to the nation, Yahya

announced his decisions on three basic issues which, he said, had to be resolved before national elections could be held. He yielded to the growing demands for the dissolution of the one unit in West Pakistan, promising to restore the original four provinces in that part of the country, namely the Punjab, Sind, the North West Frontier Province, and Baluchistan. He accepted the principle that the general elections should be on the basis of 'one man, one vote', and he agreed to grant greater autonomy to the provinces. All three of these concessions were particularly favorable to East Pakistan, where the majority of the people of the entire country lived.[21] Yahya also announced that elections to the National Assembly, on the basis of 'one man, one vote,' would be held on 5 October 1970, that the Assembly would be given 120 days to complete the framing of a new constitution, that if it was unable to meet this timetable, it would be dissolved and a new Assembly would be elected, and that elections to provincial Assemblies would be held after the National Assembly had completed its task of constitution-making. Martial law would continue until all these steps had been taken, but full political activity would be permitted from 1 January 1970. Up to that time political parties were banned, and political activity was almost non-existent. After 1 January 1970, a larger number of so-called parties began to organize and operate, and to prepare for the promised general elections in October.

On 30 March 1970, Yahya Khan promulgated a famous document, the so-called Legal Framework Order. In this he laid down five 'fundamental principles' on which the new Constitution would be based. These were (1) that Pakistan would be 'a Federal Republic to be known as the Islamic Republic of Pakistan;' (2) that Islamic ideology would be preserved and that the Head of the State would be a Muslim; (3) that 'adherence to fundamental principles of democracy shall be ensured by providing direct and free periodical elections to the Federal and Provincial legislature on the basis of population and adult franchise,' and that fundamental rights of the citizens would be guaranteed; (4) that the provinces would be assured 'maximum autonomy;' and (5) that 'the people of all areas in Pakistan shall be enabled to participate fully in all forms of national activities' and that 'economic and all other disparities between the Provinces and between different areas in a Province' would be removed.[22]

Thus direct, nationwide elections became one of the 'fundamental principles' of the new order which Yahya was seeking to bring into being, and would in fact be the first major step in the process. The Legal Framework Order specified that the National Assembly would be composed of '313 members of whom 300 shall be elected to fill general seats and thirteen to fill seats reserved for women.' It also specified the membership of the five provincial Assemblies, which Yahya announced in an address on 28 March would be elected on 22 October 1970, seventeen days after the elections to the National Assembly. Except for the election of members from centrally administered tribal areas, the members of the National and provincial Assemblies to be elected to general seats would be chosen 'from territorial constituencies by direct election on the basis of adult franchise.'[23]

Impact of the Cyclone Tragedy of November 1970. Because of floods in East Pakistan in August, the elections to the National Assembly were postponed from 5 October to 7 December, with the elections to the provincial Assemblies to come no later than 19 December. In mid-November the revised time-table was again threatened because of one of the greatest natural disasters of the twentieth century – a cyclone and tidal wave that devastated coastal areas and offshore islands of East Pakistan, killing hundreds of thousands (perhaps as many as a million people) and leaving many more hundreds of thousands homeless and in danger of starvation. All East Pakistani parties except the Awami League demanded that the national elections be further postponed, on the ground that fair elections were impossible in the immediate aftermath of such a massive tragedy, and it seemed that it would be almost impossible logistically to hold these elections in the stricken areas. 'But the government stuck to the December date, primarily because of the AL's threat to launch a mass movement if polls were postponed and also Yahya's desire to establish his regime's bonafides as a non-perpetuating interim government.'[24] Elections to nine Assembly seats from the worst hit areas were, however, postponed until mid-January 1971.

In protest against the decision to hold the elections in December, as scheduled, several East Pakistani parties, including the National Awami Party led by Maulana Bhashani, the only really formidable rival to Sheikh Mujibur Rahman in East Pakistan, decided to boycott the December elections. This gave Sheikh Mujib and his party, the Awami League, a clear field in East Pakistan, and an unparalleled opportunity to capitalize on the increased anti-Western feelings aroused by the cyclone tragedy and especially by the alleged failure of the central governmenc and the West Pakistanis to give prompt and adequate relief to their fellow-countrymen in the cyclone-affected areas of East Pakistan. Undoubtedly this feeling, and the effective way in which Sheikh Mujib and the Awami League exploited it, had a profound effect on the outcome of the elections in East Pakistan. Before the cyclone hit, it seemed likely that the Awami League would get 60 or 70 per cent of the seats from East Pakistan, but no one predicted that it had any chance for a virtually clean sweep in that province. This result was made possible in large part by the natural disaster of November, and the Government's dilatory and inadequate response. It provides an outstanding example of the effects of a unique and unexpected event – or of what are sometimes called stochastic factors – on an electoral outcome.[25] To the extent that the cyclone tragedy of November 1970 helped to account for the success of the Awami League in winning a majority of all the seats in the National Assembly, it clearly had significant political as well as physical consequences, and was a factor in the break-up of the country.

The Campaign. Before the cyclone struck East Pakistan, some 1,570 candidates for the 300 Assembly seats, including 319 Independent candidates and representatives of twenty-five political parties, were involved in the electoral campaign. It soon became apparent that the only two parties that really mattered were the Pakistan People's Party and the Awami League. Neither could claim to be a truly national party. The PPP ran candidates only in West Pakistan, and had real support only in the Punjab and Sind. The Awami League ran seven candidates in West Pakistan, but not a single candidate from that part of the country was successful.

For a time it was thought that the three different branches of the Muslim League might be major factors in the campaign in West Pakistan, the National Awami Party under Maulana Bhashani in East Pakistan, and the Jamaat-i-Islami under the colorful Maulana Maudoodi and other conservative Muslim parties in various parts of both wings; but none of these parties did well in the elections, and, as has been noted, the National Awami Party (Bhashani) did not even contest the election in the final stages. Altogether more than 1,500 candidates, including 319 Independents, contested the 300 general seats (thirteen more seats were reserved for women), but only eight parties put up more than 100 candidates.

The Awami League was the voice of Bengali nationalism. Provincial autonomy was the most controversial issue of the campaign. The League demanded such an extreme degree of autonomy for East Pakistan that it seemed highly unlikely that Pakistan could remain a united country if its six-point program, which it had first advanced in 1966 and which it made the basis of its campaign appeal, was accepted. The famous six points were as follows:

1. The character of the Government shall be federal and parliamentary.
2. The Federal Government shall be responsible only for defense and foreign affairs.
3. There shall be two separate currencies mutually or freely convertible in each wing.
4. Fiscal policy shall be the responsibility of the federating units.

5. Separate accounts shall be maintained of the foreign exchange earnings of each of the federating units.

6. Federating units shall be empowered to maintain a militia or paramilitary force.[26]

In East Pakistan Sheikh Mujib in effect converted the election into a referendum on the six points. This gave him a powerful basis of appeal to the East Pakistani voters, and raised demands that the federal government could hardly meet, even if that government had not been firmly in the hands of the West Pakistani élite. The demand for the six points in the end gave Mujib little room for maneuver or compromise with the representatives of the central government or of West Pakistan. The six points, which at one time might have been regarded as maximum demands, in time became minimum demands, and Sheikh Mujib might not have been able to remain in control in East Pakistan if he had compromised these points in any way. Hence in the end the distinction between provincial autonomy of the type envisioned in the six points and secession and separatism became a very fine one indeed.

In West Pakistan the PPP was not as solidly entrenched, but it gradually emerged as the strongest party in that part of the country. It was under the inspired, if often erratic, leadership of Zulfikar Ali Bhutto. Bhutto had been Foreign Minister in Ayub Khan's cabinet, but he broke with Ayub and was imprisoned for a few months in the latter part of Ayub's reign. Although he was Western-educated, with wide international experience and outlook, he took an anti-Western and pro-Chinese, as well as anti-Indian, stance. Although he was the scion of a distinguished family of wealthy landlords in Sind, many of whose members had had leading roles in the politics of that province, he appealed to the masses of West Pakistanis and opposed the 'vested interests' in the military, the bureaucracy, and the business leaders and landed gentry. He raised the slogan of 'Islam, Democracy and Socialism,' which, however incompatible its three principles might be, aroused widespread popular support. His 'appeal was not so much leftist as nationalistic in the sense of being statist. . . . Like Mujib's in the East, Bhutto's major constituencies in the West were student and petty bourgeois groups who were outside the system and demanded an immediate share in power.'[27]

The Verdict of the Polls. Considering the lack of experience in direct nationwide elections and the troubled conditions that prevailed, Pakistan's first direct elections, on 7 December 1970, were conducted in an impressive manner, with an overall turnout of about 60 per cent and with relatively few irregularities or acts of violence.[28] Since no political party had had a chance previously to test its real strength, the results were particularly interesting and revealing. In East Pakistan the Awami League scored an almost clean sweep, winning all but two of the 153 seats that were being contested (it also won all of the nine seats in the cyclone affected areas that were chosen in mid-January, plus all seven of the seats reserved for women from East Pakistan). The PPP won eighty-three of the 138 seats from West Pakistan, including sixty-four of eighty-two seats in the Punjab. No other political party got more than nine seats. Hence the elections gave the Awami League an unchallengeable position in East Pakistan, and the PPP a dominant position in West Pakistan, thereby polarizing the political forces in the country and creating an almost unbridgable gap between the two wings. This picture was confirmed in the elections to the provincial Assemblies on 17 December, with the Awami League gaining 268 of the 279 seats that were contested at that time (elections for the remaining twenty-one seats were held in mid-January) and the PPP obtaining 148 of the 300 seats in the four provincial Assemblies in West Pakistan. As in the elections to the National Assembly, the PPP got no seats at all from Baluchistan and only a nominal representation in the N.W.F.P., but it got the majority of seats in the Punjab and Sind. In the two frontier provinces (N.W.F.P. and Baluchistan) the Pakistan Muslim League (Qayyum), the National Awami Party (Wali), and a local religious party made the best showing.[29]

Almost all political parties except the PPP and the Awami League, including all three parties that emerged from the once-united Muslim League, the spearhead of the independence movement, fared badly in the elections. The voters repudiated the old leaders and the old parties, including religious parties. As a correspondent of the London *Daily Telegraph* reported, 'forty million Pakistani electors have voted overwhelmingly for a completely new leadership with a drubbing at the polls for almost every politician and vested interest linked with the past.'[30]

The leading newspaper of Pakistan described the elections as an 'historic achievement.'[31] The Chief Election Commissioner – who, incidentally, was an East Pakistani – declared immediately after the voting for members of the National Assembly that as a result of the successful conduct of its first direct and free national elections Pakistan could lay claim to being 'the world's third largest democracy.'[32] The London *Times*, in a leading article prophetically entitled 'The First and Perhaps Last Election,' stated that 'No one need doubt Pakistan's political capacity to express the popular will through the democratic process;' but it warned: 'What is disturbing about this first general election is that it had demonstrated seemingly unbridgable differences between the two halves of the country.'[33] This was indeed the 'great divide,' which the elections widened rather than helped to bridge.

Table 8.ii

RESULTS OF GENERAL ELECTIONS IN PAKISTAN, DECEMBER 1970: NATIONAL ASSEMBLY

Total seats	*Baluchistan* 4	*NWFP* 25	*Punjab* 82	*Sind* 27	*West Pakistan* 138	*East Pakistan* 153[a]	*Pakistan* 291
A.L.	–	–	–	–	–	151	151
P.P.P.	–	1	64	18	81	–	83
Q.M.L.	–	7	1	1	9	–	9
C.M.L.	–	–	7	–	7	–	7
J.U.P.	–	–	4	3	7	–	7
J.U.P.(H)	1	6	–	–	7	–	7
N.A.P.(W)	3	3	–	–	6	–	6
J.I.	–	1	1	2	4	–	4
P.M.L.(C)	–	–	2	–	2	–	2
P.D.P.	–	–	–	–	–	1	1
Independents	–	7[b]	3	3	13	1	14

(*a*) Elections to nine seats in cyclone-affected areas were postponed to mid-January 1971.
(*b*) No party nominated any candidate for the seven seats in the centrally administered tribal areas.

A.L. Awami League
P.P.P. Pakistan People's Party
Q.M.L. Pakistan Muslim League (Qayyum Group)
C.M.L. Council Muslim League
J.U.P. Jamiatul Ulema-i-Pakistan
J.U.P.(H) Jamiatul Ulema-i-Pakistan (Hazarvi Group)
N.A.P.(W) National Awami Party (Wali Group)
J.I. Jamaat-i-Islami
P.M.L.(C) Pakistan Muslim League (Convention)
P.D.P. Pakistan Democratic Party

Post-Election Negotiations and the Break-up of Pakistan. Although no all-Pakistan party emerged from the elections, in view of the fact that the Awami League got an overwhelming majority of seats in the National Assembly it seemed quite likely that Sheikh Mujibur Rahman would become Prime Minister of Pakistan, possibly with some kind of understanding with the PPP or even the participation of the PPP in a coalition government. After the elections the destinies of Pakistan seemed to rest in the hands of three men, and no longer primarily in the hands of one. Yahya Khan, who had no party and who had taken no part in the election, except to determine its ground rules and to supervise its conduct, took the initiative in entering into negotiations with Sheikh Mujib and Bhutto for the convening of the newly-elected National Assembly, as the next major step along his charted course toward constitutional government.[34]

For a time it seemed that the negotiations among the three leaders, although conducted mostly at long range because of Mujib's refusal to come to West Pakistan, were making progress, in spite of the obvious personal and programmatic differences between Bhutto and Mujib; but by mid-February it became apparent that a political crisis was at hand. On 15 February Bhutto announced his decision to boycott the opening of the National Assembly, which Yahya had called for 3 March.

On 1 March, yielding to Bhutto's pressure, Yahya made a fateful announcement that the opening of the Assembly would be postponed. This announcement aroused the old suspicions in East Pakistan of the intentions of the West Pakistani and central governmental leaders, and led to general strikes, public protest meetings and demonstrations, and demands for a unilateral declaration of Independence. At a mass meeting in Dacca on 7 March Shiekh Mujib disappointed some of his followers by not endorsing this demand, but he did call for non-violent non-cooperation, which virtually gave East Pakistan a parallel government, and he laid down four conditions that must be met before the Awami League would agree to participate in the National Assembly, which on 5 March Yahya had called for 25 March. These conditions were: (1) the ending of martial law, (2) the return of the Pakistani troops in East Pakistan to their barracks, (3) a public enquiry into alleged massacres in East Pakistan by the West Pakistani armed forces, and (4) the immediate transfer of power to the elected representatives of the people.

On 14 March Yahya came to Dacca and agreed to accept these four conditions, 'in principle'; but a week later negotiations involving Yahya, Mujib, and Bhutto went badly, and apparently Yahya thereupon gave the final orders for the course of action that led to the tragic events of the coming months. On 25 March Yahya suddenly returned to West Pakistan, and on that night Pakistani troops, acting on his orders to 'restore law and order' in East Pakistan, began a campaign of ruthless repression and mass killing that soon led to a bloody civil war in that part of the country, the exodus of millions of East Bengali refugees into India, India's strong support for the East Pakistanis, and eventually war between India and Pakistan, the defeat of Pakistan, the fall of Yahya Khan and the assumption of power by Z. A. Bhutto, the independence of Bangladesh, a new political order in both parts of what had been a united country, and a new order of power in South Asia.

In the light of the unhappy events that followed it, the general elections in Pakistan in December 1970 loom as a less impressive achievement than they seemed at the time, and as an event that had destabilizing rather than stabilizing effects. Instead of paving the way for the next steps along the road to constitutional government, the elections proved to be both the beginning and the end of the constitutional process. They were, however, a necessary beginning, and not an inevitable end. While there is a clear relationship between the elections and the events that followed, even including the break-up of the country, the relationship is not necessarily a casual one. The elections might not have led to these tragic results. They might have been a major step in nation-building and political development, rather than in national disintegration and political decay. They changed the political environment in Pakistan, and through the process of civil war and disruption they had some impact on the political order in the two countries that emerged from what had been a united Pakistan.

The Seventh General Elections in Ceylon

Whereas the 1971 elections in India seemed to have definitely stabilizing effects upon the political system, and the 1970 elections in Pakistan definitely destabilizing and disruptive effects, the 1970 elections in Ceylon seemed to have definitely stabilizing effects, only to be followed in less than a year by 'the greatest challenge to the power of institutionalized authority in recent Ceylonese history'[35] and by a higher degree of systemic instability than independent Ceylon had experienced in any previous period. As in India and Pakistan the Ceylonese elections of 1970 seemed to clarify a confused political picture and to give a decisive majority to political parties which had deep roots in popular support, but they had a very different impact and systemic effect than did the elections in the larger South Asian states.

For various reasons the government of the United National Party, which had come into power in 1965 with less than a majority of the membership in the House of Representatives, had become increasingly unpopular, and the economic situation in the country had become increasingly precarious. Of particular concern were the rising cost of living, the alarmingly high rate of unemployment, especially among the educated youth in a country with more than a 70 per cent rate of literacy, and the desperate foreign exchange situation. The government's action, on grounds of economic necessity, in cutting down the subsidized amount of rice from two measures (about four pounds) for 50 Ceylonese cents to one free measure had evoked widespread protest, and perhaps more than any other single factor was responsible for its decisive repudiation in the elections of 1970. For this was *par excellence* a 'rice election,' and Mrs. Sirimavo Bandaranaike's promise to restore the rice ration was a major reason for her overwhelming victory.

But there were many reasons for the outcome of the 1970 elections, some tangible, like the promise to restore the rice ration, and some intangible, like the swing away from the UNP, and Mrs. Bandaranaike's personal image and appeal. Another major reason was the success of the Sri Lanka Freedom Party, which she headed, in forming a United Front with two other important parties, the Lanka Sama Samaja Party (a Trotsykite party) and the Ceylon Communist Party (a pro-Soviet party). The United Front had a strongly left-of-center orientation and was thus able to appeal to the radical sentiments in the country. It also was able to appeal to the dominant Sinhalese population on the slogan 'Save the Sinhala nation,' to the Buddhists in a country where the vast majority of the people were Buddhists, and to the young voters who had been enfranchised since the last general elections by the lowering of the voting age to eighteen (this added some 800,000 new voters, about one-fifth of the total number, to the electorate).

Campaign Promises and Appeals. During the campaign Mrs. Bandaranaike and her supporters made all kinds of sweeping promises and pledges to the electorate. (This is reminiscent of similar sweeping pledges made by Mrs. Gandhi in the 1971 elections in India and by Sheikh Mujibur Rahman and Z. A. Bhutto in the Pakistan elections in December 1970.) Among these promises, in addition to the most politically potent pledge to restore the rice ration, were: to nationalize eight foreign banks (five of them British); to control the export–import trade; to tighten controls over the plantation industries – the tea, rubber, and coconut estates that were mostly owned by foreigners; to set up 'people's committees' to supervise the actions of local officials and to give Ceylon a more genuine 'participatory democracy'; to give Ceylon a new Constitution which would make the country a Republic, thus ending Dominion status; to abolish the Senate, the upper House of the Ceylonese Parliament; to suspend relations with Israel until that country withdrew from Arab-occupied territory; to recognize the Communist regimes in North Korea and North Vietnam and the

People's Revolutionary Government in South Vietnam, and in general to support 'national liberation struggles'. These were all popular positions, which appealed to those Ceylonese who wanted more nationalistic and socialistic policies, with a greater degree of 'distributive justice', to use a term popular in India, and of genuine national independence (meaning, apparently, independence from 'imperialistic' controls and pressures from the Western countries and India).

In his appeal to the voters Prime Minister Dudley Senanayake, head of the UNP, charged that 'the United Front was attempting to fasten the iron collar of authoritarianism on the people,' and, as has been noted, he warned that a victory for the UF would mean 'the end of our democratic set-up.' Mrs. Bandaranaike and other UF leaders referred repeatedly to the 'misdeeds' and the 'misrule' of the UNP, and they also occasionally alleged that they had information that the armed forces might try to take over the government, even before the elections could be held, if there were clear indications of a UF victory, or immediately after the elections if the UNP government was defeated.[36]

Most observers thought that the elections would be close, with the majority giving an edge to the UNP. As in India and Pakistan, the election prognostications proved to be wide of the mark. (It would be interesting to examine the reasons for remarkably wrong electoral predictions on the part of informed analysts, including pollsters, journalists, scholars, and others, whose record in most electoral predictions is generally quite good.)

The Voting – and After. The voting was held on 27 May 1950. The turnout was the highest in Ceylon's history – 85.2 per cent. Although it got only 49 per cent of the total vote, the UF won 116 of the 151 seats – 77 per cent – in the House of Representatives. The SLFP alone won ninety-one seats, with 36.9 per cent of the popular vote. The UNP got even more votes than the SLFP – 37.9 per cent of the total – but it was able to win only seventeen seats. (In the 1965 elections it won sixty-six seats with 288,000 fewer votes.) Ten Ministers and nine Deputy Ministers in the UNP Cabinet were defeated. Even Prime Minister Senanayake won re-election by an amazingly narrow majority.[37]

Like the elections of 1956, which had first given electoral proof of the shifting balance of political forces in the country and which had brought the SLFP, then led by its founder, S. W. R. D. Bandaranaike, Mrs. Sirimavo Bandaranaike's husband, into power, the elections of 1970 were obviously of special significance. Possibly they could even be called a 'critical election', as V. O. Key used the term.[38] Like the 1956 elections, they were a 'ruralizing' election, but in a somewhat different sense. Their broad significance is well stated by a leading Ceylonese political scientist: 'Ceylon has effected a social revolution by ballot of great magnitude and uniqueness. Radicalization has up to this time taken place only in the urban areas of Ceylon. The significance of the UF victory of May 1970 is that the rural areas have for the first time showed convincing evidence of the same radicalization.' He also pointed out that 'economic issues have prevailed over others relating to language, religion, etc.,' and he sagely observed: 'The air is filled with mounting expectations: Can the Government satisfy them?'[39]

This was indeed the question on almost everyone's mind as a new government, headed by Mrs. Bandaranaike, assumed office. Even though the SLFP by itself held 60 per cent of the seats in the House of Representatives, the other two parties in the United Front were also given representation in a 'ministry of all the talents from the radical forces in Ceylon politics.'[40] The veteran Trotskyite, Dr. N. M. Perera, became Minister of Finance, and the leader of the Ceylon Communist Party, Peter Keuneman, Minister of Housing. Mrs. Bandaranaike immediately took steps to implement her many election pledges, both in domestic and foreign policy. The rice ration was increased to two measures, as promised, but the increase in price to 75 cents a measure provoked some grumbling, even within the ranks of her own supporters. The high expectations that had been raised could not possibly be realized, and within a few months of its overwhelming victory, there were many signs of a growing disillusionment with the new government. 'We have not forgotten the promises we made to the people,' said Mrs. Bandaranaike. 'But you must give us a little more time.'[41]

Table 8.iii

RESULTS OF GENERAL ELECTIONS IN CEYLON, MAY 1970: HOUSE OF REPRESENTATIVES

Parties	*No. of seats won*	*Per cent of valid votes polled*	*No. of valid votes cast*
United National Party	17	37.9	1,892,525
Sri Lanka Freedom Party	91	36.9	1,839,979
Lanka Sama Samaja Party	19	8.7	433,224
Federal Party	13	4.9	245,727
Ceylon Communist Party	6	3.4	169,199
All Ceylon Tamil Congress	3	2.3	115,567
Mahajana Eksath Peramuna	—	.9	46,571
Independents	2	5.0	249,006
Total	151	100	4,991,798

Source: Report on the Seventh Parliamentary General Election in Ceylon (Colombo: Department of Government Printing, May 1971).

The JVP and the April 1971 Uprising. This appeal received a positive response from many quarters, but not from many of the young people who had supported the UF in the 1970 elections. 'Significantly enough, it was from the politics of the ballot-box that the frustration of the Sinhalese youth articulated itself in 1965 and it was the election of 1970 which accelerated the growth of this frustration.'[42] This frustration was most evident among the more radical young people who had formed the Janata Vimukti Peramuna – the People's Liberation Front, or JVP, popularly but somewhat erroneously referred to as Che Guevarists.

As early as the fall of 1970, in spite of their support of the UF in the elections, the JVP leaders were planning a revolution. In August 1970 they promised full support of the Government provided it solved the 'problem of unemployment, landlessness of peasants, malnutrition and general economic problems.'[43] This was obviously a large order, one that the Government could not possibly carry out *in toto*. But the JVP leaders would settle for nothing less than a complete package, and they were soon openly voicing their disillusionment, not only with the Government but with the entire political system. In February 1971 one of their spokesmen said at a public rally: 'We helped to form the UF Government merely to make the masses realise how futile it was to have to usher in socialism through the parliamentary process.'[44] By this time the JVP was moving towards a major uprising, and the Government, alarmed by evidences of such preparations, without giving adequate attention to them, declared a state of emergency in the country and arrested the best-known leader of the JVP, Rohan Wijeweera, a 'drop-out' from the Patrice Lumumba University in Moscow.

On 5 April 1971, the 'Che Guevarists' launched a series of attacks on police stations, security patrols, and government buildings. The uprising seemed to be badly coordinated, and was perhaps even premature, but for a time it seemed likely to topple the Government and to create a revolutionary situation in the country. After some indecision the Government, with the support of the army and police and with aid immediately provided by several foreign countries with very different political systems, the immediate challenge was met. Thousands of insurgents were killed, and at least 15,000 were captured and placed in confinement. Even a year later thousands of young Ceylonese were still in 'concentration camps,' and the basic discontent that led to the abortive uprising still remained. This created a continuing threat to the political system that the UF government has not been able to deal with satisfactorily. Its continued confinement of thousands of young insurgents provoked much criticism, and much embarrassment to the government of a democratic state that claims to be a government of the 'common man'.[45]

Sri Lanka and the New Political Framework. On 22 May 1972, a new Constitution was approved by the House of Representatives, and Ceylon officially became the 'Republic of Sri Lanka'. The new Constitution was a tough one, which in the opinion of some critics imposed serious limitations on the democratic political system. It 'does away with the various checks and balances inhibiting the legislature from giving effect to the "will of the people" expressed through elected representatives. The supremacy accorded to the unicameral legislature – called the National State Assembly – is evident from the fact that the new constitution has, in effect, abolished the right of judicial review (in the sense that it exists in India or the United States).'[46]

The 'basic tenets of the Constitution,' as Urmila Phadnis has pointed out, 'were primarily a response to the insistent demands of the indigenously educated rural élite in the island, which was largely responsible for the overwhelming success of the UF in the general election.'[47] But it still remains to be seen whether the new regime ushered in under the new Constitution will be acceptable to the disgruntled and dissatisfied elements in the country, including the radical youth. In a peculiar way the 1970 elections gave the country a stronger and more popularly-based government, which in turn gave Ceylon a new political framework and a new economic and social orientation, but which still could not cope adequately with the economic problems or with underlying unrest. Thus the Republic of Sri Lanka is faced simultaneously with various crises of development, to adopt the terminology of the Committee on Comparative Politics of the Social Science Research Council, including the crises of legitimacy, authority, participation, and national integration.

Three Elections: Similarities and Differences

The three general elections that were held in three South Asian countries in 1970 and 1971 had many similarities and many differences. They were held under conditions of political instability and uncertainty, with political regimes of dubious authority or legitimacy trying without much success to cope with growing political, economic, and social difficulties. They all led to results that surprised and confounded political analysts and prognosticators. They all produced overwhelming majorities for particular political parties, and seemed to clarify the political situation and to pave the way for greater political stability. Yet they led to very different results. They changed the political environment in each country in different ways. They gave majority support to parties and leaders who were generally much more radical than the parties or groups that were in power before the elections were held. In a sense, this may have been confirmation of a trend that seems to be apparent in many developing countries, namely the trend toward a growing radicalization of politics as well as of economic policies.

The victorious parties had closer links with the masses of the people, and with numerically dominant social groups and classes, than those parties or leaders which were in power prior to the voting. They catered to the masses by championing the causes which were of greatest concern to them. By raising slogans of socialist democracy or by appealing to national or sub-national sentiments they posed as champions of the 'common man' against the élitist groups that had been in power previously. They made all kinds of sweeping pledges and promises in the course of the electoral campaigns – for example, Mrs. Gandhi's pledge to 'abolish poverty', Sheikh Mujib's to win all of the famous six points, Bhutto's to give Pakistan 'Islam, Socialism, and Democracy,' Mrs. Bandaranaike's to establish 'participatory democracy' and socialism. These pledges returned often in the post-election weeks and months to haunt those who made them, for no matter how sincerely they tried to fulfill their campaign promises, these promises were beyond their capacity to redeem in full.

Because of the crisis with Pakistan in 1971 Mrs. Gandhi had a reprieve of about a year before she really had to face the test of performance and begin to redeem her campaign pledges seriously and comprehensively. Sheikh Mujib and Bhutto could take refuge in the argument, which obviously had some real basis, that their primary task was one of nation-building under the changed circumstances resulting from the post-election developments, including the civil war and the break-up of the country into two nations. Mrs. Bandaranaike did not have much of a reprieve, although she had some response to her pleas to give her 'a little more time.'

For all of the governments that came to power after the three elections of 1970–1, however, time is fast running out, and the test of performance is becoming one that cannot long be evaded. For all of them the problem of performance is particularly difficult, because the promises that they made are probably impossible to fulfill under the existing circumstances, because under much more favorable circumstances it would still be most difficult to achieve both political stability and significant political, economic, and social change, and because they have all raised expectations to a level that is almost certain to lead to non-fulfillment and disillusionment. The observation of Professor Wilson about the post-election situation in Ceylon, already quoted, is applicable to all three countries: 'The air is filled with mounting expectations: Can the Government satisfy them?'[48]

As has been noted, elections are usually treated as a dependent variable, but they may also be considered as intervening or as independent variables. The three general elections in South Asia in

1970 can be analyzed in all three ways. As dependent variables they were affected by the nature of the political and social systems of which they were a part. As intervening variables they provided links between the political and social system. As independent variables, they affected the nature of political development in all three countries.

Yet we come back to the interesting phenomenon that these three general elections, held within the same time period in the same part of the world, with many similarities in conditions, conduct, and results, had very different impact upon the political systems. The intriguing question therefore keeps recurring: Why were these elections at once so similar and yet so different? The answer clearly must be sought in the different experiences, the different circumstances, and the different political and social systems in the three South Asian states, and in the different roles that elections have played in these different systems. These three case studies therefore provide us with further evidence and with another timely reminder of the basic point that elections may have different kinds of systemic impact and that they must be analyzed within the framework of the larger systems of which they are a part.

9

THE INDIAN VOTER — A PROFILE

In any democratic country a national election is a major and much-publicized event. It tends to highlight and dramatize the entire political process, and to a considerable extent the underlying cultural and social milieu. It involves larger numbers of people in political activity than any other single national endeavor. For the time being, at least, it brings political leaders – and aspirants for political leadership – into more direct contact with the masses of the citizens than in any other way, and it gives the average citizen at least a temporary sense of having a real say in the choice of his political leaders and of genuine participation in the political process. As V. M. Sirsikar has observed, 'the general elections endow a temporary personality to the common voters. They are crowned as "the sovereign voters."' But, alas, as Sirsikar points out, 'the sovereignty is very transient. It lapses on the day the polling is over.'[1]

National elections in India have aspects of special interest and fascination. The spectacle of millions of ordinary Indians, most of whom are illiterate, isolated both geographically and socially, and unaccustomed to democratic ways, participating in 'the world's largest democratic elections' is a truly impressive demonstration of democracy in action in the largest non-Communist underdeveloped nation. No other experience throws so much light on the nature of the Indian political system, or on Indian political development. No other better illustrates – and indeed dramatizes – the successes and failures, the prospects and the handicaps, of the uphill Indian effort to achieve 'progress through democracy.'

As D. L. Sheth has noted, the 'political development of voters can be observed at two levels: [the] collective level of the electorate and [the] individual level of a voter;' and he calls attention to 'the need to probe further into the elements of "voter development" and to systematically conceptualise the collective and individual aspects of voter development as independent variables influencing other elements and processes in the larger systems.'[2] Most electoral and voting behavior studies, in India as in other countries, have emphasized the collective aspects of voter development. This is illustrated in India by the lengthy reports of the

Election Commission on every national election (consisting mostly of aggregate statistical data and generalized analysis), numerous studies of elections in various States, again relying heavily on aggregate data, as well as on extensive survey research, and the more conventional and more historically-oriented historical and descriptive studies. A vast amount of valuable material on the Indian voters, as individuals participating in a particular political process in a particular social and political milieu, is available in these more general studies, but the available data are seldom used to throw light on the attitudes and behavior patterns of the Indian voters, as individual citizens in a given social and political setting. Nor has sufficient attention been given to the classification and characteristics of Indian voters, or to their development, if any, as a result of their growing experience and growing familiarity with the electoral process over time.

The Indian Voter – General Characteristics

What sort of a person is the Indian voter? What does the vote, and the experience of participating in the electoral process, mean to him (or her)? How has he changed with the passing of time, from the pre-independence to the post-independence generation, from unfamiliarity with the voting experience to acceptance of it as a regular part of political life? And what evidences, indexes, measurements, and tests can be applied to throw light on his attitudes and behavior patterns as a citizen of the world's largest democracy, when in a sense both he and his country are at an early stage of political development?

It is not difficult to draw in broad strokes a profile of the 'average' Indian voter (to whom the male pronoun will be applied, although this is in a sense misleading, since the 'average' Indian voter is almost as likely to be a woman as a man. In all general elections in India the number of men who have voted has exceeded the number of women, but while the numbers of members of both sexes who have voted have increased both relatively and absolutely, the number of women voters has increased more rapidly than the number of male voters, even though more men still vote than women.) The 'average' Indian voter is a Hindu, is a member of a lower caste, lives in a rural area (probably in a village), is an agriculturist (probably a small farmer or a landless laborer), is illiterate, has seldom if ever in his life been far from his place of birth, is under thirty-five years of age, is married and has several children, has an income of under $100.00 a year, is not a member of any political party but has some kind of political preference (more likely to be in favor of the Congress than any other party), has a low level of political interest and awareness, and does not participate in political life in any way other than voting.

A more specific and empirically validated list of attributes of the Indian voter has been compiled by Ramashray Roy, on the basis of data obtained from the national sample interviewed in the 1967 election study of the Centre for the Study of Developing Societies in Delhi. According to these data, in 1967 more than four-fifths of the Indian voters were Hindus; 77.26 per cent came from rural areas; 51.29 per cent had received no formal education; 33.49 per cent had had seven years or less of schooling; 40.88 per cent were farm owners or cultivators; 12.46 per cent were landless laborers; 35.24 per cent had monthly incomes of less than 100 rupees; 26.93 per cent of between 101 and 200 rupees; only 8.70 per cent 400 rupees or above; and 30.87 per cent had been born in the third decade of the century, or later ('In other words, these voters were socialized into matters political after Independence when partisan politics replaced politics of nationalism').[3]

A disturbing picture of an uninformed, generally unparticipant, and largely apathetic citizenry emerged from a major sample survey in four States – Andhra Pradesh, Gujarat, Uttar Pradesh, and West Bengal – in 1966, involving interviews with 2,637 respondents, mostly in rural areas, belonging to some fifteen different castes (with no single caste accounting for more than 8 per cent of the sample).[4]

The level of political knowledge of the respondents was very low. Only 38.7 per cent could give the name of the Prime Minister of India (even as well-known a figure as Mrs. Indira Gandhi, who came from U. P.), only 19 per cent could give the name of the Chief Minister of their State, and only 25 per cent knew to which party the Chief Minister belonged. Only 15.2 per cent could name the main opposition party in the State Legislative Assembly. Only 24.4 per cent knew when the next general election would be held, even though it was scheduled for only a few months hence.

A rather dim view of political parties and a lack of party affiliation were also reflected in the results of the survey. 90 per cent said that they were not members of any political party, although 31.3 per cent thought that the Congress Party would do more good for the people than any other party; 46.8 per cent indicated that they supported the Congress; 50.2 per cent said they would vote in the next general elections for Congress candidates for the State Assembly and 48.1 per cent for Congress candidates for the Lok Sabha. Only 29 per cent expressed satisfaction with political parties. 36 per cent felt that political parties are necessary in India, but 21 per cent favored a no-party system and more than 35 per cent gave a 'don't know' response to this question. 54.8 per cent expressed the view that political parties had made no contribution to solving the problems of their villages or towns.

The respondents were much more favorably disposed toward the government than toward parties. 51.3 per cent believed that the national government understood the needs of the people well. The comparable figure for the assessment of the State government – in a State that was characterized by a great deal of political instability and inefficiency – was 52 per cent. 46.2 per cent were convinced that the government was contributing much to the progress of the Indian people. These replies reflected a surprising degree of satisfaction with government performance, and an apparent general acceptance of the legitimacy of the political system.

Obviously the respondents had a very low sense of political efficacy. 43.7 per cent thought that people like them could have little effect on what the government does, and another 16.5 per cent gave a 'don't know' answer to this question. The majority seemed to feel even less efficacious politically in their own localities. 56.9 per cent thought they had no influence on the policies or actions of the local panchayats or municipalities. Yet, paradoxically, 44 per cent thought that the way people vote has a great deal of effect on what the government does.

On the whole the respondents seemed to have little interest in political affairs. 48.2 per cent stated quite frankly that they had no interest in politics, and another 18.3 per cent said that they were only 'somewhat interested.' When asked about what were the most important things a citizen of India must do, the majority simply said they didn't know; another 9 per cent said 'do one's work well,' and a slightly lower number said that as citizens they had no obligations at all. The great majority were obviously quite apolitical, and had little sense of civic obligation, as well as of political efficacy, two characteristics that are often linked. Yet it is interesting to note that 41 per cent said that if they had a son who was thinking of going into politics, they would encourage him to do so, and only 25.4 per cent said that they would discourage him.

In spite of the low level of political interest and awareness, the voting record of the respondents was quite good. 71.5 per cent indicated that they voted in one or more national elections – 46.4 per cent 'every time,' 12.9 per cent 'most of the time,' and 12.2 per cent 'rarely.' Their turnout in panchayat or municipal elections was slightly lower.

Voting, however, was almost the only act of political participation in which the respondents had engaged. 86.4 per cent said that they had never attended a political meeting or rally 'during an election or at any other time.' 91.1 per cent, in fact, claimed that they had never engaged in any activity in a political campaign. A rather surprising number – 21 per cent – indicated that they had given money 'for a political cause.' 90 per cent stated that they had never contacted any representative or governmental official at block, district, or state level. Most seemed to think that such contacts would do no good, unless one had 'connections.' 93.8 per cent said that they had never contacted any party leaders 'about some need or problem.' Even more surprising, 90.9 per cent reported that no party leader or government official 'from the village/town or outside' had even contacted them. These figures suggest both a low degree of political participation, aside from voting, and of effective campaigning on the part of the various parties and candidates.

Changing Character of the Indian Electorate

Important changes have taken place in the character of the Indian electorate since independence. The most obvious change is a generational one. In the first three post-independence general elections the majority of the voters were of the pre-independence generation; by 1967 – and certainly by 1971 – the majority were of the post-independence generation, having been born, or at least having reached adulthood, after or shortly before 1947. As the Director of the Indian Institute of Public Opinion pointed out in 1967, the face of the electorate changed slowly prior to 1962, but drastically between 1962 and 1967.[5] The broad nature of the change is suggested in a report of the 1967 general elections in the Punjab and Haryana: 'The voters seemed to be less interested in the past achievements of the party (e.g., during the national freedom movement) and were also less under the charisma of any national leader than in the earlier elections. Thus, a trend was visible that they were increasingly concerned with the contemporary events and problems. Voters were more problem oriented this time.'[6]

In several democratic countries generational changes have led to significant shifts in political alignment and allegiance. Apparently this has happened in Britain, to cite one example. Butler and Stokes have emphasized the 'role which the replenishment of the electorate has played in the great changes of alignment that have dramatized British politics in this century.'[7] No such changes in voter alignment have taken place on a long-time basis in India. The results of the general elections of 1967 seemed to indicate that such a change might have occurred, as large numbers of voters who normally supported the Congress Party, including members of several minority groups, gave their support to non-Congress candidates; but the results of the fifth general elections in 1971 and the State Assembly elections of 1972 and 1974 showed that most of these dissidents had returned to the Congress fold – or, more accurately, had been won back by the new image that Mrs. Gandhi had been able to give to the wing of the former undivided Congress that she headed. There are some evidences that the Congress – even Mrs. Gandhi's Congress – had relatively little support among urban intellectuals and other highly educated Indians, and among large numbers of young people. In time this could lead to a considerable erosion of strength for the Congress, for all of these groups are growing in numbers and in political importance. But it is still too soon to attempt to chart the kind of political changes and realignments that Butler and Stokes described in Britain. With few variations – notably in 1967–71 on the national level, and in several States at different periods – the basic political pattern in India since independence, namely that of a diffuse party system with one party clearly dominant and with the opposition weak and badly divided, has persisted. If basic changes in political loyalties and alignments are in the making, their nature and significance are still unclear.

Even the nearly all-powerful Congress Party, however, has learned a basic political lesson, namely that the Indian voter, however much he may be influenced by custom and ascriptive ties and loyalties, cannot be taken for granted. He has shown an increasing degree of independence, and he has often surprised the political pundits. Butler and Stokes have called attention to an increasing volatility on the part of the British voters. The same tendency can be discerned in India. This tendency seems obvious to even the casual observer, and it is confirmed by electoral results and voting behaviour studies. The increasing volatility of the Indian voter is a significant political development. It may in time give a new cast to Indian politics, certainly in the style of politics, the nature of political campaigns and political appeals, and perhaps even in more fundamental aspects and trends in Indian political life.

Almost all students of voting behavior in India, however, have called attention to what they regard as the increasing politicization of Indian life. The Indian voter is becoming increasingly politicized, whether he realizes or wishes this or not. He is becoming more and more a political animal, and is being increasingly exposed to political influences and forces. He is already showing signs of reacting to this process in more than a negative way. One might say that the Indian voter is decreasingly merely a subject of politics and is becoming an object, a positive factor in shaping his own political destiny, choosing his political representatives, and to some extent in affecting governmental policies and priorities. The process of politicization has produced, and has stemmed from, what D. L. Sheth has called 'certain attitudinal and behavioural changes in the electorate.' Sheth's analysis of the nature and extent of politicization in India, and its meaning, is well worth noting:

> The process of politicisation, however, is 'adaptive' rather than 'transformative'. The traditional categories of social belonging are transferred to political and civic life introduced by modern political institutions. But these traditional categories do not remain immutable in the face of the demands made by modern democratic institutions.
>
> Confrontation with these new environmental conditions and institutional stimuli has produced certain attitudinal and behavioural

changes in the electorate. These changes pertain to the growth of political identification, increased salience of politics in their psychological environment, and growth of certain enduring orientations which are 'political' in nature. In this process of adaptation, the ritualistic and religious aspects of group living are undermined in favour of political articulation of group interests, including even the more primordial group interests. This is sought through identification with larger collectivities like political parties and pressure groups.[8]

The phenomenon of increasing politicization is due to many factors. Some are deeply rooted in the Indian political and social system. A major factor certainly has been the growing participation of more and more Indians in the electoral process. But it may be that India is an overpoliticized polity, at the present and likely future stages of political development. Some observers seem to fear the consequences of growing politicization in a polity for a new and still rather tentative democratic structure. Their fears have been accentuated by growing evidence of increasing tensions in Indian society and increasing instability in the political system. 'This continuing instability,' warns Ramshray Roy, 'is likely to accentuate politicization without a concomitant increase in commitment to democratic norms and indeed perhaps leading to an erosion of whatever attachment to democratic principles is still there.'[9] Too little politicization is unhealthy for an evolving polity, but too much is also undesirable, at least in the early stages of political development.

For better or for worse, the character of the Indian electorate is changing in many ways, some quite obvious, others still unclear. Some of the major changes are the result of the changing character of Indian society and of Indian life generally, under the impact of the changing conditions inside the country and of the changing external environment. The generational change and the changes consequent upon increasing urbanization, modernization, population growth, etc., are of particular long-range significance. The Indian voter has become more mature politically, more self-confident in his role as a citizen, more volatile and independent, and more highly politicized. He is also becoming more performance oriented. In the coming years, as Rajni Kothari has predicted, the test of performance may prove to be more important than most, if not all, of the other factors that have determined his voting behavior and his political loyalties and allegiance.

Political Stratification of the Indian Electorate

As Bashiruddin Ahmed has stated, 'The electorate is not an undifferentiated mass of voters. On the contrary, it is an entity which is stratified on the dimensions of political involvement and hence political influence.'[10] The political stratification of the electorate is a subject that has been analyzed in many countries. Although it is still a rather underdeveloped subject in most Indian election studies, it has by no means been neglected. In fact, the subject is a particularly fascinating one in India, where the voters are so numerous, so varied, and increasingly so volatile and unpredictable. 'In India, as elsewhere, politics is a remote phenomenon for most citizens. Political matters evoke interest, concern and informed participation only from a segment of the electorate, and it is this "involved" segment rather than the entire electorate which plays an important role both in elections and politics. To say this, however, is not to suggest that the mass of the citizenry does not count.'[11]

One can attempt to place Indian voters along a political spectrum, ranged according to degrees of political activism. In his interesting analysis of the political stratification of the Indian electorate, Bashiruddin Ahmed has divided voters into five categories – apathetics, peripherals, spectators, auxiliaries, and politists – and on the basis of a sample survey of nearly 2,000 voters in about ten per cent of the parliamentary constituencies in India during the fourth general elections in 1967 he has obtained the following results:[12]

Table 9.i

DISTRIBUTION OF THE ELECTORATE BY DIFFERENT POLITICAL STRATA (PER CENT)

Strata

LOW 1 *Apathetics*	2 *Peripherals*	3 *Spectators*	4 *Auxiliaries*	*HIGH* 5 *Politists*	*Total*
20.8	20.0	29.8	17.6	11.8	100
N 401	383	573	340	227	1926

Source: Ahmed, 'Political Stratification of the Indian Electorate,' p. 258.

Apathetics are 'those who are not involved psychologically in politics' and either engage in no political activity, or 'only vote without any political involvement.' This category obviously includes both the non-voters – who are numerous in India, as in most democratic systems, and whose motivations for non-participation in the political process require further examination – and also large numbers of Indians who vote, at least occasionally, without real interest, involvement, or enthusiasm. This category calls for further refinement. On the face of it, it seems that more than one-fifth of those who are eligible to vote in India should be placed in this category. The fact is that no Indian general election has involved four-fifths of the Indian electorate, as indicated by figures of voting turnout, which have ranged from less than 50 per cent to around 60 per cent. And certainly many of those who have cast votes in at least some elections should also be considered as apathetics. For them voting is a routine and rather meaningless act, and involves little or no real participation at all.

Peripherals have 'either some knowledge *or* some information,' but they only vote, and are not otherwise involved in the electoral process. They may also be regarded as persons with a very low level of political involvement, or, as the term suggests, with only a peripheral or marginal involvement.

According to this survey, spectators form the largest single category. These are persons 'who only vote and have some interest *and* information, along with a few who with moderate levels of motivation, vote and engage in one other activity.' Auxiliaries 'vote and engage in one or two other activities with medium levels of interest and information.' They 'are much more involved both psychologically and behaviourally in the processes of the system,' but they are simple 'auxiliaries' to the real actors, who are called politists. These last two groups – auxiliaries and politists – are the decisive element in the electorate. 'It is these two groups, constituting about 29 per cent of the electorate, who together shape and influence political outcomes.'[13]

Another analysis of the 1967 data gathered by the Centre for the Study of Developing Societies in Delhi, as well as of 1969 data gathered during the mid-term elections in four Indian States, classified voters into four categories: (1) Partisan voters who voted for the same party or candidate successively in two elections, and could report their preference by naming the party or candidate and/or its symbol; (2) The 'shifters' who switched their support from one party to another in the next election, compared to their preference in the prior election, and could accurately report about their choice; (3) The 'new voters' who did not vote in the prior election for whatever reason (either they were too young to vote or, though eligible, abstained from voting), but voted in the next one. Their party allegiances have not developed over a period and their electoral involvement is marginal; and (4) The 'uncommitted' electorate who either did not vote and/or failed to recall their preference for both the elections, or at least for the immediate one.[14]

According to this study the more than 3,500 voters in the samples used were divided as shown in Table 9.ii.[15]

These figures show a relatively low degree of partisan committment on the part of the Indian voters, and large numbers of voters whose political allegiance is uncertain, and often shifting. They also indicate that the relative percentages of voters in each category seem to vary considerably, even in two elections held only two years apart.

Table 9.ii

PROPORTIONS OF PARTISAN VOTERS, SHIFTERS, NEW VOTERS AND UNCOMMITTED VOTERS IN THE ELECTORATE ACCORDING TO POST-ELECTION REPORT ON VOTING RECORD OF 1967 AND 1969 ELECTIONS

Voting Record	*Partisans*	*Shifters*	*New Voters*	*Uncommitted Voters*	*Total (per cent)*
1962–7 ($N = 2287$)	32	17	21	30	100
1967–9 ($N = 1309$)	51	19	13	17	100

Source: D. L. Sheth, 'Political Development of Indian Electorate,' *Economic and Political Weekly*, V (Annual Number, January 1970), 139.

These results suggest the tentative nature of election findings, even those which are based on 'hard data.' Apparently these findings may vary considerably from election to election, and quite obviously they would vary even more from constituency to constituency and even in the same constituency over time. They do, however, throw some light on the character, and political stratification, of the Indian electorate, and may be compared with more general voting studies, and aggregate data based on several elections, which may be helpful in charting broad changes in the character of the electorate, in electoral results, and perhaps even in the political system itself, over longer periods of time.

In analyzing the 'political development of Indian electorate' D. L. Sheth has singled out five 'dimensions of voter development' to illustrate the 'political characteristics of the electorate.' Based on the sample survey carried out in 1967 by the Centre for the Study of Developing Societies the 'levels of voter development' for each of these dimensions were found (see Table 9.iii).[16]

In another analysis based on the same national sample survey Sheth discussed the 'political development' of a citizen on the basis of five items: '(1) general involvement in public life and politics, (2) involvement in election campaign, (3) awareness of competitive politics, (4) legitimacy of parliamentary institutions, and (5) satisfaction with the performance of the system.'[17]

Table 9.iii
POLITICAL CHARACTERISTICS OF THE ELECTORATE – 1967
(percentages)

	Levels of Voter Development			
Dimensions of Voter Development	*High*	*Medium*	*Low*	*Total*
Party identification	33	39	28	100
Political understanding	33	51	16	100
Issue orientation	67	28	5	100
Political involvement: (A) Awareness level	43	27	30	100
Political involvement: (B) Participation level	5	20	75	100

Source: Sheth, 'Political Development of Indian Electorate,' p. 143.

Drawing upon this list of indicators of the 'political development' of the Indian electorate, and upon other indicators that are commonly employed in similar analyses of voter profiles and characteristics in other political systems, the following indicators will be singled out for special treatment: (1) the political awareness level – the level of information; (2) the degree of interest in politics; (3) the political participation level, including participation in election campaigns; (4) the degree of political understanding, including what Sheth has referred to as 'awareness of competitive politics'; (5) the degree of psychological involvement in the electoral process; (6) party identification; (7) the sense of civic duty regarding voting and other acts of political participation; (8) political efficacy; (9) the attitudes toward the legitimacy of the political system; and (10) the degree of satisfaction with the performance of the government and of the political system, including attachment to or alienation from the system. Indices will be suggested as a means of testing some of these indicators, and some of the relevant findings of empirical research will be summarized. Such an analysis of these ten indicators should throw considerable light upon the character and behavior of the Indian voter, as well as upon the 'collective level of the electorate,' to use Sheth's words, and the nature of the Indian political system.

Level of Political Awareness

What is the level of political awareness, or the 'cognitive map,' of Indian voters? To what extent do they have the knowledge and the information that they need in order to function as informed citizens?

One would assume that in India, where rates of literacy are so low, where mass media and other channels of communication are so limited, and where the majority of the people seem to live in very restricted worlds, the 'cognitive map' would be a hazy and distorted one, and the level of information and awareness very low indeed. Participant observation would tend to confirm this impression. Empirical studies, however, seem to indicate that while this picture is generally true, the Indian voters have a higher level of political awareness – especially on matters that really count and that are really meaningful to them – than less systematic methods of investigation would indicate.

One of the most detailed empirical studies of political behavior at district and sub-district levels was carried out by Dr. Yogesh Atal in three communities in a western district of Uttar Pradesh on the eve of the fourth general elections in 1967. This study focussed on the elections, and it had significant macro as well as micro aspects and implications. 'Rather than analysing only the voting behaviour of the sample population, it seeks to relate political behaviour with communication development and other processes of modernization.'[18] The communities that were selected for special study were the capital of a district, a 'centre of the community' (COC) of about 25,000 people, a 'link community' (LC) or 'nucleus' village of about 2,500 people, and a 'nagla' or satellite village, a 'small community' (SC) of less than 400 people. Detailed interviews were conducted with 120 persons in the COC, sixty-five in the LC and thirty in the SC, in three waves, one in January 1967, one in mid-February on the eve of the elections, and one in March. Indexes were developed to test political awareness, among many other things, with questions designed to test the voters' knowledge of international, national, and regional issues and developments. Awareness of the international milieu was measured by responses to a set of four questions, concerning the names of world leaders, the names of countries considered to be friendly to India, the names of countries considered to be hostile to India, and major world events. The national awareness score was based on responses to questions about the date of the coming general elections, the names of national leaders, and a listing of problems faced by India. Regional awareness was tested by ten questions, including an awareness of one's registration as a voter, knowledge of winning candidates for the Lok Sabha and the State Assembly in the three previous general elections, the names of contesting candidates and of regional and provincial leaders, information about the last municipal elections, factors likely to determine the outcome of the election, and 'problems expected to be highlighted.'

The results of the survey were most interesting. Based on the first wave of interviews, international awareness was rated as medium to low in the COC, and low in the other two communities. National awareness was about equally divided among all three categories, with more in the low category than in any other. The national awareness index was constructed on the basis of replies to questions about three national problems, the anti-cow slaughter movement, student agitation, and food, and about the rights of citizens. Based on these questions the national awareness index was high in the COC, mostly high and medium in the LC, and also in the SC.

The third wave of interviews, after the elections, used knowledge about the winning MLA and MP for regional awareness, and knowledge about States where the Congress Party had lost its hold (a sensational result of the general elections), and about defeated national, State, and local leaders for national awareness. On these bases regional awareness was high to medium (more medium than high) in both the COC and LC, and medium in the SC, and national awareness medium to low (more low than medium) in the COC and LC, and low in the SC.[19]

Using fewer indicators but a much wider sample, on a national rather than a single district level, D. L. Sheth found a higher level of political awareness among the voters. Three specific indicators were used: '(1) whether he [the voter] perceives that there are important differences in the programmes and policies of various political parties, (2) whether he identifies a winning party or a candidate by name or symbol, and (3) whether he is able to relate his own position on specific issues with that of a political party as representing his views on these issues.'[20] He found that 30.6 per cent of the voters sampled perceived differences among parties, 68 per cent identified the winning party or candidate in the constituency correctly, and over 56 per cent related a specific party with an issue position on the issues of government controls and cow slaughter. He also found that strong partisans scored somewhat higher than weak partisans on all of these questions, and much higher than non-partisan voters.

Using data from the same national sample and also from a sample taken during the mid-term elections in four large States in 1969 Sheth derived a level of awareness from responses to two items: 'whether a respondent could correctly report the name and symbol of the candidate who won the election in his constituency (i) for the Lok Sabha and (ii) for the legislative assembly.'[21] About 43 per cent were able to make the correct identifications. This result is considerably less impressive than his previous findings, especially in view of 'the simple nature of information required of our respondents on these items.'

From these and other empirical election studies we may conclude that the level of political awareness in India is higher than one might expect, but still by no means satisfactory; that it is stronger among partisans than non-partisans; and that any findings of even empirical studies vary too greatly, depending on the time the studies are conducted, the nature of the sample, the indicators used, and many other factors, to warrant more than very tentative conclusions.

Interest in Politics

Survey data confirm the impression that general observation suggests, that the majority of the Indian electorate have little or no real interest in politics. Unfortunately, this is the situation with voters in most democratic countries, including those where the democratic system has been firmly established for many decades. Perhaps the most remarkable fact about Indian voters in this connection is not so much that their level of interest in politics is regrettably low, but that it is not much lower than in many other democratic states. In a country like India, whose people are inexperienced in the ways of democracy and whose society is in many respects a remarkably non-participatory one, this is indeed an impressive fact.

Perhaps the most comprehensive empirical data that can be presented in this connection are derived from the Project on Social and Political Change, conducted in 1966 as a party of a major cross-national study. In the survey interviews in support of this Project 2,637 people in four Indian States were asked: 'How interested are you in the politics and affairs of the nation?' The results were as follows:[22]

	Number of Respondents (weighted sample)	*Per cent*
No interest	4587	48.2
Somewhat interested	1745	18.3
Very interested	2184	22.9
Don't know	812	8.5
No response	193	2.1
Total	9521	100.0

It is a rather depressing fact that, on the basis of these findings, it seems that nearly one-half of the Indian electorate have 'no interest' in politics and national affairs, and that almost 80 per cent are not 'very interested'; but aside from the fact that the number of respondents who gave 'don't know' or no answers to this question is relatively quite high, the results are not very much out of line with the findings of similar surveys in other democratic states. These surveys show the same low levels of interest in politics. They also indicate a higher degree of interest among men than among women, among urban than among rural dwellers, among members of the middle class than among workers. A survey made in England in the early 1960s, based on interviews with 1,496 respondents, produced the findings shown in Table 9.iv.[23]

In commenting on these findings Richard Rose has pointed out that 'The small but important section who describe themselves as "very interested" appear to be distinguished as much by their sex as by their education or economic class.' He also has called attention to a significant psychological factor that may lead to the conclusion that in England, and in other democracies, the level of real political interest may be even lower than survey research findings have indicated. 'The pattern of responses in the life-history interviews suggests that many people were overestimating their consistent interest in politics in order to gain esteem in an interview situation.'[24] This is probably especially true in India, where persons who are asked about such strange matters as the extent of their interest in politics will probably be inclined to indicate a much higher degree of interest than they actually have, either 'to gain esteem in an interview situation,' as Rose suggests, or to give the interviewer the answer which they think he hopes to obtain.

In any event, the degree of voter interest in politics in India is disturbingly low, even though it does not compare as unfavorably with the situation in other democratic countries as one might expect. There is some evidence, however, to support a conclusion which Samuel J. Eldersveld advanced in 1964, namely that political interest is increasing among almost all social groups, with the 'urban wealthy' as the 'only exception.[25]

Level of Political Participation

As has been noted, political participation may refer to a wide spectrum of political activities and commitments, ranging from the simple act of voting, which may in itself indicate little or extensive involvement, to widespread political activism and involvement in the political process. Here we shall consider it mainly with relation to the electoral process. Even in this limited area the conclusions may vary greatly. If voting turnout is taken as the index, political participation will be quite high. If other acts of electoral participation are the basis of evaluation, the index will be very low indeed. If voting turnout and other participatory acts are considered, the composite index will be somewhere in between, depending on the acts selected, the relative weighting, if any, assigned to each indicator, and other factors.

In spite of these limitations, some useful findings have emerged from empirical voting behavior studies in India. Based on the national sample of the Indian electorate in 1967 D. L. Sheth composed an Index of

Table 9.iv

SELF–ASSESSED INTEREST IN POLITICS
(*percentages*)

	Total ($N = 1496$)	*Men*	*Women*	*Middle class*	*Working class*	*Left school*	
						Under 16	*16 and over*
Very interested	15	21	8	17	14	14	19
Interested	37	39	35	52	30	32	53
Not really interested	33	29	38	22	38	37	22
Not at all interested	15	11	19	9	18	17	6
Total	100	100	100	100	100	100	100

Source: Richard Rose, *Politics in England* (Boston: Little, Brown, 1964), p. 87.

Political Involvement, based on political participation, of five items: '(i) how much he [the voter] cared personally who won the election in his constituency; (ii) how much interest he took in politics and public affairs in non-election times; (iii) how much interested he was in the 1967 election campaign; (iv) how many election meetings he attended in 1967 elections; and (v) whether he actually participated in campaign activities.'[26]

These items may not be specific and relevant enough to form the basis for the construction of an Index of Political Participation. They seem to be even more relevant to other aspects of the political development of the Indian voter that are being considered, especially the degree of political involvement, more broadly considered (including the awareness level), the degree of psychological involvement, and the extent of a voter's interest in politics and political affairs. But the results, for whatever they may be worth, are nevertheless quite interesting: 'Only 5 per cent respondents obtained high scores on most of these items, and 20 per cent secured high scores only on a few items and low on others and were placed in the middle. The scores on items tapping actual participation in electoral activities were generally low for all respondents in this category. Nearly 75 per cent of the voters performed badly on all of these items, manifesting low level of personal involvement in politics and lack of activism.'[27]

In another analysis of the same data, concentrating more specifically and in greater detail on actual participation in the 1967 campaign, Sheth found that 11.8 per cent of the voters in the national sample reported participation in the campaign in one form or another (apart from voting). Of those who were identified as strong partisans 20.6 per cent reported some form of participation other than voting, whereas only 3.2 per cent of the non-partisans were included in this list of participants.[28]

Dr. Yogesh Atal's less comprehensive but more intensive survey during the 1967 election period in a single district in Uttar Pradesh produced some findings that are useful refinements of the question of political participation in connection with nationwide electoral campaigns. In his first wave of interviews, in January 1967, he developed a participation index on the basis of responses to questions about organizational membership, voting experience in the three previous general elections, and in elections to local bodies, and participation in electioneering and advice giving and discussion in the preliminary stages of the 1967 campaign. On the basis of these indicators the participation index ranged from medium to low in all three communities where Dr. Atal conducted his interviews.

The second wave of interviews, on the eve of the voting in mid-February 1967, indicated that the level of participation had increased; but this was probably due not so much to the effects of the campaign and the excitement of election eve as to the different questions which were asked as a basis for the construction of the participation index. At this stage only four rather election-specific and simple questions were asked: '(1) Are you known to any local leaders? (2) With whom do you talk on matters related to election? (3) Are you working for any candidate? (4) Are you going to vote?' 58 per cent of the sample population claimed that they were known to local leaders, and the great majority (87.8 per cent) said that they intended to vote; but less than half of the respondents said that they had engaged in any political discussions, even with members of their families or friends, and only 10.1 per cent indicated that they were actively working for any candidate.

The participation index constructed on the basis of the third wave of interviews, after the voting, indicated a lower level of participation in all three communities than either of the two previous indexes had suggested, and this in spite of the fact that in this index, for the first time, the indicator of actual participation in the act of voting was included. Only a handful of respondents in any of the three communities had a high score on the participation index. In the COC there were more than twice as many with a low as with a medium rating, and in the LC and SC almost all respondents had low scores. Three questions were asked in the construction of this participation index: '(1) Did you participate in any of the processions? (2) Did you attend any of the election meetings? (3) Did you vote?' Only thirteen of 203 respondents stated that they had participated in processions and only twenty-one that they had attended election meetings, but 89.1 per cent of the respondents in all three communities stated that they had voted – a figure far above the national average.[29]

These studies confirm the general impression of the Indian voter as one with a very low level of actual participation in politics, with the single outstanding exception of the voting act itself.

Psychological Involvement in Politics

The relationship of psychological involvement to political participation is a much discussed subject in political analysis. As Lester Milbrath has stated, 'Just as psychological involvement (interest in and concern about politics) is a central variable determining exposure to political stimuli, so is it a central attitudinal variable relating to participation in politics.'[30] There is overwhelming evidence to indicate that that relationship is a positive and an important one. Some of the findings are succinctly summarized by Milbrath:

> Persons have a general valence (positive or negative) toward politics. At least nine studies in four or more countries . . . have shown that *persons who are more interested in or concerned about an election*

> *are more likely to vote.* . . . Furthermore, *persons who are more psychologically involved in politics are more likely to engage in political and campaign activities beyond voting.* . . . *Persons of higher socioeconomic status (SES), especially higher education, are more likely to become highly involved psychologically in politics than persons of lower status.* . . . *Men are more likely to be psychologically involved in politics than women.* . . . This difference is more pronounced at the lower educational levels than at the upper, where it is nearly obliterated in modern industrial societies.

There is also a clear relation between psychological involvement and a feeling of political efficacy: '. . . *persons who are psychologically involved in politics are more likely to feel efficacious about political action.*'[31]

Using data from a 1956 study of the American electorate conducted by the Survey Research Center at the University of Michigan, Milbrath constructed a Psychological Involvement Index 'from answers to questions asking how interested the respondent was in the election and whether he cared who won.' The Index showed that 'only about one-fourth of the American electorate could be considered highly involved in the election.' He also called attention to the fact that one of the first empirical studies of voting behavior, conducted in Elmira, New York, during the Presidential election of 1952, 'reported about one-third of the electorate as greatly interested in the election and about one-fifth as believing it would make a good deal of difference who won.'[32] Subsequent empirical studies in other countries as well as in the United States have revealed approximately the same overall pattern. Obviously, in all of these countries the extent of psychological involvement varies greatly in ways Milbrath suggested in his general statements, and in other ways as well – including in some cases marked changes over time.

These generalizations and findings, in broad outline, would apply as fully to India as to other democratic countries, 'developed' or 'underdeveloped'. Obviously, in India as elsewhere the level of psychological involvement is shockingly low. The interviews with 2,637 Indians carried out in 1966 by interviewers associated with the Project on Social and Political Change revealed that nearly half of the respondents stated that they had no interest at all in politics and the affairs of the nation. The first three indicators in the five-item scale which D. L. Sheth used in developing his Index of Political Involvement/Participation related directly to psychological involvement, since they probed the voters' 'interest in and concern about politics,' which Milbrath used as the basis for his Psychological Involvement Index. The results of Sheth's analysis showed the same low degree of psychological as well as political involvement: 'Nearly 75 per cent of the voters performed badly on all or most of these items, manifesting low level of personal involvement in politics and lack of activism.' Sheth therefore drew the inescapable conclusion: 'It seems politics has not yet become the object of affective orientation for the Indian voter.'[33]

The fairly impressive turnout of voters in general elections does not modify this conclusion in any significant way. The act of voting, as has often been pointed out, may not be a very meaningful act of political participation, and it certainly does not indicate any high degree of psychological involvement by the voters in the political system. Moreover, there may be a high degree of political involvement and at the same time a low degree of psychological involvement.

Political Understanding

A citizen may have a high degree of political awareness, for this is determined mainly by his level of political information (such as knowledge of the outcome of the voting, at least in his constituency), without having any extensive political understanding, for this involves an understanding of the general nature and workings of the party system and the political process and some real perception of the issues and stakes in the elections. In India political understanding is quite high in some respects, and surprisingly seems to compare favorably with that in much more developed countries with greater experience in the democratic process and with a much more highly educated and experienced electorate.

This conclusion is in fact more of an hypothesis than an established fact. It seems to be contravened by the overall political behavior of the Indian voters and by first-hand reports and observations. Yet it is borne out by a number of empirical surveys, including the largest national sample survey in connection with a general election that has yet been made in India. Scholars at the Centre for the Study of Developing Societies have analyzed the data collected in this 1967 survey to determine the level of political understanding, among many other items of interest. They selected five questions which respondents were asked for this particular purpose. These questions concerned the perception of differences in the policies and programs of the various political parties, the perception of elections and of parties as a means of making the government responsive to the needs of the people, and the perceived value of elections and parties in India. Of the respondents 33 per cent were rated as having a high level of political understanding, receiving high scores on all five items, and 51 per cent were given a medium rating, receiving 'high score values on some items, especially those on the necessity of elections and political parties in India but low values on others (differences between political parties and meaning of elections) which require greater sophistication in the respondents' understanding of the functioning of the larger political system.' Only 16 per cent of the respondents were given a low rating, scoring low on all or most items.[34]

Analyzing the same data in a somewhat different way, in order to determine the 'awareness of competitive politics' – closely related to political understanding – D. L. Sheth based his findings on the responses to three specific items, testing whether respondents perceived important differences in the programs and policies of various political parties, could identify a winning party or candidate by name or symbol, and could relate their own positions on specific issues with that of a political party representing the same views on these issues (the issues selected were those of government controls and cow slaughter). He found that 30.6 per cent of the respondents could perceive differences between parties, 68 per cent could identify the winning party or candidate in their constituencies, and somewhat over 56 per cent could relate their position to that of a specific political party on the issues of government control and cow slaughter.[35] The answers to the second question would seem to be primarily a test of the level of political information rather than political understanding, in a broader sense, but the replies to the first and third questions certainly reflected a considerable amount of political understanding, as well as information. In another analysis of the respondents' positions on the issues of government controls, cow slaughter, and fasts as legitimate instruments for influencing governmental action, Sheth found that 'Nearly 67 per cent of the respondents took definite positions on all these issues, 28 per cent could express their opinion on one or two issues, whereas 5 per cent either failed to form any opinion on these issues or were totally unaware of their existence.'[36] Since these three issues were very much to the forefront of public attention during the 1967 election campaign, it is perhaps not surprising that so many of the respondents were aware of them and took definite positions regarding them. This finding reflects a rather high degree of issue orientation, in this case at least, but of course it does not necessarily tell us much about the levels of political understanding or of political participation. One must conclude, however, that the level of political understanding of the Indian electorate seems to be much higher than one would expect. Moreover, it seems to be increasing, and to be becoming more sophisticated.

Party Identification

As pointed out in one of the earliest empirical studies of voting behavior in the United States, party identification 'is a psychological force with important relationships to political behavior.'[37] It has been a focus of attention in voting behavior studies in many countries. These studies have uniformly demonstrated that it is an important, but by no means an exclusive or even a determining factor, in political behavior. They have also shown that it varies considerably in different political systems; for example, it is high in Britain and the United States but low in France and Italy – and in India. It also varies considerably among different groups within a political system. Quite clearly it is affected by the social environment, and by the underlying nature of the political culture.

Party identification is related to, but separate from, such important factors as degree of partisanship or partisan choice, party membership, active participation in party affairs, party support at the polls, and social identification.

W. Phillips Shively has quite rightly warned against confusing party identification with partisan choice, especially because a number of studies have shown that party identification may have a different meaning in different political systems. In most European democracies, for example, it seems to involve less long-range psychological attachment to political parties than in the United States. 'The European version appears to be much less stable over time than American party identification, and it seems to refer more often simply to the party the respondent intends to vote for, rather than one he feels an enduring attachment to.'[38]

In India, as elsewhere, partisanship is often related to the political development of the electorate. It is sometimes taken as a basis for computing party identification. In analyzing data gathered in the 1967 national sample survey D. L. Sheth used almost the same indicators to draw up indexes of party identification and of partisanship. Party identification was obtained from responses to five questions: '(i) whether he [a respondent] would vote for the same party again in the next election; (ii) whether there were parties for which he would never vote; (iii) whether there was any party he felt particularly close to; (iv) how strong was his preference for that party; and (v) was there ever a time when he felt closer to another party.' This analysis indicated that 33 per cent of the Indian voters were quite high in their party identification, 39 per cent were medium, and 28 per cent were low. 'It should be pointed out that on all items of party identification except one, our electorate scored quite high. . . . The one item on which the respondents scored quite low was about their personal dislike and opposition for any party'[39] (which might be taken as evidence of considerable tolerance and sophistication, if not of party loyalty). Using the first four items, and substituting information about the respondents' vote in the 1967 elections in place of the fifth item, on which the scores had been very low, Sheth found that 36 per cent of his sample could be classed as strong partisans, 34 per cent as weak partisans, and 30 per cent as non-partisans. And he drew conclusions which throw light on party identification as on political partisanship:

> These figures suggest that a substantial segment of our voter population possesses a high degree of partisanship. Roughly speaking, one in every three Indian voters manifests strong partisan commitment and loyalty. Of the remaining two-thirds of the population, one-third is at least attitudinally inclined to favour a specific party although this inclination may or may not be backed by voting preference in the past election and/or by voting intentions for future elections. The Indian electorate, therefore, is not a mass of free-floating voters who would only respond to inducements and promises made at the time of the election. A great majority of them have developed partisan attitudes which are difficult to undermine by short-term campaign tactics of parties and candidates.[40]

Those who identify themselves with particular parties are obviously far more numerous than those who are actually party members. The number of formal members of political parties is very low in most democratic polities, depending on the conditions of membership and on many factors in the political culture. In India, with an electorate of more than a quarter of a million people, no political party has a sizeable membership. According to official party reports, primary members of the Indian National Congress numbered around 17 million in 1949–50, and again in 1965, but in no other year did they exceed 11.1 million, and in 1959 and 1963 they fell below three million. Active members have never exceeded 400,000, and have fallen as low as less than 41,000.[41] Other parties, of course, have had far fewer members, although some have issued some rather preposterous figures. Presumably most members could be classed as strong partisans, but obviously not all voters who are classed as strong partisans are party members.

Party identification does not necessarily involve active participation in party affairs. This is clearly impossible, for there are few real political activists in Indian politics, and most of those who identify themselves with a party seem to feel no impulsion toward an active role in that party. In many cases the attachment is more of a psychological than an active one. Nor is party identification a necessary proof of actual voting behavior, as measured by the ways a citizen casts his vote. Presumably a person who identifies himself with a particular party will vote for that party, but of course this is not always the case, especially in elections where, as in the fourth general elections in India in 1967, large numbers of voters who normally support and are identified with a particular party become disenchanted with the party and either refrain from voting or give their support to rival parties and candidates. If this proves to be a temporary phenomenon, the election may be described as a deviating election. If it connotes a basic change in political loyalties, the election in which the change first becomes manifest on a major scale may be described as a critical or a realigning election.

The relationship between party identification and voting varies considerably in different countries. Studies have shown that party identification is more nearly an expression of voting intention in Britain and Norway than in the United States.[42] In all three countries a change in party identification is usually accompanied by a change in voting patterns; but in the United States, according to the Survey Research Center's panel for 1956, 1958, and 1960, 'a change in voting was accompanied by a change in party identification only 27 per cent of the time,' whereas in Britain, according to the Nuffield College's panel for 1963, 1964, and 1966, the comparable figure was 62 per cent.[43] In India there seems to be a definitely positive correlation between party identification and party vote. D. L. Sheth computed from the data in the 1967 national sample survey that in the 1967 election – which was marked by large-scale deflections from the Congress – the correlation was $r = .6$ for the Congress and Jana Sangh and .5 for other major parties.[44]

As B. S. Khanna and Satya Deva have observed, 'A citizen's political decision or behaviour might be conditioned by an interplay of his political and non-political loyalties.'[45] A well-known comparative study of 'Party Identification in Norway and the United States' revealed that in the United States party identification was stronger than social identification, whereas in Norway 'basic class loyalties are fairly strong and therefore there is a conjoining of a citizen's party identification with his class loyalties in influencing his behaviour.'[46] This particular relationship has not been examined in most studies of voting behavior in India. One of the few exceptions is the study by Khanna and Deva of the 1967 election to State legislatures in the Punjab and Haryana. These investigators found that in India, as elsewhere, urbanization and education 'are conducive to the growth of party identification'; that, contrary to the situation in the United States and Norway, according to the study of these two countries by Campbell and Valen, party identification in India is stronger among men than among women; and that whereas in the United States the strength of party identification tends to increase with age, among both men and women, 'our data do not indicate a definite and regular association between party identification and age.'[47]

Clearly party identification in India has to be considered against the background of 'the political character of the Indian electorate and the party system in general.' D. L. Sheth has suggested some special aspects and limitations in the Indian setting:

> In a society where political parties do not enter as elements of one's early socialization in the family or peer group (as, for instance, is the

case in the United States), but become meaningful only in one's adulthood, largely through electoral participation itself, party identification as verbally expressed cannot be taken as indicating stable voting dispositions of the citizens. Moreover, there are numerous political parties not clearly distinguishable among themselves in terms of the appeals they make and the image they project to the voters. To develop a fairly stable identification for one among these several parties requires a relatively high level of political awareness and involvement. In the absence of this, party identification as verbally expressed would remain fairly tenuous and would fail to inform voting decisions of citizens in any stable and reliable manner.[48]

Sense of Civic Duty

There seems to be a definitely positive correlation between a sense of civic duty, or civic obligation, and actual political participation, although in every political system there is obviously a gap between civic norms and civic behavior. As Milbrath points out, 'Feeling a duty to participate seems to carry over to political action: several studies show that *persons feeling a duty to participate are more likely to do so.*'[49] Feelings of civic duty vary with the degree of political awareness, interest, understanding, and party identification, and also with education, income, occupation, race, type of community, and usually with religion, age, and sex. They also vary greatly in different political systems. 'Feelings of citizen duty are instilled by the political socialization process and have their roots both in society and in personality. The data from the five-nation study . . . clearly indicate that some political cultures more probably instill this sense of duty than others.'[50]

The five-nation study to which reference is made is the cross-national study of political attitudes and democracy in the United States, the United Kingdom, Germany, Italy, and Mexico, which is reported in the volume entitled *The Civic Culture*. In general there is a high sense of civic duty in the first two countries, and a low sense in the last two, with Germany being in between. But only 22 per cent of the 963 persons polled in Germany felt that the ordinary man should be active in his community, whereas the comparable figures were 26 per cent for Mexico, only 10 per cent for Italy, 30 per cent for the United Kingdom, and 51 per cent for the United States. The following table[51] summarizes the responses in the five nations to the question: 'We know that the ordinary person has many problems that take his time. In view of this, what part do you think the ordinary person ought to play in the local affairs of his town or district?'

Table 9.v

WHAT ROLE SHOULD THE ORDINARY MAN PLAY IN HIS LOCAL COMMUNITY, BY NATION
(*percentage*)

Percentage who choose	*US*	*UK*	*Germany*	*Italy*	*Mexico*
ACTIVE PARTICIPATION IN LOCAL COMMUNITY					
Take part in activities of local government	21	22	13	5	11
Take part in activities of political parties	6	4	4	1	5
Take part in nongovernmental activity and in organizations interested in local affairs	32	17	9	5	10
MORE PASSIVE COMMUNITY ACTIVITIES					
Try to understand and keep informed	21	11	24	6	29
Vote	40	18	15	2	1
Take an interest in what is going on	3	13	6	15	4
PARTICIPATION IN CHURCH AND RELIGIOUS ACTIVITIES	12	2	2	–	–
Total percentage of respondents who mention some outgoing activity[a]	83	72	61	32	59
Total number of respondents	970	963	955	995	1,007

(*a*) Total percentages are less than the total of individual cells, since the latter involve multiple responses.

Source: Gabriel A. Almond and Sidney Verba, *The Civic Culture: Political Attitudes and Democracy in Five Nations* (Princeton, N.J.: Princeton University Press, 1963), p. 171.

Of particular interest are the wide variations in the responses to the question regarding the duty to vote. Forty per cent of the American respondents felt that the ordinary man has a duty to vote, but the comparable percentages for the United Kingdom were eighteen, for Germany fifteen, for Italy only two, and for Mexico only one. Voting is properly listed under 'more passive community activities', and it is by far the most frequent act of political participation; yet only in the United States, among five major democracies of the Western world, did any significant number of the respondents express the view that the ordinary citizen should regard voting as a civic obligation.

Most students of voting behavior who have tried to construct an index of the sense of civic duty have adopted the indicators first developed by the Survey Research Center at the University of Michigan, and first applied on a nationwide scale in a study of the American Presidential election of 1952. This index is constructed on the basis of responses to four statements, requiring a simple 'Agree' or 'Disagree' response. The statements are:

1. It isn't so important to vote when you know your party doesn't have a chance to win.
2. A good many local elections aren't important enough to bother with.
3. So many other people vote in the national elections that it doesn't matter much to me whether I vote or not.
4. If a person doesn't care how an election comes out he shouldn't vote in it.[52]

Obviously, a respondent's sense of civic duty will be determined by the extent of his disagreement with these statements.

These statements, or statements along similar lines, have been tried out in India in a number of surveys, and the responses have indicated a very high sense of civic duty among Indians. The first and third statements were used in an all-India survey of the Indian Institute of Public Opinion in January and February 1971, just before the fifth general elections. 73 per cent of the 6,300 respondents disagreed with the first statement, and 75 per cent with the third. There was considerable variation in the reactions of respondents in different States. Disagreement was greatest among respondents in the Punjab, Haryana, Uttar Pradesh, Mysore, and Kerala, and lowest in Rajasthan, Gujarat, Orissa, West Bengal, and Bihar.[53]

Yogesh Atal's three-community study in 1967 produced similar findings. In reply to the question whether the respondents considered it important to vote, 75 per cent replied in the affirmative, and only 14.1 per cent in the negative.[54]

If framed in a more specific way, involving the itemization of duties which a citizen should be expected to perform, the results are usually quite different, indicating a far lower sense of civic duty than the standard Index of Civic Duty would suggest. This is certainly true in India, whenever the more specific approach has been used. One of the questions asked of 2,637 Indian respondents by interviewers associated with the Project on Social and Political Change in 1966 was: 'Now thinking of the duties the government expects a citizen to perform what would you say are the most important things you must do as a citizen of this country?' The answers were tabulated as follows:[55]

	Number of Respondents (weighted sample)	*Per cent*
Don't know	4,869	51.0
Do one's work well	853	9.0
Nothing is owed the government	751	7.9
Defend nation	330	3.5
Produce more	287	3.0
No response	2,431	25.6
Total	9,521	100.0

Since more than three-fourths of those interviewed either gave a 'don't know' answer to this question, the results may seem to be rather meaningless. On the other hand, the fact that very few gave any specific answers at all, and that 6.5 per cent of those who did mentioned only 'defend nation' or 'produce more', may be significant evidence that Indian voters have a very vague sense of civic obligation, even though their responses to more general statements may suggest the contrary. It is possible, however, that this question was too complicated and vague for the respondents, and that their failure to mention any specific civic obligations, beyond two rather general ones, was more an indication of their bewilderment than of any lack of a sense of civic duty. More research is needed in this area, for it is obviously important to understand how Indian voters think of their obligations and duties as citizens.

Sense of Political Efficacy

One of the most intriguing and important questions regarding voters in any democratic polity relates to their sense of political efficacy. This is a term that was developed, and operationalized, by students of voting behavior at the Survey Research Center at the University of Michigan. It is similar to the 'sense of civic competence' which was a major subject of investigation in the study of political attitudes in *The Civic Culture*. It is a useful concept for investigation in any political system, for it throws light both on the characteristics of the individual voters and on their role in and attachment or lack of attachment to the political system as a whole. Fortunately it has been analyzed in some detail in several Indian voting behavior studies, in ways that make the analyses useful for cross-cultural and cross-national comparisons as well as for probing into the inner workings of the Indian polity and the characteristics of the Indian electorate.

A sense of political efficacy, to cite one of the first empirical studies of voting behavior, 'may be defined as the feeling that individual political action does have, or can have, an impact upon the political process, i.e., that it is worth while to perform one's civic duties. It is the feeling that political and social change is possible, and that the individual citizen can play a part in bringing about this change.'[56] Its importance is well stated in one of the best empirical Indian studies of voting behavior: 'The sense of political efficacy on the part of the electorate constitutes the heart of a democratic political system. In fact the voting act is at once the cause and the effect of the sense of political efficacy that citizens of a country have in their democratic polity. The more the citizens feel that they matter in the polity of their country . . . , the more stakes they develop in their political system and its survival.'[57]

Quite clearly a sense of political efficacy is positively related to political participation. As Milbrath has pointed out, a number of voting behavior studies in the United States and other countries, and several cross-national studies, have demonstrated that '*persons who feel efficacious politically are more likely to become actively involved in politics.*'[58] According to Almond and Verba, a 'subjectively competent citizen is more likely to be an active citizen. . . . The more subjectively competent an individual considers himself, the more likely he is to be politically active.'[59] Their five-nation study clearly revealed this relationship. They found that both the sense of political efficacy and the extent of political participation were highest in the United States and the United Kingdom, and lowest in Mexico and Italy, with the Federal Republic of Germany in between on both counts. Obviously the sense of political efficacy varies considerably across nations and across cultures. It also varies considerably within a nation, in accordance with a large number of demographic and socioeconomic variables.

A well-known American study, based on 1952 Presidential election data, tested 'Demographic Correlates of Sense of Political Efficacy,' and came up with some interesting findings. A sense of political efficacy was higher among males than among females and among whites than among blacks; it was evenly distributed among younger and middle age groups, but lower among persons fifty-five years of age and older; it was definitely related to levels of education and of income, increasing with more education and more income; it was higher among professional, managerial, and other white-collar groups than among skilled, semi-skilled, and unskilled workers and farm operators; it was lower in the South than in the Northeast, the Midwest, or the Far West; and it was higher in metropolitan areas and in cities and towns than in the 'open country.'[60]

These findings are similar to those obtained from electoral research in other countries, with occasional variations that can usually be explained on the basis of differences in national cultures. The greatest differences between nations that seem to be rooted in differences in political cultures, however, tend to be of a more general nature, relating to group habits and behavior and basic attitudes and values. For example, the Almond-Verba study found, as did the American study just cited, that a sense of political efficacy – which was called a sense of civic competence in this particular study – varied in all five countries where research was carried on rather similarly with education and occupation, but varied quite dissimilarly on such grounds as group cooperation. 'Political competence thus grows with higher education and occupational status, but cooperative competence seems to be rooted in specific national political cultures.'[61]

In attempting to develop criteria for measuring the sense of political efficacy the scholars at the University of Michigan's Survey Research Center developed, in connection with their study of the 1952 Presidential election, a list of five statements, calling for a simple 'Agree' or 'Disagree' response. These statements are:[62]

1. I don't think public officials care much what people like me think.
2. The way people vote is the main thing that decides how things are run in this country.
3. Voting is the only way that people like me can have any say about how the government runs things.
4. People like me don't have any say about what the government does.
5. Sometimes politics and government seem so complicated that a person like me can't really understand what's going on.

'Disagree' responses to Statements 1, 3, 4, and 5, and an 'Agree' to Statement 2 were coded as 'efficacious.' Hence an index of a sense of political efficacy, usually rated simply as 'high', 'medium', and 'low', could be constructed on the basis of reactions to these five statements.

These items, frequently with some modifications, have been used in interviews in several countries, including India, and the results have invariably been significant and revealing, although by no means conclusive. The data are too unreliable, and the scaling too crude, to warrant anything more than tentative conclusions. But the results have been suggestive, and they have provided bases for the checking, and often the confirmation, modification, or rejection, of prevailing generalizations and hypotheses about voting behavior and its concomitants.

Using the same, or essentially the same, criteria for operationalization, several Indian studies have demonstrated that the sense of political efficacy in India is generally very low, and that, as in other democratic countries, it varies considerably in accordance with various demographic and SES variables. Interviewers in the 1966 Project on Social and Political Change changed the fourth statement in the American list into the following questions: 'How much effect do you think people like you can have on what the government does? Do you have no effect, some effect, or a great deal?' The responses of the 2,637 persons interviewed broke down as follows:[63]

	Number of Respondents (weighted sample)	*Per cent*
None	4,122	43.3
Great Deal	1,894	19.9
Some	1,800	18.9
Don't know	1,568	16.5
No response	137	1.4
Total	9,521	100.0

Another question asked in this survey is reminiscent of Statements 2 and 3 in the American study: 'How much effect does the way people vote have on what the government does? Does it have no effect, some effect, or a great deal?' The answers were as follows:[64]

	Number of Respondents (weighted sample)	*Per cent*
None	1,306	13.7
A lot	4,228	44.4
A little	1,367	14.4
Don't know	2,446	25.7
No response	174	1.8
Total	9,521	100.0

The answers to these two questions seem to be contradictory. Whereas according to the responses to the first question less than 20 per cent of the respondents could be said to have a high sense of political efficacy, according to the responses to the second question nearly 45 per cent would fall within this category. Apparently the way a question is framed and asked can influence a respondent's reply. It is also significant that one-fourth of the respondents gave 'don't know' replies to the interviewers. One wonders what questions of this kind mean to ordinary Indians.

A detailed survey of the 1967 general elections in Rajasthan, based mainly on interviews with 610 respondents in all districts of the State, and using four of the same statements as the American study, reported the following results:[65]

1. People like me have no say in what the government does.
   35.19 per cent agreed, 15.8 per cent disagreed, 49.1 per cent no response among voters. 17.5 per cent agreed, 12.5 per cent disagreed, 70.0 per cent no response among non-voters.
2. Voting is the only way through which people like me can have any say in what the government does.
   40.5 per cent agreed, 12.7 per cent disagreed, 46.8 per cent no response among voters. 32.5 per cent agreed, 5.0 per cent disagreed, 62.5 per cent no response among non-voters.
3. Sometimes politics and government are so complicated that people like me cannot understand it.
   42.1 per cent agreed, 7.8 per cent disagreed, and 50.1 per cent no response among voters. 25 per cent agreed, 10 per cent disagreed, and 65 per cent no response among non-voters.
4. Public officials do not care much for what people like me think.
   43.9 per cent agreed, 7.3 per cent disagreed, 48.8 per cent no response among voters. 31.3 per cent agreed, 10.0 per cent disagreed, 58.7 per cent no response among non-voters.

These findings indicate an exceedingly low level of political efficacy among the citizens of Rajasthan. Not only did very few – usually less than ten per cent – disagree with these four statements, but almost half of the voters and between 58 and 70 per cent of the non-voters gave no response at all, indicating that the statements were rather meaningless to them or that they did not choose to answer, for whatever reason. The findings also confirm the expected fact that non-voters have a lower sense of political efficacy than voters, but this is overshadowed by the depressingly low sense of political efficacy among the respondents generally.

In his study of attitudes in three communities in a district in western Uttar Pradesh, at three different levels, during the 1967 general elections Yogesh Atal asked the following questions, again obviously modeled after the American study, of approximately 200 respondents:

1. It is now being said that Government officials have become more considerate towards [the] public. What do you think?

2. Does the public have any means to influence the Government? What are they?

3. Is it possible for the people to change the Government, if they so will?

4. Some people believe that it would not matter whether one votes or not. What is your opinion?

5. Do you consider it desirable for people to participate in politics?

Positive responses to Items 1, 2, 3, and 5, and a negative response to Item 4 were regarded as 'efficacious' and given a score of 1 each. The results were as follows:[66]

	Score	*Frequency*	
High	5	23	23
Medium	4	68	104
	3	36	
Low	2	26	40
	1	14	
No, or unascertained	0	31	31

These findings seem to indicate a medium, rather than a low, sense of political efficacy among the respondents in this particular sample. On the other hand, less than half of the respondents had a rating of 5 or 4 on the scale; and Atal himself, in summarizing his findings and impressions in a preliminary report, stated that 'an overwhelming majority of the respondents did not seem to have personal confidence in the utility of their vote in influencing public policies or governmental action.'[67]

A medium rather than a low sense of political efficacy is also indicated in the findings of the Centre for the Study of Developing Societies study of the 1969 mid-term elections in four major Indian States, including Uttar Pradesh. This is clearly indicated in Table 9.vi,[68] presented by Ramashray Roy, which also brings out another important point, namely that the level of political efficacy varies greatly from State to State (as it does, no doubt, from district to district, and from constituency to constituency).

As Roy points out, the Table shows that 'between one-fifth and one-fourth of our respondents feel "highly" politically efficacious. It is only in the case of Punjab that the proportion of highly politically efficacious respondents is as high as 45 per cent. . . . The moderately efficacious one, however, is high in each State.'[69] The Table brings out clearly the variations in the levels of political efficacy in the four States

Table 9.vi

LEVEL OF POLITICAL EFFICACY BY STATE
(*percentage*)

States	Bihar				Punjab				UP				West Bengal			
SES \ *Political efficacy*	*High*	*Medium*	*Low*	*Total*	*High*	*Medium*	*Low*	*Total*	*High*	*Medium*	*Low*	*Total*	*High*	*Medium*	*Low*	*Total*
High				76				61				76				61
	31.6	64.5	3.9	22.4	60.7	39.3	—	20.9	36.8	52.6	10.5	17.8	34.4	49.2	16.4	24.5
Medium				142				148				189				125
	27.5	62.0	10.6	41.8	50.7	43.2	6.1	50.7	15.3	66.1	18.5	44.2	21.6	54.4	24.0	50.2
Low				119				82				157				61
	18.5	58.0	23.5	35.0	24.4	58.5	17.1	28.1	14.6	68.8	16.6	36.7	9.8	50.8	39.3	24.5
NA				3				1				6				2
	—	—[a]	—	0.9	—	—[a]	—	0.3	—[a]	—[a]	—[a]	1.4	—	—[a]	—	0.8
Total	85	209	46	340	132	137	23	292	81	276	71	428	54	131	64	249
	25.0	61.5	13.5		45.2	46.9	2.9		18.9	64.5	16.6		21.7	52.6	25.7	

(*a*) Too few cases.
Source: Ramashray Roy, 'Patterns of Political Instability: A Study of the Mid-Term Elections,' *Economic and Political Weekly*, VI (Annual Number, January, 1971), 302.

under survey. It is interesting to note that it is, on the whole, highest in the Punjab and lowest in West Bengal, even though these are the two most economically developed States in the sample.

Roy also found, as have most similar studies of voting behavior in most democratic countries, 'a close relationship between socio-economic status and the strength of efficacy.'[70] This point is brought out in greater detail in Atal's study, which presents a detailed table showing 'Demographic Correlates of Sense of Political Efficacy,' obviously modeled on the similar detailed table in the American study of the 1952 Presidential election. 'Analysis of data suggests that people having a higher sense of political efficacy are in the age group 26–34 (34.8 per cent), educated up to primary level (26 per cent), in the income range of Rs. 100–300 per month (56.5 per cent), engaged in medium rank occupations (52.2 per cent), living in COC (69.5 per cent), native residents (73.9 per cent), and have an overall lower SES (47.8 per cent).'[71] The results were generally similar to those obtained in the American study fifteen years previously, but there were some significant differences, due mainly to different conditions and a different political culture. The Indian study, contrary to the American study, found that the most highly efficacious persons were in the twenty-six to thirty-four age group, were educated only up to primary level, with a marked decline in a sense of efficacy among the more highly educated, were in the lower income rather than the higher income groups, and in low to medium kinds of occupations rather than in types rated as 'high.' These findings throw much light on the character of the Indian voters and the nature of the Indian political culture.

Systemic and Institutional Legitimacy

The last two indicators of political development which we shall examine are the attitudes toward the legitimacy of the political institutions and the political system, and the degree of satisfaction with the performance of these institutions and of the system itself. As D. L. Sheth has stated, 'the ultimate test of a democratic order lies in the acceptance of its institutions as legitimate and in the confidence that these institutions can produce desired results.'[72] The authors of *The Civic Culture* made the same point quite effectively: 'Political systems, if they are to survive, must also be relatively effective and relatively legitimate; that is, what the government accomplishes must be at least satisfying enough to the citizens so that they do not turn against the government; and the system, if it is to have a long-run potential of survival, must be generally accepted by citizens as the proper form of government per se.'[73]

On the whole, the legitimacy of the existing political institutions, and of the political system, seems to have an amazingly high degree of acceptance. This is a significant finding, especially in view of the evidences to the contrary and of the doubts about the future of India's democratic polity that are often expressed at home and abroad.

The legitimacy and value of elections and parties seem to be accepted by the great majority of Indians. The data collected in the 1967 national sample survey by the Centre for the Study of Developing Societies indicated 'that acceptance of parliamentary institutions like elections and parties is quite widespread among the voter population.' About 74 per cent of the respondents 'expressed the view that it was necessary to have elections from time to time for making government responsible to the people,' and 65 per cent 'considered political parties necessary for making government pay attention to the people.'[74] A 1967 election study in Gujarat showed that 'The voter in Gujarat was concerned about fair and free elections. . . . On the whole, it could be said that elections and their fairness were accepted widely. . . . There was no doubt that elections as an integral part of the democratic set-up had come to stay.'[75] As the 1967 national sample survey showed, 'the legitimacy of political parties seems to be somewhat less accepted among voters than the legitimacy of elections.'[76] This survey, however, revealed a substantial acceptance of the value and legitimacy of parties. Other studies indicate a lesser acceptance, or considerable confusion regarding the value of parties. In the interviews conducted for the 1966 Project on Social and Political Change, one question was: 'Do you think political parties are necessary for India or do you think they should not be permitted?'[77] 43 per cent of the 2,637 respondents gave either 'don't know' replies or no reply at all. Of the 57 per cent who did reply, 36 per cent stated that they thought parties were necessary, while 21 per cent disagreed.

Belief in the legitimacy of the government in power at a particular time varies considerably. In general the government seems to have less widespread acceptance, and therefore perhaps less legitimacy, than elections or parties. According to the 1967 Gujarat study, 'the acceptance of elections was not accompanied by the equal degree of legitimacy for the government. . . . The voters were thus critical of the output functions of the political system.'[78] On the whole, however, the government too seems to have a fairly high degree of acceptance and legitimacy. This is certainly true for the system of government, more than for the government in power, as indicated by Table 9.vii, prepared by Ramashray Roy on the basis of data gathered by survey techniques during the 1969 mid-term elections in four Indian States. The answers to the question, 'Do you think that the present system of government is worth keeping even if it delays action?' were used as a basis for determining the 'Legitimacy of Democratic Government, by States'.[79]

This Table brings out clearly at least three important points about the feelings of Indian voters about the legitimacy of their system of government: that a considerable majority accept the legitimacy of the governmental system, that the degree of acceptance varies considerably in different States, and that the degree of acceptance is higher among persons of high socio-economic status. It is also, as D. L. Sheth has found, higher among strong partisans than among weak partisans, and among partisans of any kind than among non-partisans;[80] and it is higher in rural areas than in urban centers.[81]

Satisfaction with Institutional and Systemic Performance

'The issue of legitimacy of political institutions is inevitably linked up with the performance of the political system in generating and distributing satisfaction among the people.'[82] As Almond and Verba have suggested, 'Satisfaction with the political system can take several forms.' In their five-nation study they dealt with three types of orientation to the political system: 'orientation to the structure of political influence (the input structure), orientation to the structure of governmental output (the output structure), and a more general, diffuse orientation to the political system as a whole.' As they suggest, the third factor may be the most important of all. 'The attitude most relevant to long-term political stability may not be the individual's level of satisfaction with governmental output or with his role as participant. Rather, long-run political stability may be more dependent on a more diffuse sense of attachment or loyalty to the political system – a loyalty not based specifically on system performance.'[83]

D. L. Sheth has postulated that 'At the level of the individual citizen such satisfaction is concretely felt in two major areas: (1) governmental administration and (2) economic well-being.' On both of these bases, especially the latter, the degree of satisfaction is quite low. Analysing the 1967 and 1969 election data, Sheth found that 43.4 per cent of the respondents expressed satisfaction with local officials, 40.4 per cent with district officials, and 35.5 per cent with their present financial position. Only 35.9 per cent felt that their future financial position would be any better.[84]

Several questions asked by interviewers associated with the Project on Social and Political Change were designed to bring out the respondents' attitudes toward their national and State governments and toward the political system as a whole. 51.3 per cent of the sample expressed the view that the national government understood the needs of the people well, whereas 26.0 per cent disagreed (the rest of the

Table 9.vii

LEGITIMACY OF DEMOCRATIC GOVERNMENT, BY STATES
(*Do you think that the present system of government is worth keeping even if it delays action?*)
(*percentage*)

State	*Bihar*				*Punjab*				*UP*				*West Bengal*			
SES \ *Responses*	*Yes*	*Un-decided*	*No*	*Total*	*Yes*	*Un-decided*	*No*	*Total*	*Yes*	*Un-decided*	*No*	*Total*	*Yes*	*Un-decided*	*No*	*Total*
High				76				61				76				61
	77.6	10.5	7.9	22.4	75.4	9.8	14.8	20.9	78.9	7.9	10.5	17.8	65.6	8.2	26.2	24.5
Medium				142				148				189				125
	72.5	20.4	5.6	41.8	64.2	20.3	15.5	50.7	75.1	12.2	12.2	44.2	60.0	14.4	24.8	50.2
Low				119				82				157				61
	52.9	38.7	7.6	35.0	46.3	45.1	8.5	28.1	66.2	12.1	18.5	36.7	54.1	32.8	13.1	24.5
				3				1				6				2
NA	—[a]		—	0.8	—	—	—[a]	0.3	—[a]	—	—[a]	1.3	—	—	—[a]	0.8
Total	228	83	23	340	180	73	39	292	109	48	63	428	150	43	55	
	67.1	24.4	6.8		61.6	25.0	13.4		72.2	11.2	14.7		60.2	17.3	22.1	249

(*a*) Too few cases.
The row totals are less than 100 per cent because of 'not ascertained' and 'don't know' cases.
Source: Roy, 'Patterns of Political Instability,' p. 301.

respondents gave 'don't know' answers or none at all). The comparable figures for a similar question regarding the State government were about the same – 52.0 per cent and 25.7 per cent. 46.2 per cent thought that the government contributes much to the progress of the Indian people, and 32.1 per cent thought that it contributes little.[85] An overall evaluation question on this subject was framed as follows: 'In general, how satisfied are you with the performance of the government in providing services for the people? Are you dissatisfied with its performance or are you somewhat satisfied? The answers are revealing:[86]

	Number of Respondents (weighted sample)	*Per cent*
Very satisfied	3,776	39.7
Relatively satisfied	2,805	29.5
Dissatisfied	1,870	19.6
Don't know and no response	1,070	12.2
Total	9,521	100.0

These findings, and similar findings in other empirical studies, seem to bring out two main points: (1) most citizens of India accept the legitimacy of their political institutions and of their political system, and are fairly well satisfied with their institution and system; but (2) substantial numbers either have no discernible feelings about their institutions and political system, or are dissatisfied with, perhaps even alienated from, both. An overall conclusion might be that democratic institutions and the democratic system seem to be more strongly rooted in Indian soil than one might expect, with enough dissatisfied and even alienated elements to provide warnings of the need for constant vigilance and improvements and for continuing nation-building efforts. If one desires to accentuate the positive, he might subscribe to the conclusion of D. L. Sheth, in commenting on the responses of several thousand Indians in the 1967 and 1969 election studies: 'These responses reveal that a large proportion of Indian citizens have a general trust in the effectivity of democratic institutions and view them as desirable in Indian conditions. The proportions compare well with those of other democratic societies.'[87]

10

VOTING DETERMINANTS

In all democratic elections a voter makes two basic decisions. He first decides whether he will vote at all. If he decides to vote, then he must decide what party and/or candidate he will support. A decision not to vote is both a decision and a non-decision. Many eligible voters in democratic societies rarely, if ever, exercise their franchise privilege.

What are the factors or variables that influence eligible voters in making the two basic decisions that are involved in the electoral process? Obviously these are many and complex, and vary greatly in different political systems and in particular constituencies or regions within the same political system. They may also vary greatly over time, and in accordance with the circumstances under which elections are held. One would expect, for example, a greater popular interest and greater turnout in what V. O. Key, Jr., and others have called 'critical elections,'[1] and in other elections which to the voters are regarded as particularly exciting or in which they feel that issues of unusual importance, or at least which seem to them to be of particular importance, are at stake.

Three broad classes of factors or variables are usually considered in most analyses of the determinants of voting behavior. These are what might be called the ecological, the political, and the socio-economic or SES factors. These factors are by no means discrete categories, and their relative importance may vary greatly.

Almost all meaningful studies of voting behavior have dealt with both political and socio-economic factors as voting determinants. In general, such studies in the more developed countries, where most electoral research has been carried on, give special attention to political factors, whereas electoral studies in developing societies tend to stress the socio-economic factors; but the tendency of modern electoral research, wherever it is conducted, is to give considerable attention to both types of factors, and to assess their relative weights by more sophisticated techniques of analysis. The results have sometimes been quite startling, and have often challenged conventional wisdom and generally accepted axioms.

To these advances studies of electoral behavior, procedures, and results in developing countries have made significant contributions. Some of the early studies tended to ape the electoral research in more developed Western polities, which emphasized the political factors in voting behavior and gave inadequate attention to the socio-economic factors. Then a trend developed to go anthropological and sociological, and to concentrate quite heavily on the socio-economic factors and on the impact of the social setting and of social customs and institutions on the political behavior of the electorate. As a result political factors were not given due attention. More recent studies have considered both political and socio-economic factors, but there is still a great deal to be learned about the relative importance of these factors, and of their sub-categories, in different types of political and social systems at different times and under different conditions. Electoral research focusing on South Asia, which at least in the case of India has been very extensive in recent years, has gone through these three stages, and is still experimenting with methods of research and analysis and with tentative hypotheses which will be most suitable for revealing and reliable research.

Ecological Determinants

Not so much attention, unfortunately, is given to ecological or environmental factors. Yet these are of decisive importance, for they concern the broad cultural, social, political, and economic setting of the total social system in which the act of voting takes place. Voting behavior is everywhere greatly affected by social as well as political factors. In developing countries, like those of South Asia, in particular, this kind of behavior must be analysed almost as much from an anthropological and sociological as from a political science point of view. One certainly cannot hope to understand what motivates voters in India, for example, unless he is familiar with the history, culture, traditions, social patterns, and religious beliefs of the people of the area as well as with empirical studies of voting behavior, supplemented by extensive participant observation, in India and other democratic states.

The ecological approach lends itself to both macro and micro analysis. It may focus on the total social and political system, the characteristics of these systems and their interactions with the internal and external environment; or it may also focus on local communities and their ecological characteristics. In both senses this approach is closely related to both political and socio-economic determinants of voting behavior. The political factors influencing a citizen's vote are determined by the overall character of the political system, the place of that system in the international system, and the interactions of the internal and external forces affecting that system.

Socio-economic factors are linked to ecological analysis on both macro and micro levels in innumerable ways. For example, on the macro level both approaches are concerned with the general social setting, and with such macro characteristics as the individual and group determinants of voting behavior and the particular socio-economic factors that may be regarded as being of special importance as voting determinants.

On the micro level the ecological approach is also useful, as a frame of reference for giving the broader perspective with which to examine the influence of local factors and aspects of the 'little world' of the smaller communities. Many students of Indian elections have called attention to what one of them, Dr. Imtiaz Ahmed, has called 'the significance of the local political framework for the understanding of the political behaviour of social or communal groups in an area.'[2] More particularly, Dr. Ahmed has demonstrated, by empirical research as well as participant observation and experience, how the 'local context and situation in a particular constituency influence electoral behavior,' and he has stressed the 'significance of local social and economic cleavages in determining voting patterns and political alignments at the time of election.'[3]

These observations call attention to a point that should never be forgotten, namely that if one wishes to try to understand voting behavior in India he should make a detailed study of each constituency and each locality, for in many cases such detailed micro analysis will provide explanations or at least perspectives which cannot possibly be obtained in any other way, and will throw more light on various facets of Indian voting behavior, as linked to the overall patterns of belief and behavior, than can be obtained from any other approach. This calls attention to the limitations of voting studies that rely mainly on macro approaches, and it should make all students of psephology conscious of the limitations of their capabilities and results. But at the same time one should not get so bogged down in micro analysis that he overlooks the larger ecological setting. In short, one should avoid the individualistic as well as the ecological fallacy in election studies.

The ecological approach will help to explain what Verba, Nie, and Kim have described as 'the sharp difference between the meaning of the vote in India and elsewhere,' even though there are many similarities in campaign activity and in electoral procedures and objectives. 'The large group in India that votes – and it is similar in size to the proportion of Americans voting – is brought to the polls by a different social mechanism than that which brings the average U.S. citizen to the polls. . . . voting in the U.S. seems to be more a part of a general voluntaristic set of activities. In India, it reflects less motivation on the citizen's part.'[4]

Political Determinants

Among political factors influencing voting behavior three are conventionally emphasized: candidate orientation; issue orientation; and party identification. All of these categories have been analyzed at great length in the electoral experience of many countries. Apparently the relative weight that should be assigned to each varies greatly. In general, differences are particularly great with regard to the role of party identification. In political systems, such as the United States, where party identification is high, and where voters tend to remain in the same party, at least for long periods, the category of party identification may have special importance in determining voting behavior; but even in such systems candidate orientation – which includes the elements of personal preference and the personality of a candidate and voters' reactions to him – is usually an even more important determinant, and issue orientation is distinctly the least important of the three categories.

Candidate Orientation. Candidate orientation is not always the most salient factor in determining the way a citizen will vote, especially in systems where party organization, discipline, and attachment are high, and in constituencies or regions in countries with less party identification and regularity of support. In one-party states obviously the party and not the candidate is the determining factor. In two- or multi-party systems, especially in constituencies where one party has predominant strength, the same situation may prevail. How often it has been said, in almost every democratic system, that in some elections, in some constituencies, almost anyone – and sometimes the hyperbole extends to non-human actors, such as dogs or even inanimate objects, with lamp-posts seeming to be particularly favored – can be elected who is on a party ticket. Hence the importance of the process of the selection of candidates in the total electoral process. In India, where a one-party dominance system of parliamentary democracy has prevailed on the national level for most of the time since independence, with the possible exception of the years between 1967 and 1971, the party rather than the candidate has been the major determinant in most constituencies in most elections. This was particularly true in the fifth general elections in 1971 and in the State Assembly elections of 1972, when the 'Indira wave' swept all before it in most parts of the country and in most (but by no means all) States and constituencies.

Nevertheless, one should not underrate the importance of the personal qualities and appeal of candidates and of general candidate orientation of the voters. Where other factors, such as strong party loyalty or strong group identification, are not decisive, candidate orientation is often the most important voting determinant. This is probably true in the United States, where party identification, while high, is not strong, and where personal factors play a large role in an individualistic society. One recent study of the results of the Presidential elections of 1960 and 1964, for example, has indicated that in both elections candidate orientation was a considerably more important factor than party identification.[5] The evidence from Indian studies is mixed, as indeed is that from electoral studies in most countries. In general, Indian electoral studies indicate that candidate orientation is the second most important political voting determinant, next to party identification, in national elections, but is often the most important determinant, sometimes overwhelmingly so, in local elections and to a lesser degree in State elections.

In India, despite or perhaps because of the social system, personal factors are of great significance in elections, as in all aspects of social and political life. Most surveys suggest that the attributes that voters, especially the voters in rural areas, regard as most desirable in candidates for office are overwhelmingly two: honesty, and a concern for the welfare of the people.[6] According to these replies, such considerations as caste, party affiliation, education, residence, experience, or ability of the candidates are all of relatively minor importance. There is an obvious discrepancy between these findings and the actual behavior of the Indian voter. Certainly he often votes for candidates who are not distinguished for either of the two attributes which are professedly uppermost in the voter's mind, and he clearly is more influenced by other attributes than he cares to admit.

Issue Orientation. Almost all electoral studies indicate that issue orientation is much less significant as a voting determinant than candidate orientation and party identification. A voter seldom casts his vote on the basis of specific issues. In fact, he is usually rather ignorant of, or indifferent to, specific issues, and even if he does hold strong opinions on particular issues he may not be able to identify the stands of the parties and candidates regarding them. Thus the enormous amount of attention nominally given in election campaigns to 'the issues' is presumably of relatively little weight in influencing the minds of the voters. Cumulatively, however, issues may matter, and a voter who may show little familiarity with specific issues may be concerned with broad issues of public policy.

A recent analysis of data on the 1960 and 1964 presidential elections in the United States concluded that issue salience was in fact greater than is generally believed or than earlier voting behavior studies indicated. The author concluded that even though issue awareness among voters was low, many voters, especially those with strong party identification, were concerned with several specific issues. Moreover, he found 'a strong tendency among voters toward 'issue alignment,' which apparently lends order and meaning to the political world for most of them.'[7] His statistical analysis of the 1960 and 1964 data revealed some rather surprising conclusions regarding the relative importance of the three main political determinants that have been described:

> A multiple regression analysis performed with these data indicates that issue partisanship . . . was not as powerful in producing voting change as attitude toward candidate. The standard regression coefficient (beta weight) for the candidate variable (controlling for issues) was .48, while the coefficient for the issues variable (controlling for candidate) was .33. We should be aware, however, that party identification is a primary underlying factor contributing to the weights of both of these predictors of voting choice. If we wish to control or partial out the effect of party identification, we can simply add this variable to multiple regression equation. When this is done, the weights attached to issue partisanship and attitude toward candidate were both reduced, as expected. The new weights were .39 for candidate image (controlling for issues and party identification), .23 for issue partisanship (controlling for candidate image and party identification) and .27 for party identification (controlling for the other two factors). As expected, candidate image emerges as the most important factor in individual voting choice in 1964, but issues has a strong independent effect as well. The remarkable thing that emerges from this analysis is that *salient issues had almost as much weight as party identification in predicting voting choice.*[8]

In India there seems to be less familiarity with, or interest in, specific issues in national elections than in more experienced democratic polities. This is confirmed by almost all election studies, as well as by first-hand observation. But in local and State elections voters may be quite concerned with certain specific issues, and in national elections there may be more issue orientation than is generally believed. This is shown in the interest in broad public issues and in general ideological positions of various parties. Even issues as broad, and as impossible of realization, as *Garibi hatao*!, which figured prominently in the campaign of Mrs. Gandhi and other leaders of the Congress Party in their electoral successes in the 1971 national elections and the 1972 State Assembly elections, seemed to have helped greatly in enhancing Mrs. Gandhi's already favorable popular image as a leader genuinely interested in the welfare of the people and genuinely dedicated to economic and social change. An Indian scholar who has been prominently involved in the most eleborate and sophisticated analysis of data on the fourth general elections in 1967 has advanced the following suggestive interpretation:

> As shown in the analysis of 1967 data in the present series, there is a growing salience of issues in the country as a whole. Public issues and the position of voters on these issues have a crucial relevance for the voting act. It is for the avowed purpose of implementing certain programmes that parties seek to capture and control the seats of political power. As such, the identification of certain parties with certain ideologies and programmes in the voters' mind, even if in a very generalised and vague manner, becomes an important factor in the way different voters express their partisan choice.
>
> Leaving aside the identification of certain parties with certain political issues, there is also the question of the relevance of certain political issues for the concrete concerns and interests that inform the motivations and behavior of individual citizens. The conscious drive for modernization, the constant reference to socialist pattern of living in order to assure a better life based on economic justice and social equality, the necessity to mobilise resources for achieving declared goals – all these factors imply threats to some and hopes for others. In other words, the differential perception of particular public issues by voters placed in different life situations assumes quite an importance in determining voters' political preferences. It helps us to ascertain the prevailing climate of public opinion in a State and the relationship between this climate and expressed political preferences of the voters.[9]

Party Identification. Party identification vies with candidate orientation as the main voting determinant in most democratic political systems. This is particularly true in systems where party identification is strong. In such systems many, or even most, voters vote in accordance with their party affiliation, as the party leaders dictate. Their vote is therefore in a sense predetermined. It is little affected by electoral campaigns or by last-minute issues and developments. Under such circumstances party identification tends to override other considerations, including conflicting interests and affiliations. In the United States, where until recently nearly three-fourths of the voters were identified with political parties, it is traditionally the strongest determinant;[10] but it should be noted that according to RePass' calculations, this factor was overshadowed by candidate image in the 1964 presidential elections.[11] In England party identification is also usually the major voter determinant; but, as Butler and Stokes have pointed out, shifts have occurred in the support bases of the leading political parties, leading to the great Labor upsurge of the 1930s and 1940s and the Conservative recovery of the 1960s.[12]

In India formal affiliation with political parties is very low, and individual voters and groups of voters transfer support from one party to another, or to Independent candidates, with bewildering frequency and often without any apparent pattern. The 1967 national elections, for example, seemed to show that large minority groups, such as the Muslims, lower caste groups, and the young voters were, to use the words of Eric da Costa, 'rewriting their basic loyalties.'[13] In these elections large numbers of voters in these groups transferred their traditional support of the Congress Party to other parties and candidates. In most cases, however, this shift in loyalties proved to be transitory. Most of these groups returned to the Congress fold, or more specifically supported the New Congress headed by Mrs. Indira Gandhi, in the next general elections, in 1971.

Indian voters seem to shift their party support more extensively than voters in many other democratic states. The Indian voter is an unpredictable political animal; and the results of various elections have demonstrated that he is becoming increasingly independent in his electoral choice.

Party identification is nevertheless an important determinant of voting behaviour in India, especially in national elections. A detailed statistical analysis of responses of 1,309 voters in mid-term elections in four major Indian States in 1969 indicated that in every State attachment to a political party was the main voting determinant. In West Bengal it was slightly more important than candidate orientation, in Uttar Pradesh it was more than four percentage points higher, in Bihar the percentage differential was 28 points and in the Punjab it was 32 points. In the latter State 56.9 per cent of the respondents listed attachment to a party as the main factor influencing their voting decision.[14]

These figures give a higher relative score for party identification than is usually found in Indian voting behavior studies. They not only indicate a lower rate for candidate orientation, but also for other factors, especially caste and other socio-economic attributes, than is found in other studies of voter behavior in national elections. More importantly, they would be quite inapplicable to State and local elections, where party identification is a less determining factor and where the personal qualities and affiliations of the candidates and group associations and pressures would have far greater weight than in national elections. Even on these levels, however, party identification, or lack of identification, is an important variable.

Social Determinants

The close relationship between SES factors and voting behavior has been noted, and frequently documented, in innumerable election studies in many different political systems. Many analysts would agree with the Swedish sociologist, Gunnar Sjöblom, that 'the socio-economic factors are in most instances dominant for voting behavior.'[15] Some students, in discussing the sociological setting of political behavior, go far in the direction of what might be described as social determinism. This point is illustrated in the oft-quoted aphorism in one of the earliest and best of the empirically-based election studies in the United States: '. . . a person thinks, politically, as he is socially. Social characteristics determine political preference.'[16]

Some students of voting behavior insist on all kinds of qualifications to these interpretations, even while admitting the importance of SES factors in shaping, and perhaps even in determining to a large degree, the voting behavior of mass electorates. They certainly reject the more deterministic hypotheses, and argue that the actual factors that influence a voter are infinitely complex, and appear to arise from a vast number of conscious and unconscious forces and conditions, some of which can be easily identified – although not accurately weighed – while others are much more elusive, although they may be equally important determinants. Some students believe that in more developed political systems, where voters are largely literate and are accustomed to exercising the franchise as a normal part of their political life, voting is as much an individual as a collective act. Some argue that this may be increasingly the case even in less developed polities, with essentially illiterate voters, that, in short, this is an expected consequence of political development.

Election studies in India, even in rural areas, provide some basis for this hypothesis, although obviously in India the collective rather than the individual aspects of voting seem to predominate. And one does not have to be a social determinist to be conscious of the social basis of voting, as of all other social and political acts. Even when voting seems to be an individual and not mainly a collective action, the voter is still functioning within a given social system and obviously greatly affected by the folkways and mores (to borrow William Graham Sumner's famous terms) of that system, whether he realizes this or not. This would be particularly true in so-called underdeveloped societies, where old and often hierarchically organized and entrenched societies (as in India) exist in new and relatively underdeveloped political systems.

But even in these societies a consequence of political development might be to reduce the relative significance of social determinants of voting and to increase that of political factors. This hypothesis was suggested by D. L. Sheth when he wrote: 'If our electorate has attained a certain level of political development, its voting decisions should be more and more influenced by political considerations as against primordial group considerations.'[17] Presumably most of the 'primordial considerations' reside in the social and not the political system. Whether one could move beyond this hypothesis to another of even more dubious validity, namely that even in underdeveloped polities as political development occurs voting becomes more and more an individual rather than a collective act, is an interesting theme for speculation, but one that is very difficult to test, and certainly to substantiate. There are some evidences in this direction in India, but they are obviously still the exceptions to the prevailing voting determinants.

In a complex society such as India it is particularly important to study voting behavior patterns not just in the aggregate, on a macro and national basis, but also to bear in mind what Imtiaz Ahmed has called the 'significance of the local political framework for the understanding of the political behavior of social or communal groups in an area.'[18] And obviously the key to voting behavior within a 'local political framework' is to be found more in the social aspects of village society and life than in larger political considerations of a national and aggregate kind. This does not rule out the need for or the validity of macro studies, but it does suggest the possible limitations of such studies and it should make for a high degree of humility and tentativeness on the part of those who undertake them. On the other hand, micro studies alone can be of little more than anthropological interest, and may be of little value for the student of voting behavior unless some elements of comparability and some macro conclusions can be deduced from the local studies. This is a perennial dilemma for social scientists, and especially for social scientists who try to study such phenomena as political development. In trying to resolve it political scientists have turned into political sociologists and political anthropologists and sociologists and anthropologists have, however reluctantly, been forced to go into such ill-defined fields as political sociology and political anthropology.

The reasons why particular attention must be given to 'the local political framework for the understanding of the political behavior of social or communal groups in an area' are quite apparent in the case of India. As Myron Weiner and Rajni Kothari observed in introducing a number oı specialized studies of the third general elections in India, in 1962: 'In the largely segmented and highly parochial system which predominates in most of rural (and even urban) India, the patterns of loyalties and interests and the power structures which prevail at the village or neighbourhood level are often the most important elements of political action and can often more readily be studied through anthropological-type field inquiries than through national surveys.'[19] One might qualify this important observation by adding that while 'anthropological-type field inquiries' can provide needed data and insights for voting behavior studies, such studies must be supplemented by many other types of approaches and analyses, at both macro and micro levels, in voting behavior research.

The social determinants of voting behavior in India will be discussed at three levels. Special attention will be given to four 'primordial' factors, namely family and kinship, caste, factions, and communalism. Some consideration will also be given to such standard SES factors as age, sex, education, income, and rural-urban composition of the population. One factor of great, and even determining, importance in some polities, namely class, will not be treated as a separate factor. One can certainly analyse the social composition of the Indian electorate on the basis of class, with special attention to the class character of élite groups in Indian society, the role of the rising middle class – or classes – and the changing role of the lower classes, but such analyses in the Indian setting soon merge into the more 'primordial considerations' of kinship, caste, and faction. The class basis of Indian society is still too nebulous and too ill-defined to make a study of class and voting behavior in India particularly meaningful or significant. In time, perhaps, the class aspects of Indian society will become more apparent, but for the time being, at least, class does not seem to be as important a determinant of voting behavior or of other political acts as it obviously is, or has been, in many other polities.

In his well-known study of Ceylon Howard Wriggins stated: 'Since the mass of voters tend to retain their affiliations within the plural society, their political behavior is defined more by the group to which they traditionally belong than by their action as individuals in response to specific issues of policy.'[20] The groups that seem to be most important in shaping voting behavior, as other aspects of social and political behavior, seem to be the family or kinship groups, castes, factions, and communal affiliations. These groupings may introduce some cross-pressures, of an indigenous as well as an exogenous nature, but they are of central importance in shaping political as well as social attitudes and behavior.

Family and Kinship Ties. In rural India, in particular, family and kinship ties are perhaps the most 'primordial' of all. While they have great advantages from the social point of view, providing greater assurances of survival, identity, and 'belonging,' they obviously tend to subordinate the individual to the group and to stand in the way of larger affiliations and loyalties.

Some Western observers, and some Indians as well, have been quite gloomy about 'the prospects for democracy' in India because of the existence of these 'primordial' loyalties and the rather closed group nature of Indian social life. In his classic work on *Village Life in*

Northern India, one of the most perceptive of American anthropologists, Oscar Lewis, wrote: 'The theoretical assumption behind a democratic system based on voting is that the individual is an independent, thinking being capable and ready to make his own decision. However, in a kinship organized society . . . it is the large extended family which is the basic unit for most decision-making. At best, voting becomes an extended family process which violates the spirit of individuality inherent in the Western electoral system.'[21]

As has been noted, it is difficult to determine to what extent the act of voting is an individual act and to what extent it is a group act. In all probability, the groups aspects of voting behavior predominate in most political systems, even in those with highly developed traditions and practices of individualism. The 'spirit of individuality', to use Professor Lewis' words, may be 'inherent in the Western electoral system,' but this varies greatly in different Western countries, in different parts of many countries, and at different time periods. It is by no means the only 'spirit' inherent in Western electoral systems – it is rather misleading to speak of '*the* Western electoral system' – and it may not be as decisive even in Western democracies as Professor Lewis' comment would suggest.

It would be interesting to get reliable data regarding the extent to which votes are cast in India on a family or kinship basis. Are voting decisions made mainly by the head of the family or kinship group, and then adhered to by most of the members? Or are they generally collective decisions, in which most members of the family or group participate? How many women have voted as their husbands have suggested – or dictated? Are women gradually breaking away from a passive acceptance of their husbands' decisions when they cast their votes? Do younger voters tend to vote in accordance with the decisions of their elders? Since family and kinship ties are so close and so enduring, one would naturally expect that they would still be significant determinants of voting behavior, and there is ample evidence that this is indeed the case. There is also increasing evidence of deviations from these established norms, at least in the political field.[22]

Caste as a Voting Determinant. The group aspects of voting behavior become clearer when one enters the complicated world of caste and faction. Many of the local influentials, who to a considerable extent control voting as well as other forms of behavior, are leaders of ascriptive groups. These are the people who are generally identified as community leaders, whether or not they hold formal positions in the more 'modern' forms of governance at local levels, such as membership in panchayats under the Panchayati Raj system, in town councils or municipal corporations in towns or cities, in cooperative organizations, or in the ranks of local officials. Very often those who control the 'vote banks' and who therefore were courted by political parties are leaders of castes and factions. In many communities in India such people are still in a dominant position, but increasingly, it seems, their political power is being undermined and they are becoming less dominant and less effective.

Most voters, in most countries, 'vote in accordance with habit rather than the immediate issues at stake.'[23] And 'habits of allegiance' are usually shaped by factors that are deeply embedded in the fabric of the particular society. In some countries one factor seems to stand out above all others. In England, for example, that factor seems to be class. As Peter Pulzer has stated, this factor is 'easily the most important of all. . . . Class is the basis of British party politics; all else is embellishment and detail.'[24] This general conclusion, without the extreme positivism, is supported by the famous Nuffield studies of various British elections in the postwar years, and is a central theme of the Butler–Stokes volume, *Political Change in Britain*.[25]

Both historical and empirical studies of voting behavior in Japan have confirmed the importance of group determinants, or what has been called the 'collectivity orientation', in the voting behavior of Japanese voters, as in other aspects of Japanese life.[26] American voters are supposed to vote more on the basis of individual decisions in what is generally regarded, in spite of the proliferation of associations of all kinds, as a notably individualistic society. In other countries special emphasis has been placed on other socio-economic factors, such as race or religion.

Is there any similar determinant of 'habits of allegiance' and hence of political behavior in India? If there is, it almost certainly must be caste, perhaps the most pervasive social institution in India. Caste is obviously still a very important factor conditioning social and political values, and behavior, in contemporary India, although it is equally obviously changing its character and is perhaps declining in relative importance as a social and political force. Although it has been, and is, primarily a social institution, it has always had some political aspects, and it has undoubtedly been an important factor in the politics of independent India. Whether it occupies the central, or even determining, role that some students would ascribe to it is a matter of debate, and needs to be tested by more extensive micro and empirical research. It is clearly one of the intriguing aspects of the current Indian scene, one which many Indian scholars are inclined to play down and many foreign scholars to exaggerate.

As Paul Brass has observed, 'The role of caste in elections is easily the most discussed aspect of contemporary Indian political behavior.'[27] It is a most complex issue, penetrating to the bases of Indian society and politics, and to the interactions between a rather rigid and authoritarian social system and the system of parliamentary democracy. It is a two-way relationship, for while caste is affecting politics, politics is also affecting caste. As Rajni Kothari has suggested, instead of concentrating on the question whether caste is disappearing from the Indian scene, 'a more useful point of departure would be: what form is caste taking under the impact of modern politics, and what form is politics taking in a caste-oriented society?'[28]

In spite of its rather rigid character, caste is obviously changing in many fundamental respects under the impact of changing conditions. The general nature of these changes is suggested by Rajni Kothari: '... caste besides being a system of segmental differentiations (*'jathis'*), is also a system defining status, possesses a secular character, and is endowed with a class symbolism in the form of "*varnas*". With these latter aspects gaining in function and importance, caste is shedding some of its old-time character and is acquiring a new emphasis and orientation. While still retaining a good part of the traditional modes of integration, it has entered a phase of competitive adjustment in the allocation and re-allocation of functions and power among various social groups. The institutions of caste association and caste federation are the media through which such an adaptation of roles is taking place.'[29]

Fortunately, it is not necessary to enter into a detailed discussion of the nature of caste, and its role in Indian society. The matter becomes more complicated when caste is considered in terms of the innumerable *'jathis'* (or *'jatis'*) and not simply in terms of the major *'varnas'*. Some of the aspects or interpretations that are particularly relevant to the subject of caste and elections are four which have been developed and extensively explored by M. N. Srinivas, namely those of dominant castes, Sanskritization, Westernization, and secularization, the concept of the 'politicisation of caste,' and the role of caste associations and federations, to which Rajni Kothari referred.

(i) *Srinivas' Concepts.* As explained by Professor Srinivas, 'A caste may be said to be "dominant" when it preponderates numerically over other castes, and when it also wields preponderant economic and political power. A large and powerful caste group can be more easily dominant if its position in the local caste hierarchy is not too low.'[30] Examples of dominant castes which have played a truly dominant role in the politics of various Indian States are the Kammas and Reddis in Andhra Pradesh, the Lingayats and Okkaligas in Mysore, the Patidars in Gujarat, the Marathas in Maharashtra, the Rajputs and Jats in Rajasthan, the Nairs and Ezhavas in Kerala, the Gounders, Padayachis, and Mudaliars in Madras (Tamil Nadu), the Kayasthas and Rajputs in Bihar. Over time the dominant castes have often changed in various States. For example, the Brahmins were long the dominant caste in Madras State, whereas in more recent years all of the dominant castes in that State have been non-Brahmin. In general, there has been a trend away from dominant castes in several states, with formerly dominant castes, such as the Patidars in Gujarat, losing much of their erstwhile political influence if not social status, and with lower castes rising in influence, in part through the political process. The Ezhavas in Kerala are an outstanding example of a low caste group which has become a dominant caste, and an important factor in the confused politics of that State.

Even at local levels the dominant castes are becoming less dominant, and again a major reason for this change, and a clear evidence of it, is to be found in the role of castes in politics. Elections provide a channel for political participation for the more numerous lower castes, which are becoming increasingly conscious of their political power and increasingly confident in exercising it. 'The powerful pull of social, economic and political developments all around has largely been undermining the traditional power-holders in the village. It is true that political power in the village is still largely limited to the economically and socially dominant groups but the fact that the so-called "dominant castes" in the socio-economic sense have to make so many vital concessions in terms of social vertical mobility and change in their style of behavior towards the lower castes would not hardly qualify for the appelation given to them.'[31]

Sanskritization, according to Srinivas, is 'the process by which a "low" Hindu caste, or tribal or other group, changes its customs, ritual, ideology, and way of life in the direction of a high, and frequently, "twice-born" caste. Generally such changes are followed by a claim to a higher position in the caste hierarchy than that traditionally conceded to the claimant caste by the local community.'[32] It is a process that takes place in the traditional sector of Indian society, but it often leads to profound changes in relative social status, at least for lower castes. It brings lower castes into the mainstream of society, and enhanced social status makes them more able to function in the political arena as well and gives them greater confidence in exercising their political rights.

Westernization is a process that particularly affected the upper castes, and was reflected in the widespread adoption of Western (particularly British) ideas, institutions, and behavior.[33] Like Sanskritization it led to profound changes in the caste system, but unlike Sanskritization it was an exogenous process. Both processes have clearly been at work in Indian society for some decades, and both have also had political spillovers and impact. 'A feature of the simultaneous operation of the two influences is that while "Sanskritization" leads to a narrowing of the gap between castes, "Westernization" may narrow the gap, widen it, or leave it as before, depending upon the differential impacts on upper and lower castes.'[34]

India is a religiously-impregnated society and a secular polity. An intriguing question is the extent to which secular trends and influences have permeated Indian society, and the extent to which non-secular factors and forces are present in Indian politics, in spite of the conscious dedication to the secular approach. This is an aspect of the larger and even more intriguing question of the relative influence of tradition and modernity in India today,[35] when it seems that modernity is invading the traditional sectors and is also becoming increasingly influenced by traditional factors. Hence there is much discussion of the tradition of modernity and the modernity of tradition.

Secularization is in many respects an even more significant force than Sanskritization or Westernization.[36] 'This process holds the key to the tremendous shift that politics has brought about in Indian society. Whereas Sanskritization brought submerged caste groups out into the mainstream of society, and Westernization drew the Sanskritized castes into the framework of modernization, it is secularization of both kinds of groups through their political involvement that is leading to an erosion of the old order and its re-integration on secular-associational grounds.'[37]

(ii) *The Politicization of Caste.* Anthropologists are inclined to emphasise the pervasive influence of caste in politics, as in many other aspects of Indian life, whereas political scientists are inclined to emphasize the phenomenon commonly called 'the politicization of caste.' When caste enters the political arena, it not only affects the character of the contest in that arena, but also it is considerably affected and transformed in the process. In other words, it becomes 'politicized.'

Rajni Kothari is a leading exponent of this interpretation: 'The alleged casteism in politics is thus no more and no less than *politicization of caste.* By drawing the caste system into its web of organization, politics finds material for its articulation and moulds it into its own design. In making politics their sphere of activity, caste and kin groups, on the other hand, get a chance to assert their identity and to strive for positions. Drawing upon both the interacting structures are the real actors, the new contestants for power. Politicians mobilize caste groupings and identities in order to organize their power. They find in it an extremely articulated and flexible basis for organization, something that may have been structured in terms of a status hierarchy, but something that is also available for political manipulation. . . . Where there are other types of groups and other bases of association, politicians approach them as well. And as they, everywhere, change the form of such organization, they change the form of caste as well.'[38]

As André Béteille has pointed out, 'The political process seems to have a dual effect on caste. To the extent that the loyalties of caste or subcaste are consistently exploited, the traditional structure tends to become frozen. . . . To the extent that it leads to new associations and alliances cutting across caste, it loosens the traditional structure.'[39]

There is considerable disagreement over the effects of politics upon the caste system, and of the effect of the caste system upon politics. In each case one could argue that the effects are both constructive and destructive. No one, however, can overlook the importance of the interactions between caste and politics. These are essentially interactions between a – perhaps *the* – leading institution of the traditional social structure, and the most modern sector of Indian life. But, as has been noted, caste does not serve a wholly traditional role in Indian politics, and politics, perhaps in part because of the pervasive influence of caste, is not as modern in many aspects as it appears to be.

(iii) *Caste Associations and Caste Federations.* Two of the agencies of transmission between the traditional and modern sectors, specifically between caste and politics, are caste associations and caste federations. 'Caste associations are paracommunities that enable members of castes to pursue social mobility, political power, and economic advantage.'[40] There are many caste associations in India, some of them very influential in political as well as social affairs. 'Although the caste associations functioned in the social realm for a cause which was primarily social, they nevertheless prepared the background for transforming social identity into political identity.'[41] A caste association 'is no longer an ascriptive association in the sense in which caste taken as jati was and is. It has taken on features of the voluntary association. . . . At the same time, its followers tend in the early phases of the caste association to retain the more intense and exclusive loyalties and identities characteristic of ascriptive associations and to be, as a consequence, less subject to the crosscutting pressures that affect members of more strictly voluntary associations. With the passage of time and internal differentiation within the association, however, loyalties are diluted and the membership becomes more amenable to political mobilization from without.'[42]

Caste associations, therefore, may perform important linkage roles between the society and the polity. Some scholars, Indian and foreign, believe that they actually contribute to the modernization of the political system and to the strengthening of the democratic base of that system. This view is strongly advanced by Lloyd and Susanne Rudolph: 'It is the caste association that has given caste a new vitality and it is political democracy which has transformed caste and enabled it to play its paradoxical role in India. Rather than providing the bases for reaction caste has absorbed and strengthened some of the new democratic values. It is the association which links the mass electorate to the new democratic process and makes them comprehensible in traditional terms to a population still largely politically illiterate.'[43] Many examples could be cited of caste associations which seem to have performed this kind of 'paradoxical role.'

Caste federations are almost equally important as linkage agencies, although they have received less attention than caste associations. In contrast to caste associations, caste federations are 'composed of not one but several castes which may sometimes be socially homogeneous but which may at other times simply have some special interest or political objective in common. . . . The interesting thing about the caste federation is that, once formed on the basis of caste identities, it goes on to acquire non-caste functions, becomes more flexible in organisation as time passes, even begins to accept members and leaders from castes other than those with which it started, stretches out to new regions, and also makes common cause with other voluntary associations, interest groups and political parties. In course of time, the federation becomes a distinctly political group, wielding considerable bargaining strength and numerical power, but still able to appeal to caste sentiments and consciousness by adopting a common label . . ., claiming high status in the past and fostering a sense of deprivation in the present, and out of all this forging a strong and cohesive political group. It has gone far beyond the earlier caste associations in articulating group interests along political channels.'[44]

(iv) *Caste and Political Parties.* Caste influences permeate the Indian political process in innumerable ways. Every political party gives careful attention to caste considerations, although party spokesmen often denounce caste in politics and insist that their parties are not swayed by caste considerations. All the evidence is to the contrary. This is true even in the case of the Communists, who profess to scorn all considerations of caste and class. Selig S. Harrison documented this point in the case of the Communists in Andhra Pradesh many years ago,[45] and other studies in Andhra Pradesh and other States have provided additional evidence. Jawaharlal Nehru continually insisted that caste considerations had no place in politics, but even while he was its undisputed leader the Congress Party gave as much attention to caste as any other party. Perhaps this should not be surprising, for caste is so pervasive and so deeply entrenched in India that it inevitably permeates the political as well as the social arena. As one of the leading authorities on the subject, Professor M. N. Srinivas, declared: 'Caste is so tacitly and so completely accepted by all, including those most vocal in condemning it, that it is everywhere the unit of social action.'[46]

Perhaps the most obvious way in which caste permeates politics is in connection with the selection of candidates in various elections, at local, State, and national levels. This process of selection, especially in national elections, has been intensively studied in recent years, and the importance of caste is substantiated again and again in these studies. It would in fact be surprising if this were not the case. Parties and political leaders naturally pay a great deal of attention to the influential groups and leaders in various constituencies. Many of the influential groups are caste or caste-based groups, and many of the influential local leaders are leaders of dominant or numerically significant castes. Quite understandably, political parties often select their candidates from among the leaders of dominant or otherwise influential castes. Many other considerations may enter into the selection process, but caste is certainly one of the major ones, and it is often a determining factor. It becomes less significant as a voting determinant when two or more parties choose candidates from the same caste or castes, but it does not thereby cease to be an important fact.

The relation of particular castes to particular political parties is another aspect of caste in politics that merits special analysis. In some localities caste-based parties are occasionally active. If 'untouchables' may be considered within the framework of the caste system, broadly interpreted, at least one caste-based party has achieved some national following and recognition, although it has had little electoral success on the national level. This is the party for 'untouchables' founded by India's leading 'untouchable,' Dr. B. R. Ambedkar, in 1942. Originally known as the Scheduled Castes Federation, it later changed its name to the Republican Party. It has elected a few members to the Lok Sabha, and more to the Legislative Assemblies of several States. More importantly, political parties are sometimes identified with certain caste groups.

In general, on a national or near-national scale, considerable support can be found for such hypotheses as the following: (1) High castes tend to vote for opposition parties, not for the Congress; (2) Middle and lower castes tend to vote for the Congress; (3) Scheduled Castes and Scheduled Tribes tend to vote Congress. Hypotheses of this kind need further testing before they can be generally accepted. They seem to be generally true, but there are many exceptions, in various states, in different elections and at different levels. It should also be borne in mind that people of the same as well as different castes vote in different ways, and that voting cuts across caste behavior and is influenced by many other factors.

(v) *Caste Factors in Local and National Politics.* While caste is a pervasive factor in Indian life, its importance as a voting determinant should not be exaggerated. Except in local elections – and not always even there – caste is usually an important but not a determining influence on the Indian voter. As O. P. Goyal and many others have pointed out, 'The relevance of caste as a voting determinant keeps on decreasing as we move upwards at higher levels of politics and vice versa.'[47] 'For students of the Indian political process,' noted the authors of a detailed study of the 1967 general elections in Rajasthan, 'it would be useful to remember that caste as a distinct sub-category does not play a dominating role in influencing voting behavior at such macro levels as elections to the assembly or the Lok Sabha.'[48] About the only qualification that needs to be made to this generalization is that even in national and State Assembly elections caste factors are often determining in the selection of candidates, although usually not in the ultimate decision of most voters.

Even in the 1971 general elections, when caste factors seemed to be definitely subordinated to the response to Mrs. Gandhi's appeals, a detailed analysis of the basis of candidate selection would show that at this level, in many States, caste factors, while minimized, were still important. In a few States, however, far fewer candidates than usual were selected by the Congress Party from the dominant castes. This was notably true in Mysore, for example, where the representation of the long-dominant Lingayats and Okkaligas was reduced drastically, and where eventually a Chief Minister from one of the lesser castes was selected by Mrs. Gandhi, and not by the ruling groups in the State Congress Party.

At local levels a different style of politics seems to prevail in elections to State or national Assemblies, as contrasted to elections to local bodies. Caste considerations are less important in national and State elections than in elections to local offices. This suggests that the same voters in rural areas may follow two different styles of politics, one still largely influenced by 'primordial loyalties', of which caste is often predominant, the other influenced by larger considerations that cut across caste and other traditional lines. In one case they function in traditional ways, in the other they show an amazing ability to shift roles and views and to become more 'modern.'[49]

The effects of national elections on the style of politics in a village in western India are graphically described by Professor Somjee: '. . . the participation of the village in national politics, particularly during the general elections, was an important source of change in its own style of politics. The national politics were much less structured than the local politics. As opposed to the compelling electoral conformity of the local politics, the dialogues, the criticisms, and the emphases of contesting candidates during the general elections, in addition to the fact that no one from the village was directly involved in them, gave the villagers greater freedom of electoral choice.'[50] The likely spillover effects of this style of politics on the village electorate were quite clear: 'It was a sheer matter of time before it was demanding the same measure of electoral freedom in the local elections and politics.'[51]

Almost all observers who are familiar with rural India have noted the twofold phenomenon of the continuance of the caste system as a major factor in the life of most of the people in the country and at the same time of the declining role and importance of caste, in social and even more in political life. This is demonstrated in the behavior of rural voters in elections of all kinds. Even in local elections, where caste is obviously a more important voting determinant than in elections at higher levels, and is often still the major determinant, the pattern of loyalties and other factors conditioning popular behavior is becoming more complex. An observation that Professor A. H. Somjee made on the basis of a detailed study of a rural community in western India would seem to be rather generally valid: 'The social basis of democratic politics in the village gradually became still more complicated . . . curious group alignments based on caste, kinship, patronage, social prejudice, etc. began to play their part in the democratic politics of the village.'[52] Another detailed study of village politics, in a village in northwestern India, concluded that 'Even in rural India, caste as a determinant of voting behavior is no longer a pure category' (perhaps it never was as 'pure' a category as it once seemed to be). This study also concluded that 'the rural voter in India is sophisticated to the point of creating caste-splits at different levels of elections. Whereas caste was relevant at the level of the elections to the offices of Panches [members of the village panchayat], it was relatively less relevant for the election of the office of the Sarpanch [the chairman of the panchayat].'[53]

Caste considerations are not only more important in local elections than in State Assembly and national elections in rural areas. They are also more important for some groups than for others in rural areas, including the more traditionally oriented, and the more socially conservative, sectors of rural society. O. P. Goyal has suggested the interesting thesis that 'obedience to the caste decision has much to do with the dependence upon land and agriculture.' He has pointed out that 'industrial labour . . . is very different from agricultural labour. For industrial labour, caste is much less relevant in voting-behavior even if the origin and contacts of that labour are still in the village.'[54] This is undoubtedly due in large part to the effects of urban life upon the large numbers of persons of village origin who flock to the cities to work in factories.

Quite clearly caste is much less influential as a voting determinant, as well as a determinant of social behavior, in urban than in rural areas. An urban dweller, even if he comes from a village and/or has close contacts and family ties in a rural area, is subject to a bewildering variety of influences and pressures that would quite naturally challenge his village loyalties; and people who are born in urban areas and who are in every sense urbanites are far less subject to caste influences and patterns of behavior. Hence it is hardly surprising that caste factors are seldom a major voting determinant for them.

(vi) *Caste and Politics: Conflicing Trends.* There is considerable debate over the question of whether caste is becoming more or less important in Indian elections. A popular interpretation – and one that is advanced by almost every official Indian spokesman – is that it is becoming less and less of a factor in India's developing democracy, in which the influence of 'primordial loyalties' is declining and that of other factors, mainly political rather than social, is increasing. There is considerable evidence in support of this interpretation, at least in State and national elections. Even in village India, and even in local elections, the introduction of universal adult franchise has tended to undermine traditional social patterns, including the caste system. This point was emphasized by A. H. Somjee, on the basis of his detailed study of one rural community in western India and of his expertise as a political scientist: 'The extension of democracy to the village had its own repercussions on the existing social relationships in general and on political relationships in particular. Among various provisions which normally go with a democratic polity, the influence of universal adult suffrage . . . was about the greatest. Moreover, the influence of elections on the panchayat . . . was about the most significant. These elections not only gave a jolt to the existing social relationships, which in the preceding years were reflected in the political field as well, but they also indicated probable beginnings of some degree of *independent* political relationships; independent, though not completely or totally, of the existing and hitherto almost unchanging social relationships.'[55]

There can be little question that caste factors were very important in the early stages of India's electoral experience. As M. N. Srinivas pointed out in 1955: 'One of the short-term effects of universal adult suffrage is to strengthen caste. It is easily understandable that the villager, other things being equal, prefers to vote for his caste man.'[56] This generalization would seem to hold true in all elections under universal adult suffrage, although it does seem that many other voting determinants have become of increasing importance and that therefore 'other things' have by no means remained 'equal.' Increasingly it seemed to be true that, as F. G. Bailey, on the basis of his careful studies in Orissa, wrote, 'caste is only one of the many kinds of loyalties upon which the politician can draw, and which he must balance one against the other.'[57]

A broad conclusion for which considerable support can be found is that increasingly caste has become only one of many determinants of voting behavior, and that at least in State and national elections it is seldom if ever the most decisive factor. Some of the leading students of Indian voting behavior have gone much farther, and have argued that caste is no longer a major voting determinant at all. Harold Gould has advanced the view that caste has ceased to be a 'determinant' of politics in India, and should instead be regarded as simply an 'ethnic variable.'[58] Rajni Kothari has argued that 'Today . . . caste has turned into just another variable in politics along with many other variables.'[59] In the involved jargon of contemporary political science caste, like every other relevant factor, may indeed be considered as 'just another variable in politics,' without necessarily relegating it to such a lessened position as the statements by Gould and Kothari would suggest. Actually these two scholars, like many others, have provided substantial evidence of the continued importance of caste in politics, whatever its reduced status and role.

A different interpretation is that caste factors, after declining in importance in elections, have experienced a resurgence, as the bases of participation in politics have widened, as more and more eligible voters, most of whom live in rural areas where traditional ways are still strong, become participants in the political process, as the more numerous lower castes become more active politically, and as new and less cosmopolitan leaders, with deeper roots in rural areas and in the traditional society, rise to prominence at State and national levels. This trend was noted by a leading Indian journalist during the 1971 general elections, when many observers insisted that caste factors were less prominent than in any previous election: 'Since caste and community serve as the reference points for establishing an individual's identity in rural India, these affiliations are getting inevitably accentuated in a period when millions are being drawn into the political whirlpool. The problem is becoming more acute with each election, as the submerged groups . . . stake a claim to a share in power.'[60]

The broad picture that emerges, therefore, is a rather confusing and paradoxical one. Caste factors are still very important voting determinants, although their influence varies greatly. In some respects, in some elections, in some States, and in some communities, the importance of these factors is still great, and may be actually increasing. In other respects caste is a declining, if still significant factor – or 'variable' – in Indian political life. Certainly no study of Indian elections can ignore it. The picture is not a static one. The subject remains infinitely complex – and infinitely intriguing.

Factionalism as a Voting Determinant. A social determinant of voting decisions that is almost as important as caste – and in some cases even more so – is factionalism, 'a characteristic feature of Indian political life at all levels, from village to state and nation.'[61] Indeed, one leading authority on Indian elections has stated that 'factionalism plays a dominant role in deciding the voting pattern.'[62] There is ample evidence of its pervasive influence on voting behavior, and also considerable evidence that it is playing an increasing, rather than a declining, role in Indian elections, at least in some States. One of the best studies of State politics in India, dealing with Uttar Pradesh, is appropriately entitled *Factional Politics in an Indian State.* This is a study of the Congress Party in U.P., which is a reminder that the ruling party in India has been as much affected by factionalism as any other determining factor. It is a characteristic of almost every political party, not excluding the Communist parties.

A faction 'is a vertical structure of power which cross-cuts caste and class divisions.'[63] Factions, like caste, belong to the traditional order, and are particularly important in villages and at local levels generally; but, also like caste, they are also important at higher levels of political and social life. Hence they provide linkages between traditional and modern sectors of the society. They give political parties a base in the traditional order, while at the same time they are themselves affected, and changed, by their association with agencies of modernization.

There is a close relationship between the two main kinds or forms of factionalism that are influential as voting determinants: the traditional factionalism of Indian society, especially in rural areas, and the intense factionalism within virtually all Indian political parties. Several studies of State politics have called attention to this close relationship, and have provided empirical evidence that it does in fact exist. 'Factionalism in the Indian political parties is closely linked with village factionalism built around a kinship unit consisting of one or more extended families.'[64] It is this 'close inter-relationship between factionalism in the villages and the factionalism within the party that has made it possible for the party to sustain popular support in the midst of intense intra-party conflict.'[65] 'The factional structure of the Congress party in Uttar Pradesh reflects the adaptation of the organization to the traditional society. . . . The Congress, the agent of modernization in rural Uttar Pradesh, has been traditionalized. The traditionalization of the Congress organization does not mean that it does not perform a modernizing function in the society. Rather, there is a two-way interaction: the Congress performs its modernizing role through traditional social organization, the faction, which in turn adapts itself to modern party organization. In this two-way interaction, both the modern party organization and the traditional society are undergoing change.'[66]

Voting behavior studies have shown that intra-party factional disputes within the Congress Party have been mainly responsible for marked changes in the electoral fortunes of the party in various districts. This means, obviously, that the Congress may attract widespread support in districts and States where it is not riven by factional strife and may lose support in constituencies where factional divisions alienate many voters.

As Rajni Kothari has pointed out, 'the faction system . . . works at all levels of the Congress organization. Generally, however, the lower down we go, the more pervasive the system becomes in conditioning the political process.'[67] It is hardly surprising that factionalism should be most prevalent and influential in politics in those areas where it is most prevalent in the social structure, namely in rural areas. But it is also significant at State and even national levels. Paul Brass's study provides overwhelming evidence that it is a major factor in the fortunes of the Congress Party in Uttar Pradesh. Rajasthan provides a particularly interesting example of State-level factions in the Congress Party – especially in the days of rivalry between three faction-based groups in the Congress giving support, respectively, to Mohanlal Sukhadia, Jai Narain Vyas, and Kumbharam Ayar. Each of these factions was originally anchored in factions at local and regional levels, but in the course of time they changed their character and became inter-regional in composition.[68]

Studies of the electoral fortunes of other Indian parties have revealed a similar prevalence and a similar impact of factionism. In West Bengal, for example, the Communist parties have appealed particularly to certain factions as well as to certain castes. They have also been weakened by factional divisions and rivalries.

Thus far the divisive effects of factionalism upon electoral support, as well as upon party organization, have been stressed. It is well to bear in mind, however, that 'factions and factional conflict perform both integrative and disintegrative functions.'[69] The distintegrative functions are more obvious, and their results can be shown in fluctuations in electoral support and in party strength and morale. The integrative functions are less obvious, but no less important. 'The major integrative function . . . has been to recruit new groups into the Congress (and the same comment could be made of other parties), thereby broadening the base of political participation. . . . Most important, factions in a mass party tend to divide caste and community groups and thereby free the party from the threat of communal politics. . . . Thus, factionalism in . . . political parties has been a device for meeting the problem of political mobilization of new elites in the society.'[70]

On a more neutral level we may conclude that factionalism is an important voting determinant in both positive and negative ways. A voter may cast his vote mainly on the basis of the faction to which he belongs, whether in the social or political realm, or both. On the other hand, he may be alienated from certain political parties because of excessive factionalism within their ranks.

Communalism, Minorities, and Voting Behavior. Communalism is another pervasive force in Indian life, and it is often a powerful voting determinant. 'It is applied in different localities to groups differentiated by religion, language, region, historical origin, occupation.'[71] It thus embraces a variety of factors which have profound effects on voting behavior, including ethnic composition and ethnic minorities, religion, region, and language. 'It is above all applied to the ill-feeling existing in Hindu-Muslim relationships.'[72] This greatest of communal divides casts its shadow over many facets of Indian life, and is inevitably a powerful force in politics. On the whole, Muslims, constituting more than 10 per cent of the population of India, are underrepresented in elected bodies, at local, State, and national levels. Except in a few parts of the country the majority of Muslim voters have tended to support the Congress Party, which has been led by persons of national stature, past and present, who have been dedicated to the principle of communal harmony and minority rights (the Muslims are in a sense the largest minority in India), and which has been in a position to implement its campaign pledges. In the 1967 elections there was widespread Muslim defection from the Congress, as a part of a general anti-Congress trend, but apparently, judging from the results of later elections, this was a temporary deviation.

No Muslim political party has had any success at all on a nationwide basis. The Muslim League claims to be a national party, but its electoral successes have been confined mainly to northern Kerala, where it has been, and is, a significant political force.[73] In August 1964 an All-India Muslim Majlis-e-Mushawarat was inaugurated 'to specify the demands of the Muslim community, define its interests, and impress these upon the political parties.'[74] In the 1967 general elections it adopted a manifesto, and was active on the electoral scene in eight states. It did not function as a political party, with its own slate of candidates, but it endorsed candidates of various parties and independents who, in its judgment, would best represent 'Muslim interests'. 'The performance of the Majlis was not spectacular in terms of absolute numbers, but it was successful in influencing Muslim voters so that the bulk of them (contrary to their usual practice) did not vote for the Congress.'[75] In 1968 the U.P. unit of the Muslim Majlis-e-Mushawarat decided to form a political party called the Muslim Majlis. This decision was not approved by the national leadership of the Majlis, since it 'wanted to attract Muslim politicians who had already thrown in their lot with other national and regional parties.'[76] Instead, the national organization adopted a new constitution which transformed the Muslim Majlis-e-Mushawarat into a federation of Muslim associations.

Other minority groups have formed political parties or other types of organizations to promote their interests through electoral activity. Outstanding examples are the Republican Party (formerly the Scheduled Castes Federation), representing the interests of the Harijans or untouchables; and the Jharkhand Party, the most successful of the many tribal-based parties in India. Occasionally electoral alliances or coalitions of minority groups have been formed. In the third general elections in 1962 such an alliance was forged between Muslims and Harijans, and in the mid-term poll in U.P. in 1969 a Federation of Backward Classes, Scheduled Castes and Minorities was formed.[77] None of these groups or alliances has had much cohesion, or electoral success.

Considerations of region and language are closely intertwined in India, and both are major conditioning factors in Indian politics. The North of India is the Hindi heartland. It has been a major stronghold of the Congress Party (all of whose Prime Ministers have come from U.P.), and of the Jana Sangh, which is dedicated to a revival of Hindu culture and practices. Congress has also done well in the West of the country, and so, for a time, did the Swatantra Party, a non-communal conservative party. The Communists, especially the Left Communists, have been particularly strong in West Bengal, Kerala, and Andhra Pradesh. The non-Hindi South has been a strong opponent of Hindi domination, and in some States, notably Tamil Nadu and Kerala, the Congress has faced formidable opposition from locally-based parties or, in Kerala, from both of the main Communist parties.

Language is closely associated with region. The North is mainly Hindi-speaking, whereas most of the people of the South speak different Dravidian languages. The States of India are organized mainly on a linguistic basis. Almost every State has a dominant language, and linguistic considerations and issues are often the main voting determinants, especially in the South. There are a number of State parties based on religion, such as the Akali Dal, a Sikh party, in the Punjab, and a number based on linguistic and cultural identity, notably the Dravida Munnetra Kazhagam in Tamil Nadu.

Other SES Factors. The social determinants that have been discussed thus far – family and kinship associations, caste, factionalism, and communalism – have particular significance in India, and to a considerable degree are peculiar to that country. The standard SES factors that are usually considered as voting determinants are also relevant in India. Among these factors are age, sex, education, income, occupation, and rural or urban places of residence.[78]

In India, as in most other countries, older people tend to be more conservative in their voting habits, and younger people more radical. Age seems to be one of the significant determinants of support of the Congress Party, which seems to appeal more to older than to younger voters. In spite of its continued success, the Congress Party faces a real problem in the long run of winning greater support from the younger voters. This is a particularly important consideration in a country where half of the voters are under thirty-five years of age. It will become even more important if the voting age in India is lowered from twenty-one to eighteen, as it has been in Sri Lanka and several other countries.

In most democratic countries women are more conservatively inclined than men. They tend to participate in voting and other electoral activities less frequently than men, and they are considerably underrepresented in all elective bodies. India is certainly no exception to the general rule. Indeed, since India is a socially conservative society in which women's role, while of equal significance with men, tends to be more behind the scenes than in the center of either the social or political stage, the degree of participation in political life by women is truly impressive. Even in rural areas, where in the first general elections many women refrained from voting because of social inhibitions, women have been taking an increasingly active role in politics. They are still greatly underrepresented as candidates and even more as members of legislative and other elective bodies, but they have a proportionately larger representation in the Lok Sabha than do women in many other countries, including the United States, in the national Parliaments, and, of course, the Prime Minister is a woman. It would be interesting to know more of the determinants of voting by Indian women. To what extent are they influenced by essentially the same factors as are men? To what extent do they tend to vote as their husbands or other influential members of their families, kinship groups, castes, or other ascriptive groups suggest?

In all democracies the level of education is an important voting determinant, but of course its effects vary in accordance with many local circumstances and national conditions. In India, where the majority of people are illiterate, it is quite natural that ascriptive ties and 'primordial loyalties' are often decisive influences in determining a citizen's voting behavior. One hypothesis that seems to have been corroborated in various voting studies is that 'the lower the level of education of the family, [the] higher is the influence of the family head on [the] voting of other members of the family.'[79] With greater education people may respond more to other considerations.

Another hypothesis that also seems to be confirmed by voting studies is that 'highly educated voters tend to vote for opposition parties.' This has been a source of increasing difficulty, and some embarrassment, to the ruling Congress Party, but since most people are illiterate or have had little formal education it has not seriously affected the mass base of party support.

Among income groups, too, support for the Congress seems to vary inversely with levels of income. On the whole, the lowest income groups tend to vote for the Congress, whereas the highest income groups tend to be anti-Congress. There are, of course, many exceptions to this generalization. The Congress has consistently had the support – financial and otherwise – of many relatively wealthy individuals and organizations in India. Some of this support – from such an eminent businessman as G. D. Birla, for example – has been of long standing, and some has been of more recent origin. In the countryside, also, a significant and long-standing phenomenon has been that the 'vested interests' – mainly the larger landowners – have been pillars of the Congress. Since these interests have usually been dominant in the political as well as the economic life of the rural areas, they have been valuable 'vote banks' for the Congress; but they can also be liabilities, for they are the obvious targets of attack from the less privileged but more numerous groups in the rural areas and they are alleged to stand in the way of land reforms and other programs of 'distributive justice' to which the Congress Party is committed.

In rural areas, however, the Congress has drawn massive support from almost all sectors of the population, from landless laborers and members of lower castes (often the same people) to large landowners and other rural 'influentials'. In urban areas its support base has been consistently much weaker, especially among higher income groups, white collar workers, and intellectuals. It does have a considerable following among middle class citizens, in both urban and rural areas.

The rural-urban dichotomy is becoming an increasingly important one, as India becomes more urbanized and as the role of metropolitan areas in Indian life becomes more significant. As in many other countries, different styles of politics seem to prevail in the cities and in the countryside, and different political preferences and 'preference systems' often exist. In India, as has been noted, the rural areas are, in general, the stronghold of the Congress Party – with some exceptions – whereas the cities are centers of opposition – usually quite diversified and disunited – to the Congress. Since the Congress is an umbrella-type party, it derives support from groups in almost all sectors of Indian society, and from urban as well as rural areas; but it is still true that on the whole it fares better among less educated, lower caste, middle and lower income and rural groups than among the highly educated, the higher castes, the more affluent, and the urban dwellers. Most other parties, also, have pockets of strength in both rural and urban areas, but of course their support bases are narrower and more limited, geographically and socially. The Swatantra Party, for example, has drawn considerable support from the richer peasant castes, especially in Andhra Pradesh, but its leadership has been drawn heavily from former Princely rulers, who have often carried with them the support of the most 'feudal' elements of Indian society, from big industrialists and from intellectuals, who are based in the larger cities.

Other Determinants

Three other factors that may in some instances be very powerful voting determinants should be mentioned, although they will not be explored in any detail, partly because they are too complex, partly because they deal with behavior that is carried on in a semi-clandestine or secret manner behind the scenes and hence cannot be measured with any degree of accuracy, and partly because their role and influence in elections, and in public life generally, are too nebulous, imprecise, and controversial. These factors are corruption, money, and liquor.

Corruption is an endemic disease of Indian politics, as it is in most political systems. In India it flourishes in various forms at all levels of political life, from the petty graft of the local political leaders and public officials to the massive corruption of top central government officials and political organizations. In spite of amendments to the Companies Act that make such practices illegal, 'It is no secret that huge amounts are still collected by parties, especially the ruling party, from industrialists and businessmen,' obviously in return for expected favors and protection. 'The entire operation is conducted in black money,' and the amounts, and their use, are kept secret.[80] As the most important study of corruption in Indian politics pointed out in its 1964 report: 'This public belief in the prevalence of corruption at high political levels has been strengthened by the manner in which funds are collected by political parties, especially at the time of elections.'[81]

In this massive way money undoubtedly plays a major role in determining the shape and results of Indian elections. It is also important at lower levels, in influencing the decisions of individual voters, through the purchase of votes and the provision of favors, or through creating 'an impression of such overwhelming strength that even the voter who is not bemused and won over by the show thinks it is a waste of time to vote for any other candidate.' Hence the liberal use of money in elections 'loads the electoral scales in favour of the ruling party more heavily than ever. For only it can repay contributions in kind. Contributions to other parties are more in the nature of insurance for the future or bribes to keep parties with influence among the labour unions in good humour.'[82]

The distribution of liquor may play the same role as the distribution of money to win votes. There are innumerable indications and evidences of the widespread distribution of liquor on the eve of voting in many elections, local, State, and national, in many States and constituencies. With poorer peasants in rural areas and working classes in the cities this practice may be a very decisive factor in influencing the vote which recipients of liquor will cast on the day of voting. It is impossible to tell, however, how widespread or how influential it actually is. Certainly it is in some cases a factor that cannot be disregarded.

Voting Determinants: A Relative Assessment

After this detailed discussion of political and social determinants of voting in India, the question of the relative importance of these determinants naturally arises. One would assume that in a traditionally-oriented society such as prevails in India the social determinants would be most decisive. On the other hand, voting behavior studies in developed polities have provided evidence that social determinants of voting behavior are by no means as important as they were thought to be. Indeed, some Western psephologists would agree with one of the leading American students of voting behavior, V. O. Key, Jr., that on the whole social determinants do not in fact determine the way a citizen actually votes.[83]

However valid such a sweeping generalization might be for Western democracies, it would not hold true for India. But there is some basis for the statement of a German student of Indian politics that 'Intensive studies . . . have empirically proved that the influence of social, ethnic and religious groups [in other words, of social determinants] on the voting pattern is overestimated.'[84] There is also evidence that the influence of social determinants is declining, while that of political determinants is increasing. This may be interpreted as a sign of political development, for better or for worse. To refer again to a suggestive interpretation by D. L. Sheth, 'If our electorate has attained a certain level of political development, its voting decisions should be more and more influenced by political considerations as against primordial group considerations.'[85] The trend in India seems to be in this direction. One should bear in mind, however, that many important social determinants would not come under the heading of 'primordial considerations', and that there are many other determinants – such as those of corruption, money, and liquor that have been mentioned – that cannot clearly be classified as political or social determinants.

There is some evidence that even in rural areas voters are acting more independently, and are less influenced by group pressures and considerations. A study by D. L. Sheth of 2,287 persons 'drawn from a stratified sample of all accessible constituencies of India' produced the findings summarized in Table 10.i.[86]

These findings indicate a surprising degree of individual decision on the part of rural voters, a high degree of influence from family and kinship groups, and an amazingly small degree from caste affiliations, unless the influence of caste is reflected in the voter's own decision or in the discussions which he has within the family or in the advice he received from family elders.

Table 10.i

WAYS BY WHICH VOTING DECISIONS ARE REACHED BY RESPONDENTS, 1967

Mode of Voting Decision	*Per cent*
On advice of head or elders in the family	26
Through joint discussion in the family	20
On advice of village head or caste leaders	1
Voter's own decision	49
Don't know	2
Not ascertained	2

Source: Sheth, 'Political Development of the Indian Electorate,' p. 147.

A different picture emerges from a detailed study of the 1967 elections in Poona, based upon a random sample of some 1,000 voters in every Assembly constituency and of about 400 voters from major elite groups.[87] Of the various factors influencing voting decisions, the following received the highest percentages of response:

	Per cent
Caste	58
Money	42
Party organization	36
Party ideology	21
Candidate personality	25

These results indicate the heavy influence of caste factors, even in an essentially metropolitan area, of the political determinants of party and candidate orientation, and of the role of money.

Even more comprehensive and revealing evidence of the growing importance of political determinants, along with great variations in different parts of India, is provided in a study of the 1969 mid-term elections in the four major States of Bihar, the Punjab, U.P., and West Bengal. This is shown in Table 10.ii.[88]

This Table confirms the importance of political determinants of voting decisions, and provides further evidence in support of the proposition that social determinants – even including such basic factors as family and kinship, caste, factionalism, and communalism – are not as important voting determinants as has been commonly assumed. It also suggests that the relative importance of social determinants varies greatly from State to State. In Bihar, the Punjab, and West Bengal, for

Table 10.ii

CONSIDERATIONS INFLUENCING VOTING DECISION BY STATES
(*percentage*)

	States				
Considerations	*Bihar* *N* = *340*	*Punjab* *N* = *292*	*U.P.* *N* = *428*	*West Bengal* *N* = *349*	*Total* *N* = *1309*
Group pressures	10.6	6.8	24.7	9.2	14.13
Candidate	15.9	24.7	22.2	31.7	22.92
Attachment to Congress	26.4	31.9	19.6	10.8	22.46
Attachment to non-Congress parties	17.4	25.0	6.8	21.4	16.35
Miscellaneous	10.9	6.8	4.7	18.9	9.47
DK, NA, etc.	18.8	4.8	22.0	8.0	14.67
Total	100.0	100.0	100.0	100.0	100.00

Source: Roy, 'Patterns of Political Instability,' p. 297.

example, they seem to be of surprisingly little importance in this respect, whereas in U.P. they are still significant factors, even though less important than political determinants. The general picture that emerges is a mixed and rather confusing one, although overall trends seem to be in directions that can be clearly related to political development.

NOTES

Chapter 1. Elections and the Political System

1. James N. Rosenau, *The Dramas of Politics* (Boston: Little, Brown, 1973), p. 171.

2. V. O. Key, Jr., 'A Theory of Critical Elections,' *Journal of Politics*, XVII (February 1955), p. 3.

3. David E. Butler and Anthony King, *The British General Election of 1964* (London: Macmillan, 1965), p. 5.

4. Robert E. Lane, *Political Life: Why People Get Involved in Politics* (Glencoe, Ill.: The Free Press, 1959), p. 6.

5. Richard Rose and Harve Mossawir, 'Voting and Elections: A Functional Analysis,' *Political Studies*, XV (June 1967), 173.

6. Most of these studies were made by scholars associated with what might be called the Columbia and the Michigan schools. The first outstanding example was Paul F. Lazarfeld, Bernard Berelson, and Hazel Gaudet, *The People's Choice* (2nd edition, New York: Columbia University Press, 1948). 'The book reports on the first sophisticated application of survey techniques to a presidential election, the 1940 contest between Franklin D. Roosevelt and Wendell Willkie.' Peter H. Rossi, 'Four Landmarks of Voting Research,' in Eugene Burdick and Arthur J. Brodbeck, eds., *American Voting Behavior* (New York: The Free Press, 1959), p. 7. Professor Lazarsfeld and his associates carried out their research in Erie County, Ohio, conducting several interviews with a panel of respondents. Ten years later Lazarsfeld and Berelson, together with William McPhee, published another major contribution – *Voting: A Study of Opinion Formation in a Presidential Campaign* (Chicago: University of Chicago Press, 1954) – using substantially the same techniques in Elmira, New York, to study the 1948 presidential contest between Harry S. Truman and Thomas E. Dewey. As a result of their study they came up with no fewer than 149 findings, generalizations, or propositions regarding elections and voting, and in tabular form they summarized 209 generalizations derived from their studies of the 1940 and 1948 American presidential elections, other studies of the presidential elections of 1944, 1948, and 1952, and two British studies conducted along the lines of their own research in Erie County and Elmira, in Greenwich in 1950 and in Bristol in 1951. The first important work of the Michigan school was Angus Campbell, Gerald Gurin, and Warren E. Miller, *The Voter Decides* (Evanston, Ill.: Row, Peterson, 1954), a study of the 1952 presidential election, based on a nationwide sample, which was 'the most sophisticated nationwide

study of a presidential election' that had been made up to that time. Rossi, 'Four Landmarks,' p. 7. Six years later Campbell and Miller, with Philip E. Converse and Donald E. Stokes, published *The American Voter* (New York: John Wiley & Sons, 1960), probably the most influential book on elections that has yet been written. Using data drawn mainly from the American Presidential elections of 1948, 1952, and 1956, *The American Voter* summed up many of the findings regarding elections that had been suggested in the more rigorous election studies since the 1940s, and charted new directions for further research.

7. R. B. McCallum and Alison Readman, *The British General Election of 1945* (London: Oxford University Press, 1947); H. G. Nicholas, *The British General Election of 1950* (London: Macmillan, 1951); David E. Butler, *The British General Election of 1951* (New York: St. Martin's Press, 1952); David E. Butler, *The British General Election of 1955* (London: Macmillan, 1955); David E. Butler and Richard Rose, *The British General Election of 1959* (London: Macmillan, 1960); David E. Butler and Anthony King, *The British General Election of 1964* (London: Macmillan, 1965); and David E. Butler and Michael Pinto-Duschinsky, *The British General Election of 1970* (London: Macmillan, 1971). See also David E. Butler, *The Electoral System in Britain since 1918* (2nd edition, Oxford: Clarendon Press, 1963); and David E. Butler and Donald E. Stokes, *Political Change in Britain: Forces Shaping Electoral Choice* (New York: St. Martin's Press, 1969).

8. Examples are Seymour M. Lipset and Stein Rokkan, eds., *Party Systems and Voter Alignments: Cross-National Perspectives* (New York: The Free Press, 1967); Stein Rokkan, *Citizens, Elections, Parties* (New York: David McKay Co., 1970); Henry Valen and Daniel Katz, *Political Parties in Norway* (London: Tavistock Publications, 1964); Henry Ehrmann, *Politics in France* (Boston: Little, Brown, 1968); Juan Linz, 'The Social Bases of West German Politics' (Ph.D. dissertation, Columbia University, 1959); Sidney Tarrow, 'The Urban-Rural Cleavage in Political Involvement: The Case of France,' *The American Political Science Review*, LXV (June 1971).

9. See two special numbers of the *Political Science Review* (Department of Political Science, University of Rajasthan) on the fourth general elections in India – Vol. 6 (July–September, October–December 1967 and April–June 1969) and Vol. 7 (July–September 1968); and Aloo J. Dastur *et al.*, *Studies in the Fourth General Elections* (Bombay: Allied Publishers, 1972).

10. Professor R. B. McCallum claims that he coined the word 'psephology', in connection with the first of the Nuffield studies of British general elections. 'More as a joke than anything else, I devised a Greek name, psephology, from the Greek word *psephos*, a pebble, which was the mode in which the ancient Athenians cast their vote. Somehow the word has caught on. . . . It is always a good thing, if you start a new form of study, to find a Greek name for it. It looks

established and respectable and intellectual snobs wonder uneasily whether they ought not to pretend to have known about it all their lives.' R. B. McCallum, 'The Study of Psephology,' *Parliamentary Affairs*, VIII (Autumn 1955), 508.

11. W. J. M. Mackenzie, *Free Elections: An Elementary Textbook* (New York: Rinehart and Company, 1958), p. 175.

12. Sidney Verba, Norman H. Nie, and Jai-on Kim, *The Modes of Democratic Participation: A Cross-National Comparison* (Beverly Hills, Calif.: Sage Publications, 1971), pp. 16, 64.

13. Rokkan, *Citizens, Elections, Parties*, pp. 418, 419. Italics in original.

14. Maurice Duverger, 'The Influence of the Electoral System on Political Life,' *International Social Science Bulletin*, III (Summer 1971), p. 314.

15. Rose and Mossawir, 'Voting and Elections,' p. 173.

16. John Badgley, *Asian Development: Problems and Prognosis* (New York: The Free Press, 1971), p. 139.

17. See table in ibid., p. 145.

18. Campbell *et al.*, *The American Voter*, pp. 3–4.

19. Rose and Mossawir, 'Voting and Elections,' p. 173.

20. Lucian W. Pye, *Aspects of Political Development* (Boston: Little, Brown, 1956), p. 63. For a detailed treatment of these 'crises of development,' see Leonard Binder, James S. Coleman, Joseph LaPalombara, Myron Weiner, and Lucian W. Pye, *Crises and Sequences in Political Development* (Princeton, N. J.: Princeton University Press, 1971).

21. Pye, *Aspects of Political Development*, pp. 45–8. These themes relate to 'the development syndrome' which was developed by the members of the SSRC's Comparative Politics Committee. For an elaboration of this 'development syndrome' concept, see James S. Coleman, 'The Development Syndrome . . . ,' in Binder, *et al.*, *Crises and Sequences in Political Development*, Chap. 2.

22. Badgley, *Asian Development*, p. 186.

23. V. O. Key, Jr., *The Responsible Electorate* (Cambridge: Harvard University Press, 1966), p. 7.

24. Ashoka Mehta, in a personal discussion with the author, 27 December 1971.

25. Gopal Krishna, 'Religion in Politics' (unpublished paper), p. 27.

26. Seymour Martin Lipset, *Political Man: The Social Bases of Politics* (Anchor Books edition, Garden City, N.Y.: Doubleday and Co., 1963), p. 12.

27. Richard Harris, 'Ne'er the Twain Shall Meet, Particularly in Politics,' *The Times*, 4 May 1973.

28. Samuel P. Huntington, *Political Order in Changing Socities* (New Haven: Yale University Press, 1968), p. 7.

29. See Norman D. Palmer, 'Power of the Ballot,' *The Economic Times* (Bombay), Annual, 1972.

30. For excellent succinct commentaries on different kinds of electoral systems, see Mackenzie, *Free Elections*; Duverger, 'The

Influence of the Electoral System on Political Life;' and Stein Rokkan, 'Electoral Systems,' *International Encyclopedia of the Social Sciences*, V (New York: Macmillan, 1968).

31. André Siegfried, *Tableau politique de la France de l'ouest sous la troisième république* (Paris: Librairie Armand Colin, 1913), pp. 499–506.

32. V. O. Key, Jr., 'A Theory of Critical Elections,' *Journal of Politics*, XVII (1955), 3–18.

33. Ibid., pp. 4–16.

34. Richard Rose, *Politics in England* (Boston: Little, Brown, 1964), p. 247.

35. David E. Butler and Anthony King, *The British General Elections of 1964* (London: Macmillan, 1965), p. 1.

36. Angus Campbell, Philip E. Converse, Warren E. Miller, and Donald E. Stokes, *Elections and the Political Order* (New York, John Wiley and Sons, 1966), Chapter 4, 'Classification of Presidential Elections.'

37. Butler, *The British General Elections of 1951*, p. 1.

38. Duverger, 'The Influence of the Electoral System on Political Life,' p. 314.

39. Ibid., p. 319.

40. Gopal Krishna, 'One Party Dominance – Development and Trends,' *Perspectives*, Supplement to *The Indian Journal of Public Administration*, XII (January–March 1966), 24, 25.

41. Butler and King, *The British General Elections of 1964*, p. 30.

42. This approach has been suggested by many political sociologists, including Talcott Parsons, Seymour Martin Lipset, and Reinhard Bendix, and by several students of political development, including the members of the Committee on Comparative Politics of the SSRC. It has also been utilized by non-American political scientists who have been influenced by 'the developmental approach'. See, for example, Rose, *Politics in England*, especially Chapter V, and Rajni Kothari, *Politics in India* (Boston: Little, Brown, 1970), especially Chapter VI.

43. '. . . a person thinks, politically, as he is socially. Social characteristics determine political preference.' Lazarsfeld, *et al.*, *The People's Choice*, p. 27.

44. Key, 'A Theory of Critical Elections,' p. 17.

45. Richard Harris is quite justified in criticizing Western news media for reporting on elections in Asian countries as if these elections were directly comparable to elections in Britain, or France, or Norway, or the United States. 'Ne'er the Twain Shall Meet, Particularly in Politics,' *The Times*, 4 May 1973.

Chapter 2. Elections and the Political System: India

1. D. L. Sheth, 'Political Development of Indian Electorate,' *Economic and Political Weekly*,' V (Annual Number, January 1970), 138.

2. Imtiaz Ahmed *et al.*, 'Elections and Political Process: Studies in the Fifth Parliamentary Elections' (unpublished paper, issued by the Centre for the Study of Political Development, Jawaharlal Nehru University, n.d.).

3. See Gopal Krishna, 'One Party Dominance – Development and Trends,' *Perspectives*, Supplement to *The Indian Journal of Public Administration*, XII (January–March 1966); and Samuel J. Eldersveld, 'The 1967 Indian Election: Patterns of Party Regularity and Defection,' *Asian Survey*, X (November 1970).

4. W. H. Morris-Jones and B. Das Gupta, 'India's Political Areas: Interim Report on an Ecological Investigation,' *Asian Survey*, IX (June 1969), 399.

5. V. M. Sirsikar, 'Electoral Process in Poona 1967: A Study in Parties, Politics and Voters' (unpublished manuscript, Poona: Department of Political Science, University of Poona, n.d.), p. 182.

6. W. H. Morris-Jones, 'India Elects for Change – and Stability,' *Asian Survey*, XI (August 1971), 739.

7. The author is inclined to emphasize the importance of elections in the Indian political system, because elections are indeed central to that system, because they highlight many of the major aspects of the system, and because they provide insights into Indian politics and society. He is, however, well aware of the limitations of election studies for the study of political systems, especially in polities where non-political factors and considerations seem to be so important. It is useful to ponder the following observation by one of the leading modern students of comparative political systems (although the author does not wish to suggest that he is in full agreement with it): 'The importance of the differences arising out of the social bases and goals of the parties suggests that electoral systems have perhaps less of an impact than has been sometimes suggested and may not deserve the extensive analysis they have received.' Jean Blondel, *Comparing Political Systems* (New York: Praeger Publishers, 1972), p. 106.

8. See V. O. Key, Jr., *The Responsible Electorate* (Cambridge: Harvard University Press, 1966).

9. See W. H. Morris-Jones, 'India's Political Idioms,' in C. H. Philips, ed., *Politics and Society in India* (New York: Frederick A. Praeger, 1962); Lloyd I. Rudolph and Susanne Hoeber Rudolph, *The Modernity of Tradition: Political Development in India* (Chicago: University of Chicago Press, 1967); Rajni Kothari, *Politics in India* (Boston: Little, Brown, 1970), especially Chapter VII, 'Political Culture and Socialization.'

10. V. M. Sirsikar, *Political Behaviour in India: A Case Study of the 1962 General Elections* (Bombay: Manaktala, 1965), p. 252.

11. See references in footnote 8.

12. Samuel P. Huntington, *Political Order in Changing Societies* (New Haven: Yale University Press, 1968), pp. 444, 445.

13. Ibid., pp. 445–6.

14. Ibid., pp. 446–7. The words which Huntington quotes are from Myron Weiner, 'India's Third General Elections,' *Asian Survey*, II (May, 1962), p. 10.

15. Ranbir Sharma, 'Political Parties in Himachal Pradesh: A Study in Political Development' (unpublished Ph.D. dissertation, Punjab University, Chandigarh, 1972), p. 219.

16. Ibid., p. 220.

17. Surindar Suri, 'Towards a Theory of Indian Politics: Some Implications of the Results of the General Elections,' *Economic Weekly*, XIV (Dec. 1, 1962), 1849.

18. Gopal Krishna, 'One-Party Dominance,' pp. 9, 10–11.

19. Maurice Duverger, 'The Influence of the Electoral System on Political Life,' *International Social Science Bulletin*, III (Summer, 1951), 314.

20. See Norman D. Palmer, *The Indian Political System* (2nd edition, Boston: Houghton Mifflin Company, 1971), pp. 12, 207; Susanne Hoeber Rudolph, 'Consensus and Conflict in Indian Politics,' *World Politics*, XIII (April 1961); and Jayaprakash Narayan, 'Towards a Fuller Democracy,' *The Radical Humanist*, XXII (15 and 22 June 1958).

21. Duverger, *The Influence of the Electoral System on Political Life*, p. 319.

22. Shriram Maheswari, *The General Election in India* (Allahabad: Chaitanya Publishing House, 1963), p. 65.

23. Douglas Madsen, 'Solid Congress Support in 1967: A Statistical Inquiry,' *Asian Survey*, X (November, 1970), 1005.

24. See Robert W. Stern, *The Process of Opposition in India* (Chicago: University of Chicago Press, 1972).

25. Shiv Lal, *National Parties of India* (New Delhi: Election Archives, 1971), p. 13.

26. D. L. Sheth, 'Profiles of Party Support in 1967,' *Economic and Political Weekly*, VI (Annual Number, January, 1971), 284.

27. Ibid., pp. 284–5.

28. Kothari, *Politics in India*, p. 1.

29. Sheth, 'Political Development of Indian Electorate,' p. 148.

30. See Kothari, *Politics in India*, Chapter VI, 'Social Infrastructure'; and Rajni Kothari, 'Introduction: Caste in Indian Politics,' in Rajni Kothari, ed., *Caste in Indian Politics* (New Delhi: Orient Longmans, 1970). For an elaboration of this important theme see Chapter 10.

31. Rajni Kothari, 'Diagnosis and Design,' *Seminar*, No. 173, January, 1974, p. 29.

32. See Surindar Suri, 'Intelligentsia and the Elections,' *The Times of India*, 30 Dec. 1970.

33. See Angus Campbell *et al.*, *Elections and the Political Order* (New York: John Wiley and Sons, 1966), Chapter 4, 'Classification of Presidential Elections.'

34. The themes of each general election were dramatically presented in five cartoons by the leading political cartoonist of India – Laxman of *The Times of India* – which are reproduced in Chapter 6.

35. V. O. Key, Jr., 'A Theory of Critical Elections,' *The Journal of Politics*, XVII (February 1955), 11.

36. Kathari, *Politics in India*, pp. 153–4, 200.

37. For aggregate data on the general elections, at national, State, and constituency levels, see the reports on each general election by the Election Commission of India; for data on voting trends at district levels, see Craig Baxter, *District Voting Trends in India: A Research Tool* (New York: Columbia University Press, 1969).

38. See Stern, *The Process of Opposition in India.*

39. A. J. Milnor, *Elections and Political Stability* (Boston: Little, Brown, 1969), p. 42.

40. E. P. W. da Costa, 'The Congress "Multiplier" – a New Parameter,' and 'The "Multiplier" and Electoral Alliances,' in E. P. W. da Costa, *The Indian General Elections: The Structure of Indian Voting Intentions: January 1967* (New Delhi: Indian Institute of Public Opinion, 1967); and E. P. W. da Costa, 'The Congress Multiplier in 1971,' *Monthly Public Opinion Surveys* of the Indian Institute of Public Opinion, XVI (December, 1970, January, February, 1971), 9.

41. See 'The Erratic Splinter Factor,' in *Monthly Public Opinion Surveys* of the Indian Institute of Public Opinion, XVI (December 1970, January, February 1971), 7–8.

42. Ratna Dutta, 'The Party Representation in the Fourth Lok Sabha,' *Economic and Political Weekly*, IV (January 1969); and 'A Facelift for Parliament,' *The Times of India*, 31 March 1971.

43. 'A Facelift for Parliament.'

44. Ibid.

45. Ibid.

46. R. Chandidas, Leon Clark, Richard Fontera, Ward Morehouse, eds., *India Votes: A Source Book on Indian Elections* (Bombay: Popular Prakashan, 1968), p. vi.

47. T. E. Smith, *Elections in Developing Countries* (New York: St. Martin's Press, 1960), p. 255.

48. See Philip E. Jacob *et al.*, *Values and the Active Community: a Cross-National Study of the Influence of Local Leadership* (New York: The Free Press, 1971), especially p. 394 (Table 3, 'Value Priorities').

49. Sidney Verba, Normal H. Nie, and Jae-on Kim, *The Modes of Democratic Participation: A Cross-National Comparison* (Beverly Hills, Calif.: Sage Publications, 1971), pp. 61, 73.

50. See, for example, Alice and Yasumasa Kuroda, 'Aspects of Community Participation in Japan,' *The Journal of Asian Studies*, XXVII (February, 1968).

51. Irene Tinker-Walker, 'Himachal Pradesh,' in S. V. Kogekar and Richard L. Park, eds., *Reports on the Indian General Elections 1951–52* (Bombay: Popular Book Depot, 1956), p. 302.

52. Pran Chopra, *Uncertain India: A Political Profile of Two Decades of Freedom* (Cambridge: The MIT Press, 1968), p. 387.

53. Rajni Kothari, 'Introduction' to a series of articles on 'Voting in India: Competitive Politics and Electoral Change,' *Economic and Political Weekly*, VI (Annual Number, January 1971), p. 229.

54. Rajni Kothari, 'Democracy in Perspective: Significance of Recent Elections in India,' *Indian & Foreign Review*, 1 April 1972, p. 15.

55. Sheth, 'Political Development of Indian Electorate.'

56. Ibid., p. 11.

57. See, for example, D. N. Pathak and K. D. Desai, 'A Study of Political Behaviour in Gujarat with Special Reference to the Fourth General Elections, 1967' (unpublished manuscript, Ahmedabad: University School of Social Sciences, Gujarat University, 1970), pp. 115–16; and Satish K. Arora, 'India's Rural Politicians: Two Faces of Power,' *Economic and Political Weekly*, (Annual Number, February 1972), 250.

58. Sitasaran Singh, 'A Study of Indian Voters,' *The Illustrated Weekly of India*, XIII (26 Sept. 1971).

59. Deepal Banerjee, 'Ensuing Elections: Some Posers,' *Amrita Bazar Patrika*, 25 Feb. 1971. This article summarizes the findings of this prepoll survey, which was carried out by the Youth Press Service, an organization of students in the Journalism Department, Calcutta University.

60. Kothari, *Politics in India*, p. 193.

Chapter 3. The Functions of Elections: Political Choice and Political Participation

1. James N. Rosenau, *The Dramas of Politics* (Boston: Little, Brown, 1973), pp. 144–5.

2. W. J. M. Mackenzie, 'The Export of Electoral Systems,' *Political Studies*, V (October 1957), 255.

3. Ibid., pp. 240–57.

4. A. J. Milnor, *Elections and Political Stability* (Boston: Little, Brown, 1969), p. 7. See Peter M. Blau, *Exchange and Power in Social Life* (New York: John Wiley & Sons, 1967).

5. D. N. Pathak and K. D. Desai, 'A Study of Political Behaviour in Gujarat, with Special Reference to the Fourth General Elections, 1967' (unpublished manuscript, Ahmedabad: University School of Social Sciences, Gujarat University, 1970), p. 108.

6. Yogesh Atal, *Local Communities and National Politics* (Delhi: National Publishing House, 1971), p. 63.

7. Robert Dahl, *A Preface to Democratic Theory* (Chicago: University of Chicago Press, 1956), p. 125.

8. Peter J. Pulzer, *Political Representation and Elections in Britain* (London: George Allen and Unwin, 1967), p. 147.

9. See Warren E. Miller and Donald E. Stokes, 'Constituency Influence in Congress,' in Angus Campbell *et al.*, *Elections and the Political Order* (New York: John Wiley and Sons, 1966), pp. 351–72.

10. Jack Dennis, 'Support for the Institution of Elections by the Mass Public,' *The American Political Science Review*, LXIV (September 1970), 819–20.

11. Michael Brecher, 'Succession in India: The Routinization of Political Change,' *Asian Survey*, VII (July 1967), p. 147.

12. Pulzer, *Political Representation*, p. 147.

13. W. J. M. Mackenzie, 'The Functions of Elections,' *International Encyclopedia of the Social Sciences* (New York: Macmillan, 1968), v, 5.

14. Richard Rose and Harve Mossawir, 'Voting and Elections: A Functional Analysis,' *Political Studies*, XV, (June 1967), 186.

15. Gunnar Sjöblom, *Party Strategies in a Multiparty System* (Lund: Studentlitteratur, 1968), p. 209.

16. This thesis was advanced by Herbert Tingsten in his classic work on *Political Behavior* (London: P. S. King, 1937) and has often been repeated and expanded since the publication of Tingsten's work. Students of the politics of developing societies, in particular, have pointed out that a high degree of participation may have destabilizing, as well as stabilizing effects. In *Political Order in Changing Societies* (New Haven: Yale University Press, 1968), pp. 397–8, Samuel Huntington wrote: 'Polities which have a stable balance between participation and institutionalization at low levels of both face the prospect of future instability unless the development of political institutions keep pace with the expansion of political participation. Since the prospects of this are relatively low, such societies are presumably unstable. On the other hand, societies which have created large-scale modern political institutions with the capability of handling much more extensive political participation than exists are present are presumably stable. Societies where participation already exceeds institutionalization are, clearly, unstable, while societies with a balance between the two at high rates of both may be said to have validated stability.' According to this interpretation, in terms of democratic theory the levels of participation are associated with levels of political development, including levels of institutionalization. A fully-developed modern democratic state would require a high level of participation; a developing polity moving in the democratic direction would require lower levels of participation at the beginning and increasingly higher levels as overall political development occurs. The paradox here is that a developing society can hardly claim to be democratic without a fairly high degree of political participation, but too much participation, outpacing institutionalization and other requisites of development, could lead to greater political instability and could therefore jeopardize the efforts for democracy in that society.

17. Sidney Verba, 'Democratic Participation,' *The Annals* of the American Academy of Political and Social Science, CCCLXXIII (September 1967), p. 55.

18. Ibid.

19. Myron Weiner, 'Political Participation: Crisis of the Political Process,' in Leonard Binder *et al.*, *Crises and Sequences in Political Development* (Princeton: Princeton University Press, 1971), p. 164.

20. Ibid., p. 197.

21. See Norman D. Palmer, 'Experiments in "Democratic Decentralisation" in South Asia,' *The Indian Political Science Review*, I (October, 1966–March, 1967), 49–68.

22. Lecture on 'Political Participation' at the University of Pennsylvania, 26 Jan. 1973.

23. Verba, 'Democratic Participation,' p. 61.

24. Seymour Martin Lipset, *Political Man* (Garden City, N.Y.: Doubleday & Co., 1960), p. 184.

25. See ibid., p. 14.

26. Sidney Verba, Norman H. Nie, and Jae-on Kim, *The Modes of Democratic Participation: A Cross-National Comparison* (Beverly Hills, Calif.: Sage Publications, 1971), p. 17.

27. Lester W. Milbrath, *Political Participation* (Chicago: Rand McNally & Co., 1965), p. 18.

28. See, for example, David E. Butler and Donald Stokes, *Political Change in Britain: Forces Shaping Electoral Choice* (New York: St. Martin's Press, 1969), p. 25; and Bashiruddin Ahmed, 'Political Stratification of the Indian Electorate,' *Economic and Political Weekly*, VI (Annual Number, January 1971), 252.

29. Lewis Bowman and G. R. Boynton, 'Recruitment Patterns Among Local Party Officials: A Model and Some Preliminary Findings in Selected Locales,' *American Political Science Review*, LX (September 1966), 668.

30. See Lipset, *Political Man*, Chap. 6; Angus Campbell *et al.*, *The American Voter* (New York: John Wiley & Sons, 1960), Chap. 5; and Herbert Tingsten, *The Problem of Democracy* (Totawa: Bedminster Press, 1965), pp. 101–3.

31. Ahmed, 'Political Stratification of the Indian Electorate.'

32. Ibid., p. 258.

33. Ibid.

34. Ibid., p. 252.

35. Ibid.

36. Robert E. Lane, *Political Life: Why and How People Get Involved in Politics* (New York: the Free Press, 1965), pp. 93–94.

37. Ahmed, 'Political Stratification of the Indian Electorate,' p. 253.

38. Ibid.

39. Ibid., p. 255.

40. Ibid.

41. Rose and Mossawir, 'Voting and Elections,' p. 173.

42. Herbert Tingsten, *Political Behavior: Studies in Election Statistics* (London: P. S. King and Son, 1937).

43. Lipset, *Political Man*, p. 187.

44. Myron Weiner, 'Political Development in the Indian States,' in Myron Weiner, ed., *State Politics in India* (Princeton: Princeton University Press, 1968), p. 33.

45. 'Turnout at the polls on election day in England has been consistently high since 1885. In the four general elections of the 1950s it averaged 80 per cent.' Richard Rose, *Politics in England* (Boston: Little, Brown, 1964), p. 85. In elections in the Federal Republic of Germany the turnout has been even higher. In five elections between 1953 and 1969 the turnout ranged between 86 and 88 per cent, and in the 1972 elections it reached the remarkable figure of 91.2 per cent. 'The 1972 Bundestag Election – A Historic Event?,' a Special Service by the Editorial Department of *Inter Nationes* (Bonn-Bad Godesberg, SO 16/72), p. 19.

46. The figure for the voting turnout in India in the 1967 general elections is lower than that reported by the Indian Election Commission.

47. For aggregate data on voting turnout in many countries, see Bruce M. Russett, *et al.*, *World Handbook of Political and Social Indicators* (New Haven: Yale University Press, 1964), especially Figure 13.3 (p. 306), 'Voting Tends to Be Highest in Developed Countries, But Not in the Richest Ones.'

48. Verba, Nie, and Kim, *The Modes of Democratic Participation*, p. 43. Verba, Nie, and Kim go so far as to argue that 'the only thing to recommend the use of turnout as a measure of participation is the availability of the data.' Ibid., p. 67, n. 2. This seems to be too extreme a view.

49. Ibid., pp. 43, 51.

50. Ibid., p. 65.

51. Ibid. See Adam Przeworski and Henry Teune, 'Equivalence in Cross-National Research,' *Public Opinion Quarterly*, XXX (Winter, 1967), 551–68.

52. Bowman and Boynton, 'Recruitment Patterns Among Local Party Officials,' p. 670.

53. See Campbell, *et al.*, *The American Voter*, p. 490; and Angus Campbell, Gerald Gurin, and Warren E. Miller, *The Voter Decides* (Evanston, Illinois: Row, Peterson and Company, 1954), p. 191. For an application of the scale of political efficacy, in slightly revised form, to Japan, see Alice and Yasumasa Kuroda, 'Aspects of Community Political Participation in Japan,' *The Journal of Asian Studies*, XXVII (February 1968), 239–41. See also Gabriel Almond and Sidney Verba, *The Civic Culture: Political Attitudes and Democracy in Five Nations* (Princeton: Princeton University Press, 1963), Chap. 7, 'The Sense of Civic Competence.'

54. Ramashray Roy, 'Patterns of Political Instability: A Study of the 1969 Mid-Term Elections,' *Economics and Political Weekly*, VI (Annual Number, January 1971), 302 (Table 13: Level of Political Efficacy by State; reproduced above, p. 263). The sense of political efficacy of Indian voters is discussed more fully and more specifically in Chapter 9.

55. Almond and Verba, *The Civic Culture*, Chap. 6, 'The Obligation to Participate.' The question asked of respondents in this connection was: 'We know that the ordinary person has many problems that take his time. In view of this, what part do you think the ordinary person ought to play in the local affairs of his town or district?' In addition to those who thought that the 'ordinary person' should 'be active in his community,' 27 per cent in the United States, 31 per cent in England, 38 per cent in Germany, 33 per cent in Mexico, and 22 per cent in Italy thought that the 'ordinary person' should 'only participate passively' (for example, one ought to be interested in local affairs, try to understand them and keep informed, and vote). Ibid., pp. 171–2.

56. International Studies of Values in Politics, *Values and the Active Community: A Cross-National Study of the Influence of Local Leadership* (New York: The Free Press, 1971). See Table 3 – 'Value Priorities,' p. 394. The Indian part of this cross-national study was based mainly on answers to an elaborate questionnaire by 955 local leaders in 30 community development blocks in Gujarat, Maharashtra, and Uttar Pradesh. These answers were analyzed by various statistical techniques. Table 3 shows that participation was given a far lower rating by the Indian local leaders than by local leaders in Poland, Yugoslavia and the United States. Only in India was participation ranked as the least important of the eight values which were singled out for analysis by the ISVIP. It should be borne in mind that this finding is based on data obtained from a rather unrepresentative and limited sample, and may not in fact be an accurate reflection of Indian views on participation; but it does seem to corroborate what more general studies and participant observation have indicated as a striking phenomenon of India's non-participant but in some respects highly politicized society.

Chapter 4. The Functions of Elections: Support-Building and Linkage Patterns

1. James N. Rosenau, *The Dramas of Politics* (Boston: Little, Brown, 1973), pp. 159–60.

2. W. J. M. Mackenzie, 'The Function of Elections,' *International Encyclopedia of the Social Sciences*, (New York: Macmillan, 1968), v, 5.

3. Richard Rose and Harve Mossawir, 'Voting and Elections: A Functional Analysis,' *Political Studies*, XV (June 1967), 199.

4. See Norman D. Palmer, 'Power of the Ballot,' *The Economic Times*, Annual 1972, pp. 55–9.

5. Ibid., p. 59.

6. A. J. Milnor, *Elections and Political Stability* (Boston: Little, Brown, 1969), p. 104.

7. Ibid., pp. 99–100.

8. Palmer, 'Power of the Ballot,' p. 58.

9. Rose and Mossawir, 'Voting and Elections,' p. 186.

10. Gerald M. Pomper, *Elections in America: Control and Influence in Democratic Politics* (New York: Dodd, Mead, 1968), p. ix.

11. Ibid., p. 40.

12. Rosenau, *The Dramas of Politics*, p. 159.

13. John Stuart Mill, *Considerations on Representative Government* (New York: The Liberal Arts Press, 1958), p. 128.

14. See Herbert H. Hyman, *Political Socialization: A Study in the Psychology of Political Behavior* (Glencoe, Ill.: Free Press, 1959); Richard E. Dawson and Kenneth Prewitt, *Political Socialization: An Analytic Study* (Boston: Little, Brown, 1969).

15. See Lloyd I. Rudolph and Susanne Hoeber Rudolph, *The Modernity of Tradition: Political Development in India* (Chicago: University of Chicago Press, 1967); Rajni Kothari, *Politics in India* (Boston: Little, Brown, 1970), pp. 85–6; and Norman D. Palmer, *The Indian Political System* (2nd edition, Boston: Houghton Mifflin, 1971), pp. 8–10.

16. See Dennis, 'Support for the Institution of Elections,' pp. 819–20.

17. See Jerrold Schecter, *The New Faces of Buddha* (New York: Coward-McCann, 1967), Chap. 12, 'Japan: Soka Gakkai, Faith Equals Power.'

18. See Donald E. Smith, *India as a Secular State* (Princeton: Princeton University Press, 1963); Freeland Abbott, 'Pakistan and the Secular State,' and Donald E. Smith, 'The Sinhalese Buddhist Revolution,' in Donald E. Smith, ed., *South Asian Politics and Religion* (Princeton: Princeton University Press, 1966).

19. Keith Callard, *Pakistan: A Political Study* (London: George Allen and Unwin, 1957), p. 225.

20. See W. H. Morris-Jones, 'India's Political Idioms,' in C. H. Phillips, ed., *Politics and Society in India* (New York: Frederick A. Praeger, 1962), and W. H. Morris-Jones, *The Government and Politics of India* (Garden City, N.Y.: Doubleday and Company, 1967), pp. 40–9.

21. See Susanne Hoeber Rudolph, 'Consensus and Conflict in Indian Politics,' *World Politics*, XIII (April 1961). Professor Morris-Jones has argued that in spite of the traditional emphasis on consensus Indian society today is in reality 'a fragmented society, a society with an absence of a basic consensus,' and that that ' "absence of consensus" theme has been central to an understanding of modern Indian politics.' W. H. Morris-Jones, 'The Exploration of Indian Political Life,' *Pacific Affairs*, XXXII (December 1959), 419.

22. See Jayaprakash Narayan, 'Towards a Fuller Democracy,' *The Radical Humanist*, XXII (15 and 22 June 1958); and Palmer, *The Indian Political System*, p. 207.

23. For accounts of the 1971 general elections in India see R. L. Gupta, *Politics of Commitment* (New Delhi: Trimurti Publications, 1972); and 'The Nineteen Seventy-one Election,' *Seminar*, No. 144 (August 1971).

24. See Norman D. Palmer, 'Elections and the Political System in India: The 1972 State Assembly Elections,' *Pacific Affairs*, XLV (Winter 1972–3).

25. For accounts of the 1970 general election in Ceylon see the issues of the *Ceylon Daily News* just before and after the elections on 27 May 1970. A concise summary of and commentary on the election results may be found in *The Statesman*, 29 May 1970.

26. For accounts of the 1970 elections in Pakistan see Ahmed Husain, *Politics and People's Representation in Pakistan* (Lahore: Ferozsons, 1972), pp. 121–207, and Sharif al Mujahid, 'Pakistan: First General Elections,' *Asian Survey*, XI (February 1971).

27. Pomper, *Elections in America*, p. 41.

28. See Norman D. Palmer, 'Revolution by Ballot: The Fourth General Elections in India,' *Midway*, VIII (Autumn, 1967), 86–7.

29. Murray Edelman, *The Symbolic Uses of Politics* (Urbana, Ill.: University of Illinois Press, 1964), p. 17.

30. Henry S. Albinski and Lawrence K. Pettit, *European Political Processes*, (manuscript of revised edition), p. 117.

31. Rose and Mossawir, 'Voting and Elections,' p. 188.

32. Ibid., p. 189.

33. Ibid., p. 188.

34. Dennis, 'Support for the Institution of Elections,' p. 825.

35. See Gabriel A. Almond and Sidney Verba, *The Civic Culture* (Princeton: Princeton University Press, 1963), p. 171; Rose and Mossawir, 'Voting and Elections,' p. 189; Lewis J. Edinger, *Politics in Germany* (Boston: Little, Brown, 1968), p. 106.

36. Sidney Verba, Norman H. Nie, and Jae-On Kim, *The Modes of Democratic Participation: A Cross-National Comparison* (Beverly Hills, Calif.: Sage Publications, 1971), p. 73.

37. Ramashray Roy, 'Patterns of Political Instability: A Study of the 1969 Mid-term Elections,' *Economic and Political Weekly*, VI (Annual Number, January 1971), p. 304.

38. Ibid., pp. 304–5.

39. See Urmila Phadnis, 'Insurgency in Ceylon: Hard Challenge and Grim Warning,' *Economic and Political Weekly*, VI (8 May 1971).

40. John Plamenatz, 'Electoral Studies and Democratic Theory: A British View,' *Political Studies*, VI (February 1958), 9.

Chapter 5. The Electoral Process In India

1. *Encyclopaedia Britannica*, Vol. VIII, p. 134.

2. Ibid.

3. Mary C. Carras, *The Dynamics of Indian Political Factions: A Study of District Councils in the State of Maharashtra* (London: Cambridge University Press, 1972), p. 19.

4. Imtiaz Ahmed, 'Secularisation,' *Seminar*, No. 144 (August 1971), p. 22.

5. W. J. M. Mackenzie, *Free Elections* (London: George Allen and Unwin, 1958), p. 14.

6. For an excellent general discussion of proportional representation, see Maurice Duverger, 'The Influence of Electoral Systems in Political Life,' *International Social Science Bulletin*; III (Summer 1951). For different views on the desirability of some system of PR for India, see S. P. Sen Varma, 'A Challenge,' and Romesh Thapar, 'Reform Must Begin,' in *Seminar*, No. 159 (November, 1972), pp. 25–7, and 35–6.

7. *'The Problem,' Seminar*, No. 159 (November, 1972), p. 14.

8. Sen Gupta, 'A Challenge,' p. 25.

9. Shriram Maheshwari, *The General Election in India* (Allahabad: Chaitanya Publishing House, 1963), p. 24.

10. Ibid., pp. 24–5.

11. Ibid., p. 31.

12. T. E. Smith, *Elections in Developing Countries* (London: Macmillan, 1960), p. 3.

13. Norman D. Palmer, *The Indian Political System* (2nd edition, Boston: Houghton Mifflin, 1971), p. 242.

14. Maheshwari, *The General Election in India*, p. 84.

15. Ibid., p. 89.

16. Ibid., p. 91.

17. Ramashray Roy, 'Selection of Congress Candidates – I,' *Economic and Political Weekly*, I (31 Dec. 1966), 833.

18. Gunnar Sjöblom, *Party Strategies in a Multiparty System* (Lund: Studentlitteratur, 1968), p. 131.

19. W. H. Morris-Jones, 'Candidate Selection: The Ordeal of the Indian National Congress, 1966–1967,' in M. S. Rajan, ed., *Studies in Politics: National and International* (Delhi: Vikas Publications, 1971), p. 34.

20. Stanley Kochanek, *The Congress Party of India: The Dynamics of One-Party Democracy* (Princeton, N.J.: Princeton University Press, 1968), p. 298.

21. Ibid., p. 273.

22. Morris-Jones, 'Candidate Selection,' p. 37.

23. Kochanek, *The Congress Party of India*, p. 279.

24. Ibid., p. 275.

25. Quoted in W. H. Morris-Jones, *Parliament in India* (Philadelphia: University of Pennsylvania Press, 1957), p, 173.

26. Press conference in New Delhi, 3 Nov. 1951; quoted in Neeraj, *Nehru and Democracy in India* (Delhi: Metropolitan Book Co., 1972), p. 143.

27. *The Hindu*, 27 Sept. 1951.

28. Letter to the Chairmen of the Pradesh Election Committees, Oct. 13, 1951; quoted in Neeraj, *Nehru and Democracy in India*,, p. 143.

29. *The Hindu Weekly Review*, 7 Jan. 1957.

30. *Congress Bulletin*, Nos. 7–8, July–August 1966, p. 254.

31. Kochanek, *The Congress Party of India*, pp. 269–70.

32. Statement of Professor N. G. S. Kini, Nagpur University, at a

Seminar on Electoral and Party Behaviour, University of Rajasthan, Jaipur, December 1966.

33. See Norman D. Palmer, 'Elections and the Political System in India: The 1972 State Assembly Elections and After,' *Pacific Affairs*, XLV (Winter 1972–3), 537–8.

34. G. K. Reddy, 'Much Confusion in Cong (R) Selection of Candidates,' *The Hindu*, 7 February 1972.

35. Ibid.

36. This information regarding the processes of selection of Congress candidates in various States is culled from Indian newspapers during February, 1972.

37. S. Viswam, 'Selection of Congress Candidates,' *The Statesman*, 4 Feb. 1972.

38. Reddy, 'Much Confusion in Cong (R) Selection of Candidates.'

39. D. N. Pathak and K. D. Desai, 'A Study of Political Behaviour in Gujarat, with Special Reference to the Fourth General Elections, 1967' (Ahmedabad: University School of Social Sciences, Gujarat University, 1970, unpublished manuscript), p. 78.

40. Ibid.

41. As, for example, in Bernard Berelson, Paul F. Lazarsfeld, and William McPhee, *Voting: A Study of Opinion Formation in a Presidential Campaign* (Chicago: University of Chicago Press, 1954).

42. Pathak and Desai, *A Study of Political Behaviour in Gujarat*, pp. 78–84.

43. David E. Butler, *The British General Election of 1951* (London: Macmillan, 1952), p. 4.

44. David E. Butler and Donald Stokes, *Political Change in Britain: Forces Shaping Electoral Choice* (New York: St. Martin's Press, 1969).

45. Pathak and Desai, *A Study of Political Behaviour in Gujarat*, p. 78.

46. Yogesh Atal, *Local Communities and National Politics* (Delhi: National Publishing House, 1971), pp. 189–90.

47. Nelson W. Polsby and Aaron B. Wildavsky, *Presidential Elections* (3rd edition, New York: Charles Scribner's Sons, 1971), p. 12.

48. Atal, *Local Communities and National Politics*, pp. 244–9.

49. R. Chandidas and Ward Morehouse, eds., *India Votes (II): A Source Book on Indian Elections, 1968–1970* (Bombay: Popular Prakashan, 1971), p. 4.

50. Atal, *Local Communities and National Politics*, p. 227.

51. Ibid., pp. 227–31.

52. Ibid., pp. 189–93 and 197–231.

53. Ibid., p. 191.

54. Ibid., p. 192.

55. Ibid., p. 193.

56. Ibid.

57. Norman D. Palmer, *The Indian Political System* (Second Edition, Boston: Houghton Mifflin Company, 1971), p. 251.

58. Ibid., p. 252.

59. Ramashray Roy, 'Patterns of Political Instability: A Study of the 1969 Mid-Term Elections,' *Economic and Political Weekly*, VI (Annual Number, January 1971), 297 (Table 7).

60. Pathak and Desai, *A Study of Political Behaviour in Gujarat*, p. 22.

61. See K. C. Khanna, 'Money Makes the M.P.: Stupendous Cost of Campaigns,' *The Times of India*, 31 March 1971.

62. Maheshwari, *The General Election in India*, pp. 6–7.

63. Ibid., p. 125.

64. See V. M. Sirsikar, *Sovereigns Without Crowns: A Behavioural Analysis of the Indian Electoral Process* (Bombay: Popular Prakashan, 1973), p. 152.

65. Maheshwari, *The General Election in India*, pp. 97–8.

66. S. P. Sen Varma, 'A Challenge,' *Seminar*, No. 159 (November 1972), p. 23.

67. Ibid., p. 22.

68. Ibid., p. 20. The Chief Election Commissioner calls these charges a 'fantastic, palpably absurd and mischevious story.' Yet they were widely made in the 1971 elections, and after, especially by Balraj Madhok, then a top Jana Sangh leader (he was subsequently expelled from the Jana Sangh). See Balraj Madhok, 'Rigged or Free,' *Seminar*, VI (November, 1972), pp. 32–4.

Chapter 6. India's Electoral Experience

1. See Margaret W. Fisher and Joan V. Bondurant, *The Indian Experience with Democratic Elections* (Berkeley, Calif.: Institute of International Studies, University of California, *Indian Press Digests*, Monograph Series No. 3, December, 1956); Shriram Maheshwari, *The General Election in India* (Allahabad: Chaitanya Publishing House, 1963); and Norman D. Palmer, *The Indian Political System* (Second edition, Boston: Houghton Mifflin, 1971), Chapter 10, 'Elections and Electoral Procedures.'

2. Ajit Bhattacharjea, 'India Comes of Age,' *Hindustan Times*, 26 Jan. 1971.

3. W. H. Morris-Jones, 'India Elects for Change – and Stability,' *Asian Survey*, XI (August, 1971), 739.

4. See Verinder Groves, 'Elections in India – a Short Historical Study,' *The Indian Political Science Review*, I (April–September 1967).

5. S. Bhattacharya, *A Dictionary of Indian History* (Calcutta: Calcutta University Press, 1967), p. 166.

6. *Report on Indian Constitutional Reforms*, Cd. 9109 (1918), para. 6.

7. Bhattacharya, *A Dictionary of Indian History*, p. 168.

8. Percival Spear, *India: A Modern History* (Ann Arbor, Mich.: University of Michigan Press, 1961), p. 354.

9. See *Returns Showing the Results of Elections in India*, Cmd. 5589 (1937); *The Annual Register, 1937*, New Series (London: Longmans, Green, 1938), pp. 146–7; and S. R. Mehotra, 'The Congress and the Partition of India,' and Z. H. Zaidi, 'Aspects of the Development of Muslim League Policy, 1937–47,' in C. H. Philips and Mary Doreen Wainwright, eds., *The Partition of India: Policies and Perspectives, 1935–1947* (London: Allen & Unwin, 1970), pp. 189–90, 245–55.

10. The text of this AICC resolution is given in M. Gwyer and A. Appadoria, eds., *Speeches and Documents on the Indian Constitution, 1921–1947* (Bombay: Oxford University Press, 1957), I, 392–3.

11. For example, Maulana Abul Kalam Azad, the most famous Muslim to cast his lot with India instead of Pakistan, wrote in his autobiography, published posthumously, that 'this was a serious mistake, which strengthened the League and ultimately led to Pakistan.' *India Wins Freedom* (Calcutta: Orient, Longmans, 1959), p. 161.

12. See *The Annual Register*, 1945, New Series (London: Longmans, Green, 1946, pp. 156–9; *The Annual Register*, 1946, New Series (London: Longmans, Green, 1947), p. 165; *Indian Annual Register*, 1946, I, 229–31; Mehrotra, 'The Congress and the Partition of India,' and Zaidi, 'Aspects of the Development of Muslim League Policy, 1937–47,' in Philips and Wainwright, eds., *The Partition of India*, pp. 272–3.

13. *India, Statement by the Cabinet Mission and His Excellency, the Viceroy*, Cmd. 6821 (1946).

14. Granville Austin, *The Indian Constitution: Cornerstone of a Nation* (Oxford: Clarendon Press, 1966), pp. 13–14.

15. Ibid., p. 148.

16. Neeraj, *Nehru and Democracy in India* (Delhi: Metropolitan Book Co., 1971), p. 140.

17. Jawaharlal Nehru, *The Discovery of India* (New York: The John Day Company, 1946), p. 54.

18. Election Commission, Government of India, *Report on the First General Elections in India, 1951–52* (Delhi: Manager of Publications, 1955), I, 10.

19. 'At the time the constitution was being framed, universal suffrage appeared a privilege of doubtful value in a country where eighty per cent of the people could not even write their names. . . . But the suggestion that the franchise be limited in the initial stages and enlarged as education spread and political consciousness grew was not favored. Nehru argued in the Constituent Assembly – and others agreed with him – that adult suffrage would hasten the process of consciousness. Prevailing views regarded the danger of the illiterate masses misusing their vote as less ominous than the possibility that those who might acquire power on the basis of a limited franchise would prove unwilling to share it with others later.' Krishan Bhatia, *The Ordeal of Nationhood* (New York: Atheneum, 1971), p. 68.

20. K. M. Panikkar, *Hindu Society at the Crossroads* (Bombay: Asia Publishing House, 1955), pp. 63–4.

21. *Report on the First General Elections in India, 1951–52*, I, 10–11.

22. Neeraj, *Nehru and Democracy in India*, p. 142.

23. Palmer, *The Indian Political System*, p. 243.

24. *Report on the First General Elections in India, 1951–52*, I, 208.

25. *Tribune* (Ambala), 22 Dec. 1951.

26. *Hitavada*, 30 Dec. 1951.

27. *Hindustan Times*, 17 June 1956.

28. See Palmer, *The Indian Political System*, pp. 248–50.

29. Ibid., p. 251.

30. *The Hindu Weekly Review*, 7 Jan. 1957.

31. Palmer, *The Indian Political System*, pp. 252–3.

32. See Election Commission, Government of India, *Report on the Second General Elections in India, 1957* (Delhi: Manager of Publications, 1958).

33. See K. P. Pillai, *The Red Interlude in Kerala* (Trivandrum: The Kerala Pradesh Congress Committee, 1959).

34. *Report on the Second General Elections in India, 1957*, I, 236.

35. 'The Ballot Box: A Pointer,' *The Radical Humanist*, XXI (May 19, 1957), p. 248.

36. For a detailed account of the 1960 election in Kerala, see K. P. Bhagat, *The Kerala Mid-Term Election of 1960* (Bombay: Popular Book Depot, 1962).

37. See Election Commission, Government of India, *Report on the Third General Elections in India, 1962* (Delhi: Manager of Publications, 1966).

38. Palmer, *The Indian Political System*, p. 257.

39. Ibid., p. 258.

40. Neville Maxwell, 'India's Disintegrating Democracy,' *The Times*, 26 and 27 Jan. 1967.

41. For the results of the fourth general elections, see Election Commission, Government of India, *Report on the Fourth General Elections in India, 1967* (Delhi: Manager of Publications, 1968). See also S. P. Varma and Iqbal Narain, eds., *Fourth General Election in India*, 2 vols. (Bombay: Orient, Longmans, 1968 and 1969), and Norman D. Palmer, 'India's Fourth General Elections,' *Asian Survey*, VII (May 1967).

42. E. P. W. da Costa, 'Roots of Change in Popular Vote,' *The Hindu*, 17 March 1967.

43. Subhash C. Kashyap, *The Politics of Defection: A Study of State Politics in India* (Delhi: National Publishing House, 1969), p. 5.

44. Palmer, *The Indian Political System*, p. 262.

45. For the results of the 1968–9 mid-term elections, see R. Chandidas and Ward Morehouse, eds., *India Votes Two: A Source Book on Indian Elections, 1968–1970* (Bombay: Popular Prakashan, 1971).

46. Bhabani Sen Gupta, *Communism in Indian Politics* (New York: Columbia University Press, 1972), pp. 248–64.

47. See R. L. Gupta, *Politics of Commitment* (New Delhi: Trimurti Publications, 1972); Suresh K. Tameri, *The Wonder Elections: Indira Versus the Right* (Delhi: Vivek Publishing House, 1971); B. O. Graham, M. Johnson, and J. White, 'The Indian Election Results: 1967, 1969, 1971,' *South Asia Review*, IV (April 1971); and 'The Nineteen Seventy-one Election,' *Seminar*, No. 144 (August 1971).

48. Sham Lal, 'India's Year of Decision: A Changed International Environment,' *The Times of India*, 31 Dec. 1971.

49. Norman D. Palmer, 'Elections and the Political System in India: The 1972 State Assembly Elections and After,' *Pacific Affairs*, XLV (Winter 1972–3), 549.

50. See 'State Elections,' *Seminar*, No. 153 (May 1972); and Palmer, 'Elections and the Political System in India.'

51. Palmer, 'Elections and the Political System in India,' p. 551.

52. For the text of this message, see *India News*, XI (18 Aug. 1972).

53. Sham Lal, 'A Hurricane, Not a Wave,' *The Times of India*, 14 March 1972.

54. In April 1974, Professor Rajni Kothari, one of the most perceptive of Indian political scientists, who strongly favors the continuance of the democratic system in India, wrote: 'There is an explosion of discontent in the country. . . . These feelings . . . betray a deep sense of anxiety and consternation which relates less to any particular issue or person including Mrs. Gandhi than to the political system. The general feeling is "something has gone very wrong somewhere." . . . those who have begun to doubt the relevance of the system of its capacity to deliver the goods . . . realise that the present crisis has not greatly affected the Congress party's capacity to secure a majority in the elections which in turn has little to do with its capacity to perform. They also know that the opposition parties are as divided as ever, and that all they can think of in this situation is action aimed at obstructing civil government from carrying on its normal functions.' 'Political System on Trial,' *The Times of India*, 2 April 1974.

55. Dilip Mukerjee, at a meeting at the Indian International Centre, New Delhi, 26 March 1974. See India International Centre *News Bulletin*, V (March 1974), 3.

56. In late 1973 Rajni Kothari wrote: 'Ultimately . . . the country will have to consider adopting the indirect system of elections in a major way, with smaller electoral constituencies as the basic unit, district and State electoral colleges composed of representatives from them, on the basis of which the Vidhan Sabhas and the Lok Sabha are elected. This will both reduce electoral expenses and corruption which are present disqualify the vast majority of the people from political office and would be logically suited to a country with close to a billion people at the end of this century (when an average Lok Sabha constituency will, if the present structure continues and the voting age is lowered which cannot be denied for long, encompass almost two million people and a million voters).' 'Diagnosis and Design,' *Seminar*, No. 173, January 1974, p. 31.

57. Girilal Jain, 'What Has Gone Wrong? The 1971 Elections and After,' *The Times of India,* 1 May 1974.

58. Ajit Bhattacharjea, 'Doubts About Democracy: Achievements Overlooked,' *The Times of India*, 12 March 1974. See also W. H. Morris-Jones, 'India, the One and the Many,' *Art International* (incorporating *The Lugano Review*), XVIII (20 March 1974).

Chapter 7 The Electoral Experience of Pakistan, Ceylon, and Nepal

1. Khalid B. Sayeed, *The Political System of Pakistan* (Boston: Houghton Mifflin Company, 1967), pp. 34, 44–5.

2. Keith Callard, *Pakistan: A Political Study* (London: George Allen & Unwin, 1957), pp. 77–101.

3. *Dawn,* 12 Oct. 1956 and 25 April 1957.

4. Callard, *Pakistan*, p. 122.

5. *Gazette of Pakistan (Extraordinary)*, 24 April 1956, p. 922.

6. Callard, *Pakistan*, p. 57.

7. Ibid., p. 58.

8. Ahmed Husain, *Politics and People's Representation in Pakistan* (Lahore: Ferozsons, 1972), p. 81.

9. Muhammad Ayub Khan, 'Pakistan Perspective,' *Foreign Affairs*, XXXVIII (July 1960), 550.

10. Husain, *Politics and People's Representation*, pp. 81–2.

11. In support of its view that the Basic Democrats should not continue to be the electoral college, the Commission stated that 'the prime consideration with us is the necessity for a direction election, having regard to the role which the President plays in the country.' *Report of the Constitution Commission, Pakistan* (Karachi: Government of Pakistan Press, 1962), p. 70. The Report was not made public until nearly a year later, at the time of the promulgation of the new Constitution by Ayub Khan. See Karl von Vorys, *Political Development in Pakistan* (Princeton, N.J.: Princeton University Press, 1965), pp. 209–216.

12. von Vorys, *Political Development in Pakistan* p. 271.

13. Husain, *Politics and People's Representation*, p. 90.

14. Jacques Nevard, ' "Zindabad!" for Miss Jinnah,' *New York Times Magazine*, Nov. 8, 1964, p. 124.

15. For accounts of the 1965 election see von Vorys, *Political Development in Pakistan*, Chap. 12, 'A Guided Democracy in Action: Managing Reelection;' and K. P. Misra, M. V. Lakhi, and Virendra Narain, *Pakistan's Search for Constitutional Consensus* (New Delhi: Impex India, 1967).

16. Husain, *Politics and People's Representation*, p. 89.

17. See Election Commission, Pakistan, *Results of Elections to Provincial Assemblies of East and West Pakistan* (Rawalpindi: Government of Pakistan Press, 1965).

18. Husain, *Politics and People's Representation*, p. 90.

19. See Rounaq Jahan, *Pakistan: Failure in National Integration* (New York: Columbia University Press, 1972); Husain, *Politics and People's Representation*, pp. 93–119.

20. Statement of 25 March 1969; in *Dawn*, 26 March 1969.

21. The text of the Legal Framework Order is given in *Dawn*, 30 March 1970.

22. These views were expressed to me with remarkable candor by several Pakistanis with whom I talked during a visit to Pakistan in August, 1970.

23. For accounts of the 1970 general election in Pakistan see Sharif al Mujahid, 'Pakistan: First General Elections,' *Asian Survey*, XI (February 1971); 'General Elections, 1970,' an eight-page supplement in *Dawn* 29 Nov. 1970; Hazon Ahmed Shah, 'Pakistanis Prove True Democrats,' *Dawn* 9 Dec. 1970; *Pakistan Affairs*, XXIV (15 Jan. 1971); Husain, *Politics and People's Representation*, pp. 121–207.

24. Husain, ibid., pp. 209–35; Khurshid Hyder, 'Pakistan under Bhutto,' *Current History*, LXIII (November 1972).

25. See *The Constitution of the Islamic Republic of Pakistan* (Karachi: Manager of Publications, 1973).

26. S. Arasaratnam, 'The Ceylon Insurrection of April 1971: Some Causes and Consequences,' *Pacific Affairs*, XLV (Fall 1972), p. 356.

27. Urmila Phadnis, 'Ceylon' (unpublished manuscript), p. 66. I am indebted to Professor Phadnis for letting me read this manuscript, and for many insights into developments in Ceylon.

28. Howard Wriggins, *Ceylon: Dilemmas of a New Nation* (Princeton, N.J.: Princeton University Press, 1960), p. 460.

29. Ibid., p. 82.

30. *Report of the Special Commission on the Constitution of Ceylon, 1931* (Cmd. 3131).

31. Wriggins, *Ceylon*, p. 85.

32. Calvin A. Woodward, *The Growth of a Party System in Ceylon* (Providence: Brown University Press, 1969), p. 44.

33. *Ceylon: Report of the Commission on Constitutional Reform*, 1945 (Cmd. 6677).

34. For an account of the Ceylonese elections of 1947 see Woodward, *Growth of a Party System in Ceylon*, pp. 69–70; Sir Ivor Jennings, 'Ceylon General Elections of 1947,' *University of Ceylon Review*, VI (April 1947).

35. S. Arasaratnam, *Ceylon* (Englewood Cliffs, N.J.: Prentice-Hall, 1964), p. 24.

36. Ibid., p. 25.

37. For accounts of the Ceylonese elections of 1952 see Woodward, *Growth of a Party System in Ceylon*, pp. 87–8; I. D. S. Weerawardana, 'The General Elections in Ceylon, 1952,' *Ceylon Historical Journal*, II (July, October 1952); K. P. Mukerji, 'Parties and Politics in Ceylon,' *Foreign Affairs Reports*, II (October, November 1953).

38. Arasaratnam, *Ceylon*, p. 13.

39. Wriggins, *Ceylon*, p. 366.

40. D. Peiris, *1956 and After: Background to Parties and Politics in Ceylon Today* (Colombo: Associated Newspapers of Ceylon, 1958), p. 10. Quoted in Woodward, *Growth of a Party System in Ceylon*, p. 107.

41. See Jerrold Schecter, *The New Face of Buddha* (New York: Coward-McCann, 1967), especially Chap. 7, 'Ceylon: The Buddhist Revival;' and Donald E. Smith, ed., *South Asian Politics and Religion* (Princeton, N.J.: Princeton University Press, 1972), Part IV, 'Ceylon: The Politics of Buddhist Resurgence.'

42. For accounts of the Ceylonese general election of 1956 see Wriggins, *Ceylon*, Chap. IX, 'The General Election of 1956;' Woodward, *Growth of a Party System in Ceylon*, pp. 101–26.

43. Arasaratnam, *Ceylon*, p. 26.

44. Wriggins, *Ceylon*, p. 327.

45. Samuel Huntington, *Political Order in Changing Societies* (New Haven: Yale University Press, 1968), p. 448.

46. Robert N. Kearney, 'The New Political Crises of Ceylon,' *Asian Survey*, II (June, 1962), 19.

47. Wriggins, *Ceylon*, p. 366.

48. A. M. Rosenthal, 'Ceylon Follows India into Neutralist Camp,' *New York Times*, 8 April 1956.

49. Wriggins, *Ceylon*, p. 462.

50. For an account of the two general elections in Ceylon in 1960 see Woodward, *Growth of a Party System in Ceylon*, pp. 141–57.

51. For an account of the Ceylonese election of 1965 see ibid., pp. 167–70.

52. For accounts of the Ceylonese election of 1970 see the issues of the *Ceylon Daily News* just before and after the election on 27 May 1970; and *The Statesman*, 29 May 1970.

53. See Urmila Phadnis, 'Insurgency in Ceylon: Hard Challenge and Grim Warning,' *Economic and Political Weekly*, VI (8 May 1971); and Urmila Phadnis, 'Sri Lanka Today,' *Current History*, LXIII (November 1972).

54. Bhuwan Lal Joshi and Leo E. Rose, *Democratic Innovations in Nepal* (Berkeley, Calif.: University of California Press, 1966), p. 41.

55. Ibid., p. 39.

56. Leo E. Rose and Margaret W. Fisher, *The Politics of Nepal* (Ithaca, N.Y.: Cornell University Press, 1970), p. 45.

57. Quoted in ibid., pp. 46–7.

58. Ibid., p. 46.

59. Ibid., p. 167.

60. For an account of the 1959 general election in Nepal, see Joshi and Rose, *Democratic Innovations in Nepal*, pp. 295–6; Anirudha Gupta, *Politics in Nepal: A Study of Post-Rana Political Developments and Party Politics* (Bombay: Allied Publishers, 1964), pp. 139–48. Only about 42 per cent of the eligible voters actually voted in this election.

61. Joshi and Rose, *Democratic Innovations in Nepal*, p. 512.
62. Ibid., p. 513.
63. Rose and Fisher, *The Politics of Nepal,* p. 53.
64. Joshi and Rose, *Democratic Innovations in Nepal*, p. 513.

Chapter 8 Three Elections: Variations in Systemic Impact

1. Samuel P. Huntington, 'Political Development and Political Decay,' *World Politics*, XVII (April 1965).

2. Dilip Mukerjee, 'The Year That Was: Politics of Fission and Fusion,' *The Times of India*, 2 Jan. 1971.

3. See Norman D. Palmer, 'India's Fourth General Elections,' *Asian Survey*, VII (May 1967).

4. See Subhash C. Kashyap, *The Politics of Defection: A Study of State Politics in India* (Delhi: National Publishing House, 1969).

5. See Norman D. Palmer, *The Indian Political System* (2nd edition, Boston: Houghton Mifflin, 1971), pp. 262–3.

6. See M. M. Rahman, *The Congress Crisis* (New Delhi: Associated Publishing House, 1970).

7. The text of this broadcast is given in *The Times of India* and other Indian newspapers of 28 Dec. 1970.

8. 'Mrs. Gandhi's Gamble,' *New York Times*, 29 Dec. 1970. After the elections had begun a correspondent of the *Christian Science Monitor*, writing from Bombay, made an equally gloomy assessment: 'Not since 1947 has the stability of the world's largest democracy and probably Asia's most politically conscious electorate been so distressingly threatened by political turmoil. Unless stable government is forthcoming there are grave fears that India may veer toward communism or, in the midst of communal violence, provoke an Army take-over.' David Winder, 'Most Crucial Test Since '47: India Votes on "Socialism",' *Christian Science Monitor*, 3 March 1971.

9. S. Nihal Singh, 'Mrs. Gandhi at the Centre of the Stage,' *The Statesman Weekly*, 13 Feb. 1971.

10. 'This, however, was only one side of the picture. The Marxists got 700,000 more popular votes in 1970 than in 1967, and the CPI-Congress alliance 300,000 fewer votes in 1970 than in 1967. For the first time in Kerala, the Communists' popular vote surpassed that of the Congress party – the CPI(M) alone polled more popular votes than the two Congress factions put together. . . . The Indian press hailed the results as a great victory for Mrs. Gandhi's Congress faction and the CPI, as a debacle for the Marxists. What the election actually demonstrated, however, was that electoral politics had rendered political alignments in Kerala extremely unstable; and that the Communist movement, despite impressive gains, had arrived at a stalemate which could hardly be resolved without further radical change in social relationships.' Gupta, *Communism in Indian Politics*, pp. 192, 194.

11. E. P. W. da Costa, 'Fifth Lok Sabha Elections: 3 New Factors,' *The Times of India*, 9 Jan. 1971.

12. S. Nihal Singh, 'Mrs. Gandhi at the Centre of the Stage.'

13. 'The Choice Is Clear,' *The Hindu*, 1 March 1971.

14. See Iqbal Narain, 'Democratic Interlude for Nation Building: Fifth Lok Sabha Elections,' *Economic and Political Weekly*, VI (18 Sept. 1971); 'Democracy's Proud Moment in India,' *India News*, IX (19 March 1971); 'India: A Clear Mandate for Mrs. Gandhi,' *Time*, 22 March 1971, pp. 22–3; 'Clean Sweep,' *The Indian Express*, 16 March 1971; Frank Moraes, 'The People's Verdict,' *The Indian Express*, 12 March 1971.

15. 'Democracy's Proud Moment in India,' *India News*, IX (19 March 1971).

16. Developments since the fifth general elections have provided further indications of the return of a one-dominant-party system, but it is still advisable to heed the suggestion of a leading Indian political scientist, made shortly after the 1971 elections: 'We should, therefore, keep our analytical options open in regard to the re-emergence of the one-party dominance situation.' Iqbal Narain, 'Democratic Interlude for Nation-Building,' p. 2027.

17. The Director of the Institute for Defence Studies and Analyses in New Delhi, for example, argued that India had 'no option' but to go to war with Pakistan. See K. Subrahmanyam, 'Bangla Desh & India's National Security – the Options for India,' *Foreign Affairs Report*, XXI (January 1972), 2–14. This was originally prepared as a paper for an off-the-record seminar on Bangladesh that was held at the Indian Council on World Affairs in New Delhi on 3 July 1971. A copy reached Peter Hazelhurst, the London *Times*' correspondent in South Asia, and Hazelhurst published a fairly detailed summary of the paper in *The Times*, 13 July 1971.

18. W. Howard Wriggins, *Ceylon: Dilemmas of a New Nation* (Princeton: Princeton University Press, 1960), p. 460.

19. *Gazette of Pakistan Extraordinary*, 24 April 1956, p. 922.

20. The text of this broadcast is given in *Dawn*, 27 March 1969.

21. The text of this broadcast is given in *Dawn*, 29 Nov. 1969.

22. The text of the Legal Framework Order is given in *Dawn*, 31 March 1970.

23. Legal Framework Order, paragraph 6 (1).

24. Sharif al Mujahid, 'Pakistan: First General Elections,' *Asian Survey*, XI (February, 1971), p. 168.

25. See Ronald D. Brunner and Garry D. Brewer, *Organized Complexity: Empirical Theories of Political Development* (New York: The Free Press, 1971), p. 116.

26. The six-point program had been advanced by the Awami League as early as February 1966. See *Dawn*, 12 Feb. 1966. They were the central demands of the Awami League during the 1970 elections.

27. Rounaq Jahan, 'Elite in Crisis: An Analysis of the Failure of

Mujib-Yahya-Butto Negotiation' (unpublished paper, 1972), p. 9.

28. The turnout varied considerably in the different provinces. It was 57.6 per cent in East Pakistan, 68.7 per cent in the Punjab, 60 per cent in Sind, 48.1 per cent in the N.W.F.P., and only 40.5 per cent in Baluchistan. Valid votes throughout the two wings were about 57 per cent. See Mustaq Ahmad, *Politics without Social Change* (Karachi: Space Publishers, 1971), p. 148.

29. The election results were fully reported in *Dawn* and other Pakistani newspapers.

30. David Lushak, *Daily Telegraph* (London), 10 Dec. 1970.

31. *Dawn*, 9 Dec. 1970.

32. Quoted in Hazon Ahmed Shah, 'Pakistanis Prove True Democrats,' *Dawn*, 9 Dec. 1970.

33. *The Times*, 9 Dec. 1970.

34. For an account of these negotiations and of the developments that led to the civil war in East Pakistan, from different points of view, see Rounaq Jahan, 'Elite in Crisis,' pp. 15–34; *White Paper on the Crisis in East Pakistan* (Islamabad: Government of Pakistan Press, August 1971); and Zulfikar Ali Bhutto, *The Great Tragedy* (Karachi: Pakistan People's Party, 1971).

35. Urmila Phadnis, 'Insurgency in Ceylon: Hard Challenge and Grim Warning,' *Economic and Political Weekly*, VI (8 May 1971), 967.

36. See 'Charges in Ceylon Against Opposition Dominate Campaign,' *The New York Times*, May 17, 1970; and Sydney H. Schanberg, 'Ceylon's Leftist Government Finds Its Promises Have Added to Economic Problems,' *The New York Times*, 18 Oct. 1970.

37. See *Ceylon Daily News*, 28 and 29 May 1970; and *The Statesman*, 29 May 1970. For the detailed official results, see *Report on the Seventh Parliamentary General Election in Ceylon 27th May, 1970,* Sessional Paper No. VII – 1971 (Colombo: Department of Government Printing, May, 1971).

38. V. O. Key, Jr., 'A Theory of Critical Elections,' *Journal of Politics*, XVII (1955).

39. A. Jeyaratnam Wilson, 'Recent Political Developments in Ceylon,' *Round Table*, No. 241 (January, 1971), p. 145.

40. Ibid., p. 141.

41. Schanberg, 'Ceylon's Leftist Government Finds Its Promises Have Added to Economic Problems.'

42. Phadnis, 'Insurgency in Ceylon,' p. 966.

43. *Ceylon Daily News*, 11 Aug. 1970.

44. Ibid., 28 Feb. 1971.

45. See Urmila Phadnis, 'Sri Lanka Today,' *Current History*, LXIII (November 1972), 211.

46. Ibid., p. 210.

47. Ibid.

48. Wilson, 'Recent Political Developments in Ceylon,' p. 145.

Chapter 9. The Indian Voter: A Profile

1. V. M. Sirsikar, '*Electoral Process in Poona 1967*: A Study in Parties, Politics and Voters', (Poona: Department of Political Science, University of Poona, 1971), p. 182. I am indebted to Professor Sirsikar for letting me examine this unpublished manuscript. See also V. M. Sirsikar, *Sovereigns without Crowns* (Bombay: Popular Prakashan, 1973).

2. D. L. Sheth, 'Political Development of Indian Electorate,' *Economic and Political Weekly*, V (Annual Number, January 1970), 138, 148.

3. Ramashray Roy, 'Elections, Electorate and Democracy in India,' *Perspectives*, Supplement to *The Indian Journal of Public Administration*, XVII (October–December 1971), 14–15. See Table 5 (p. 14), 'Attributes of the Electorate.'

4. This was a part of a major cross-national Project on Social and Political Change, involving collaborative research in four countries, under the general direction of Gabriel A. Almond and Sidney Verba. In a sense it was a sequel to the five-nation cross-national study which led to the well-known volume *The Civic Culture: Political Attitudes and Democracy in Five Nations*, by Almond and Verba (Princeton, N.J.: Princeton University Press, 1963). The research in India was carried out in collaboration with scholars at the Centre for the Study of Developing Societies in Delhi. I am indebted to Dr. Bashiruddin Ahmed of the Centre for making available to me the print-out sheets summarizing the responses of the 2,637 persons in India who were interviewed in connection with this Project. For purposes of analysis the sample was appropriately weighted, giving a total of 9,521.

5. E. P. W. da Costa, 'The Changing Face of the Indian Electorate,' in *The Indian General Elections 1967* (New Delhi: Indian Institute of Public Opinion, 1967), p. 1.

6. B. S. Khanna and Satya Deva, 'Elections to State Legislatures in Punjab and Haryana: A Study in Political Behaviour (unpublished manuscript, Chandigarh: Department of Public Administration, Punjab University, n.d.), p. 205.

7. David Butler and Donald Stokes, *Political Change in Britain: Forces Shaping Electoral Choice* (New York: St. Martin's Press, 1969), p. 274.

8. Sheth, 'Political Development of Indian Electorate,' p. 148.

9. Ramashray Roy, 'Patterns of Political Instability: A Study of the Mid-Term Elections,' *Economic and Political Weekly*, VI (Annual Number, January, 1971), 304.

10. Bashiruddin Ahmed, 'Political Stratification of the Indian Electorate,' *Economic and Political Weekly*, VI (Annual Number, January 1971), 251.

11. Ibid.

12. Ibid., p. 258, Table 7.

13. Ibid., 258.

14. Sheth, 'Political Development of Indian Electorate,' p. 139.

15. Ibid.

16. Ibid., p. 143.

17. D. L. Sheth, 'Partisanship and Political Development,' *Economic and Political Weekly*, VI (Annual Number, January 1971, p. 263).

18. Yogesh Atal, *Local Communities and National Politics* (Delhi: National Publishing House, 1971), p. v.

19. Ibid., pp. 143–60, 238–44, 270–4.

20. Sheth, 'Partisanship and Political Development,' p. 265.

21. Sheth, 'Political Development of Indian Electorate,' p. 145.

22. Questionnaire used in interviews conducted in India in connection with the cross-national Project on Social and Political Change, 1966, Question No. 40.0.

23. Richard Rose, *Politics in England* (Boston: Little, Brown, 1964), p. 87.

24. Ibid., p. 86.

25. Samuel J. Eldersveld, 'The Political Behaviour of the Indian Public,' *Monthly Public Opinion Surveys* of the Indian Institute of Public Opinion, IX (1964), 5.

26. Sheth, 'Political Development of Indian Electorate,' p. 145.

27. Ibid.

28. Sheth, 'Partisanship and Political Development,' p. 265 (Table 2: 'Involvement in Election Campaign Against Strength of Partisanship').

29. Atal, *Local Communities and National Politics*, pp. 164–7, 249–51, 278–9.

30. Lester W. Milbrath, *Political Participation* (Chicago: Rand McNally, 1965), p. 50.

31. Ibid., pp. 51, 53–4. Italics in original.

32. Ibid., pp. 51–2. The study to which Milbrath referred is Bernard E. Berelson, Paul F. Lazarsfeld, and William N. McPhee, *Voting* (Chicago: University of Chicago Press, 1954).

33. Sheth, 'Political Development of Indian Electorate,' p. 145.

34. Ibid.

35. Sheth, 'Partisanship and Political Development,' pp. 265, 267.

36. Sheth, 'Political Development of Indian Electorate,' p. 145.

37. Angus Campbell, Gerald Gurin, and Warren E. Miller, *The Voter Decides* (Evanston, Ill.: Row, Peterson and Company, 1954), p. 92.

38. W. Phillips Shively, 'Party Identification, Party Choice, and Voting Stability: The Weimar Case,' *The American Political Science Review*, LXVI (December, 1972), 1205.

39. Sheth, 'Political Development of Indian Electorate,' p. 143. 'On the party loyalty question, i.e., whether they would vote the same party again, 52 per cent replied in the affirmative. On the direct identification question, i.e., whether they felt close to any party, 61 per cent had only one specific party to mention which they identified. And on the question relating to strength of their identification, 52 per cent responded that their preference for the party was very strong.' Ibid.

40. Sheth, 'Partisanship and Political Development,' p. 261.

41. Stanley Kochanek, *The Congress Party of India: The Dynamics of One-Party Democracy* (Princeton, N.J.: Princeton University Press, 1968), p. 343.

42. See Butler and Stokes, *Political Change in Britain*, pp. 40–3; and Angus Campbell and Henry Valen, 'Party Identification in Norway and the United States,' in Angus Campbell, *et al.*, *Elections and the Political Order* (New York: John Wiley and Sons, 1966), pp. 245–68.

43. Shively, 'Party Identification, Party Choice, and Voting Stability,' p. 1206; see also Butler and Stokes, *Political Change in Britain*, pp. 41–2.

44. Sheth, 'Partisanship and Political Development,' pp. 260–1.

45. Khanna and Deva, *Elections to State Legislatures in Punjab and Haryana*, p. 90.

46. Campbell and Valen, 'Party Identification in Norway and the United States,' p. 268.

47. Khanna and Deva, *Elections to State Legislatures in Punjab and Haryana*, p. 94.

48. Sheth, 'Partisanship and Political Development,' p. 261.

49. Milbrath, *Political Participation*, p. 61. Italics in the original.

50. Ibid., p. 63.

51. Almond and Verba, *The Civic Culture*, p. 171.

52. Campbell, Gurin, and Miller, *The Voter Decides*, p. 194.

53. 'The Fifth Lok Sabha Elections: An Analysis of Indian Political Behaviour,' *Monthly Public Opinion Surveys* of the Indian Institute of Public Opinion, XVI (December 1970, January, February 1971), 74–81.

54. Atal, *Local Communities and National Politics*, p. 288.

55. Question No. 57.0.

56. Campbell, Gurin, and Miller, *The Voter Decides*, p. 187.

57. S. P. Varma and Associates, 'Voting Behaviour in Rajasthan (An Empirical Study of the Fourth General Election)' (unpublished manuscript, Jaipur: Department of Political Science, University of Rajasthan, n.d.), p. 410.

58. Milbrath, *Political Participation*, p. 56.

59. Almond and Verba, *The Civic Culture*, pp. 182, 236.

60. Campbell, Gurin, and Miller, *The Voter Decides*, pp. 191–2 (Table A.2: 'Some Demographic Correlates of Sense of Political Efficacy').

61. Almond and Verba, *The Civic Culture*, p. 213. See also Alice and Yasumasa Kuroda, 'Aspects of Community Participation in Japan,' *The Journal of Asian Studies*, XXVII (February 1968).

62. Campbell, Gurin, and Miller, *The Voter Decides*, pp. 187–8.

63. Question 53.0. When the question was applied to local government, and framed in terms of influence rather than effect, an even higher percentage of the respondents showed a lack of feeling of political efficacy. The questions were: 'How much influence do you think you can have on politics and actions of the panchayat/munici-

pality? A lot of influence, a little influence or none at all?' The results were as follows (Question 63.1.0):

	Number of Respondents (weighted sample)	*Per cent*
None at all	5,413	56.9
A lot	930	9.8
A little	1,640	17.2
Don't know	1,364	14.3
No response	173	1.8
Total	9,520	100.0

64. Question 59.0.
65. Varma and Associates, *Voting Behaviour in Rajasthan* pp. 412–18, Tables 9-I, 9-II, 9-III, and 9-IV.
66. Atal, *Local Communities and National Politics*, pp. 289–90.
67. Yogesh Atal, 'Citizens' Sense of Political Efficacy,' *Economic and Political Weekly*, IV (Annual Number, January, 1960), 175.
68. Roy, 'Patterns of Political Instability,' p. 302.
69. Ibid., p. 404.
70. Ibid.
71. Atal, *Local Communities and National Politics*, p. 291.
72. Sheth, 'Partisanship and Political Development,' p. 267.
73. Almond and Verba, *The Civic Culture*, p. 230.
74. Sheth, 'Partisanship and Political Development,' p. 267.
75. D. N. Pathak and K. D. Desai, 'A Study of Political Behaviour in Gujarat, with Special Reference to the Fourth General Elections, 1967' (unpublished manuscript, Ahmedabad: University School of Social Sciences, Gujarat University, 1970) pp. 116, 134.
76. Sheth, 'Partisanship and Political Development,' p. 267.
77. Question 48.1.0.
78. Pathak and Desai, *A Study of Political Behaviour in Gujarat*, p. 134.
79. Roy, 'Patterns of Political Instability,' p. 301.
80. Sheth, 'Partisanship and Political Development,' p. 267. See especially Table 4: 'Legitimacy of Parliamentary Institutions Against Strength of Partisanship.'
81. Pathak and Desai, *A Study of Political Behaviour in Gujarat*, pp. 34, 116.
82. Sheth, 'Partisanship and Political Development,' p. 267.
83. Almond and Verba, *The Civic Culture*, pp. 242, 246.
84. Sheth, 'Partisanship and Political Development,' p. 268. See especially Table 5: 'Satisfaction with System Performance Against Strength of Partisanship.'
85. Questions 54.0, 55.0, and 56.0.
86. Question 62.0.
87. Sheth, 'Political Development of Indian Electorate,' p. 145.

Chapter 10. Voting Determinants

1. V. O. Key, Jr., 'A Theory of Critical Elections,' *The Journal of Politics*, XVII (February 1955).
2. Imtiaz Ahmed, 'Elections and Political Change: A Statistical Analysis of a U.P. Constituency' (unpublished paper).
3. Imtiaz Ahmed, 'Elections and the Political Process' (unpublished paper). I am indebted to Professor Ahmed for making this paper, and the paper listed in the previous footnote, available to me.
4. Sidney Verba, Norman H. Nie, and Jae-On Kim, *The Modes of Democratic Participation: A Cross-National Comparison* (Beverly Hills, Calif.: Sage Publications, 1971), pp. 61, 73.
5. David E. RePass, 'Issue Salience and Party Choice,' *The American Political Science Review*, LXV (June 1971).
6. See Yogesh Atal, *Local Communities and National Politics* (Delhi: National Publishing House, 1971), pp. 162–3.
7. RePass, 'Issue Salience and Party Choice,' p. 399.
8. Ibid., p. 400. Italics in original.
9. Ramashray Roy, 'Patterns of Political Stability: A Study of the 1969 Mid-Term Elections,' *Economic and Political Weekly*, VI (Annual Number, January 1971), p. 302.
10. See Angus Campbell, *et al.*, *The American Voter* (New York: Holt, Rinehart & Winston, 1960), pp. 143–5; and Walter Dean Burnham, *Critical Elections and the Mainsprings of American Politics* (New York: W. W. Norton, 1970), p. 120.
11. RePass, 'Issue Salience and Party Choice,' p. 400.
12. David E. Butler and Donald Stokes, *Political Change in Britain: Forces Shaping Electoral Choice* (New York: St. Martin's Press, 1969), Chaps. 11 and 12.
13. E. P. W. da Costa, 'The Prospects of a Non-Violent Revolution Disestablishing the Establishment?,' in *The Indian General Elections 1967* (New Delhi: Indian Institute of Public Opinion, 1967), p. XXIII. This is the last in a series of fifteen articles which appeared originally in *The Times of India* from October 1966 to January 1967.
14. Roy, 'Patterns of Political Instability, p. 247 (Table 6: 'Considerations Influencing Voting Decisions by States').
15. Gunnar Sjöblom, *Party Strategies in a Multi-Party System* (Lund: Studentlitteratur, 1968), p. 232.
16. Paul Lazarsfeld, *et al.*, *The People's Choice* (New York: Duell, Sloan and Pearce, 1944), p. 27.
17. D. L. Sheth, 'Political Development of the Indian Electorate,' *Economic and Political Weekly*, V (Annual Number, January 1970), p. 147.
18. Ahmed, 'Elections and Political Change.'
19. Myron Weiner and Rajni Kothari, eds., *Indian Voting Behaviour; Studies of the 1962 General Elections* (Calcutta: Firma K. L. Mukhopadhyay, 1965), p. 1.
20. W. Howard Wriggins, *Ceylon: Dilemmas of a New Nation* (Princeton, N.J.: Princeton University Press, 1960), p. 460.

21. Oscar Lewis, *Village Life in Northern India* (New York: Vintage Books, 1965), p. 149.

22. See, for example, Sheth, 'Political Development of the Indian Electorate,' p. 147, Table 4: 'Ways by Which Voting Decisions Are Reached by Respondents.' This Table is reproduced and commented upon above, pp. 299–300.

23. Peter G. J. Pulzer, *Political Representation and Elections in Britain* (London: Allen and Unwin, 1967), p. 133.

24. Ibid., p. 98.

25. See Butler and Stokes, *Political Change in Britain*, especially Chaps. 4, 5, and 6. 'The preeminence of class in electoral alignments is not a universal fact of modern politics. There are many countries and party systems where race, or religion, or region, or other lines of potential cleavage are more important than class in defining electoral support.' Ibid., p. 123.

26. See Alice and Yasumasa Kuroda, 'Aspects of Community Participation in Japan,' *The Journal of Asian Studies*, XXVII (February 1968), 233.

27. Paul R. Brass, *Factional Politics in an Indian State: The Congress Party in Uttar Pradesh* (Berkeley: University of California Press, 1965), p. 155.

28. Rajni Kothari, 'Introduction,' in Rajni Kothari, ed., *Caste in Indian Politics* (New Delhi: Orient Longmans, 1970), p. 4.

29. Rajni Kothari and Rushikesh Maru, 'Federating for Political Interests: The Kshatriyas of Gujarat,' in Kothari, ed., *Caste in Indian Politics*, p. 93. 'It has been emphasized, and quite rightly, that the operating caste system in India functions not along the *varna* typology found in the texts but along the Jati lines of primary marriage groups.' Ibid., p. 96. In this connection see Irawati Karve, *Hindu Society: An Interpretation* (2nd edition, Poona: Deshmukh Prakashan, 1968); David G. Mandlebaum, 'Concepts and Methods in the Study of Caste,' *The Economic Weekly*, XI (Special Number, January 1959); and Harold Gould, 'Toward a "Jati" Model for Indian Politics,' *Economic and Political Weekly*, IV (February 1969).

30. M. N. Srinivas, 'The Social System of a Mysore Village,' in McKim Marriott, ed., *Village India* (Chicago: University of Chicago Press, 1955), p. 18. See also M. N. Srinivas, 'The Dominant Caste in Rampura,' *American Anthropologist*, LXI (1959); and M. N. Srinivas, *Social Change in Modern India* (Berkeley: University of California Press, 1966), pp. 151–2.

31. Pravin N. Sheth, 'Impact of Politics on Lower Castes,' *Vidya*, XI (1969), 50–1.

32. Srinivas, *Social Change in Modern India*, p. 6. Chap. 1, 'Sanskritization.'

33. See ibid., Chap. 2, 'Westernization.'

34. Kothari and Maru, 'Federating for Political Interests,' p. 97.

35. See Lloyd I. Rudolph and Susanne Hoeber Rudolph, *The Modernity of Tradition: Political Development in India* (Chicago: University of Chicago Press, 1967); and Rajni Kothari, *Politics in India*

(Boston: Little, Brown, 1970), especially Chap. III, 'Approach to Modernization,' and Chap. VII, 'Political Culture and Socialization.'

36. See Srinivas, *Social Change in Modern India*, Chap. 4, 'Secularization.'

37. Kothari, *Politics in India*, p. 248.

38. Ibid., p. 225. 'Where caste itself becomes a political category, it is futile to argue as to whether caste uses politics or politics uses caste.' Ibid., p. 226.

39. André Béteille, 'Caste and Political Group Formation in Tamilnad,' in Kothari, ed., *Caste in Indian Politics*, p. 291.

40. Rudolph and Rudolph, *The Modernity of Tradition*, p. 29.

41. Ramashray Roy, 'Caste and Political Recruitment in Bihar,' in Kothari, ed., *Caste in Indian Politics*, p. 237.

42. Rudolph and Rudolph, *The Modernity of Tradition*, pp. 33–4.

43. Lloyd I. Rudolph and Susanne Hoeber Rudolph, 'The Political Role of India's Caste Associations,' *Pacific Affairs,* XXXIII (March, 1960).

44. Rajni Kothari, 'Introduction,' in Kothari, ed., *Caste in Indian Politics*, p. 21.

45. See Selig S. Harrison, 'Caste and the Andhra Communists,' *The American Political Science Review*, L (June 1956); and Selig S. Harrison, *India: The Most Dangerous Decades* (Princeton: Princeton University Press, 1960).

46. M. N. Srinivas, 'Caste in Modern India,' *Journal of Asian Studies*, XVI (1956–7), 548.

47. O. P. Goyal, 'Caste and Politics – A Theoretical Framework,' a paper prepared for the Punjab Studies Conference, held at the University of Pennsylvania, May 5–8, 1971, p. 4.

48. S. P. Varma and Associates, *Voting Behaviour in Rajasthan (An Empirical Study of the Fourth General Election)* (Jaipur, Rajasthan: Department of Political Science, University of Rajasthan, 1971), p. 402.

49. See W. H. Morris-Jones, 'India's Political Idioms,' in C. H. Philips, ed., *Politics and Society in India* (New York: Frederick A. Praeger, 1962), pp. 133–54; and A. H. Somjee, *Democracy and Political Change in Village India* (New Delhi: Orient Longmans, 1971), Chapter One, 'The Framework of Village Politics.'

50. Ibid., p. 12.

51. Ibid.

52. Ibid., p. 19.

53. Goyal, 'Caste and Politics,' p. 4.

54. Ibid.

55. Somjee, *Democracy and Political Change in Village India*, p. 13.

56. M. N. Srinivas, *Report of the Seminar on Casteism and Removal of Untouchability* (1955), p. 137.

57. F. G. Bailey, 'Politics and Society in Contemporary Orissa,' in Philips, ed., *Politics and Society in India*, p. 106.

58. Harold A. Gould, 'Changing Political Behavior in Rural Indian

Society,' *Economic and Political Weekly*, II (Special Number, August, 1967), 1523.

59. Kothari, *Politics in India*, p. 241.

60. Dilip Mukherjee, 'Politics of Manipulation: Arithmetic of Caste and Community,' *The Times of India*, 20 Feb. 1971.

61. Myron Weiner, 'Village and Party Factionalism in Andhra: Ponnur Constituency,' in Weiner and Kothari, ed., *Indian Voting Behaviour*, p. 177.

62. V. M. Sirsikar, 'Electoral Process in Poona 1967 (A Study in Parties, Politics and Voters' (unpublished manuscript, Poona: Department of Political Science, University of Poona, 1971), p. 25.

63. Brass, *Factional Politics in an Indian State*, p. 236. See also D. F. Miller, 'Factions in Indian Village Politics,' *Pacific Affairs*, XXXVIII (Spring 1965), p. 125.

64. Ranbir Sharma, 'Political Parties in Himachal Pradesh: A Study in Political Development' (Ph.D. dissertation, Department of Political Science, Punjab University, 1972), p. 261.

65. Myron Weiner, *Party Building in a New Nation: The Indian National Congress* (Chicago: University of Chicago Press, 1967), p. 159.

66. Brass, *Factional Politics in an Indian State*, p. 3.

67. Rajni Kothari, 'Party System,' *The Economic Weekly*, XIII (3 June 1961), p. 849.

68. See Richard Sisson and Lawrence L. Shrader, *Legislative Recruitment and Political Integration: Patterns of Political Leadership in an Indian State* (Berkeley: Center for South and Southeast Asia Studies, University of California, 1972).

69. Sharma, *Political Parties in Himachal Pradesh*, p. 310.

70. Ibid., pp. 311–12.

71. W. Norman Brown, *The United States and India and Pakistan* (Cambridge, Mass.: Harvard University Press, 1953), p. 112.

72. Ibid., p. 113.

73. See Theodore P. Wright, Jr., 'The Muslim League in South India Since Independence: A Study in Minority Group Political Strategy,' *The American Political Science Review*, LX (September 1966).

74. Zaheer Masood Quraishi, 'Electoral Strategy of a Minority Pressure Group: The Muslim Majlis-e-Mushawarat,' *Asian Survey*, VIII (December 1968).

75. Zaheer Masood Quraishi, 'Emergence and Eclipse of Muslim Majlis-e-Mushawarat,' *Economic and Political Weekly*, VI (19 June 1971), 1232.

76. Ibid., p. 1233.

77. See Surindar Singh Suri, *1962 Elections: A Political Analysis* (New Delhi: Sudha Publications, 1962), pp. 153ff.; and *Hindustan Times*, 14 Oct. 1968.

78. For data on SES factors and the strength of partisanship, see D. L. Sheth, 'Partisanship and Political Development,' *Economic and Political Weekly*, VI (Annual Number, January 1971), 269–70.

79. This hypothesis seemed to be confirmed in Professor Sirsikar's

study of the 1967 elections in Poona, as reported in his 'Electoral Process in Poona 1967'.

80. Ajit Bhattacharjea, 'Poisoning the Roots: Black Money and the Elections,' *The Times of India*, 15 Feb 1973.

81. *Report of the Committee on the Prevention of Corruption* (The Santhanam Report) (New Delhi: Ministry of Home Affairs, Government of India, 1964).

82. Bhattacharjea, 'Poisoning the Roots.'

83. 'On the question of social determinants – whether people vote according to economic status, religion, education, urban, suburban, or rural residence, and membership in minority and ethnic groups – Key rejects the idea that any of these factors determines a person's vote.' Roger Hilsman, *The Politics of Policy Making in Defense and Foreign Affairs* (New York: Harper and Row, 1971), p. 94.

84. Horst Hartmann, *Political Parties in India* (Meerut: Meenakshi Prakashan, 1971), p. 35. Hartmann cites the following works as examples of the kind of studies which present this point of view: Weiner and Kothari, eds., *Indian Voting Behaviour*; V. M. Sirsikar, *Political Behaviour in India – A Case Study of the 1962 General Election* (Bombay: Manaktalas, 1965); and S. P. Varma and C. P. Bhambhri, *Elections and Political Consciousness in India – a Study* (Meerut: Meenakshi Prakashan, 1967).

85. Sheth, 'Political Development of the Indian Electorate,' p. 147.

86. Ibid.

87. Sirsikar, *Electoral Process in Poona 1967*, p. 142.

88. Roy, 'Patterns of Political Instability,' p. 297 (Table 6).

INDEX